Polar Bear Café

COLLECTOR'S EDITION

1

STORY & ART BY
ALOHA HIGA

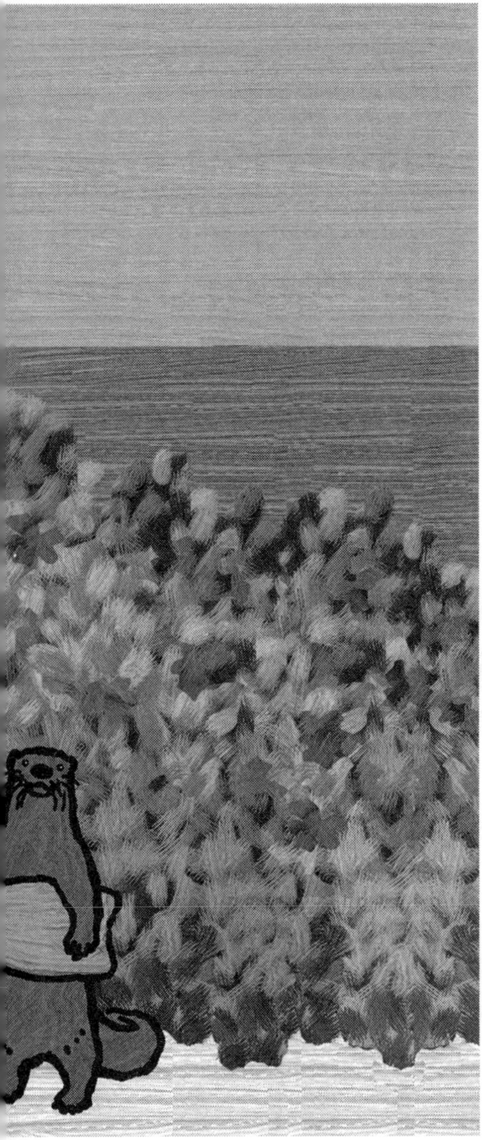

MENU

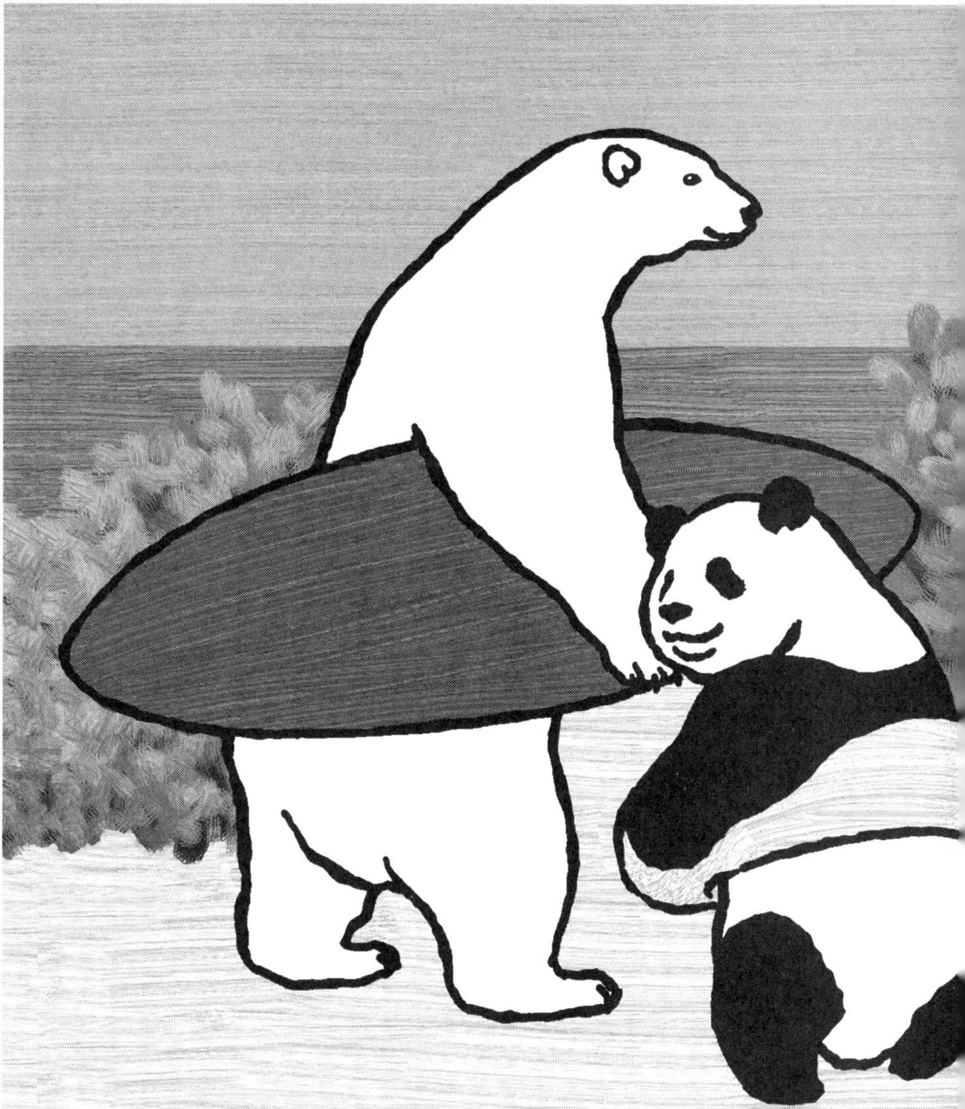

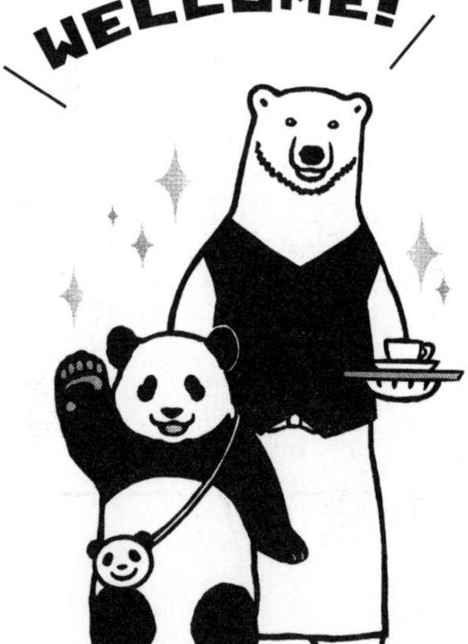
WELCOME!
Polar Bear Café

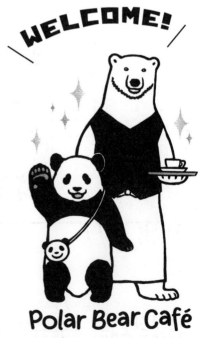

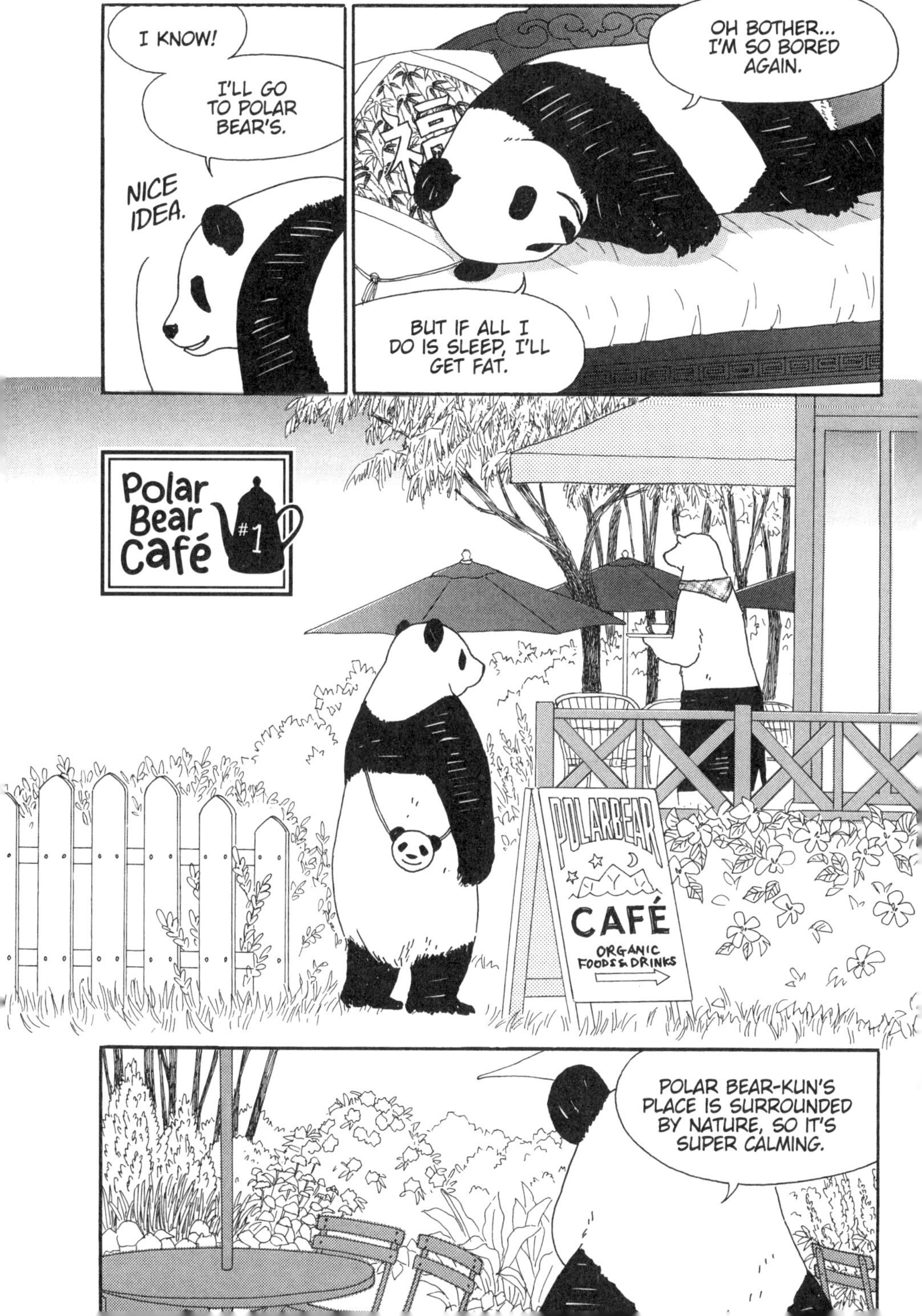
OH BOTHER... I'M SO BORED AGAIN.
BUT IF ALL I DO IS SLEEP, I'LL GET FAT.
I KNOW!
I'LL GO TO POLAR BEAR'S.
NICE IDEA.
Polar Bear Café #1
POLARBEAR
CAFÉ
ORGANIC FOODS & DRINKS
POLAR BEAR-KUN'S PLACE IS SURROUNDED BY NATURE, SO IT'S SUPER CALMING.

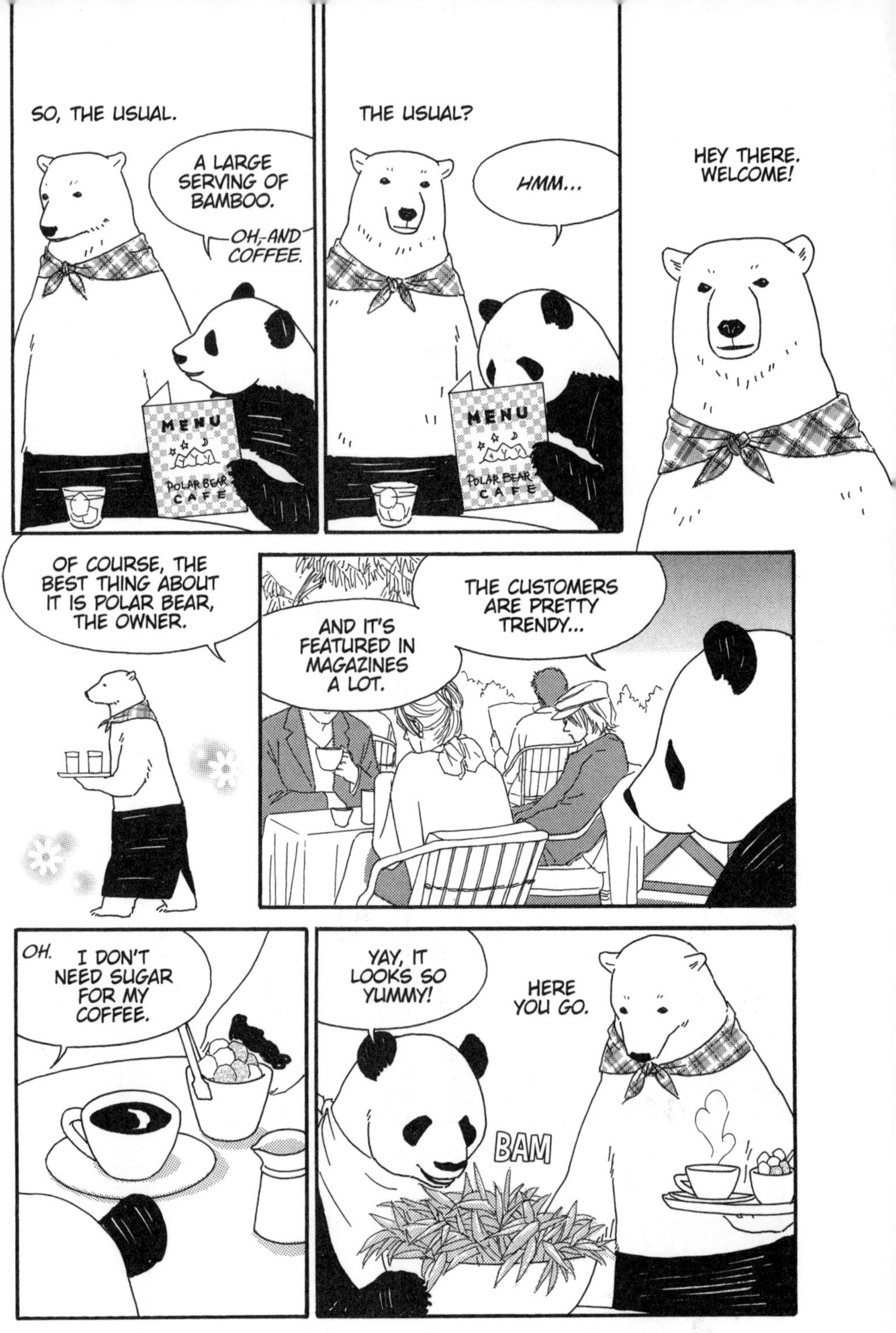
HEY THERE. WELCOME!
THE USUAL?
HMM...
SO, THE USUAL.
A LARGE SERVING OF BAMBOO.
OH, AND COFFEE.
THE CUSTOMERS ARE PRETTY TRENDY...
AND IT'S FEATURED IN MAGAZINES A LOT.
MENU
POLAR BEAR CAFE
OF COURSE, THE BEST THING ABOUT IT IS POLAR BEAR, THE OWNER.
HERE YOU GO.
YAY, IT LOOKS SO YUMMY!
BAM
OH.
I DON'T NEED SUGAR FOR MY COFFEE.

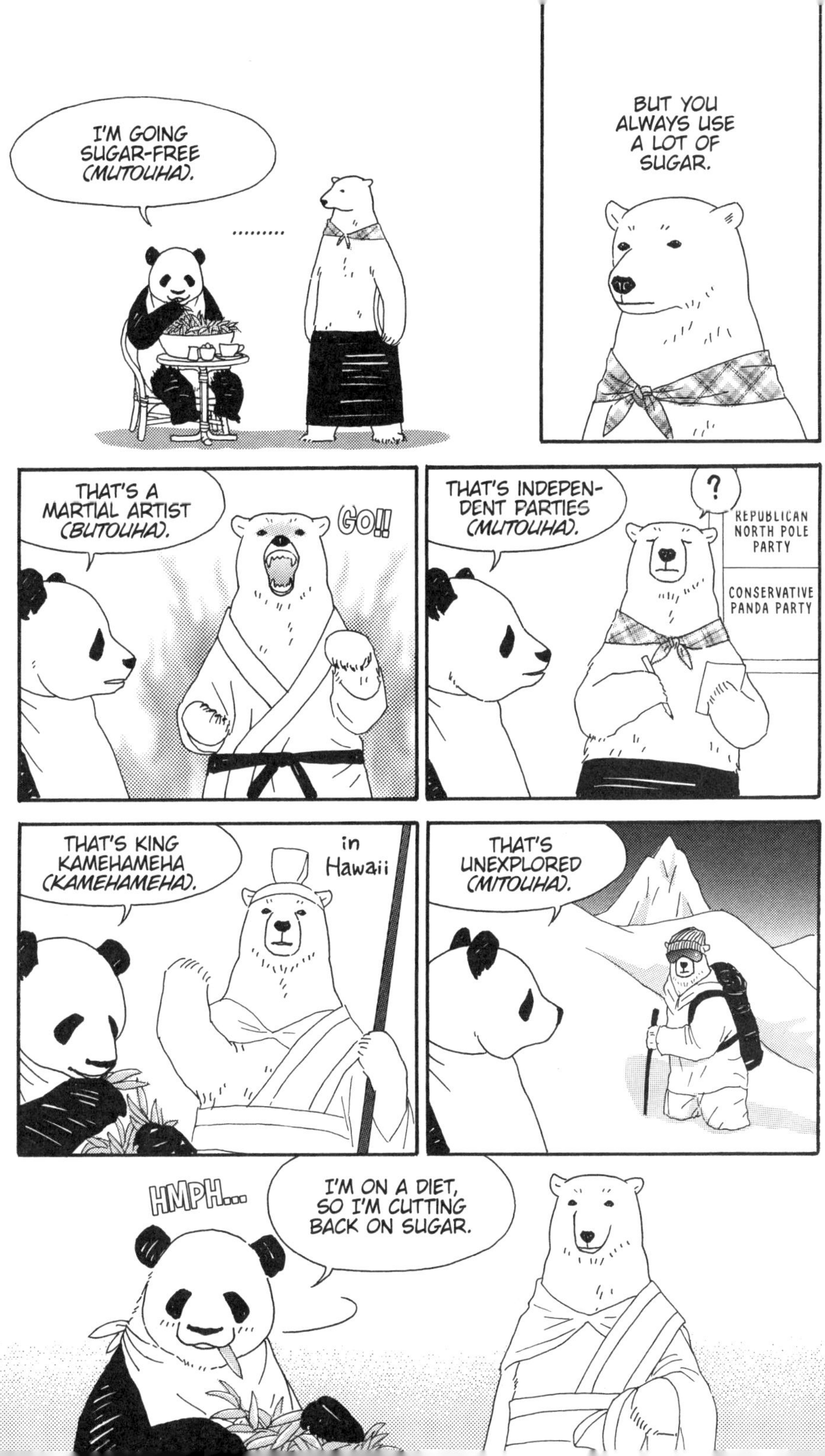
BUT YOU ALWAYS USE A LOT OF SUGAR.
I'M GOING SUGAR-FREE (MUTOUHA).
....
?
REPUBLICAN NORTH POLE PARTY
CONSERVATIVE PANDA PARTY
THAT'S INDEPENDENT PARTIES (MUTOUHA).
GO!!
THAT'S A MARTIAL ARTIST (BUTOUHA).
THAT'S UNEXPLORED (MITOUHA).
in Hawaii
THAT'S KING KAMEHAMEHA (KAMEHAMEHA).
I'M ON A DIET, SO I'M CUTTING BACK ON SUGAR.
HMPH...

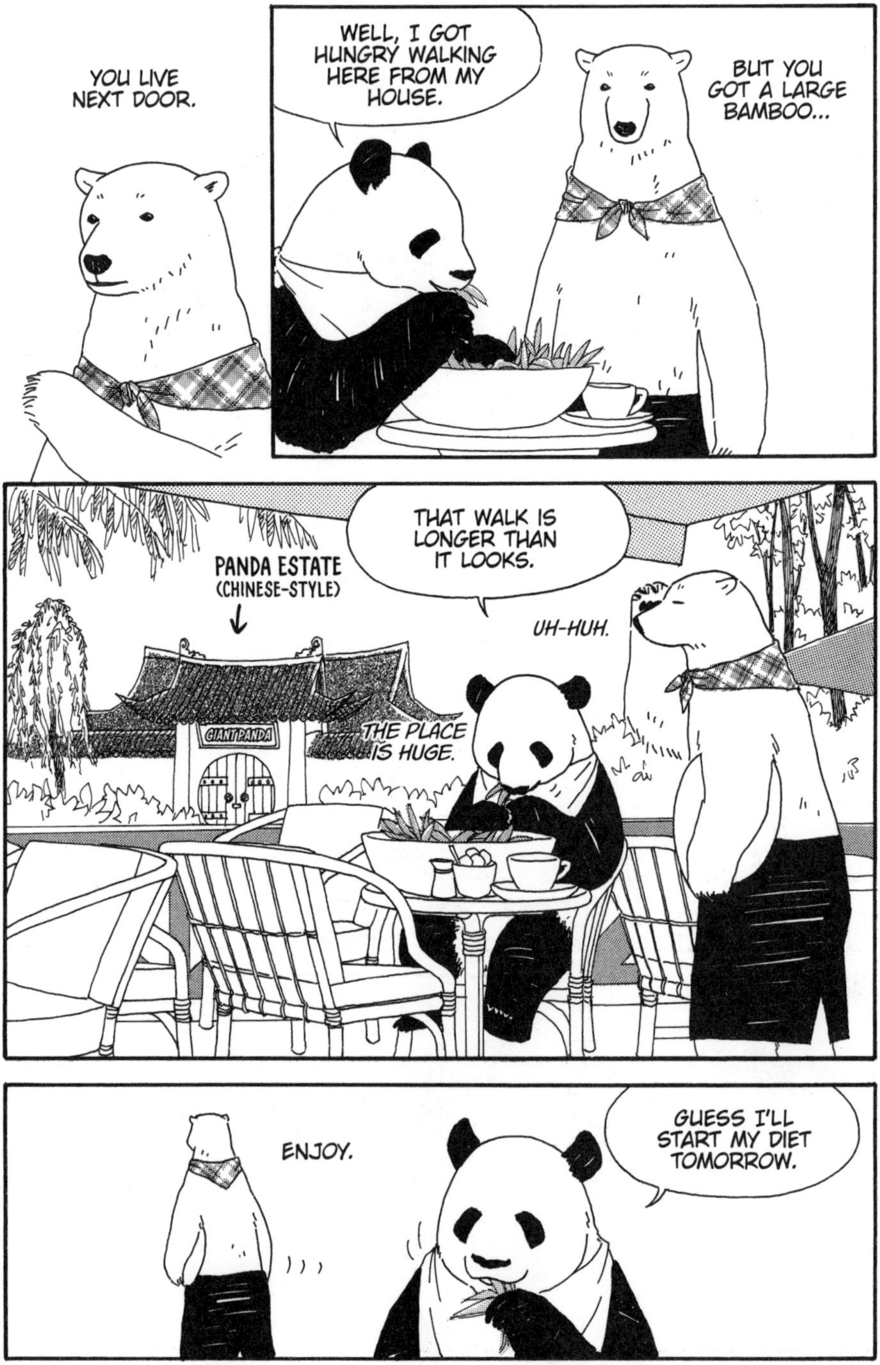
BUT YOU GOT A LARGE BAMBOO...
WELL, I GOT HUNGRY WALKING HERE FROM MY HOUSE.
YOU LIVE NEXT DOOR.
THAT WALK IS LONGER THAN IT LOOKS.
UH-HUH.
PANDA ESTATE (CHINESE-STYLE)
THE PLACE IS HUGE.
GIANT PANDA
GUESS I'LL START MY DIET TOMORROW.
ENJOY.

EVERYONE'S DIET ALWAYS STARTS "TOMORROW."

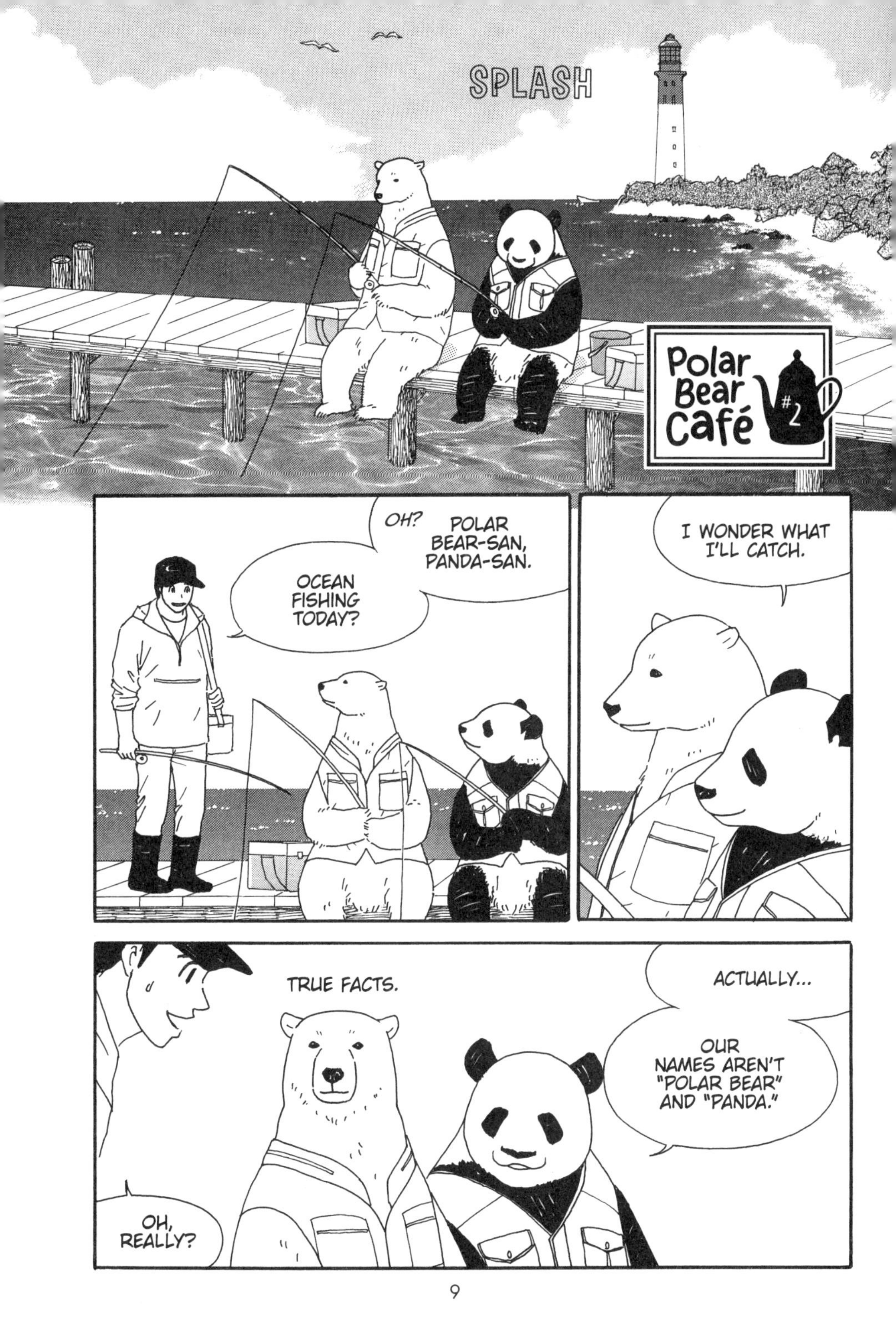
SPLASH
Polar Bear Café #2
I WONDER WHAT I'LL CATCH.
OH? POLAR BEAR-SAN, PANDA-SAN.
OCEAN FISHING TODAY?
ACTUALLY...
OUR NAMES AREN'T "POLAR BEAR" AND "PANDA."
TRUE FACTS.
OH, REALLY?

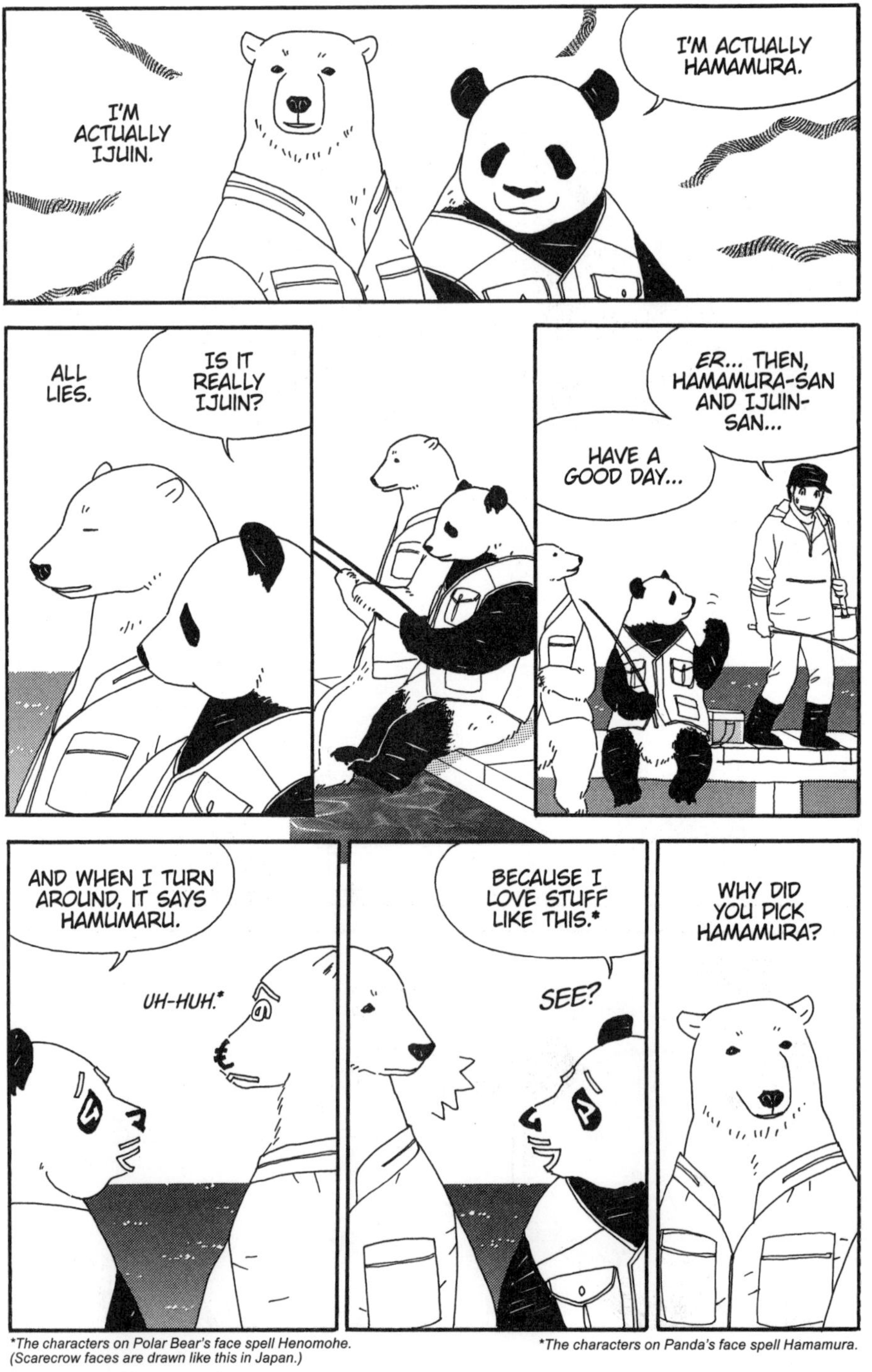
I'M ACTUALLY HAMAMURA.
I'M ACTUALLY IJUIN.
ER... THEN, HAMAMURA-SAN AND IJUIN-SAN...
HAVE A GOOD DAY...
IS IT REALLY IJUIN?
ALL LIES.
WHY DID YOU PICK HAMAMURA?
BECAUSE I LOVE STUFF LIKE THIS.*
SEE?
AND WHEN I TURN AROUND, IT SAYS HAMUMARU.
UH-HUH.*

*The characters on Panda's face spell Hamamura.

*The characters on Polar Bear's face spell Henomohe. (Scarecrow faces are drawn like this in Japan.)

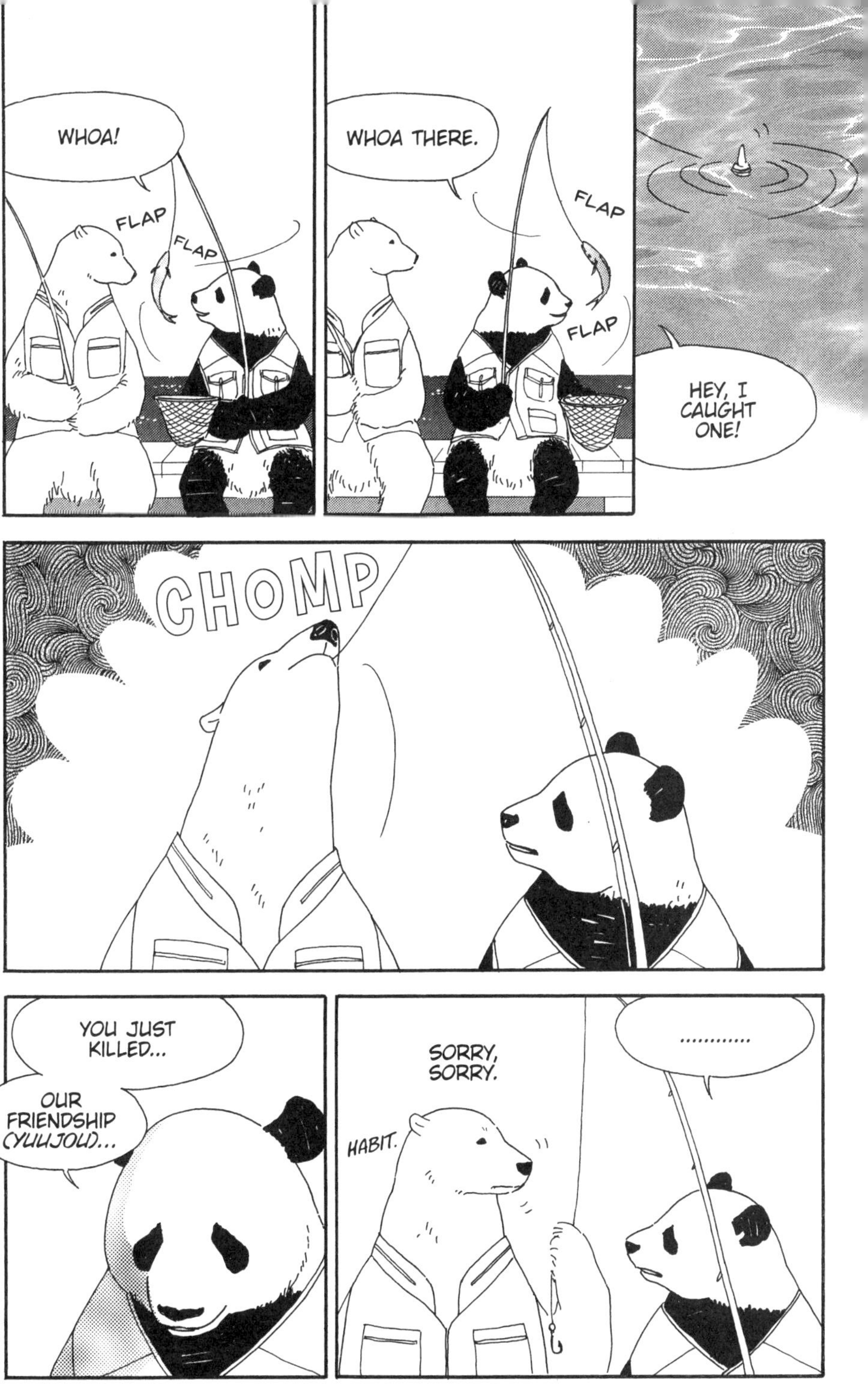
HEY, I CAUGHT ONE!
WHOA THERE.
FLAP
FLAP
WHOA!
FLAP
FLAP
CHOMP
....
SORRY, SORRY.
HABIT.
YOU JUST KILLED...
OUR FRIENDSHIP (YUUJOU)...

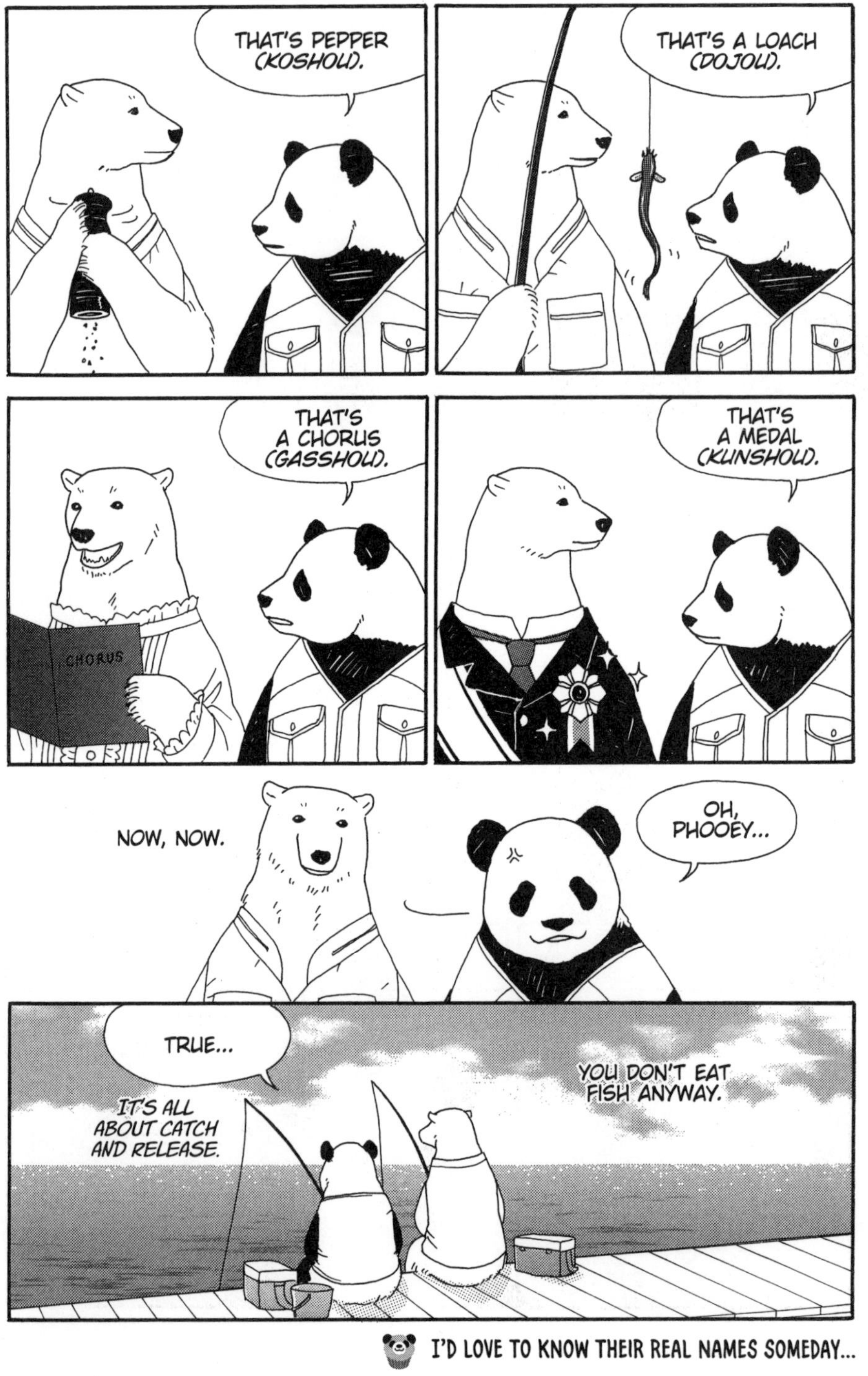
THAT'S A LOACH (DOJOU).
THAT'S PEPPER (KOSHOU).
THAT'S A MEDAL (KUNSHOU).
THAT'S A CHORUS (GASSHOU).
CHORUS
OH, PHOOEY...
NOW, NOW.
YOU DON'T EAT FISH ANYWAY.
TRUE...
IT'S ALL ABOUT CATCH AND RELEASE.

I'D LOVE TO KNOW THEIR REAL NAMES SOMEDAY...

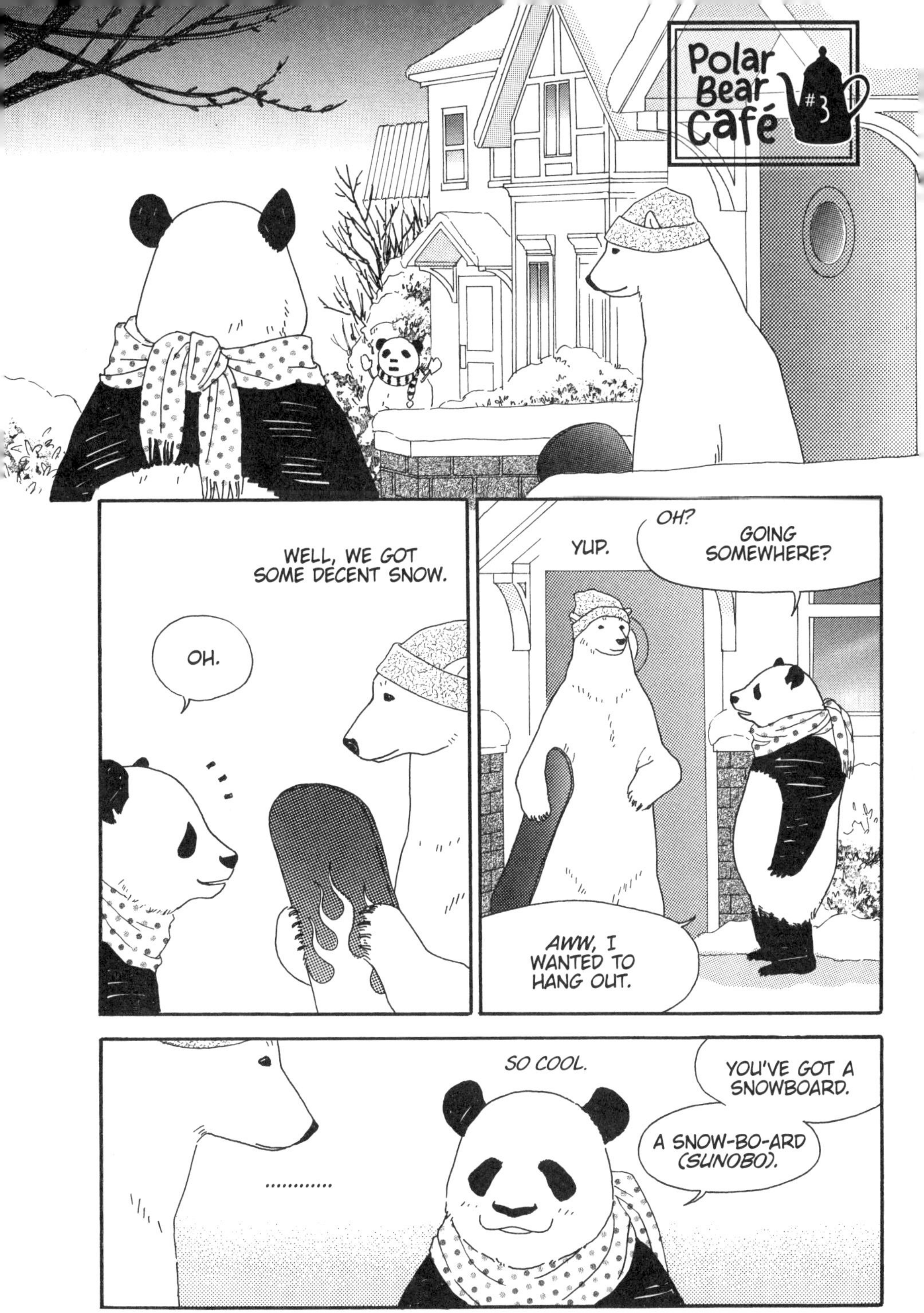
Polar Bear Café
#3
OH? GOING SOMEWHERE?
YUP.
AWW, I WANTED TO HANG OUT.
WELL, WE GOT SOME DECENT SNOW.
OH.
YOU'VE GOT A SNOWBOARD.
A SNOW-BO-ARD (SUNOBO).
SO COOL.
....

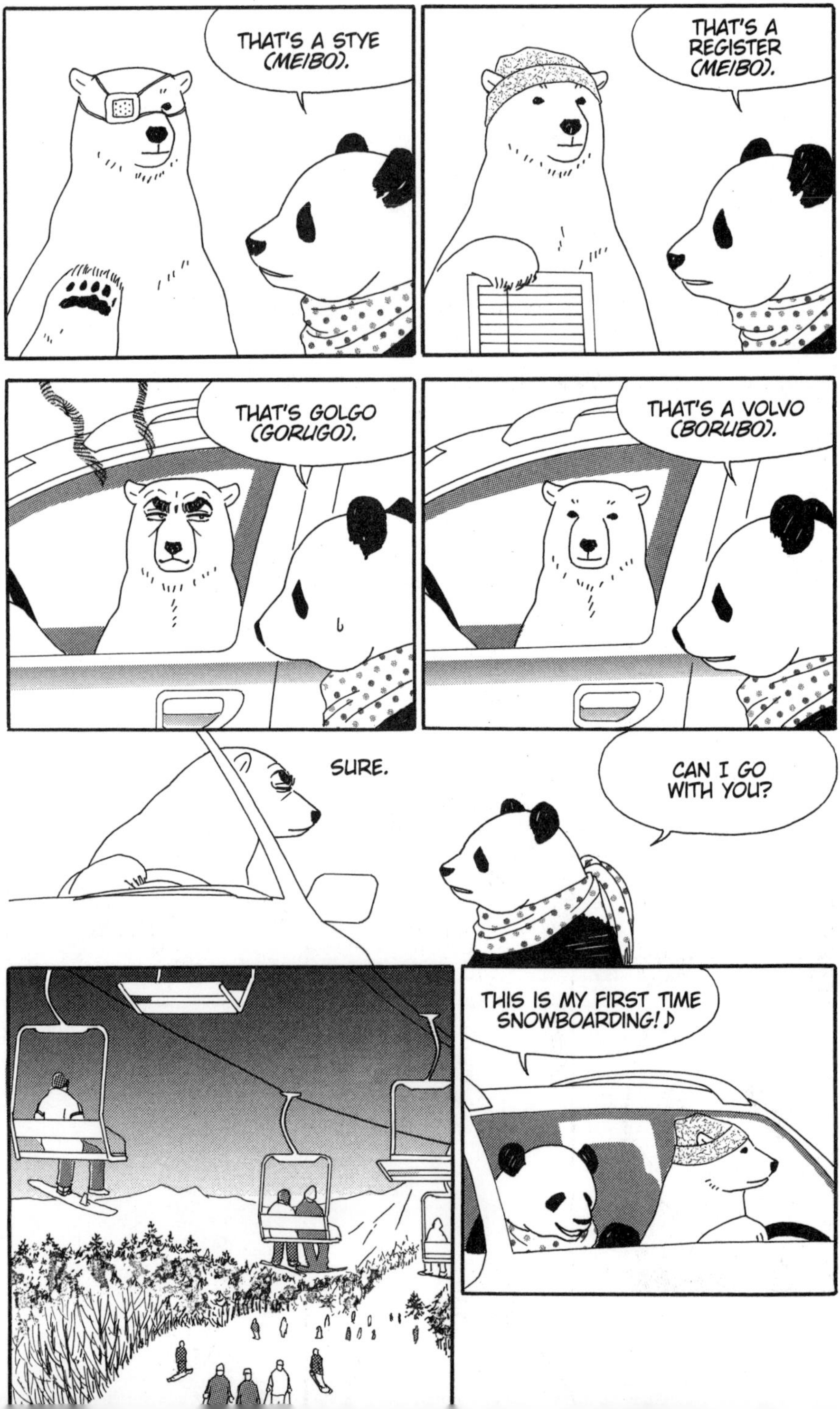
THAT'S A REGISTER (MEIBO).
THAT'S A STYE (MEIBO).
THAT'S A VOLVO (BORUBO).
THAT'S GOLGO (GORUGO).
CAN I GO WITH YOU?
SURE.
THIS IS MY FIRST TIME SNOWBOARDING!♪

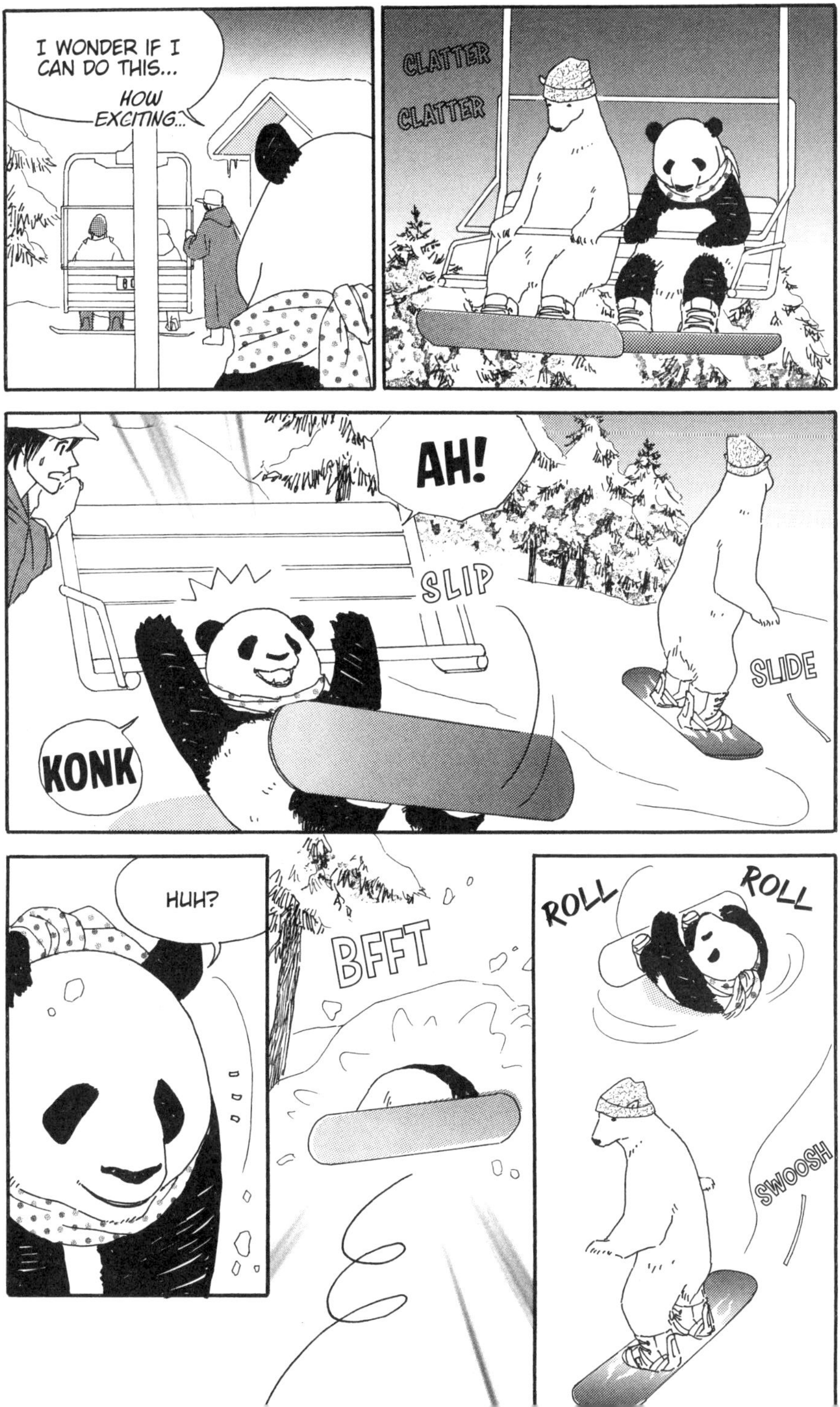
CLATTER
CLATTER
I WONDER IF I CAN DO THIS...
HOW EXCITING...
AH!
SLIP
SLIDE
KONK
ROLL
ROLL
SWOOSH
BFFT
HUH?

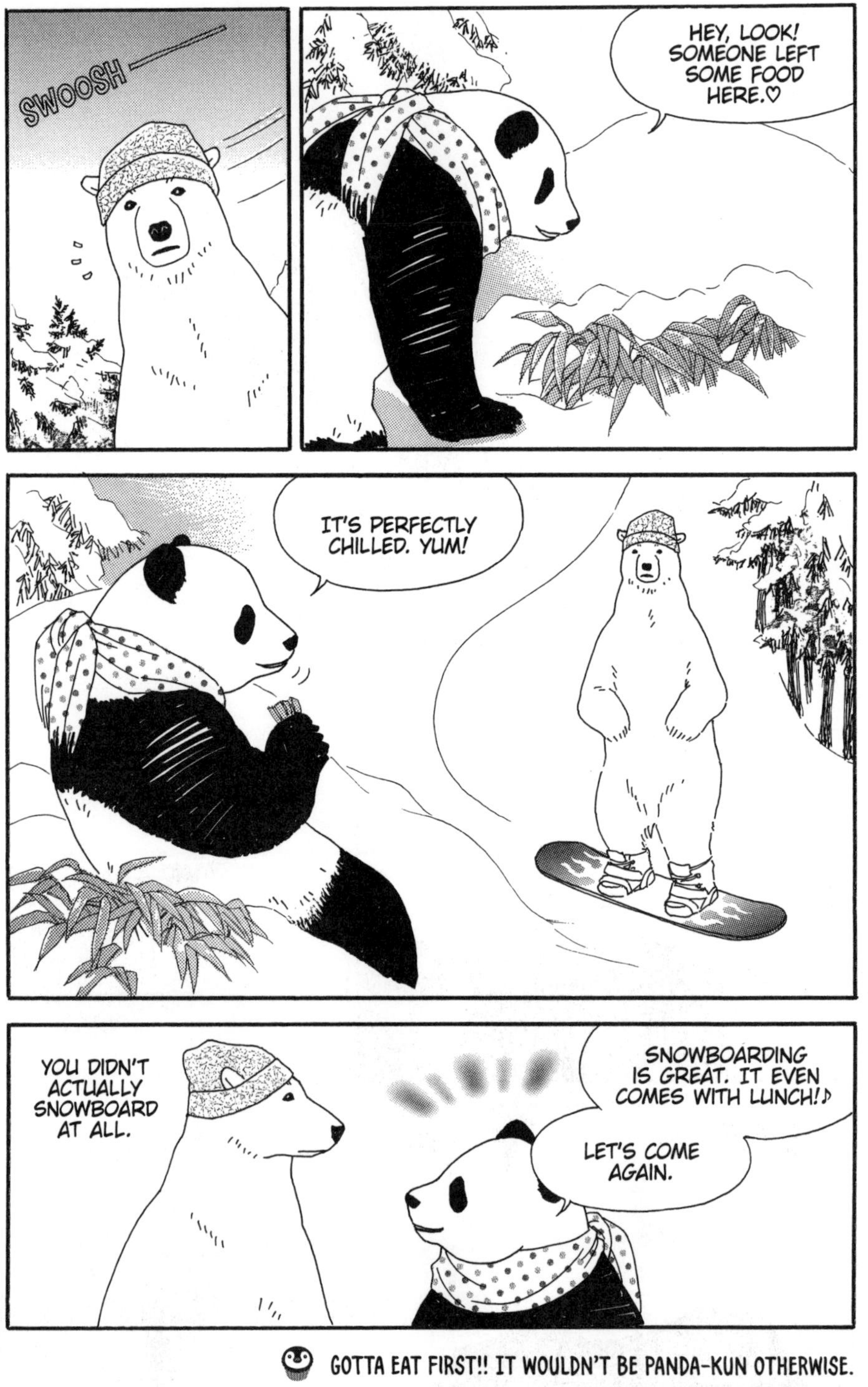
HEY, LOOK! SOMEONE LEFT SOME FOOD HERE.♡
SWOOSH
IT'S PERFECTLY CHILLED. YUM!
SNOWBOARDING IS GREAT. IT EVEN COMES WITH LUNCH!♪
LET'S COME AGAIN.
YOU DIDN'T ACTUALLY SNOWBOARD AT ALL.

GOTTA EAT FIRST!! IT WOULDN'T BE PANDA-KUN OTHERWISE.

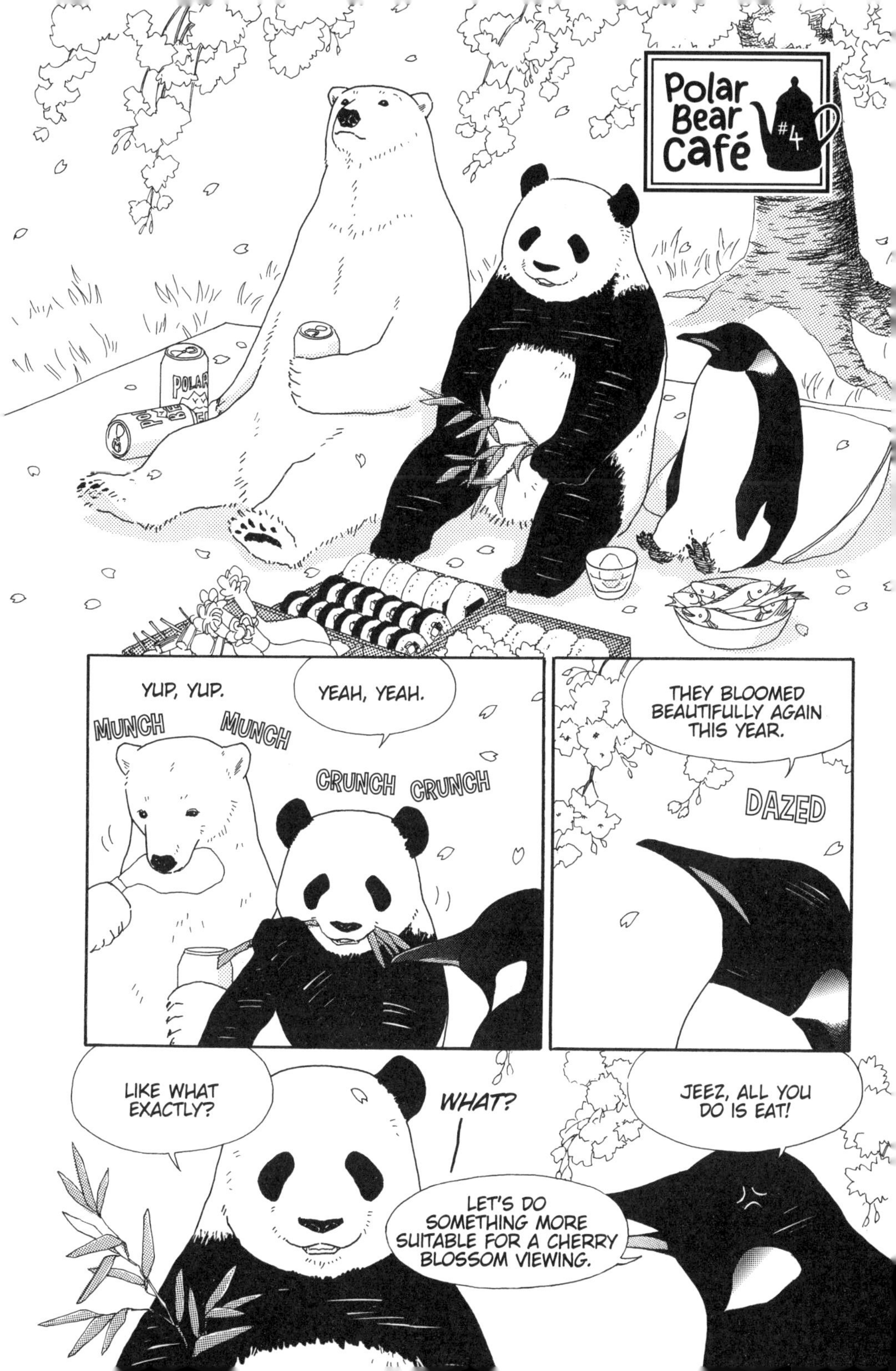
Polar Bear Café
#4
POLAR BEER
THEY BLOOMED BEAUTIFULLY AGAIN THIS YEAR.
DAZED
YEAH, YEAH.
YUP, YUP.
MUNCH
MUNCH
CRUNCH
CRUNCH
JEEZ, ALL YOU DO IS EAT!
WHAT?
LET'S DO SOMETHING MORE SUITABLE FOR A CHERRY BLOSSOM VIEWING.
LIKE WHAT EXACTLY?

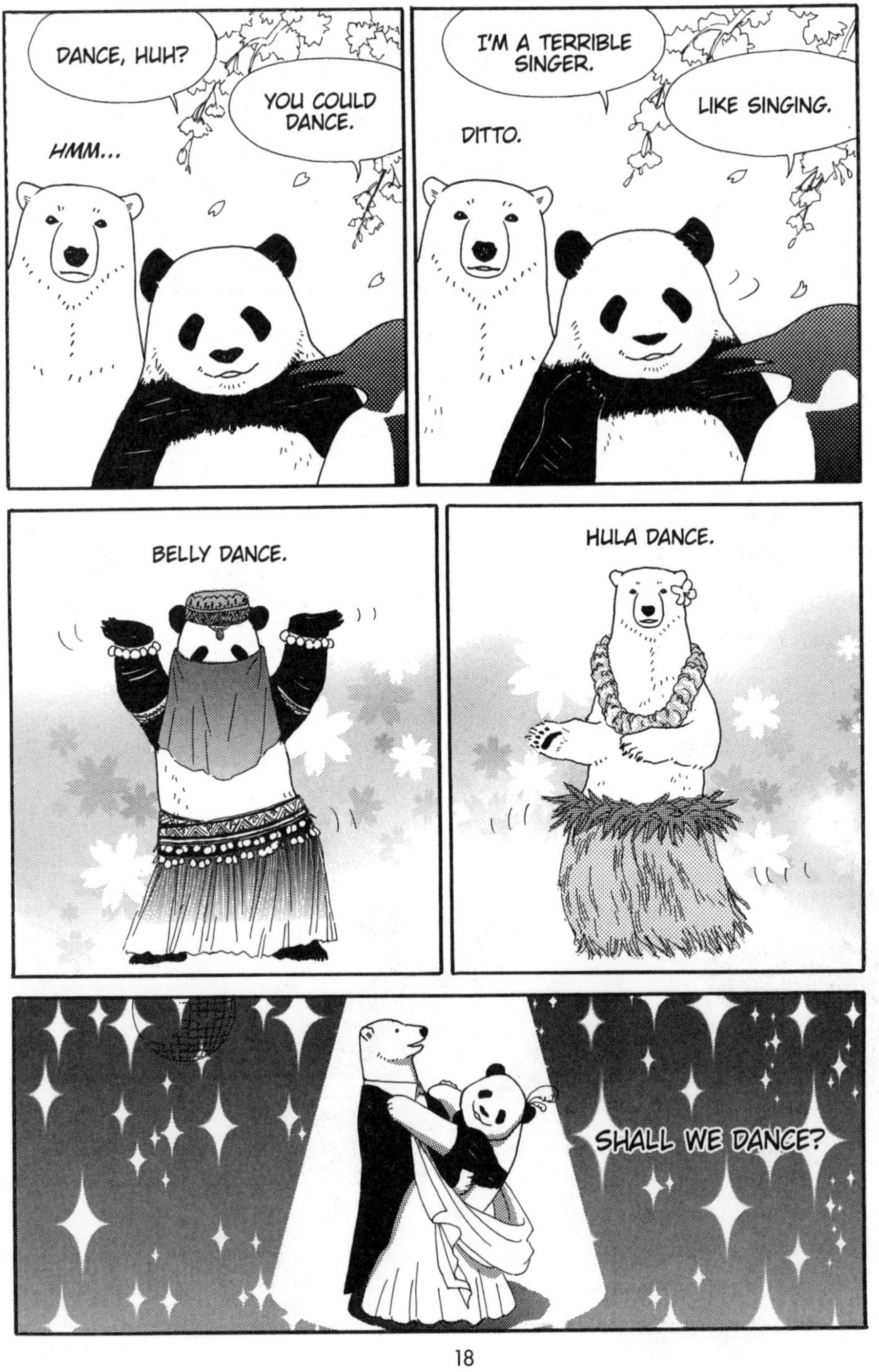
LIKE SINGING.
I'M A TERRIBLE SINGER.
DITTO.
YOU COULD DANCE.
DANCE, HUH?
HMM...
HULA DANCE.
BELLY DANCE.
SHALL WE DANCE?

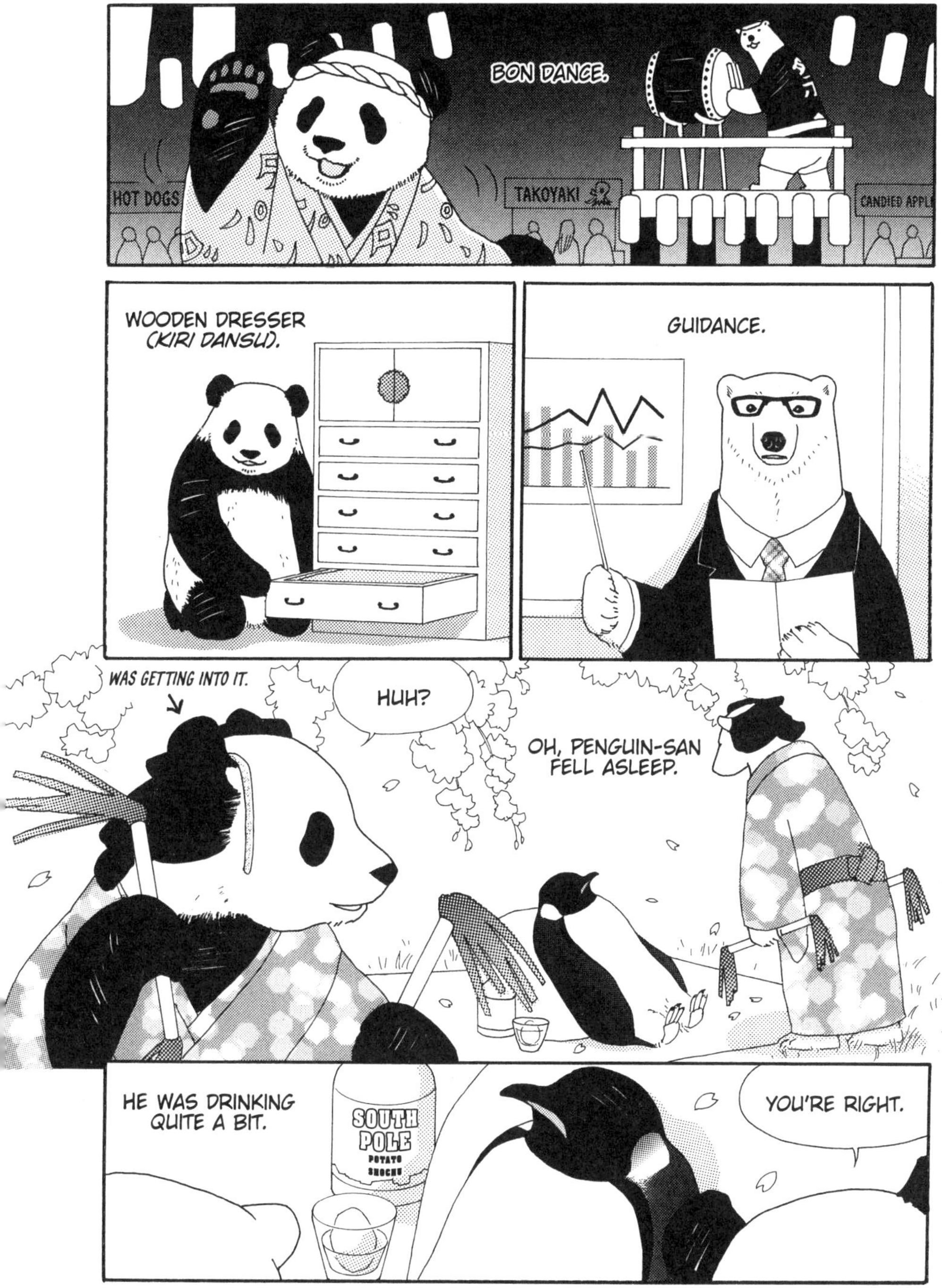

BON DANCE.
CANDIED APPL
TAKOYAKI
HOT DOGS
GUIDANCE.
WOODEN DRESSER (KIRI DANSU).
OH, PENGUIN-SAN FELL ASLEEP.
HUH?
WAS GETTING INTO IT.
YOU'RE RIGHT.
SOUTH POLE POTATO SHOCHU
HE WAS DRINKING QUITE A BIT.

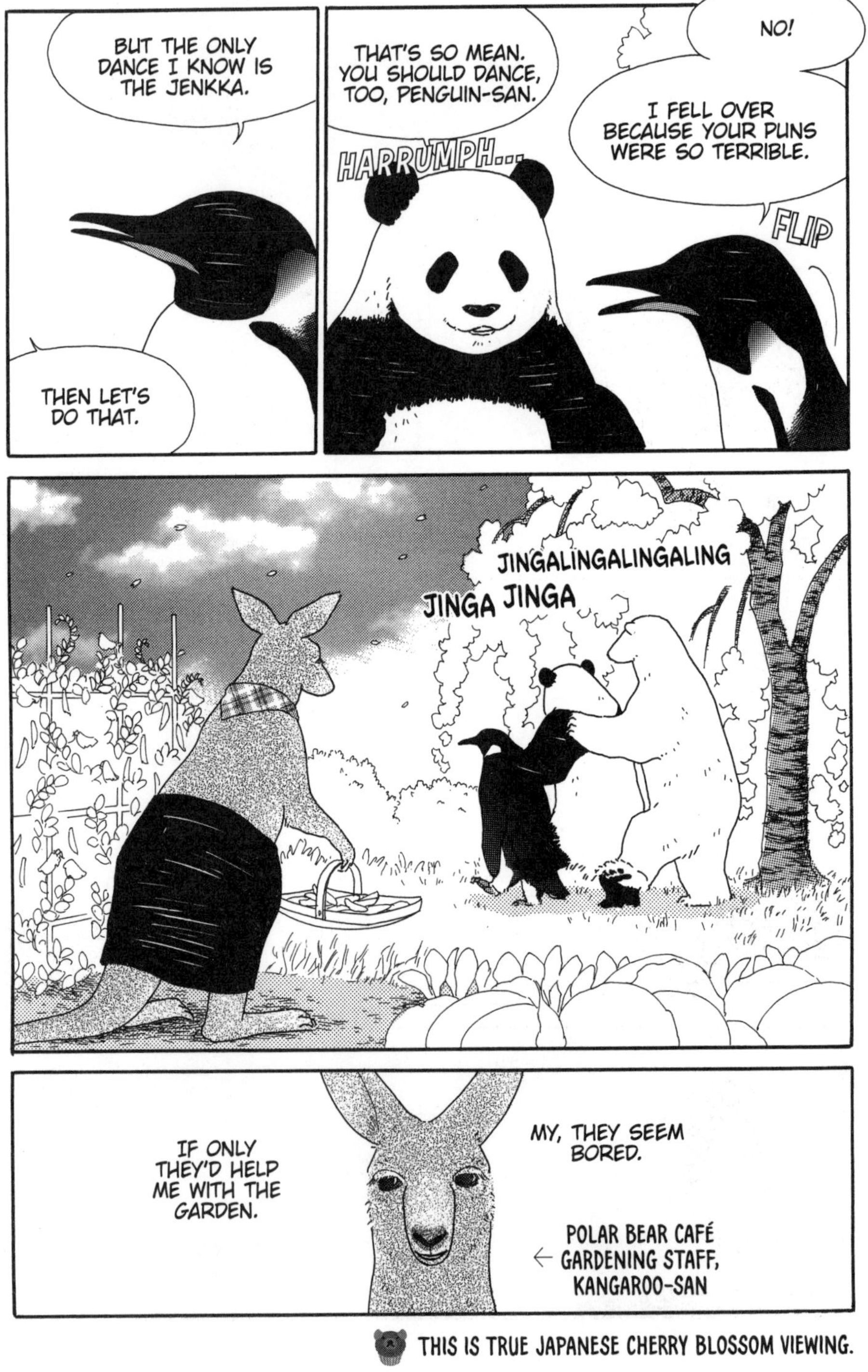
THAT'S SO MEAN. YOU SHOULD DANCE, TOO, PENGUIN-SAN.
HARRUMPH...
NO!
I FELL OVER BECAUSE YOUR PUNS WERE SO TERRIBLE.
FLIP
BUT THE ONLY DANCE I KNOW IS THE JENKKA.
THEN LET'S DO THAT.
JINGALINGALINGALING
JINGA JINGA
MY, THEY SEEM BORED.
IF ONLY THEY'D HELP ME WITH THE GARDEN.
← POLAR BEAR CAFÉ GARDENING STAFF, KANGAROO-SAN

THIS IS TRUE JAPANESE CHERRY BLOSSOM VIEWING.

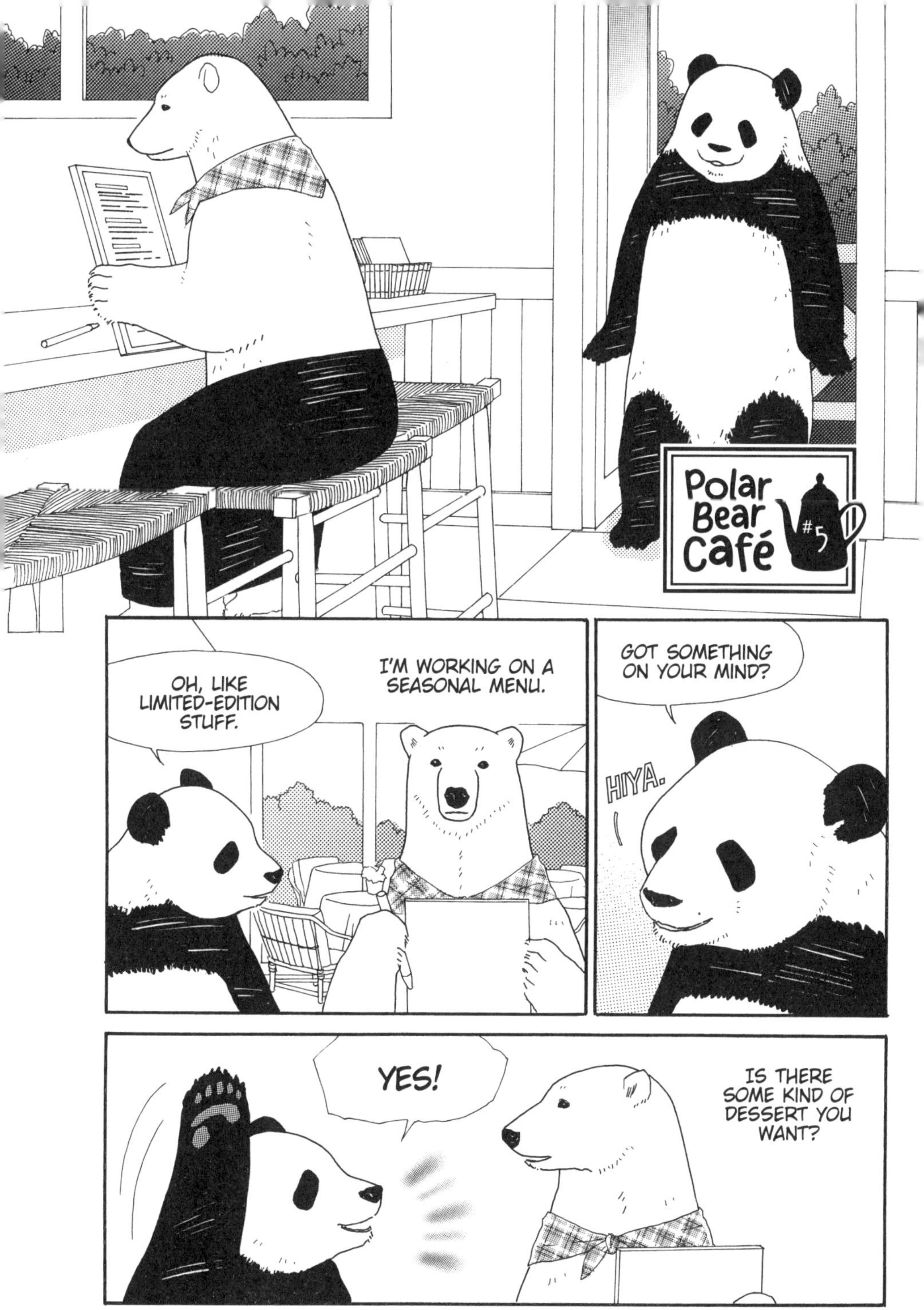
Polar Bear Café
#5
GOT SOMETHING ON YOUR MIND?
HIYA.
I'M WORKING ON A SEASONAL MENU.
OH, LIKE LIMITED-EDITION STUFF.
IS THERE SOME KIND OF DESSERT YOU WANT?
YES!

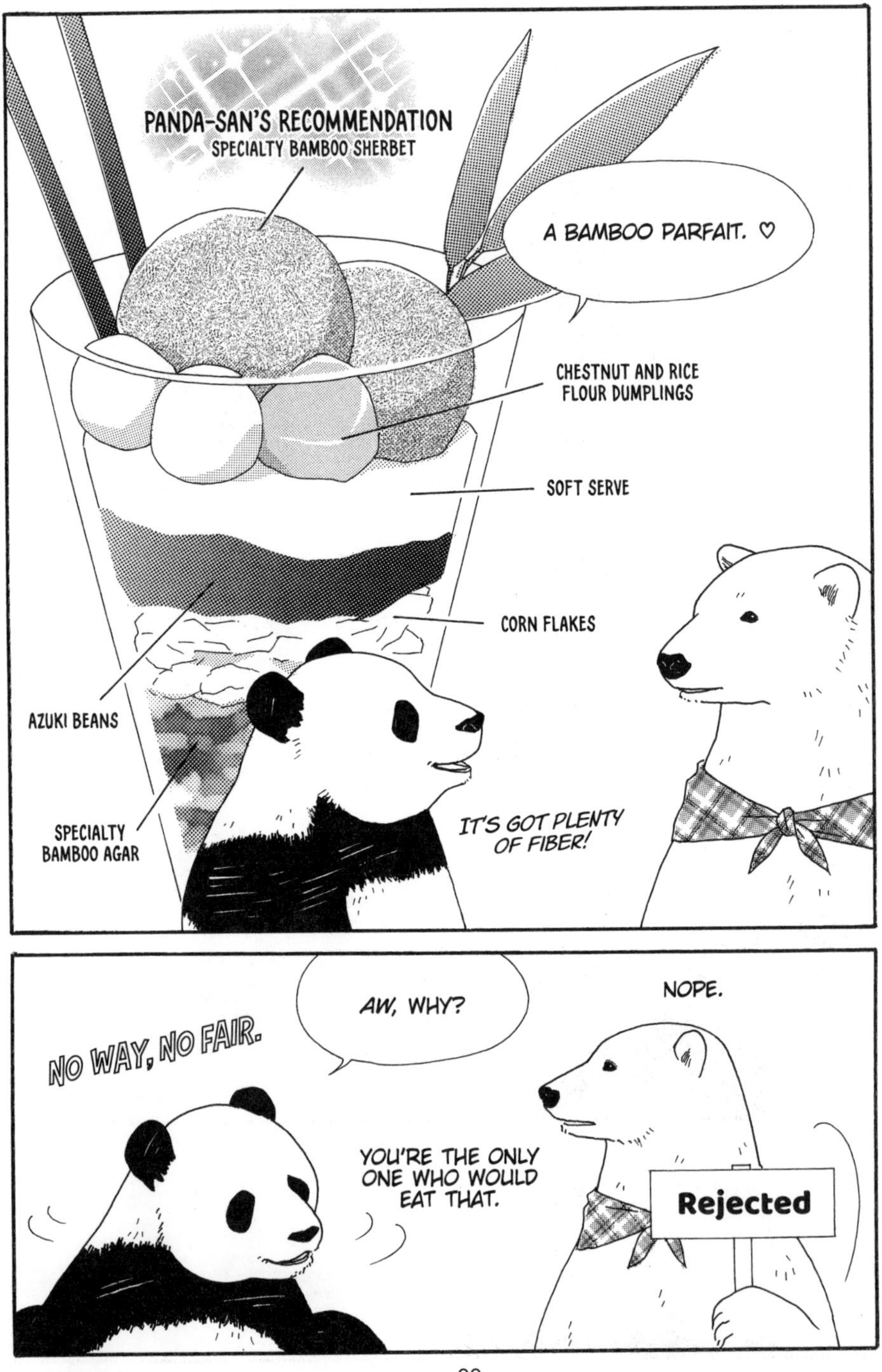
A BAMBOO PARFAIT. ♡
PANDA-SAN'S RECOMMENDATION
SPECIALTY BAMBOO SHERBET
CHESTNUT AND RICE FLOUR DUMPLINGS
SOFT SERVE
CORN FLAKES
IT'S GOT PLENTY OF FIBER!
AZUKI BEANS
SPECIALTY BAMBOO AGAR
NOPE.
Rejected
YOU'RE THE ONLY ONE WHO WOULD EAT THAT.
AW, WHY?
NO WAY, NO FAIR.

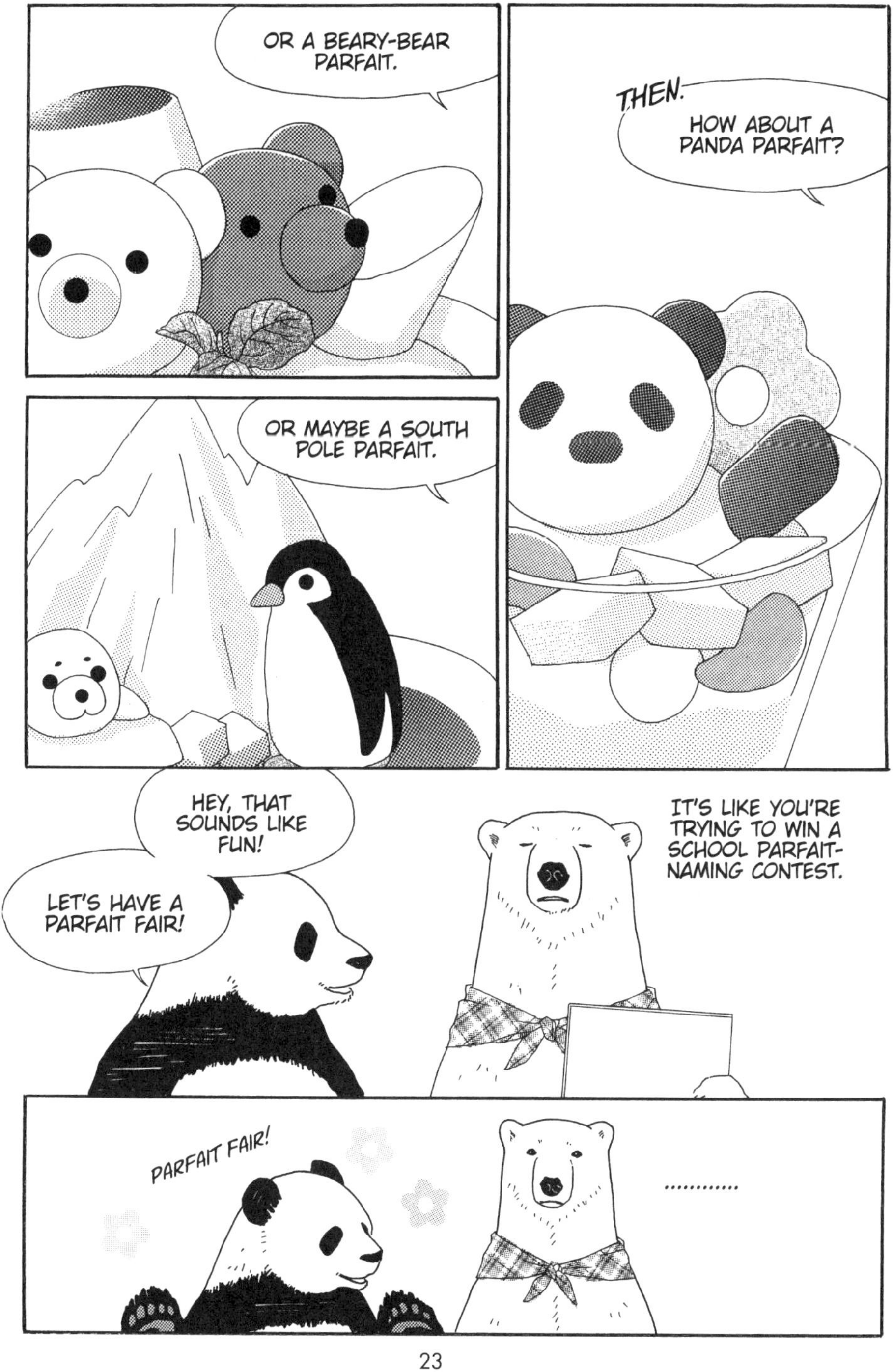
THEN.
HOW ABOUT A PANDA PARFAIT?
OR A BEARY-BEAR PARFAIT.
OR MAYBE A SOUTH POLE PARFAIT.
IT'S LIKE YOU'RE TRYING TO WIN A SCHOOL PARFAIT-NAMING CONTEST.
HEY, THAT SOUNDS LIKE FUN!
LET'S HAVE A PARFAIT FAIR!
....
PARFAIT FAIR!

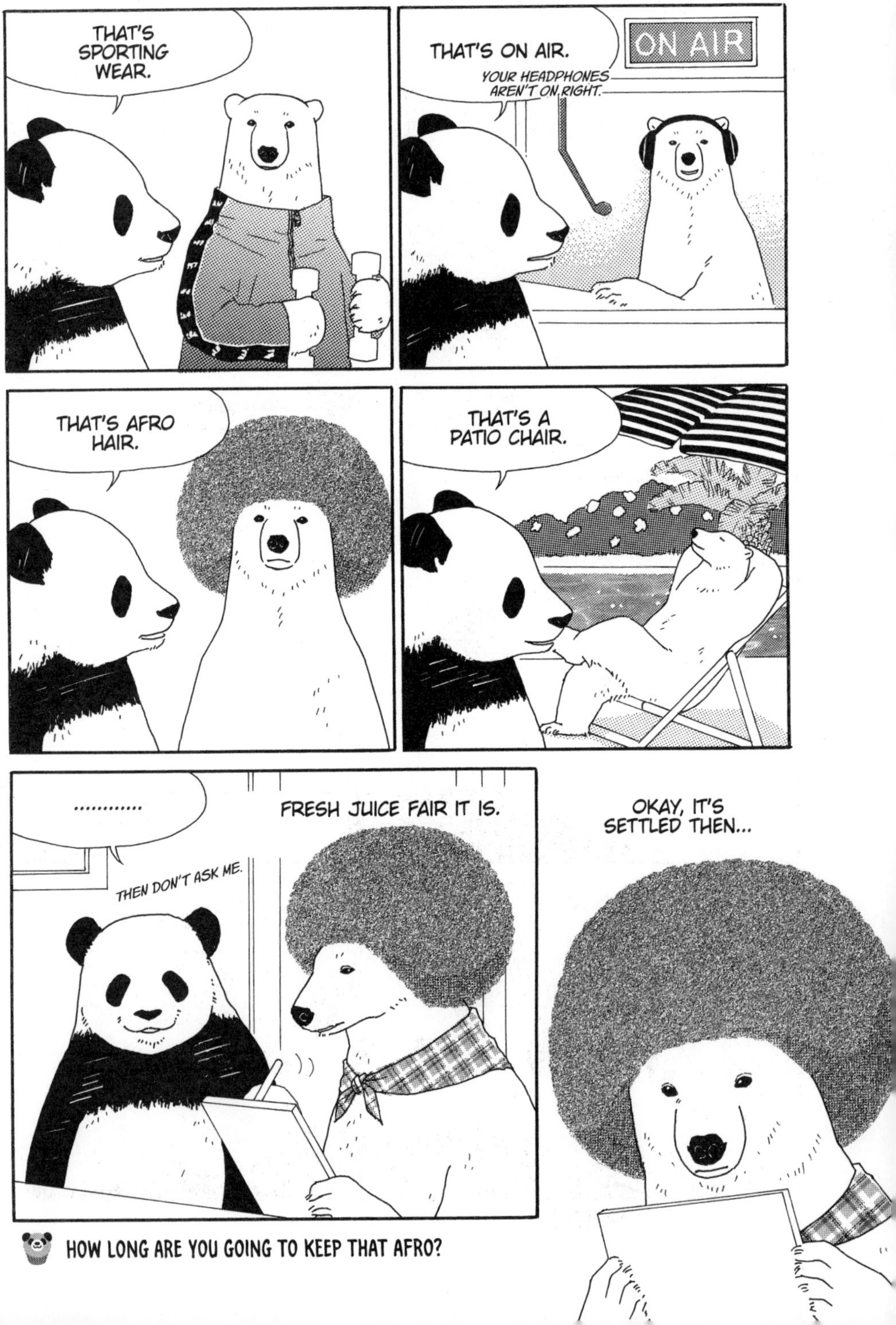
ON AIR
THAT'S ON AIR.
YOUR HEADPHONES AREN'T ON RIGHT.
THAT'S SPORTING WEAR.
THAT'S A PATIO CHAIR.
THAT'S AFRO HAIR.
OKAY, IT'S SETTLED THEN...
FRESH JUICE FAIR IT IS.
....
THEN DON'T ASK ME.

HOW LONG ARE YOU GOING TO KEEP THAT AFRO?

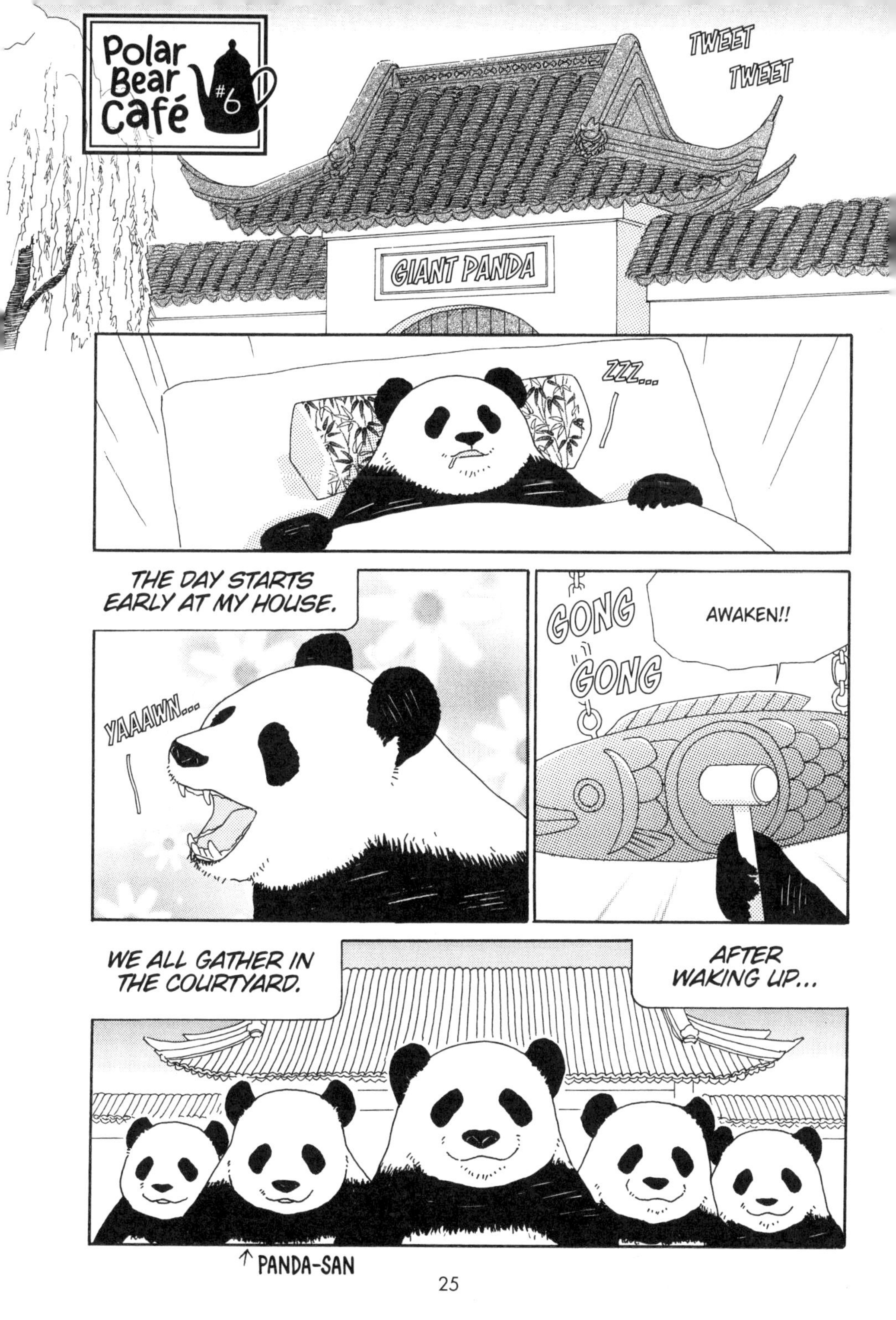
Polar Bear Café #6
TWEET TWEET
GIANT PANDA
ZZZ...
GONG GONG
AWAKEN!!
THE DAY STARTS EARLY AT MY HOUSE.
YAAAWN...
AFTER WAKING UP...
WE ALL GATHER IN THE COURTYARD.
↑ PANDA-SAN

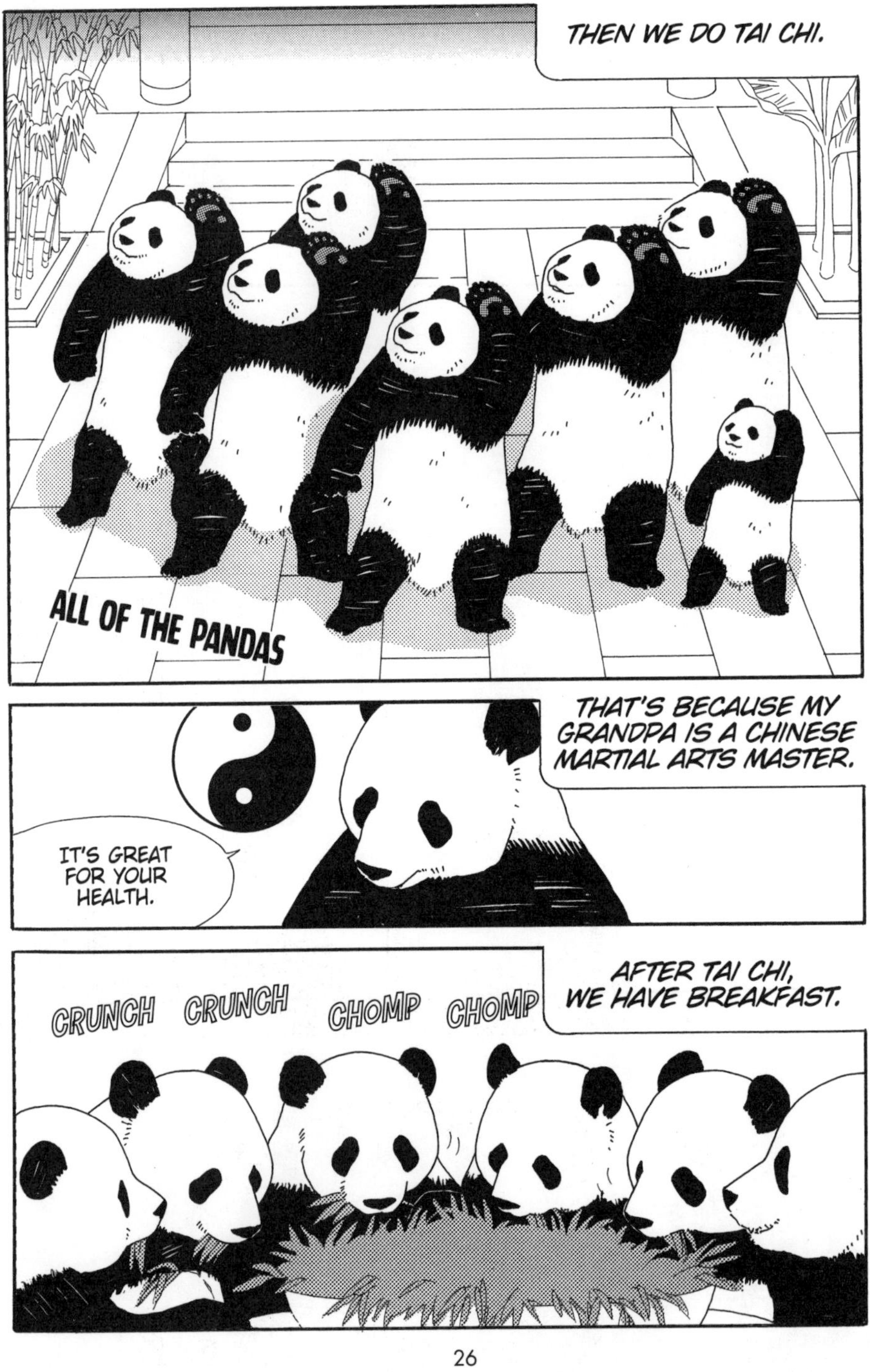
THEN WE DO TAI CHI.
ALL OF THE PANDAS
THAT'S BECAUSE MY GRANDPA IS A CHINESE MARTIAL ARTS MASTER.
IT'S GREAT FOR YOUR HEALTH.
AFTER TAI CHI, WE HAVE BREAKFAST.
CHOMP
CHOMP
CRUNCH
CRUNCH

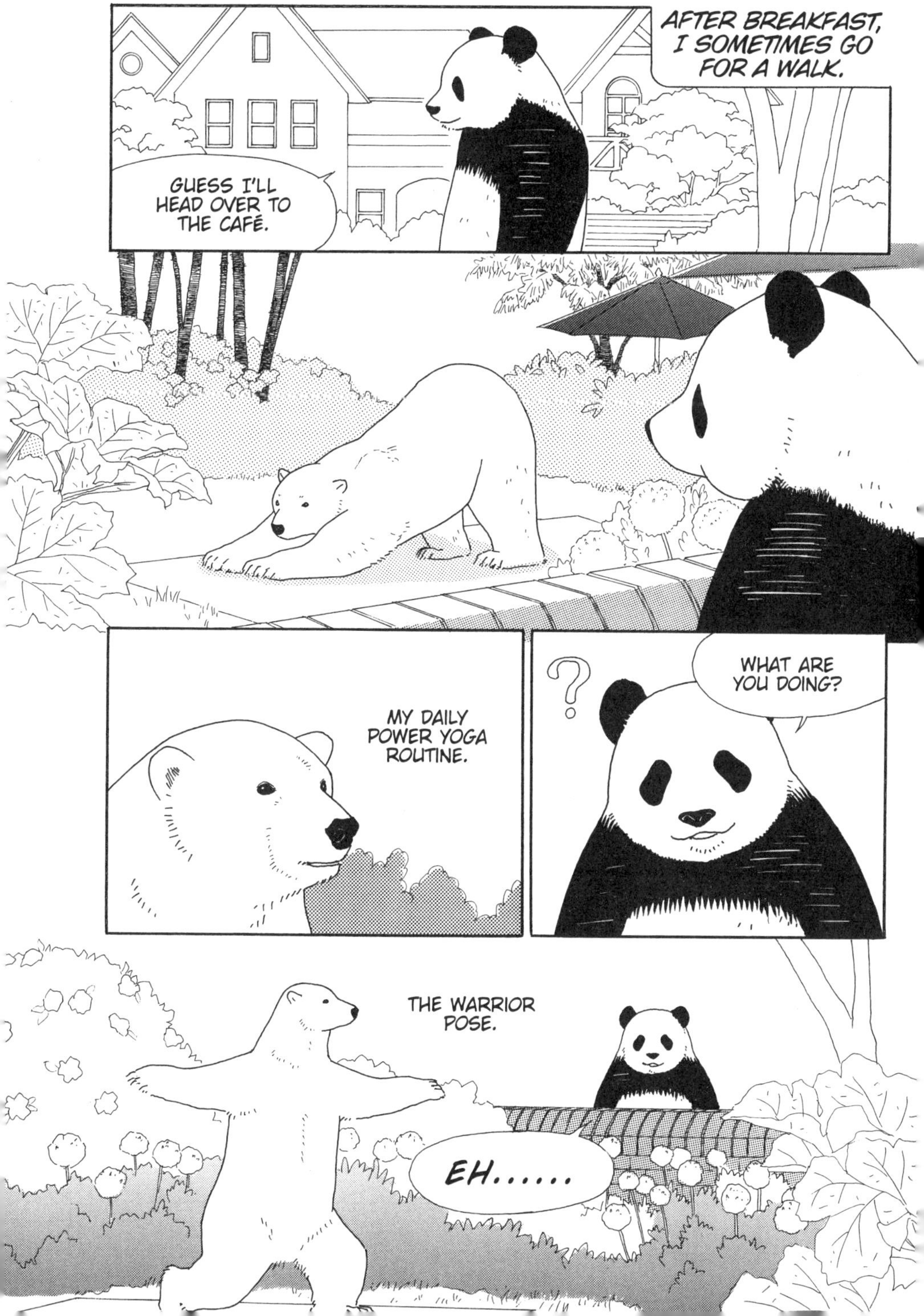
AFTER BREAKFAST, I SOMETIMES GO FOR A WALK.
GUESS I'LL HEAD OVER TO THE CAFÉ.
WHAT ARE YOU DOING?
MY DAILY POWER YOGA ROUTINE.
THE WARRIOR POSE.
EH......

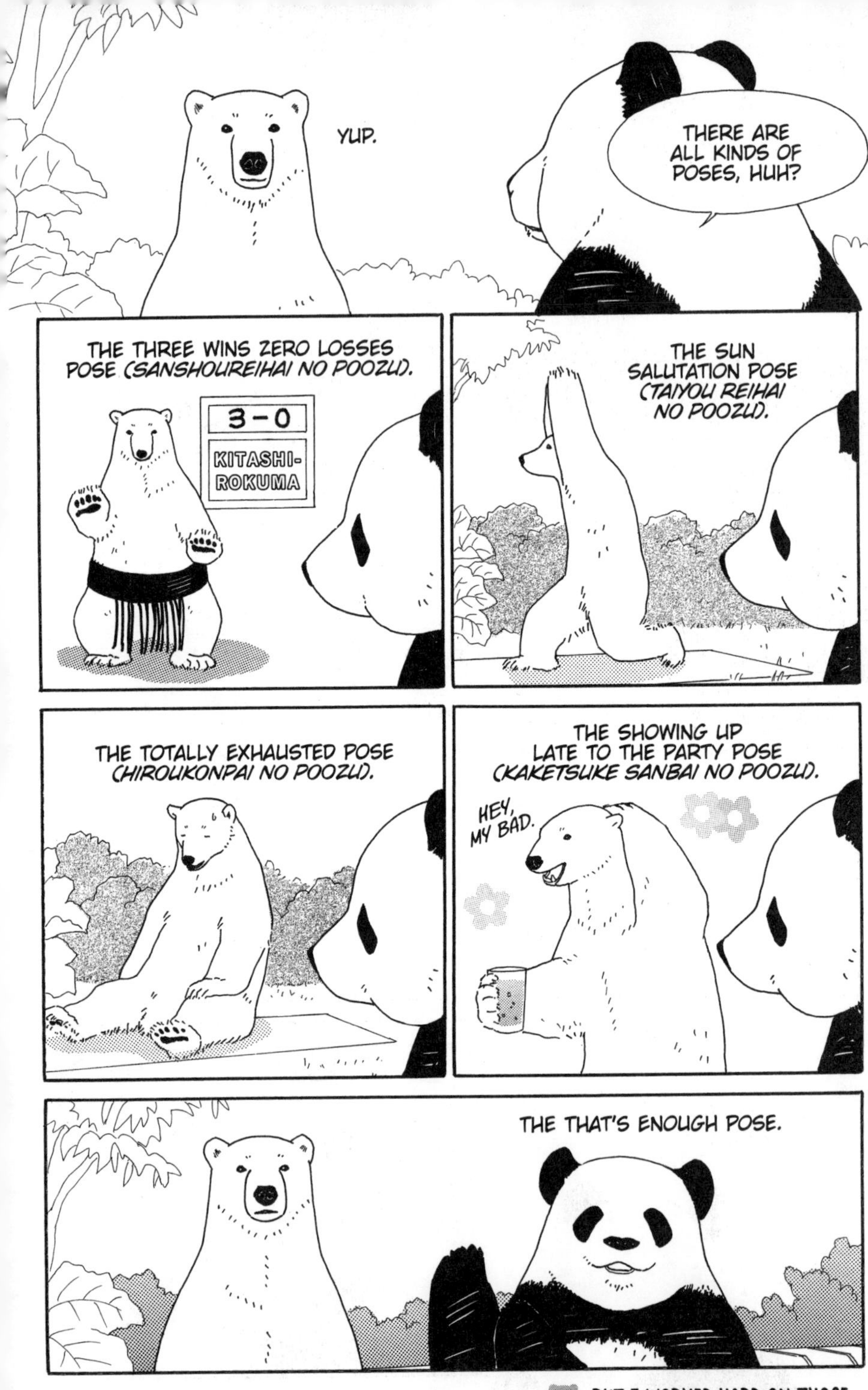
THERE ARE ALL KINDS OF POSES, HUH?
YUP.
THE SUN SALUTATION POSE (TAIYOU REIHAI NO POOZU).
THE THREE WINS ZERO LOSSES POSE (SANSHOUREIHAI NO POOZU).
3-0
KITASHI-ROKUMA
THE SHOWING UP LATE TO THE PARTY POSE (KAKETSUKE SANBAI NO POOZU).
HEY, MY BAD.
THE TOTALLY EXHAUSTED POSE (HIROUKONPAI NO POOZU).
THE THAT'S ENOUGH POSE.

BUT I WORKED HARD ON THOSE...

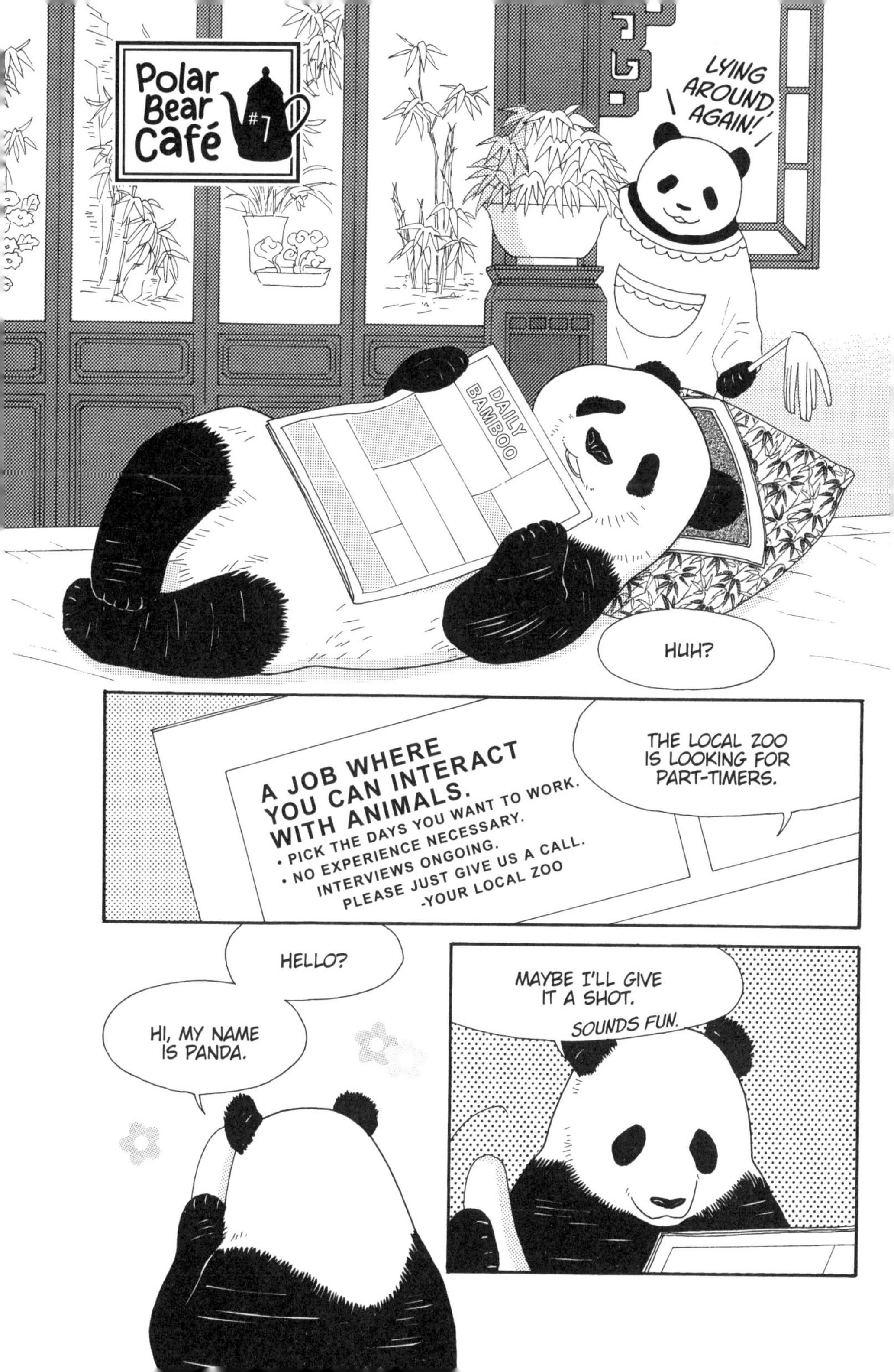
LYING AROUND, AGAIN!
Polar Bear Café #7
DAILY BAMBOO
HUH?
THE LOCAL ZOO IS LOOKING FOR PART-TIMERS.
A JOB WHERE YOU CAN INTERACT WITH ANIMALS.
• PICK THE DAYS YOU WANT TO WORK.
• NO EXPERIENCE NECESSARY.
INTERVIEWS ONGOING.
PLEASE JUST GIVE US A CALL.
-YOUR LOCAL ZOO
MAYBE I'LL GIVE IT A SHOT.
SOUNDS FUN.
HELLO?
HI, MY NAME IS PANDA.

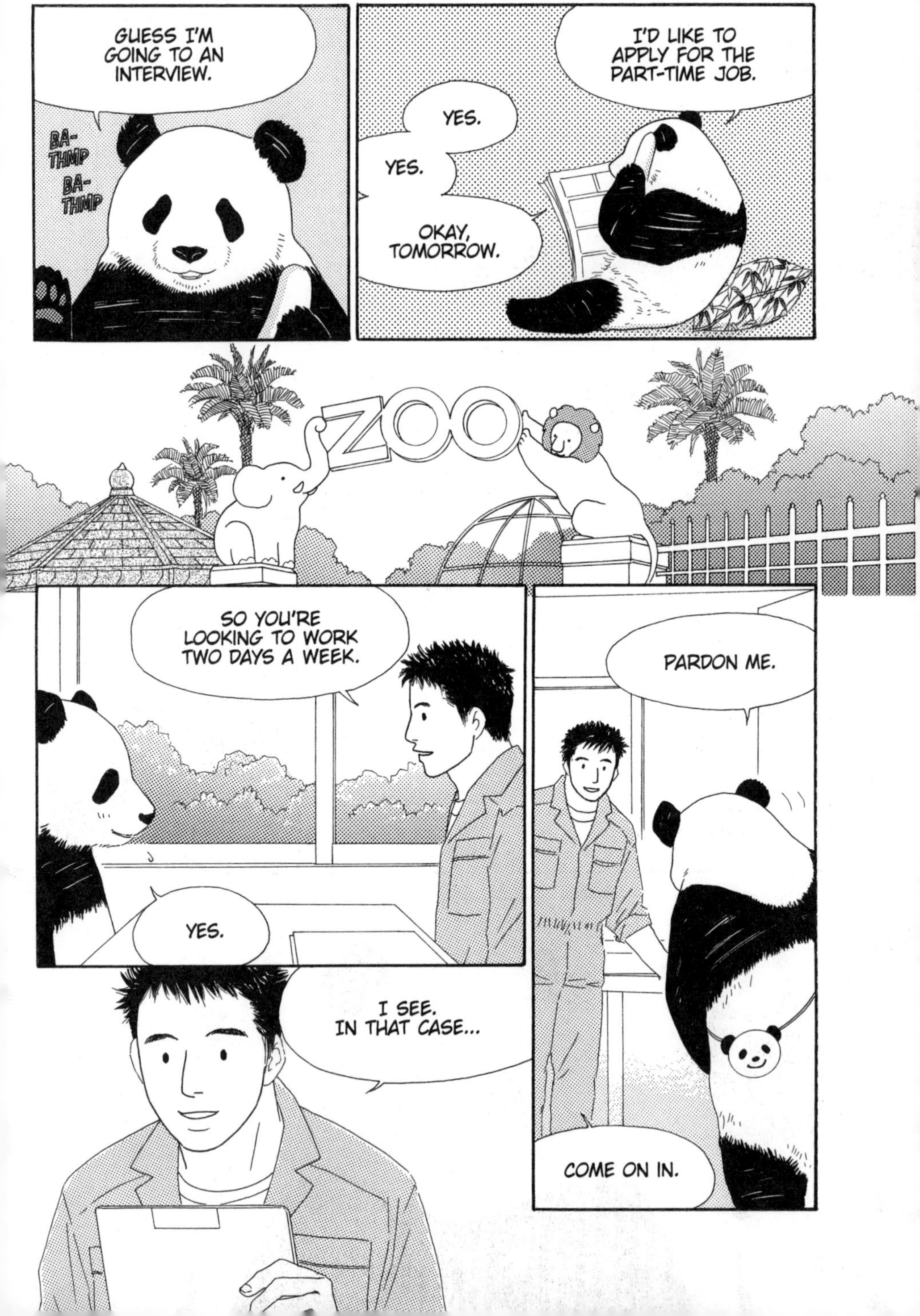
I'D LIKE TO APPLY FOR THE PART-TIME JOB.
YES.
YES.
OKAY, TOMORROW.
GUESS I'M GOING TO AN INTERVIEW.
BA-THMP
BA-THMP
ZOO
PARDON ME.
COME ON IN.
SO YOU'RE LOOKING TO WORK TWO DAYS A WEEK.
YES.
I SEE. IN THAT CASE...

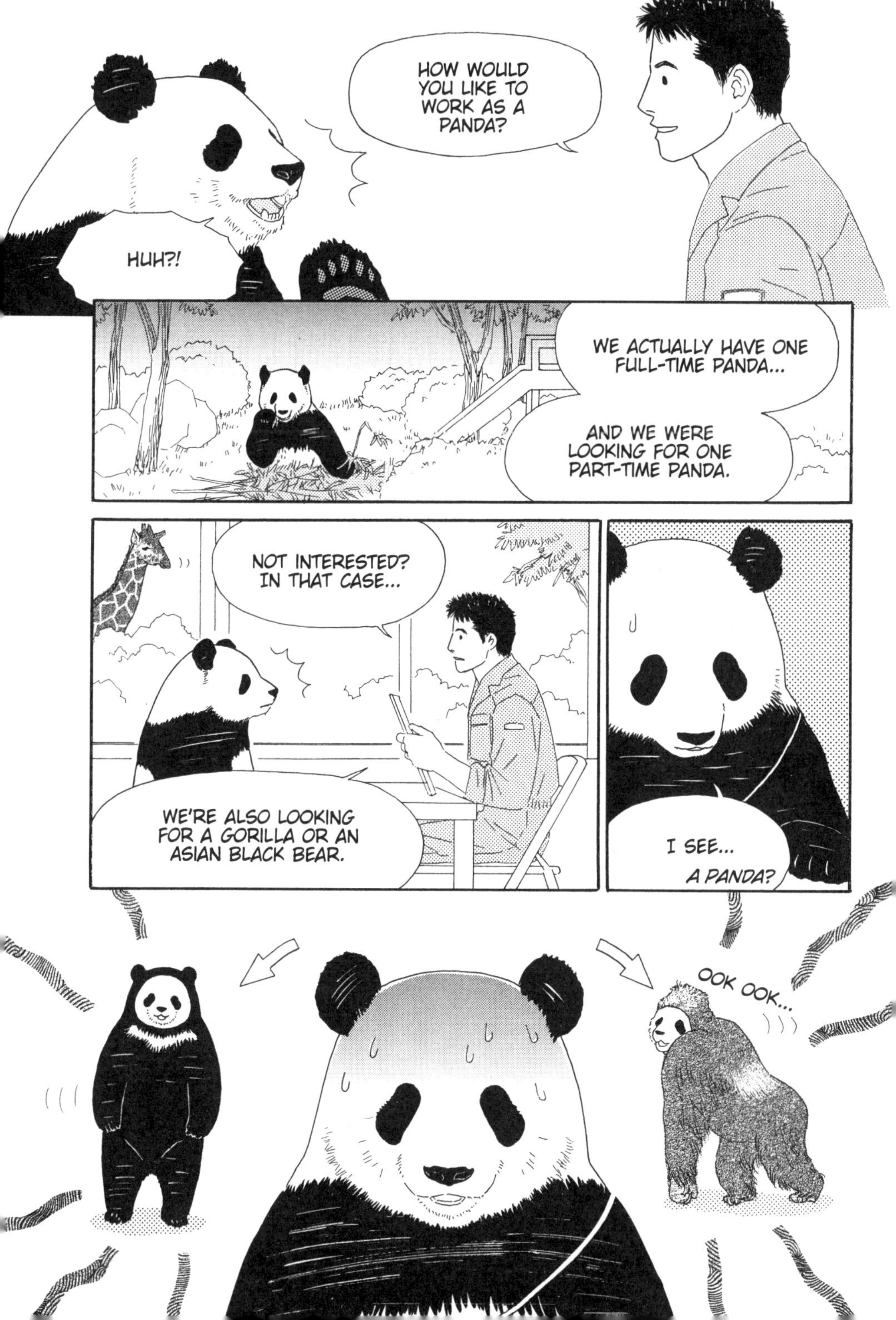
HOW WOULD YOU LIKE TO WORK AS A PANDA?
HUH?!
WE ACTUALLY HAVE ONE FULL-TIME PANDA...
AND WE WERE LOOKING FOR ONE PART-TIME PANDA.
I SEE... A PANDA?
NOT INTERESTED? IN THAT CASE...
WE'RE ALSO LOOKING FOR A GORILLA OR AN ASIAN BLACK BEAR.
OOK OOK...

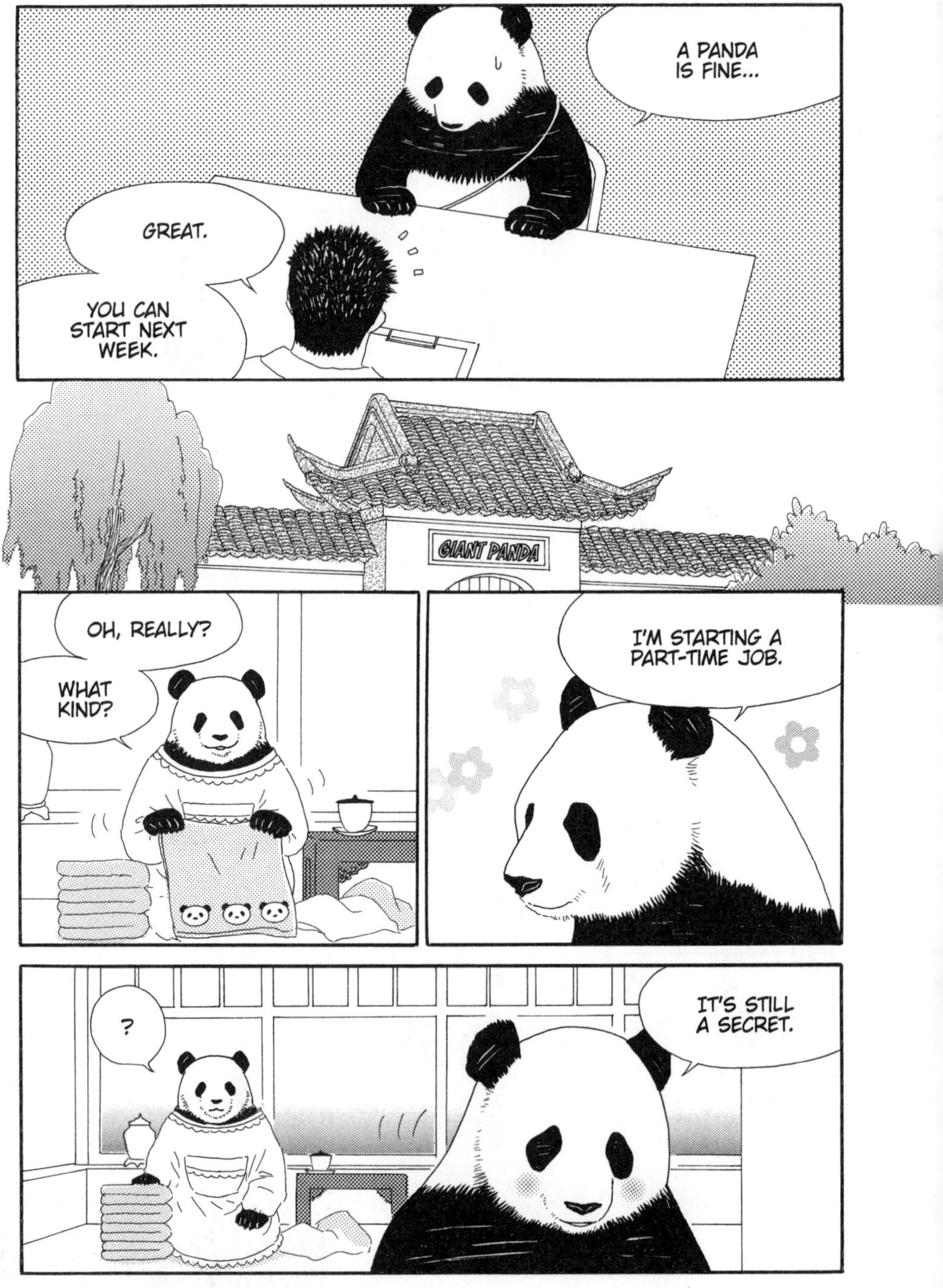
A PANDA IS FINE...
GREAT.
YOU CAN START NEXT WEEK.
GIANT PANDA
I'M STARTING A PART-TIME JOB.
OH, REALLY?
WHAT KIND?
IT'S STILL A SECRET.
?

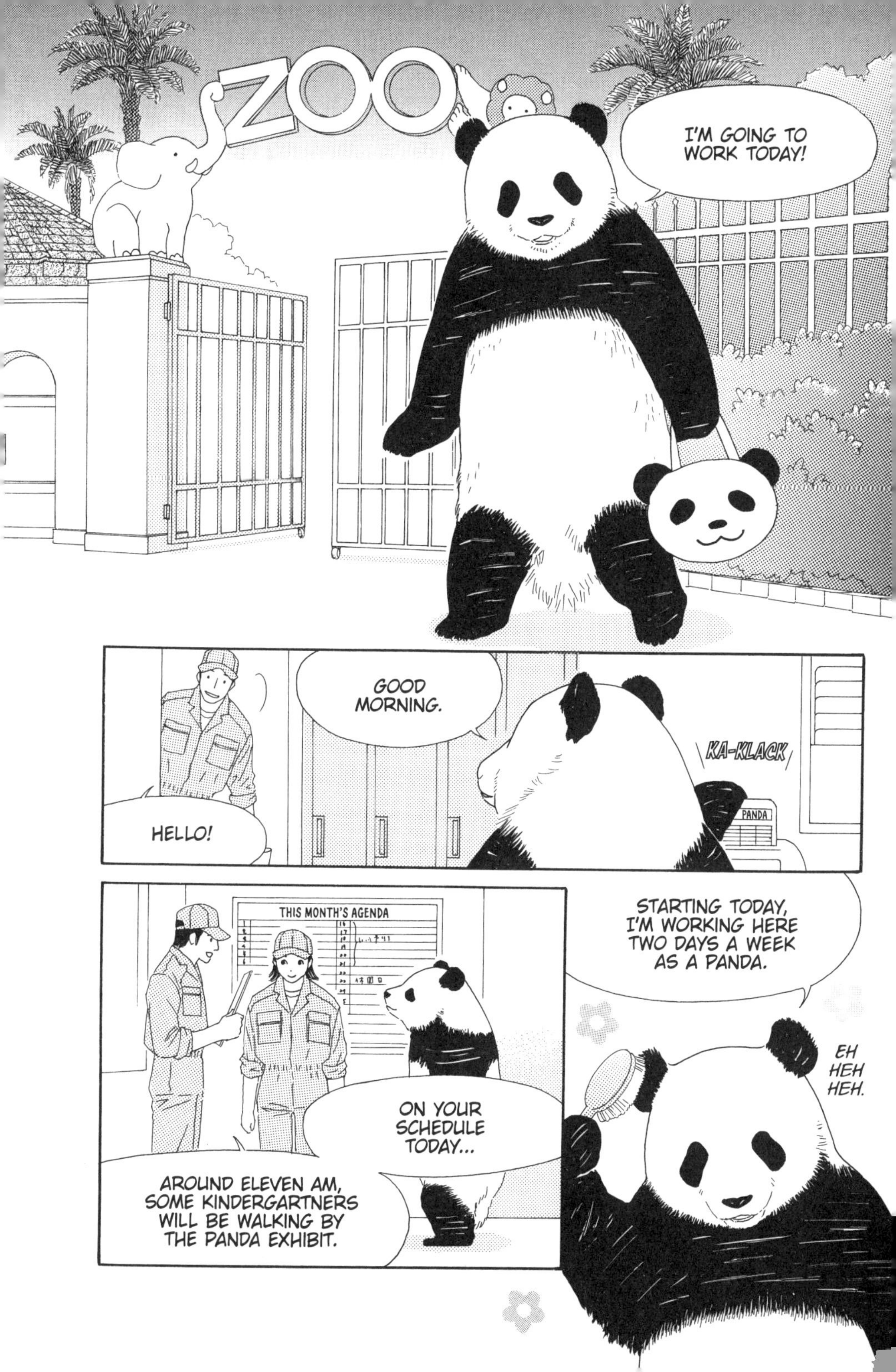
ZOO
I'M GOING TO WORK TODAY!
KA-KLACK
GOOD MORNING.
PANDA
HELLO!
STARTING TODAY, I'M WORKING HERE TWO DAYS A WEEK AS A PANDA.
EH HEH HEH.
THIS MONTH'S AGENDA
ON YOUR SCHEDULE TODAY...
AROUND ELEVEN AM, SOME KINDERGARTNERS WILL BE WALKING BY THE PANDA EXHIBIT.

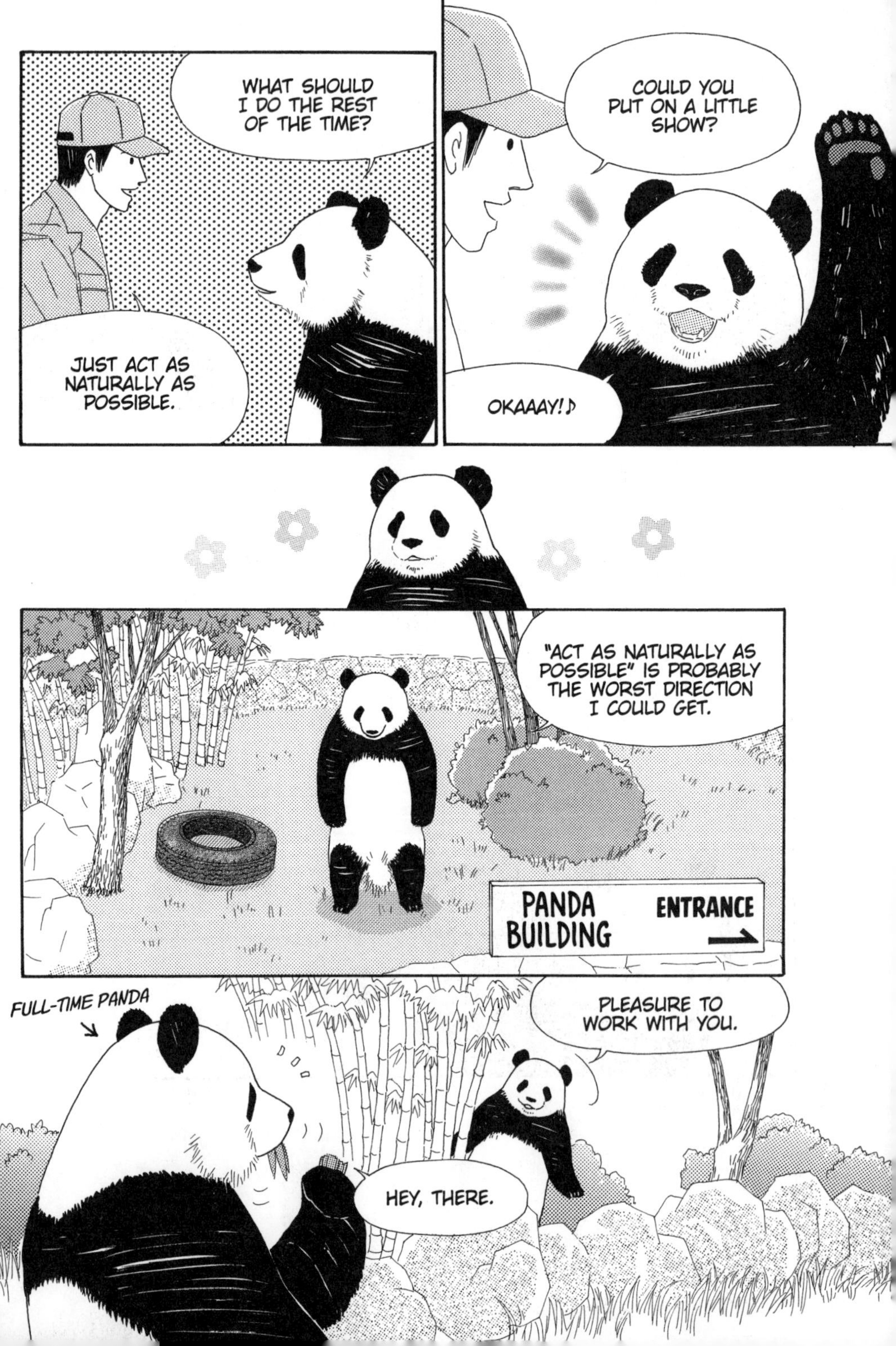
COULD YOU PUT ON A LITTLE SHOW?
OKAAAY!♪
WHAT SHOULD I DO THE REST OF THE TIME?
JUST ACT AS NATURALLY AS POSSIBLE.
"ACT AS NATURALLY AS POSSIBLE" IS PROBABLY THE WORST DIRECTION I COULD GET.
PANDA BUILDING
ENTRANCE
PLEASURE TO WORK WITH YOU.
FULL-TIME PANDA
HEY, THERE.

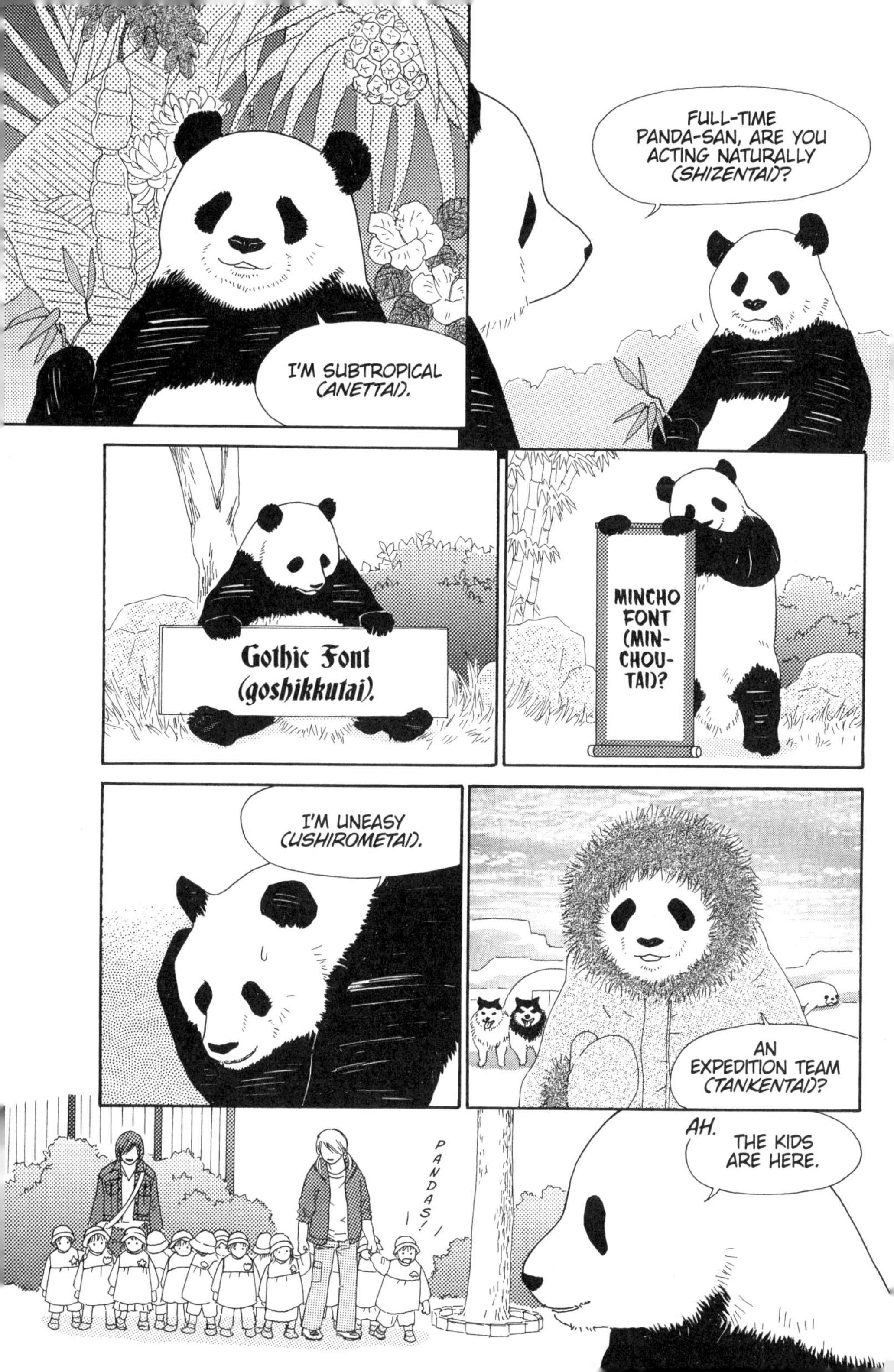
FULL-TIME PANDA-SAN, ARE YOU ACTING NATURALLY (SHIZENTAI)?
I'M SUBTROPICAL (ANETTAI).
MINCHO FONT (MIN-CHOU-TAI)?
Gothic Font (goshikkutai).
AN EXPEDITION TEAM (TANKENTAI)?
I'M UNEASY (USHIROMETAI).
AH.
THE KIDS ARE HERE.
PANDAS!

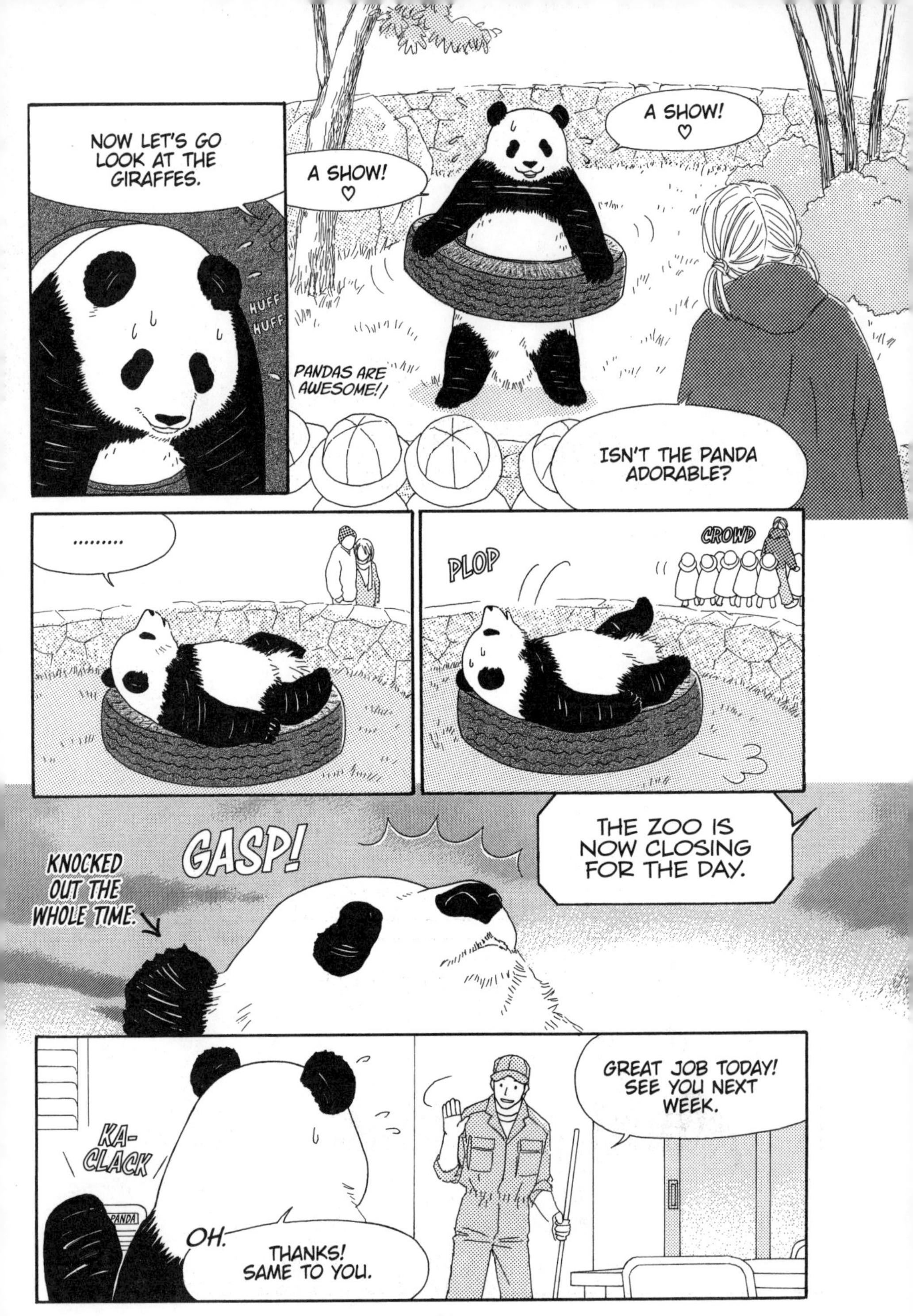
A SHOW! ♡
A SHOW! ♡
PANDAS ARE AWESOME!
ISN'T THE PANDA ADORABLE?
NOW LET'S GO LOOK AT THE GIRAFFES.
HUFF HUFF
CROWD
PLOP
....
THE ZOO IS NOW CLOSING FOR THE DAY.
GASP!
KNOCKED OUT THE WHOLE TIME.
GREAT JOB TODAY! SEE YOU NEXT WEEK.
KA-CLACK
PANDA
OH.
THANKS! SAME TO YOU.

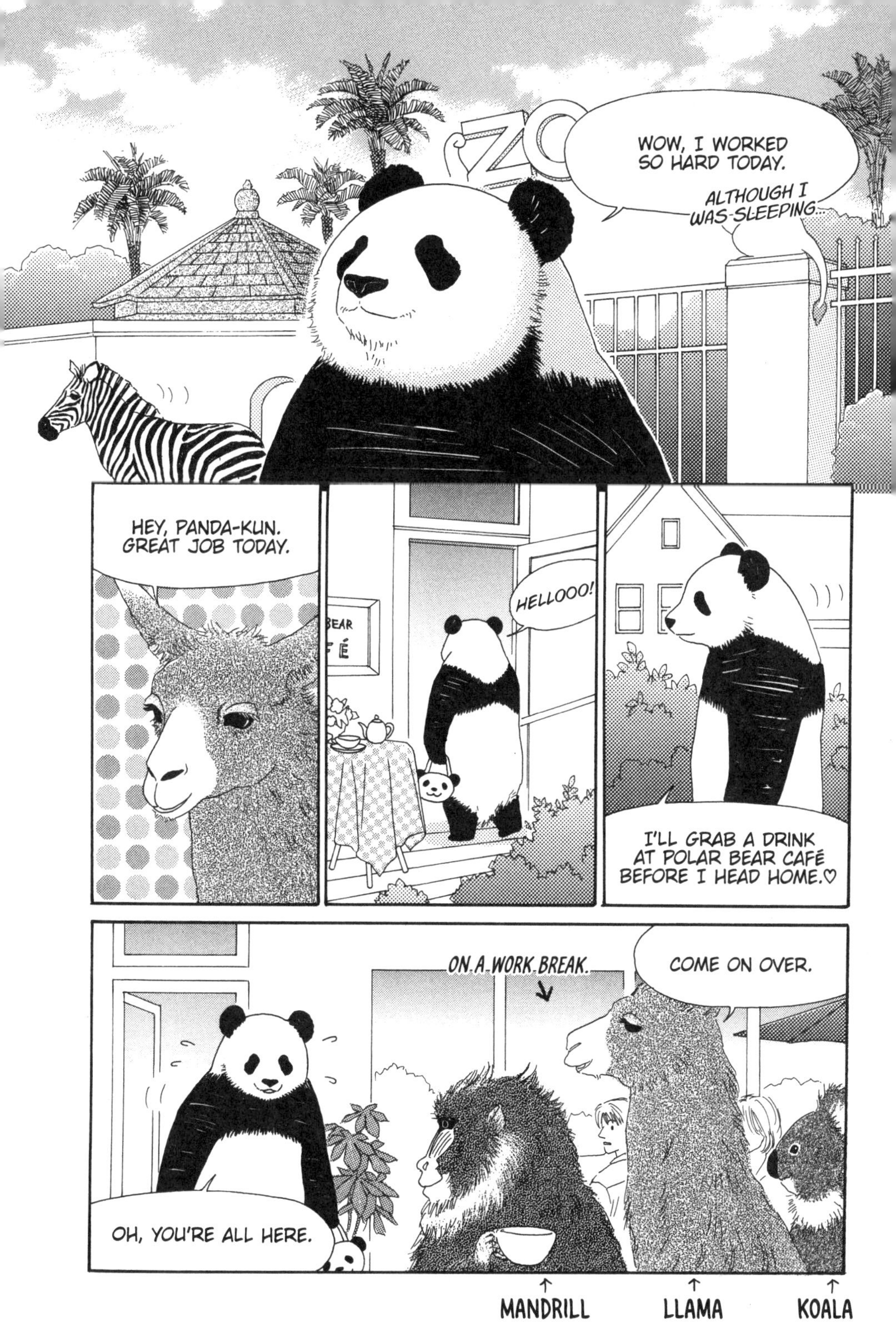
WOW, I WORKED SO HARD TODAY.
ALTHOUGH I WAS SLEEPING...
I'LL GRAB A DRINK AT POLAR BEAR CAFÉ BEFORE I HEAD HOME.♡
HELLOOO!
HEY, PANDA-KUN. GREAT JOB TODAY.
COME ON OVER.
ON A WORK BREAK.
OH, YOU'RE ALL HERE.
MANDRILL
LLAMA
KOALA

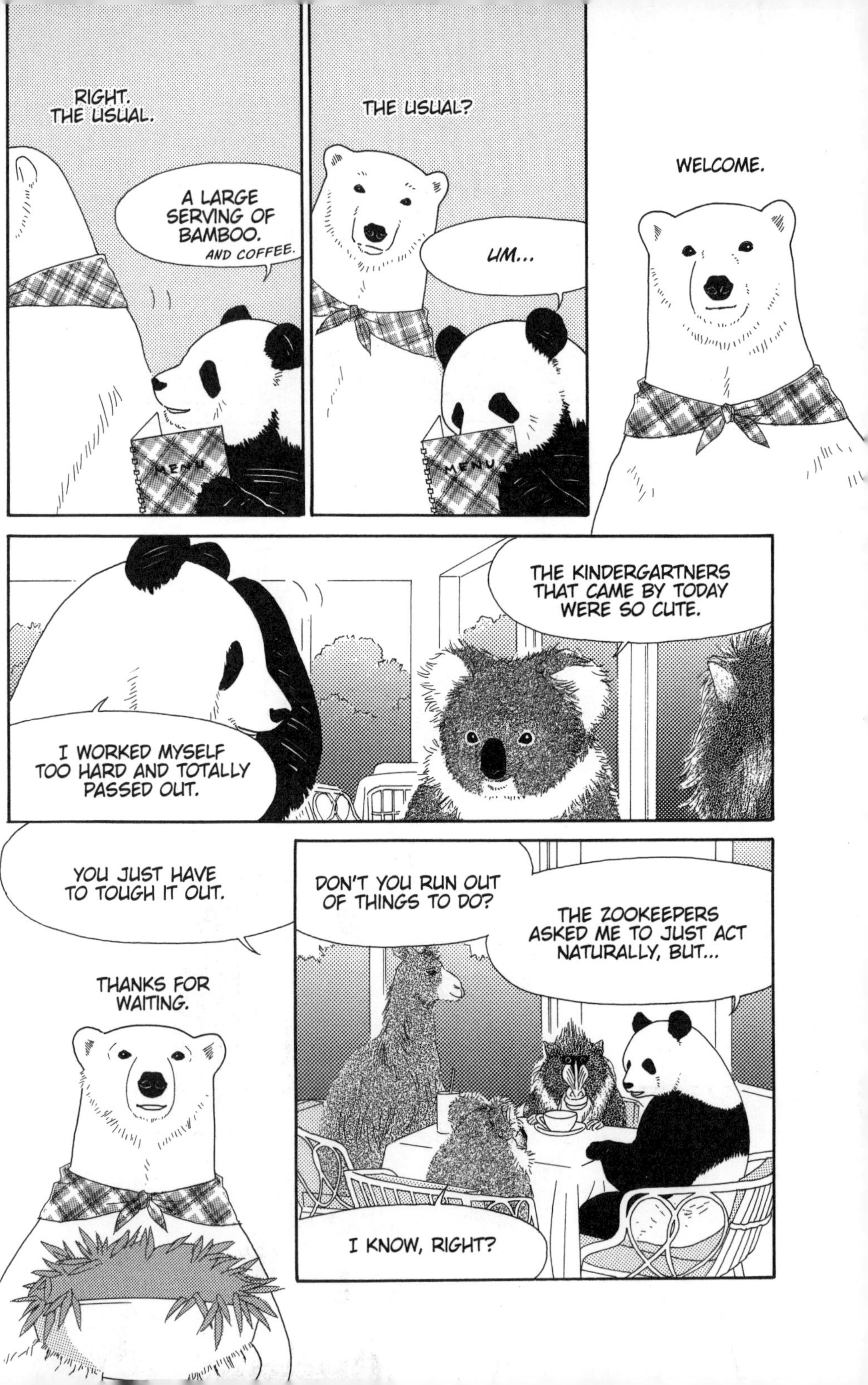
WELCOME.
THE USUAL?
UM...
A LARGE SERVING OF BAMBOO.
AND COFFEE.
RIGHT. THE USUAL.
THE KINDERGARTNERS THAT CAME BY TODAY WERE SO CUTE.
I WORKED MYSELF TOO HARD AND TOTALLY PASSED OUT.
THE ZOOKEEPERS ASKED ME TO JUST ACT NATURALLY, BUT...
DON'T YOU RUN OUT OF THINGS TO DO?
I KNOW, RIGHT?
YOU JUST HAVE TO TOUGH IT OUT.
THANKS FOR WAITING.

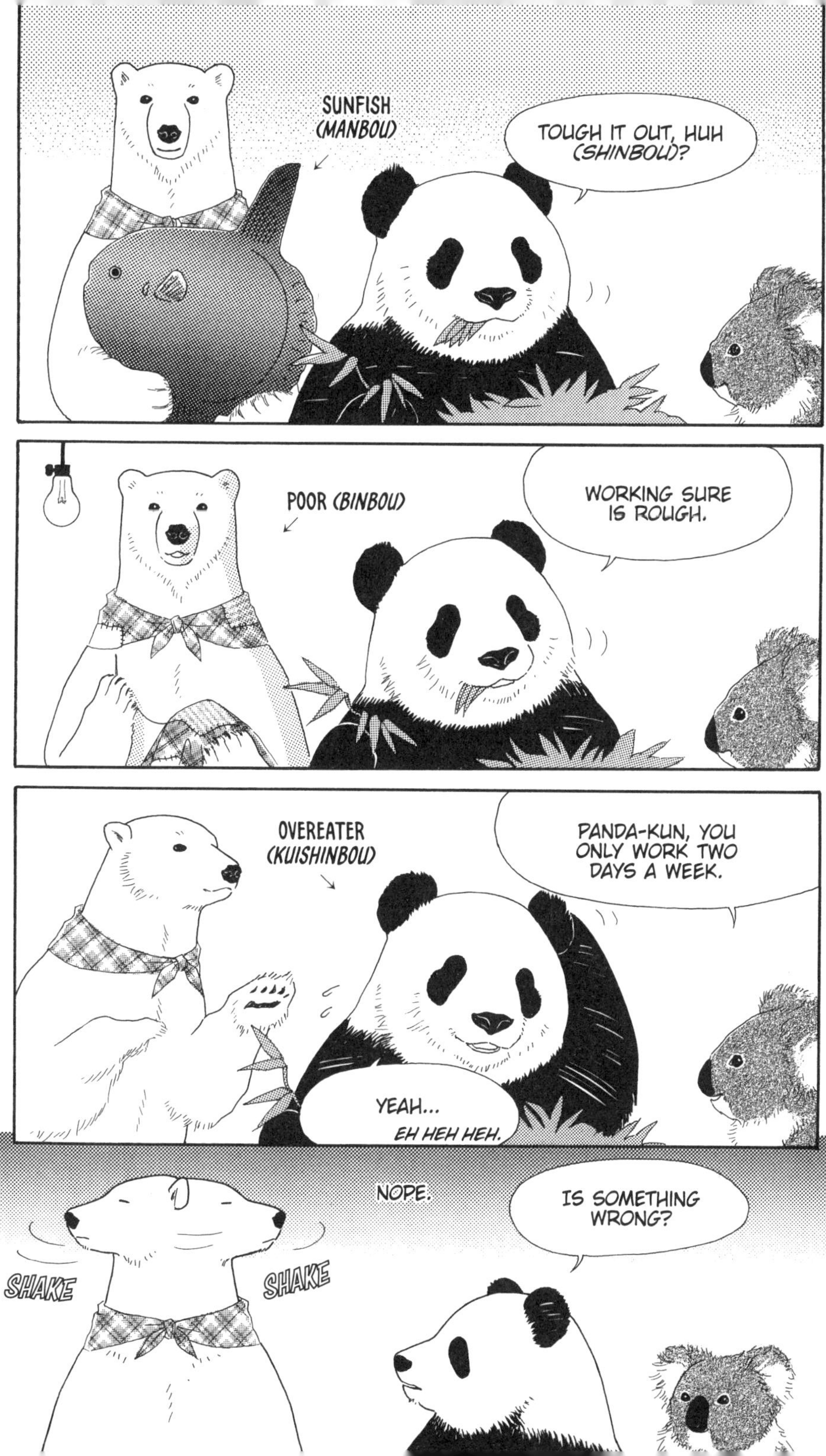
TOUGH IT OUT, HUH (SHINBOU)?
SUNFISH (MANBOU)
WORKING SURE IS ROUGH.
POOR (BINBOU)
PANDA-KUN, YOU ONLY WORK TWO DAYS A WEEK.
OVEREATER (KUISHINBOU)
YEAH...
EH HEH HEH.
IS SOMETHING WRONG?
NOPE.
SHAKE
SHAKE

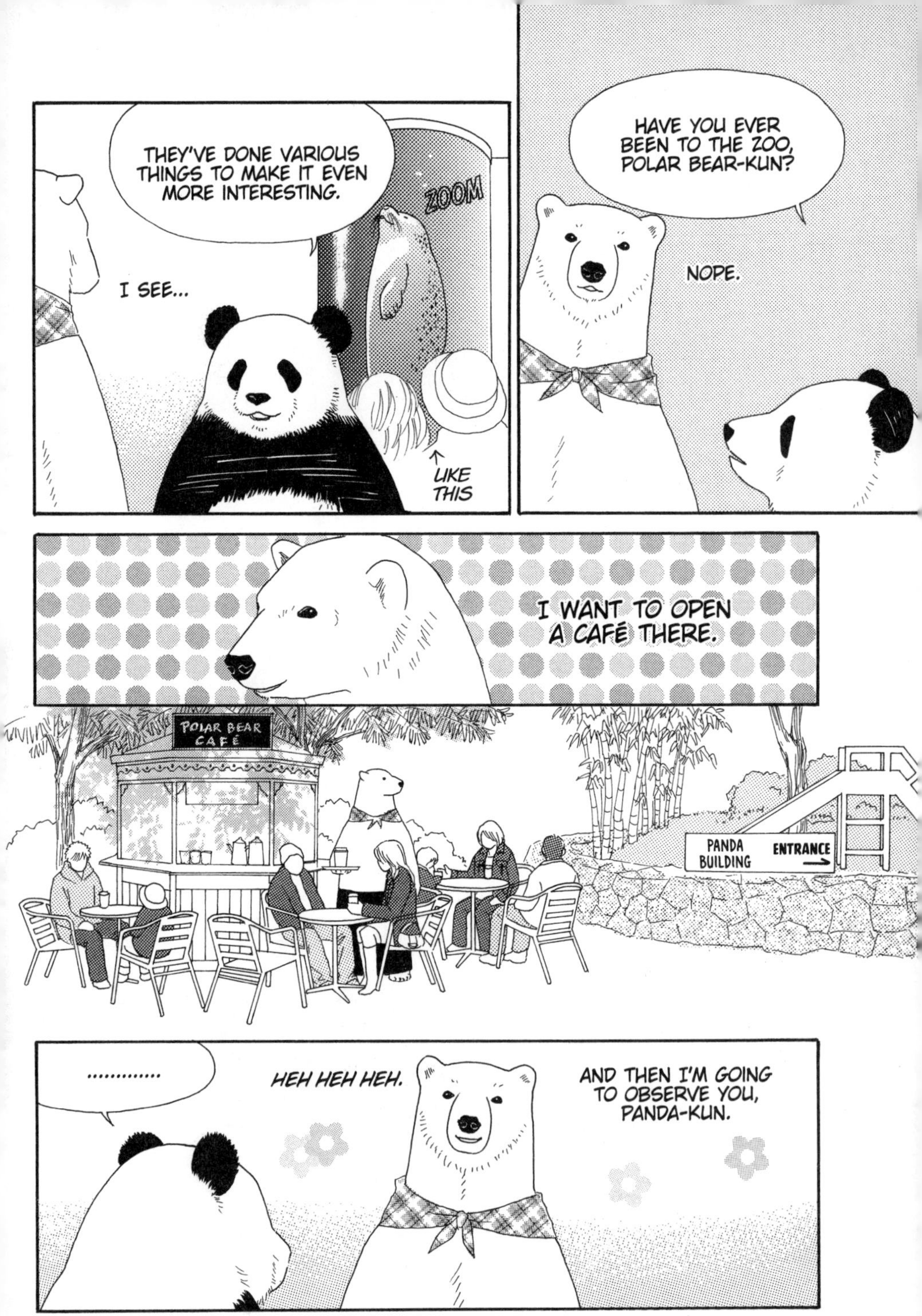
HAVE YOU EVER BEEN TO THE ZOO, POLAR BEAR-KUN?
NOPE.
THEY'VE DONE VARIOUS THINGS TO MAKE IT EVEN MORE INTERESTING.
ZOOM
I SEE...
LIKE THIS
I WANT TO OPEN A CAFÉ THERE.
POLAR BEAR CAFÉ
PANDA BUILDING
ENTRANCE
AND THEN I'M GOING TO OBSERVE YOU, PANDA-KUN.
HEH HEH HEH.
....

I MEAN, ALL HE DOES IS SLEEP, SO...?

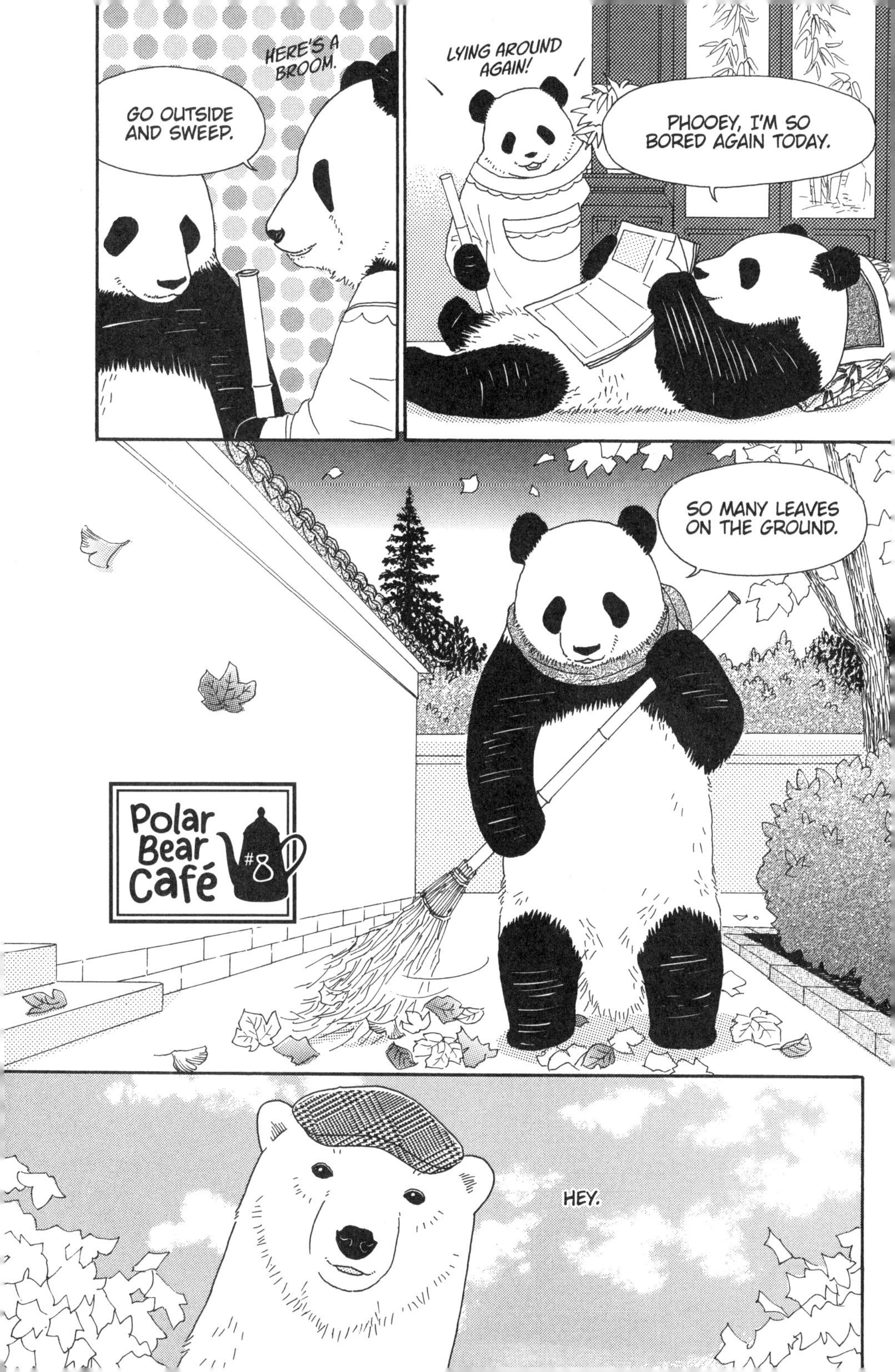
PHOOEY, I'M SO BORED AGAIN TODAY.
LYING AROUND AGAIN!
HERE'S A BROOM.
GO OUTSIDE AND SWEEP.
SO MANY LEAVES ON THE GROUND.
Polar Bear Café #8
HEY.

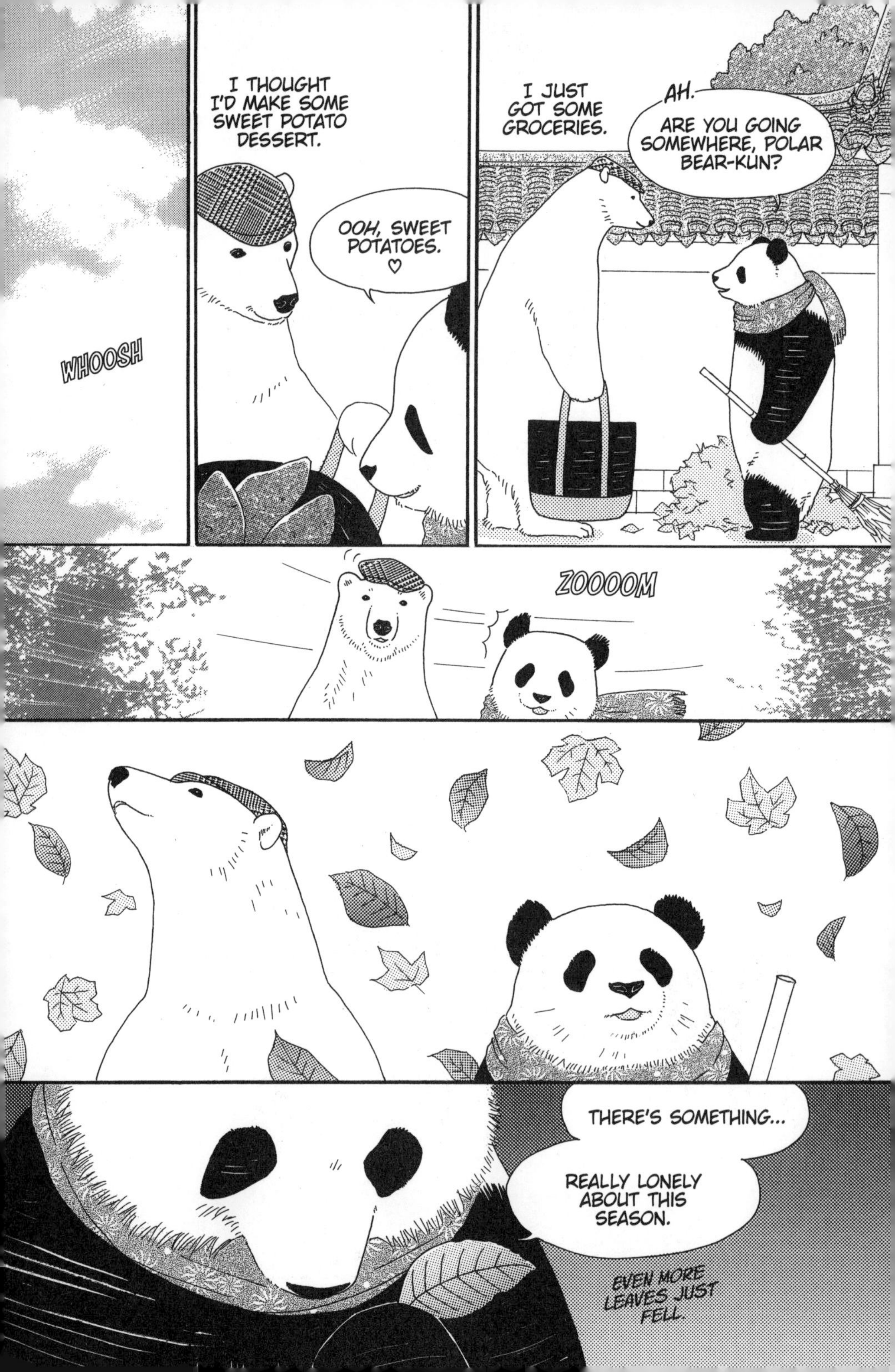
AH.
ARE YOU GOING SOMEWHERE, POLAR BEAR-KUN?
I JUST GOT SOME GROCERIES.
I THOUGHT I'D MAKE SOME SWEET POTATO DESSERT.
OOH, SWEET POTATOES. ♡
WHOOSH
ZOOOOM
THERE'S SOMETHING...
REALLY LONELY ABOUT THIS SEASON.
EVEN MORE LEAVES JUST FELL.

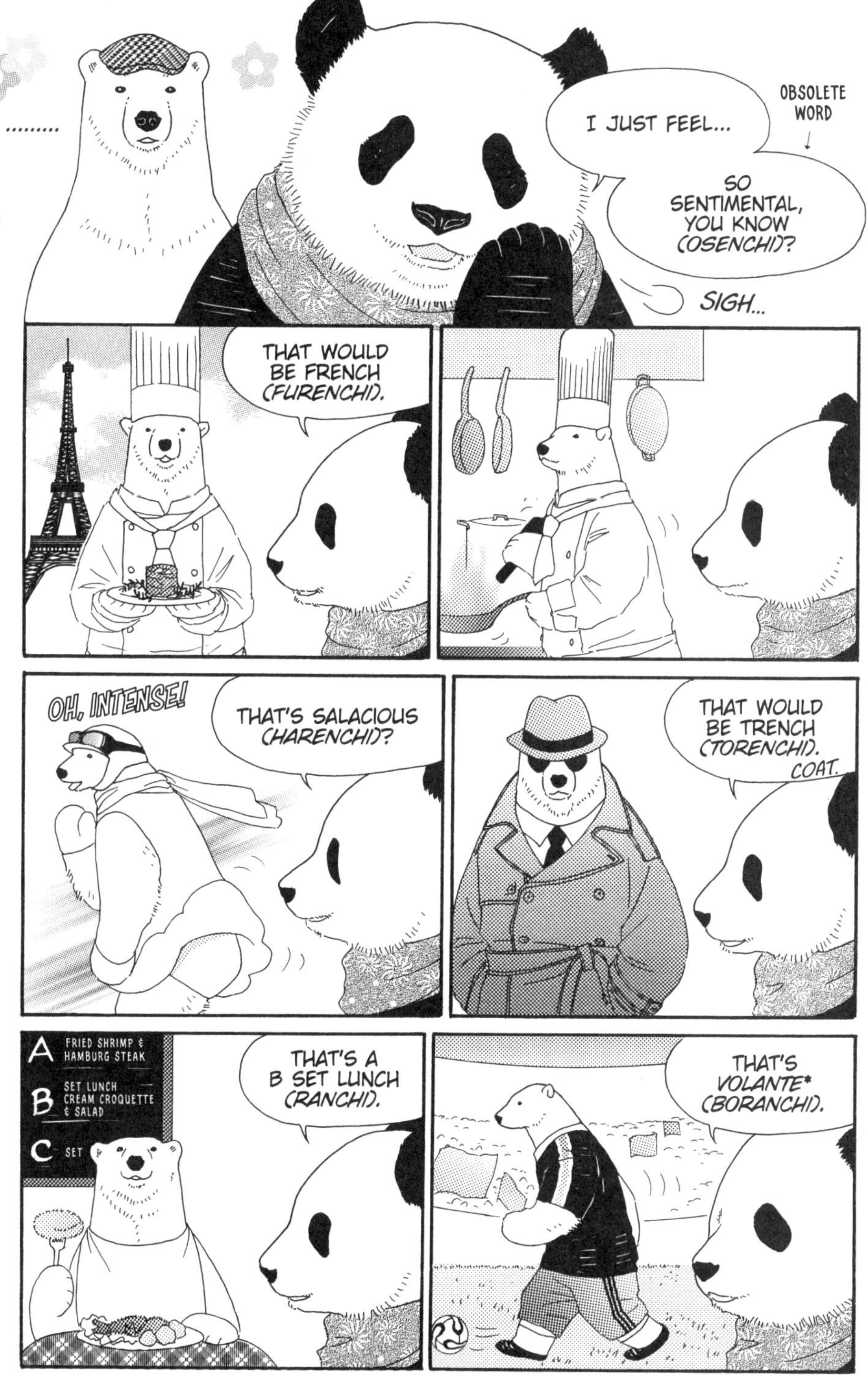
OBSOLETE WORD
I JUST FEEL...
SO SENTIMENTAL, YOU KNOW (OSENCHI)?
SIGH...
....
THAT WOULD BE FRENCH (FURENCHI).
THAT WOULD BE TRENCH (TORENCHI).
COAT.
THAT'S SALACIOUS (HARENCHI)?
OH, INTENSE!
THAT'S VOLANTE* (BORANCHI).
THAT'S A B SET LUNCH (RANCHI).
A FRIED SHRIMP & HAMBURG STEAK
B SET LUNCH CREAM CROQUETTE & SALAD
C SET

*A soccer position.

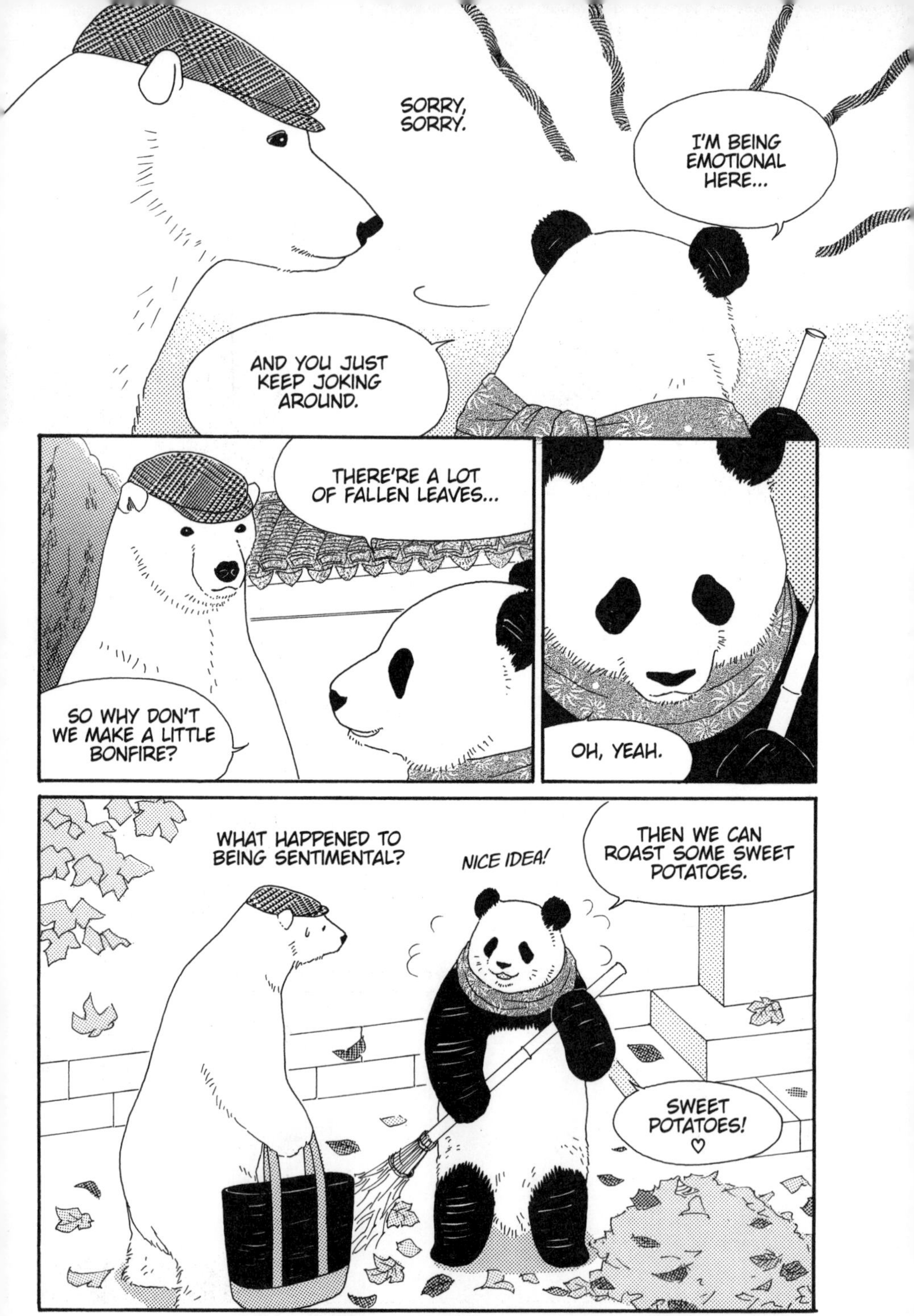
I'M BEING EMOTIONAL HERE...
SORRY, SORRY.
AND YOU JUST KEEP JOKING AROUND.
OH, YEAH.
THERE'RE A LOT OF FALLEN LEAVES...
SO WHY DON'T WE MAKE A LITTLE BONFIRE?
THEN WE CAN ROAST SOME SWEET POTATOES.
NICE IDEA!
SWEET POTATOES! ♡
WHAT HAPPENED TO BEING SENTIMENTAL?

THE JAPANESE TERM "OSENCHI" IS SHORT FOR THE ENGLISH WORD "SENTIMENTAL"! DID YOU KNOW THAT?!

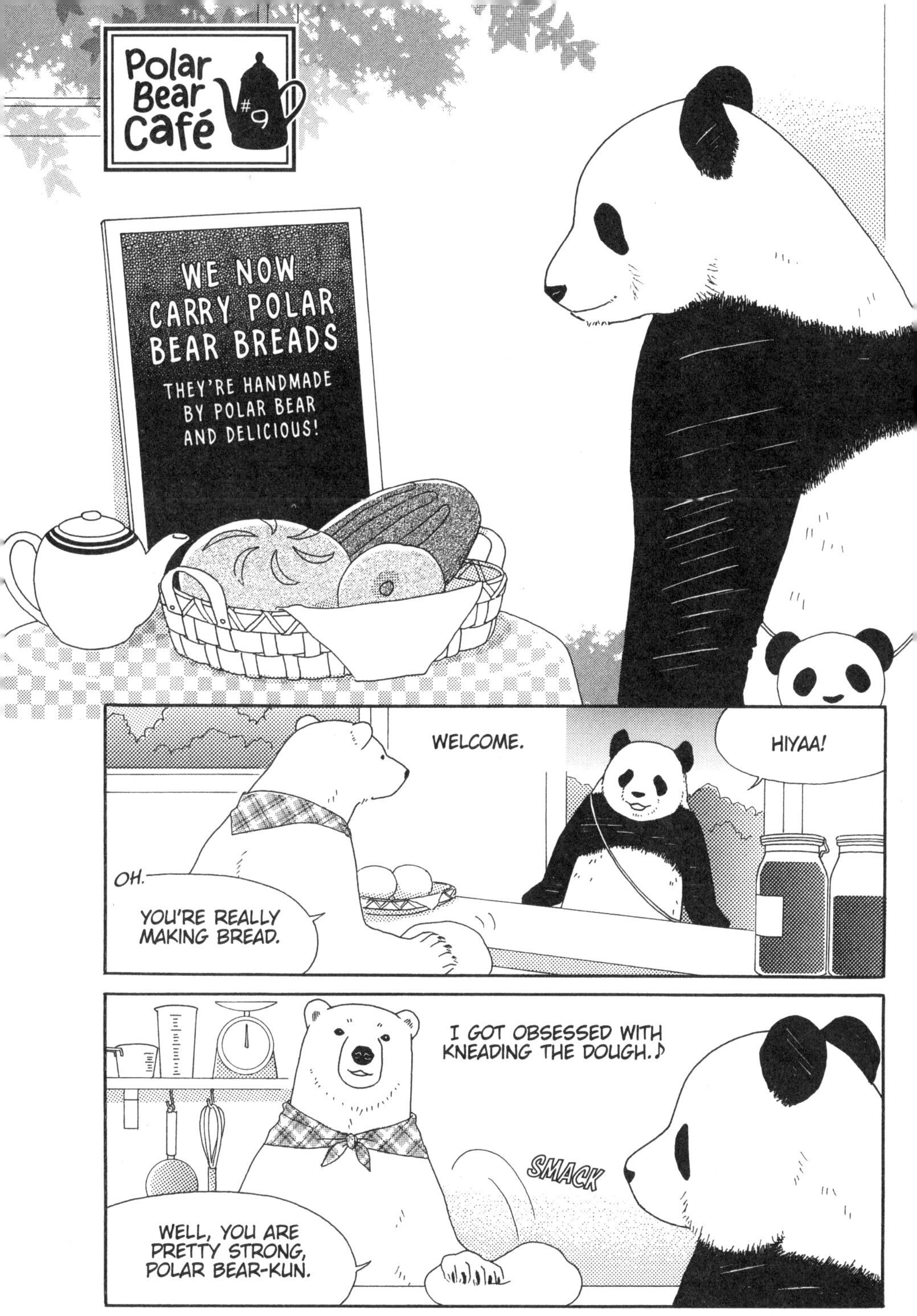
Polar Bear Café #9
WE NOW CARRY POLAR BEAR BREADS
THEY'RE HANDMADE BY POLAR BEAR AND DELICIOUS!
HIYAA!
WELCOME.
OH.
YOU'RE REALLY MAKING BREAD.
I GOT OBSESSED WITH KNEADING THE DOUGH.♪
SMACK
WELL, YOU ARE PRETTY STRONG, POLAR BEAR-KUN.

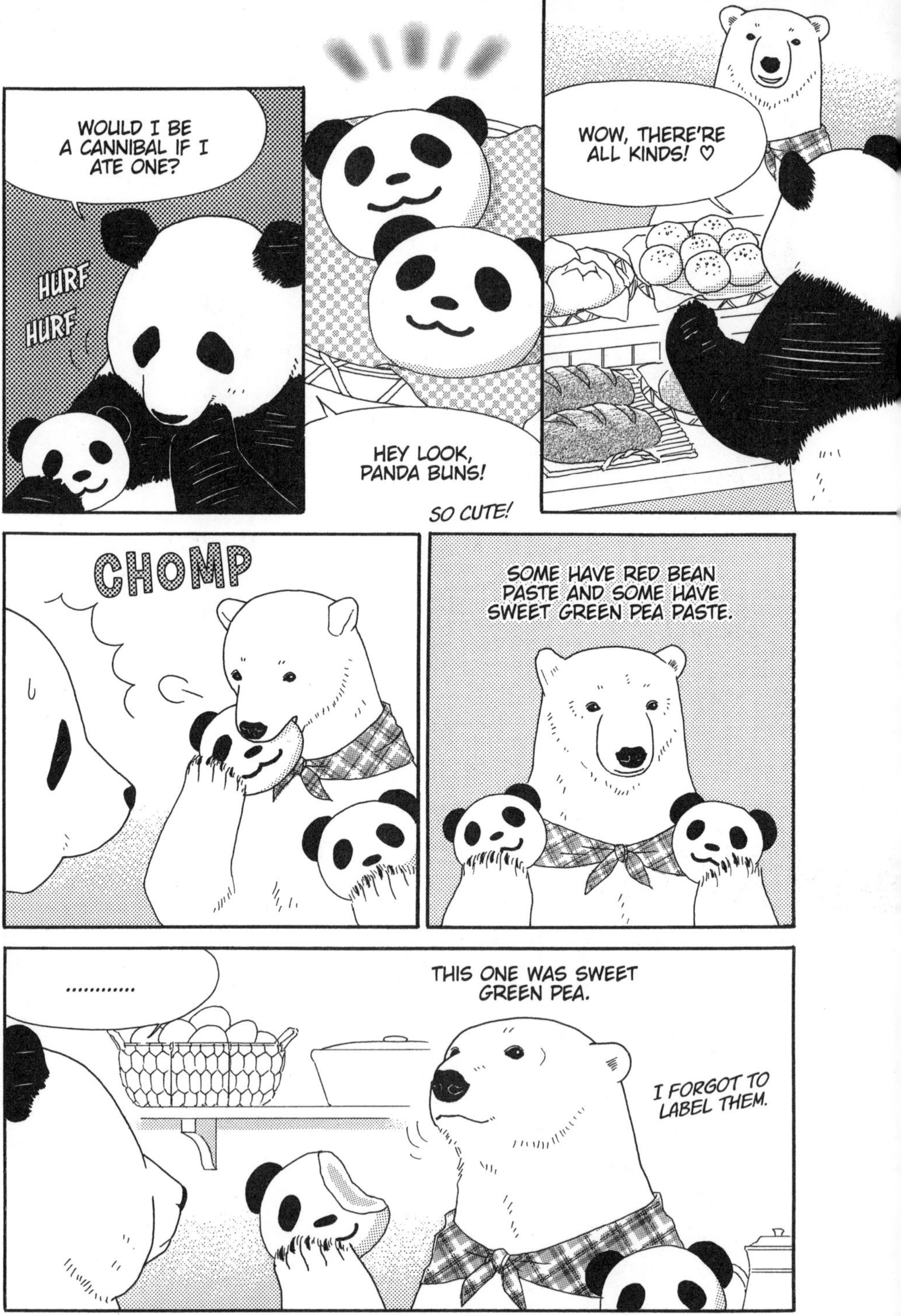
WOW, THERE'RE ALL KINDS! ♡
HEY LOOK, PANDA BUNS!
SO CUTE!
WOULD I BE A CANNIBAL IF I ATE ONE?
HURF HURF
SOME HAVE RED BEAN PASTE AND SOME HAVE SWEET GREEN PEA PASTE.
CHOMP
THIS ONE WAS SWEET GREEN PEA.
I FORGOT TO LABEL THEM.
....

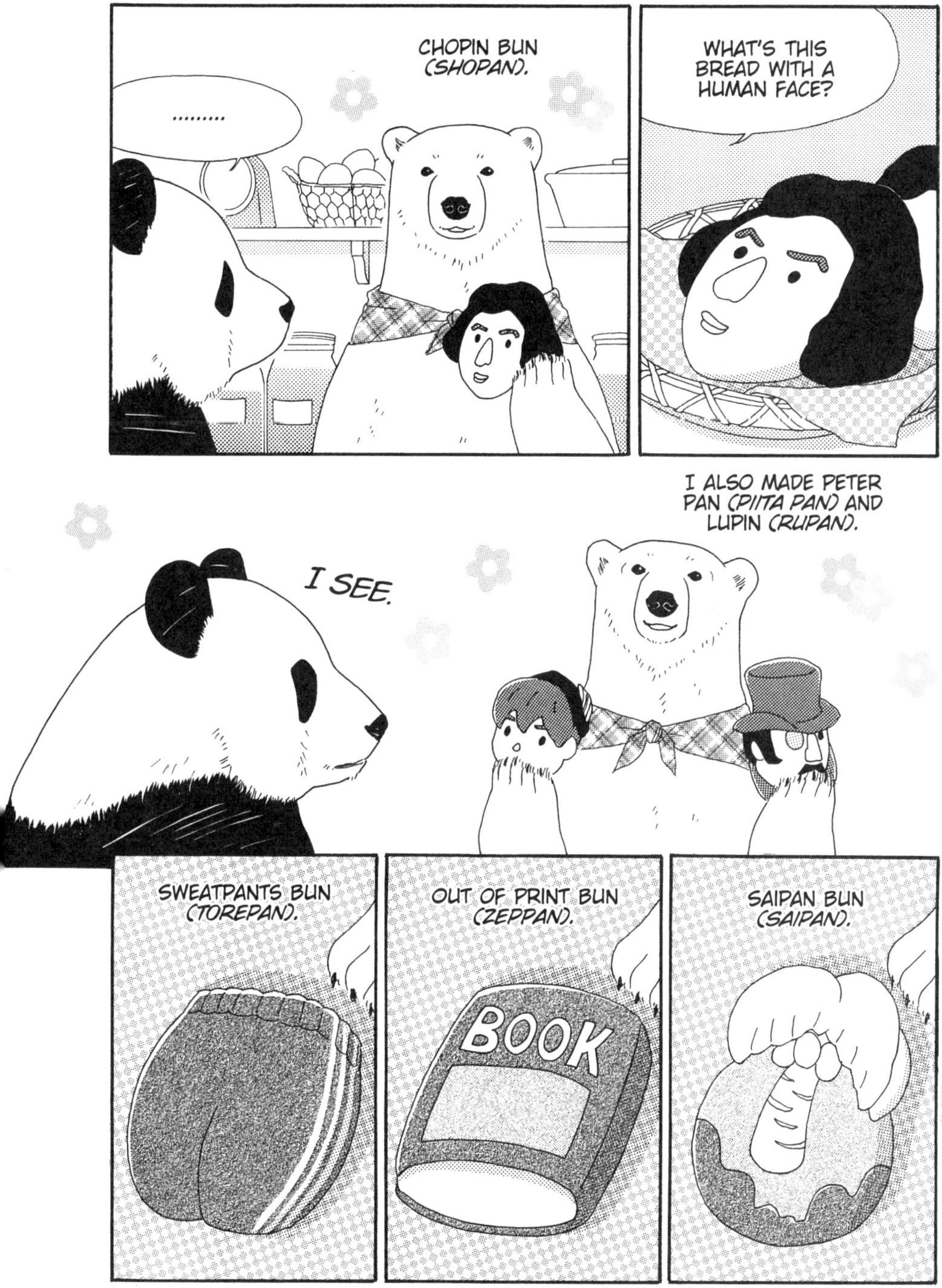
WHAT'S THIS BREAD WITH A HUMAN FACE?
CHOPIN BUN (SHOPAN).
....
I ALSO MADE PETER PAN (PIITA PAN) AND LUPIN (RUPAN).
I SEE.
SAIPAN BUN (SAIPAN).
OUT OF PRINT BUN (ZEPPAN).
BOOK
SWEATPANTS BUN (TOREPAN).

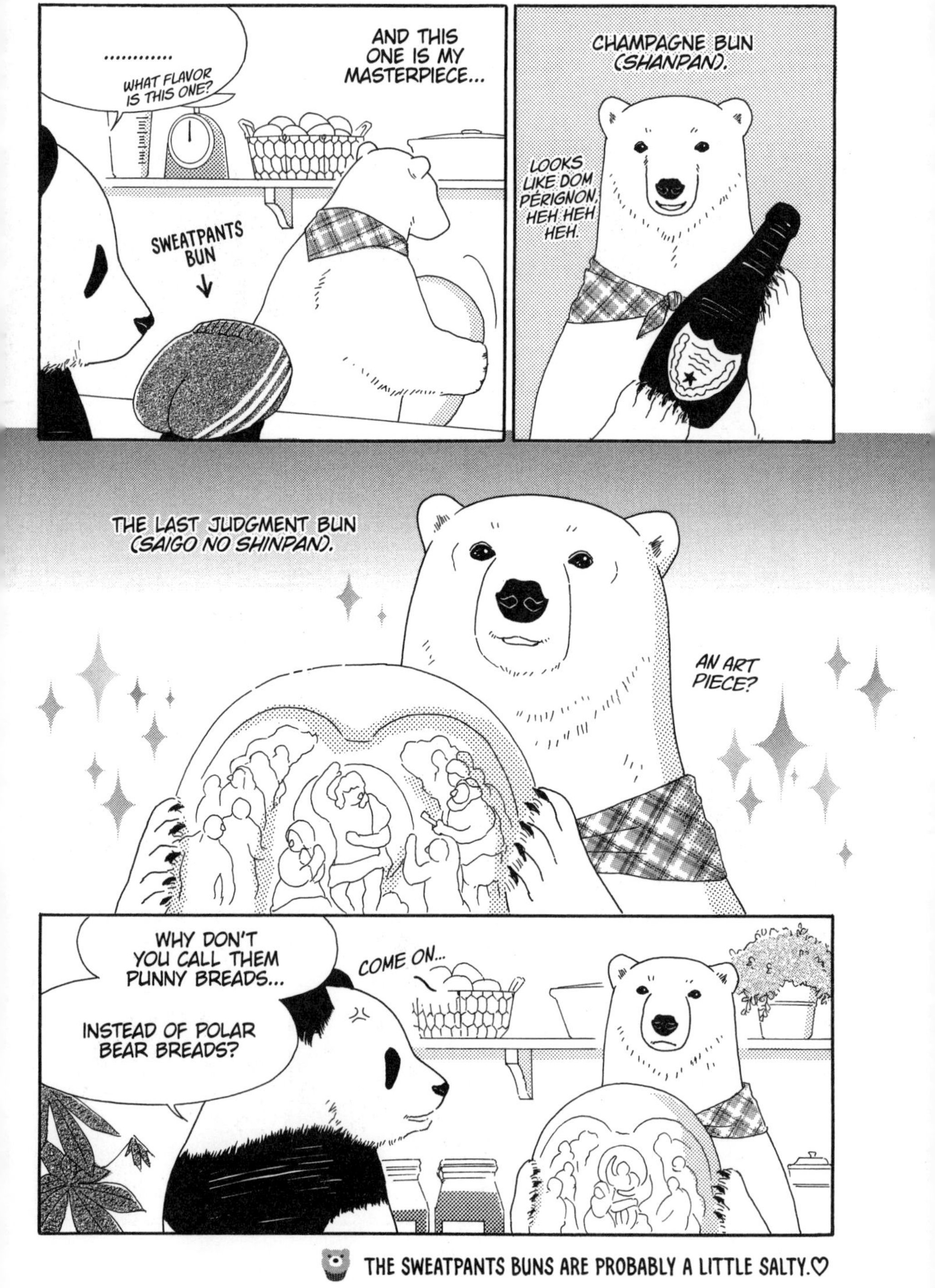
CHAMPAGNE BUN (SHANPAN).
LOOKS LIKE DOM PÉRIGNON, HEH HEH HEH.
AND THIS ONE IS MY MASTERPIECE...
....
WHAT FLAVOR IS THIS ONE?
SWEATPANTS BUN
THE LAST JUDGMENT BUN (SAIGO NO SHINPAN).
AN ART PIECE?
COME ON...
WHY DON'T YOU CALL THEM PUNNY BREADS...
INSTEAD OF POLAR BEAR BREADS?

THE SWEATPANTS BUNS ARE PROBABLY A LITTLE SALTY.♡

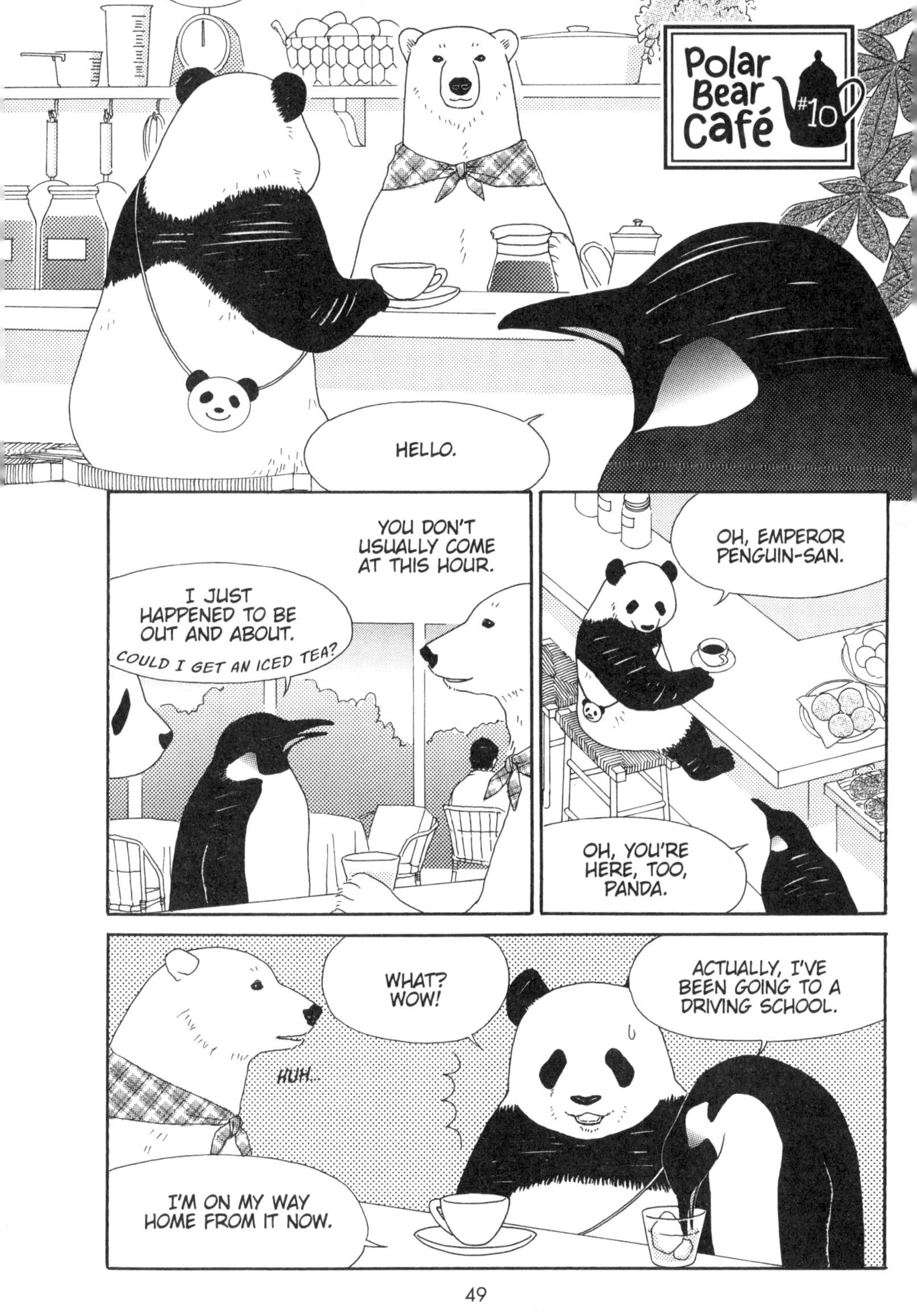

Polar Bear Café
#10
HELLO.
OH, EMPEROR PENGUIN-SAN.
OH, YOU'RE HERE, TOO, PANDA.
YOU DON'T USUALLY COME AT THIS HOUR.
I JUST HAPPENED TO BE OUT AND ABOUT.
COULD I GET AN ICED TEA?
ACTUALLY, I'VE BEEN GOING TO A DRIVING SCHOOL.
WHAT? WOW!
HUH...
I'M ON MY WAY HOME FROM IT NOW.

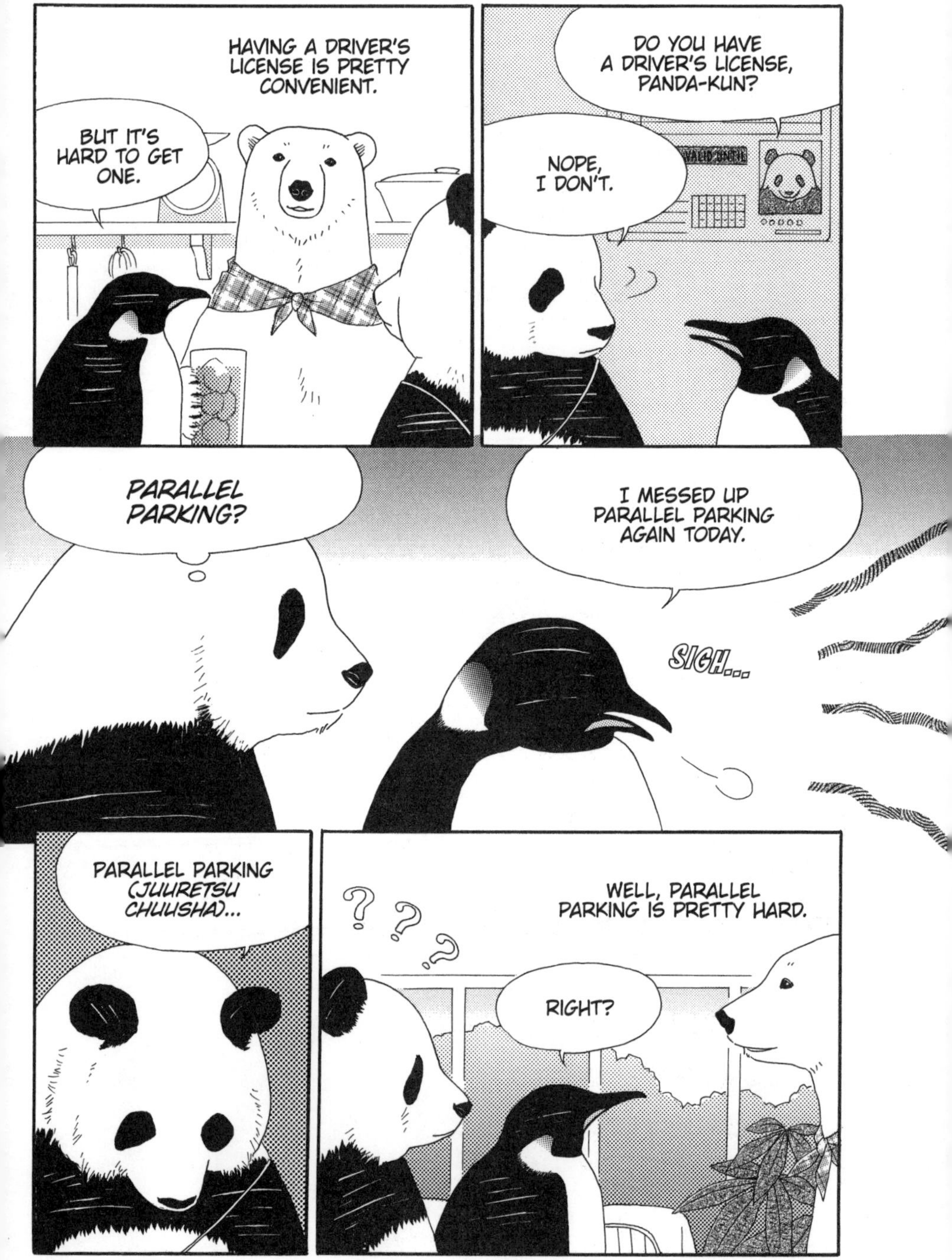
DO YOU HAVE A DRIVER'S LICENSE, PANDA-KUN?
VALID UNTIL
NOPE, I DON'T.
HAVING A DRIVER'S LICENSE IS PRETTY CONVENIENT.
BUT IT'S HARD TO GET ONE.
I MESSED UP PARALLEL PARKING AGAIN TODAY.
SIGH...
PARALLEL PARKING?
WELL, PARALLEL PARKING IS PRETTY HARD.
RIGHT?
PARALLEL PARKING (JUURETSU CHUUSHA)...

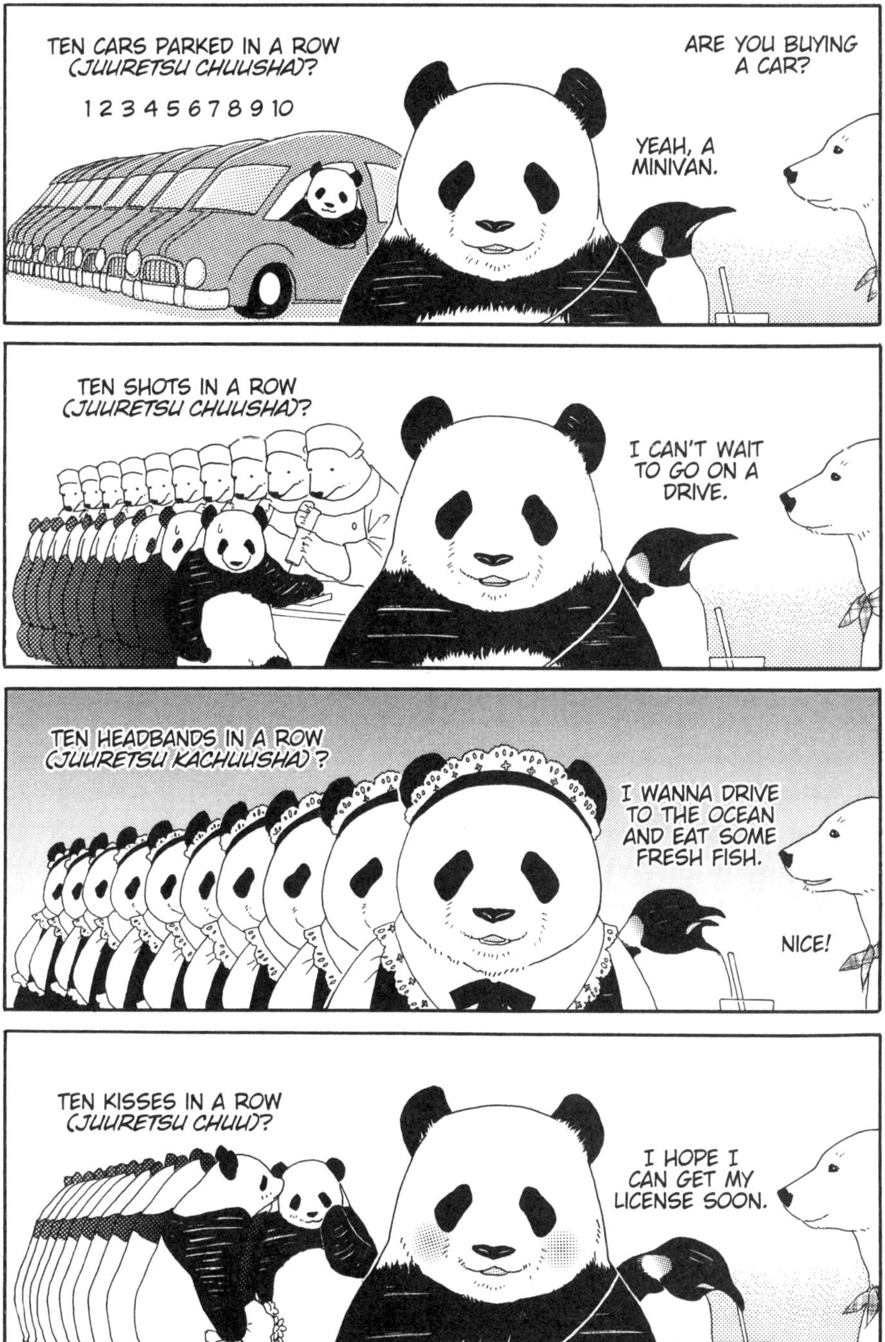
ARE YOU BUYING A CAR?
YEAH, A MINIVAN.
TEN CARS PARKED IN A ROW (JUURETSU CHUUSHA)?
1 2 3 4 5 6 7 8 9 10
I CAN'T WAIT TO GO ON A DRIVE.
TEN SHOTS IN A ROW (JUURETSU CHUUSHA)?
I WANNA DRIVE TO THE OCEAN AND EAT SOME FRESH FISH.
NICE!
TEN HEADBANDS IN A ROW (JUURETSU KACHUUSHA)?
I HOPE I CAN GET MY LICENSE SOON.
TEN KISSES IN A ROW (JUURETSU CHUU)?

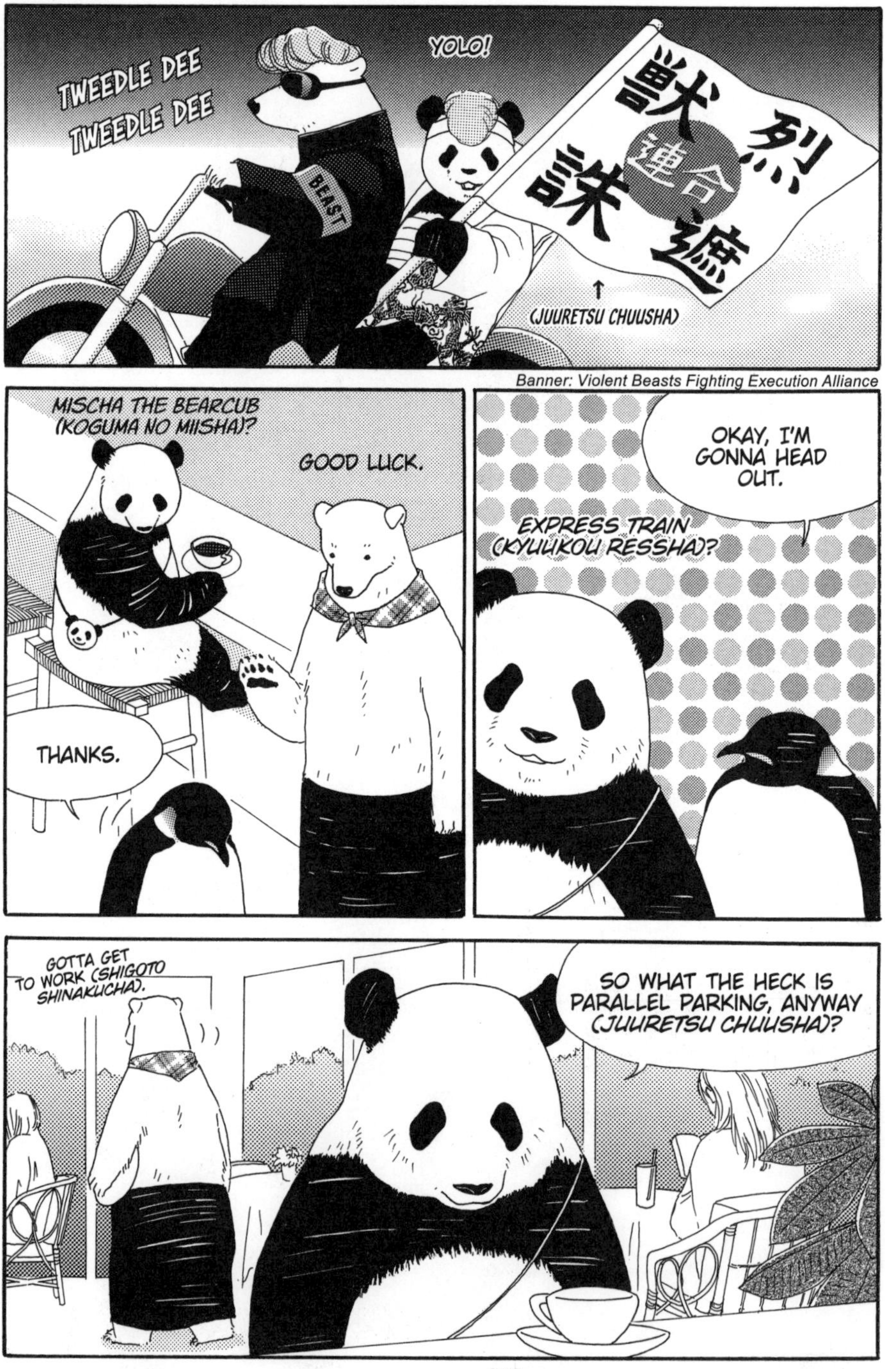
獣烈
連合
誅遮
YOLO!
TWEEDLE DEE
TWEEDLE DEE
↑
(JUURETSU CHUUSHA)
Banner: Violent Beasts Fighting Execution Alliance
OKAY, I'M GONNA HEAD OUT.
EXPRESS TRAIN (KYUUKOU RESSHA)?
GOOD LUCK.
MISCHA THE BEARCUB (KOGUMA NO MIISHA)?
THANKS.
SO WHAT THE HECK IS PARALLEL PARKING, ANYWAY (JUURETSU CHUUSHA)?
GOTTA GET TO WORK (SHIGOTO SHINAKUCHA).

THAT PUN LOST ITS WAY SOMEWHERE...

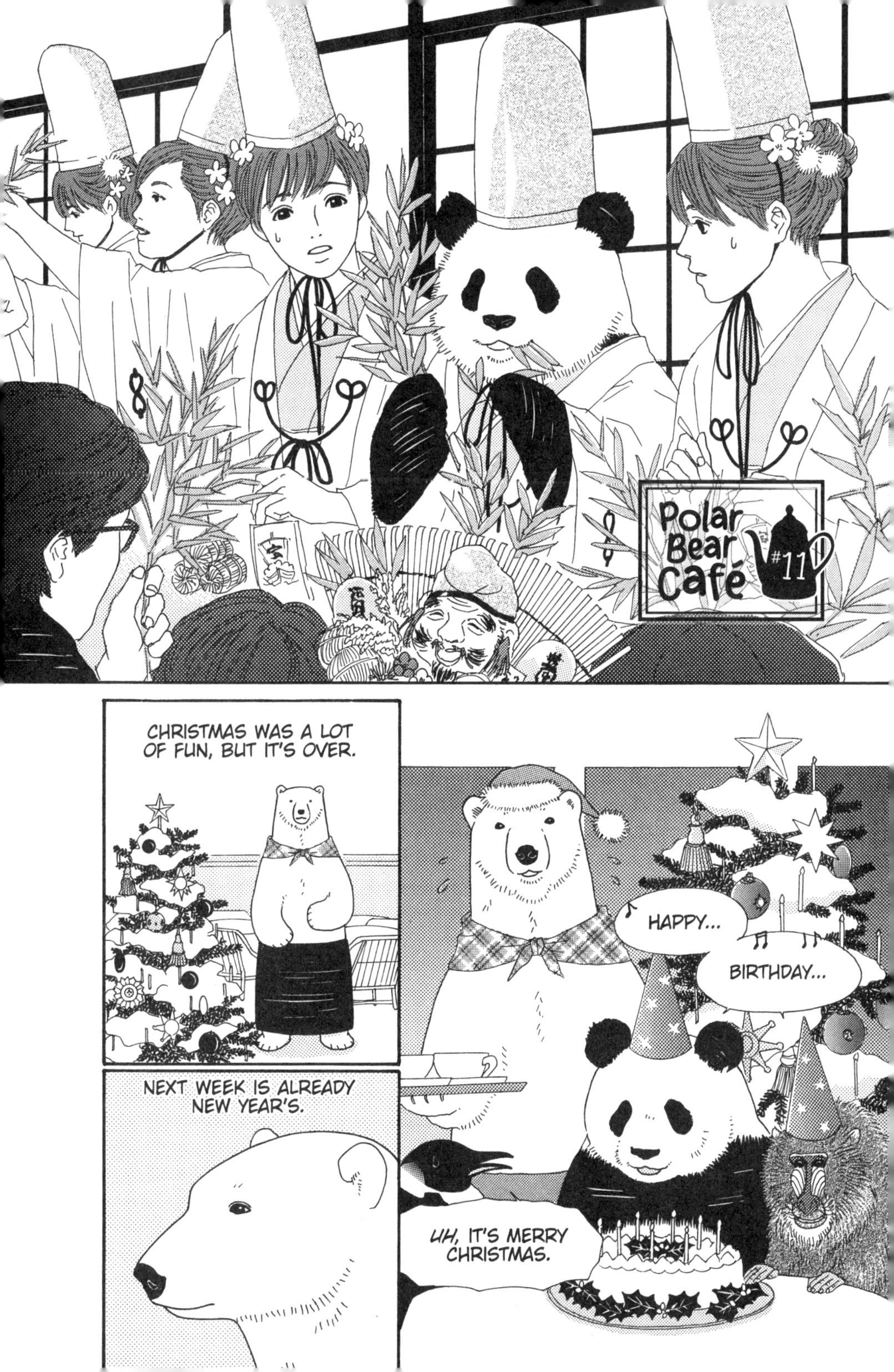
Polar Bear Café
#11
HAPPY...
BIRTHDAY...
UH, IT'S MERRY CHRISTMAS.
CHRISTMAS WAS A LOT OF FUN, BUT IT'S OVER.
NEXT WEEK IS ALREADY NEW YEAR'S.

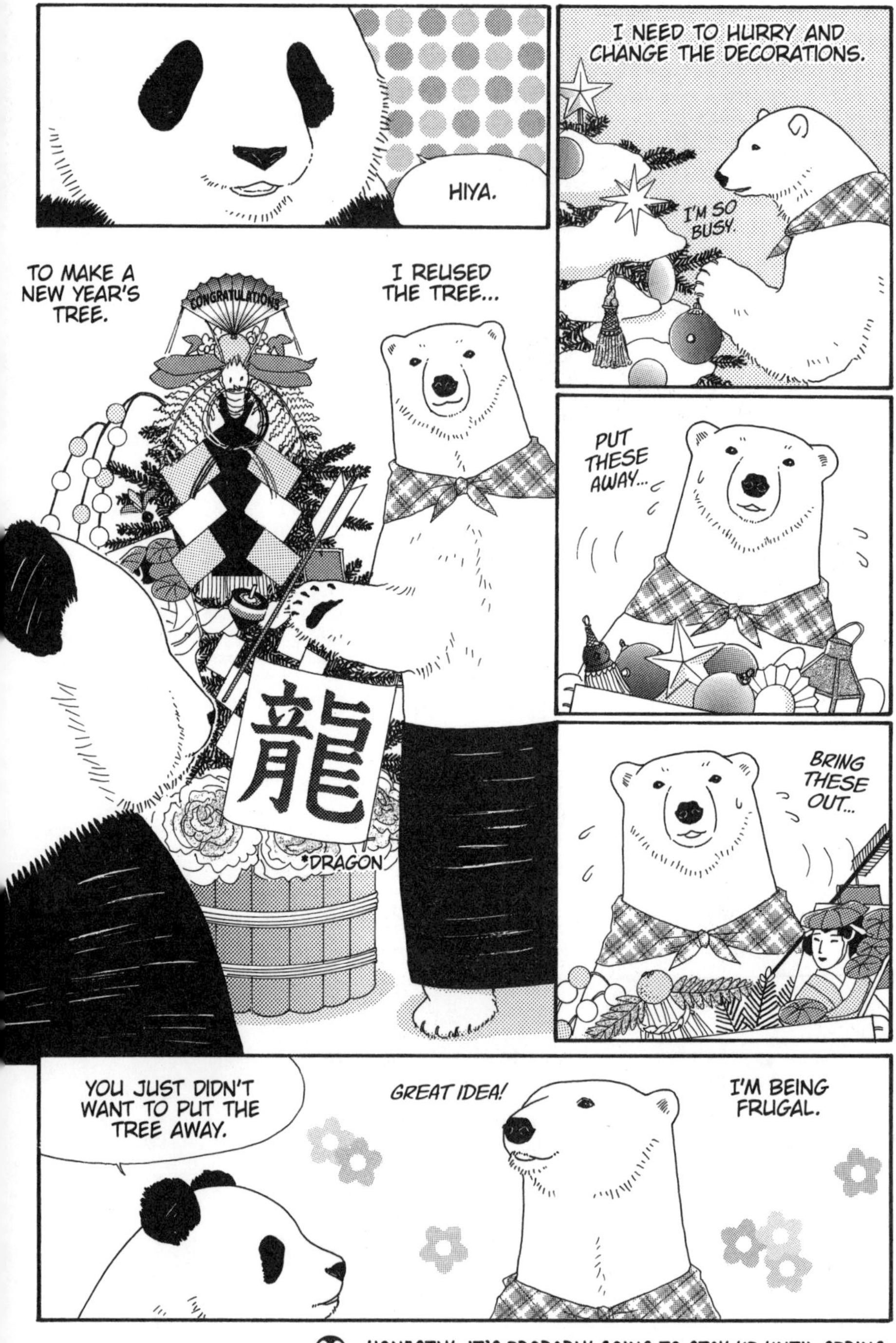
I NEED TO HURRY AND CHANGE THE DECORATIONS.
I'M SO BUSY.
HIYA.
PUT THESE AWAY...
BRING THESE OUT...
I REUSED THE TREE...
TO MAKE A NEW YEAR'S TREE.
CONGRATULATIONS
龍
*DRAGON
I'M BEING FRUGAL.
GREAT IDEA!
YOU JUST DIDN'T WANT TO PUT THE TREE AWAY.

HONESTLY, IT'S PROBABLY GOING TO STAY UP UNTIL SPRING.

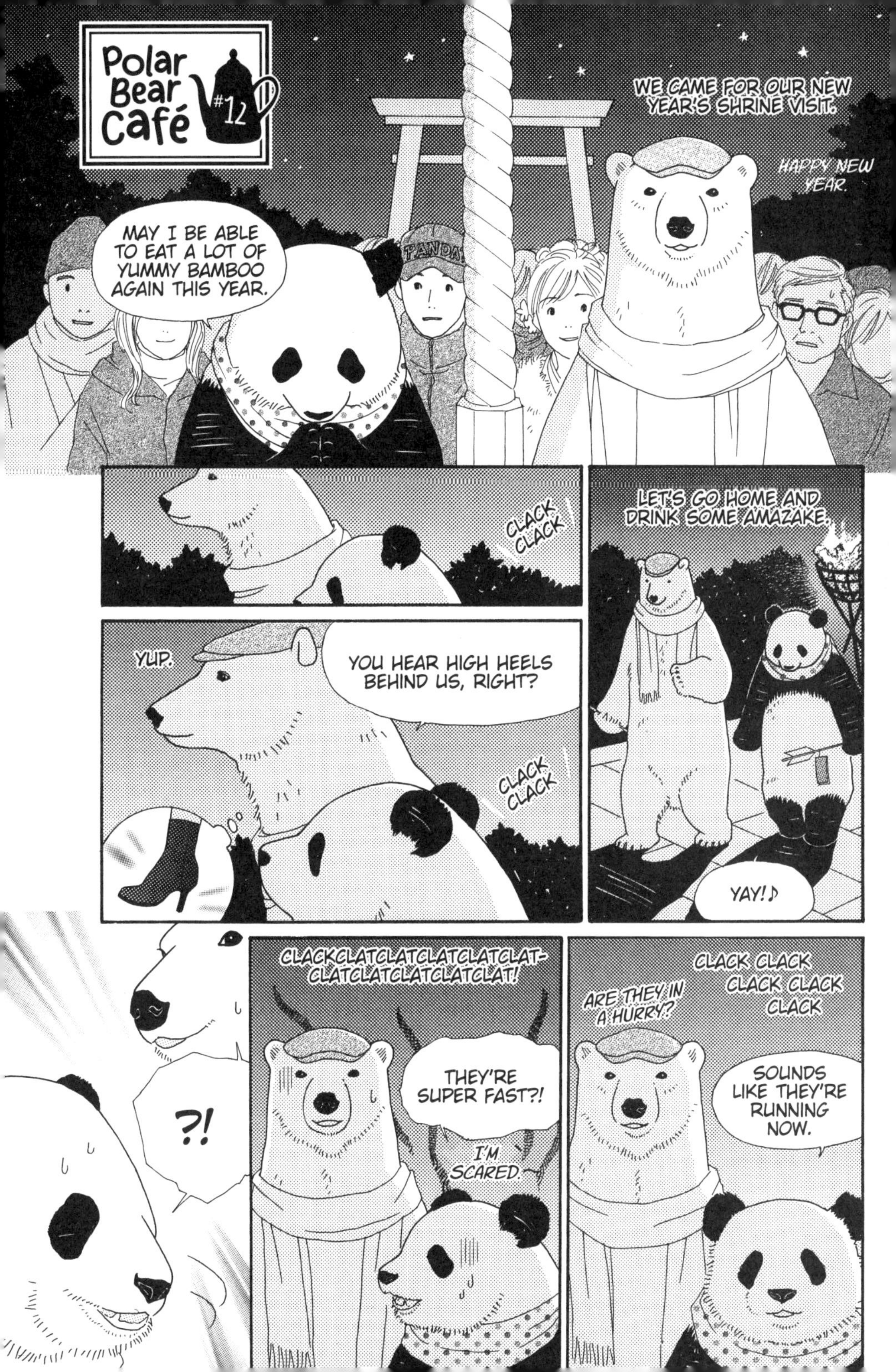
Polar Bear Café #12
WE CAME FOR OUR NEW YEAR'S SHRINE VISIT.
HAPPY NEW YEAR.
MAY I BE ABLE TO EAT A LOT OF YUMMY BAMBOO AGAIN THIS YEAR.
PANDA
LET'S GO HOME AND DRINK SOME AMAZAKE.
YAY!♪
CLACK CLACK
YOU HEAR HIGH HEELS BEHIND US, RIGHT?
YUP.
CLACK CLACK
CLACK CLACK CLACK CLACK CLACK
ARE THEY IN A HURRY?
SOUNDS LIKE THEY'RE RUNNING NOW.
CLACKCLATCLATCLATCLATCLAT-CLATCLATCLATCLATCLAT!
THEY'RE SUPER FAST?!
I'M SCARED.
?!

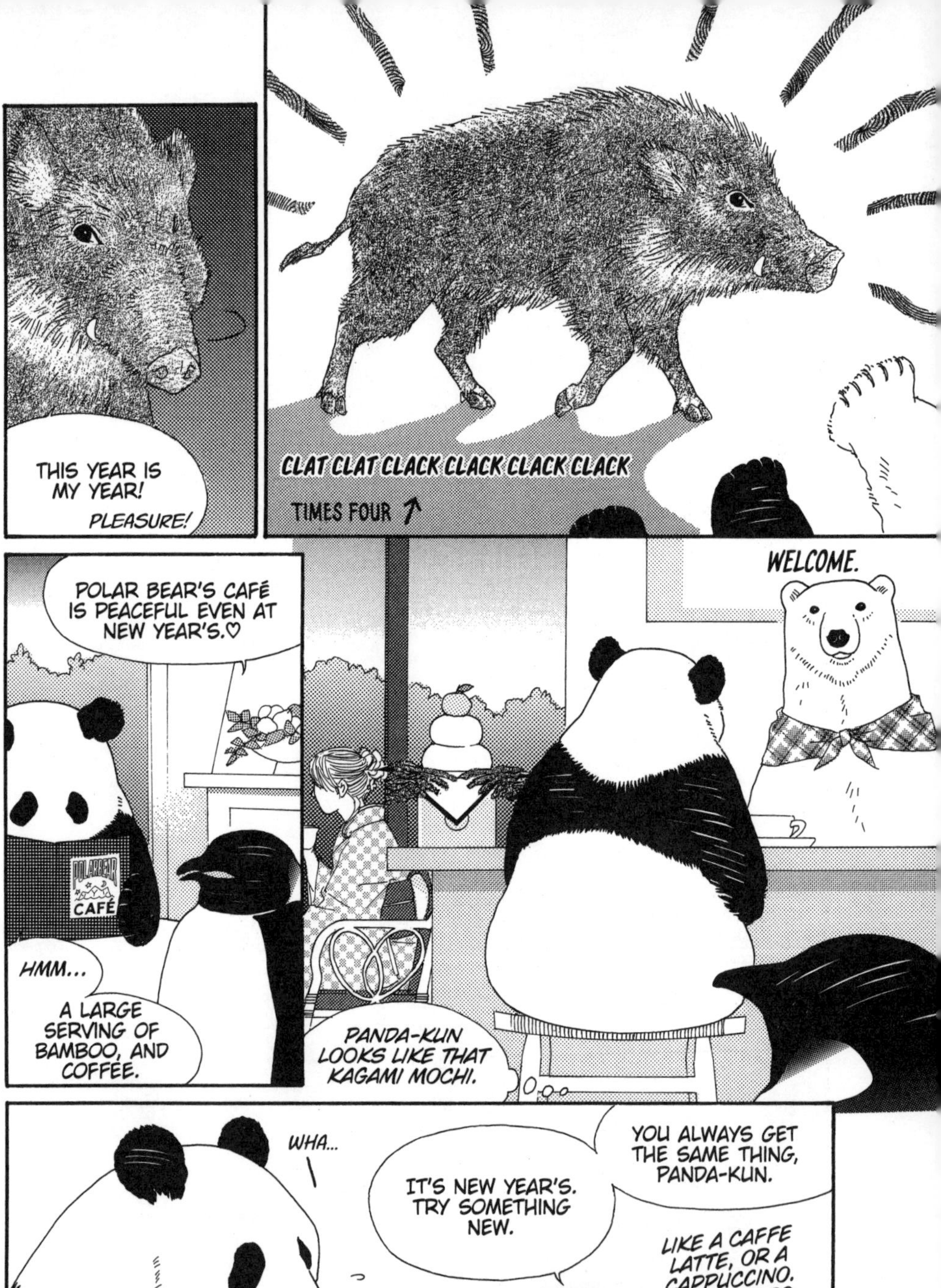
CLAT CLAT CLACK CLACK CLACK CLACK
TIMES FOUR ↗
THIS YEAR IS MY YEAR!
PLEASURE!
WELCOME.
PANDA-KUN LOOKS LIKE THAT KAGAMI MOCHI.
POLAR BEAR'S CAFÉ IS PEACEFUL EVEN AT NEW YEAR'S.♡
POLAR BEAR CAFÉ
HMM...
A LARGE SERVING OF BAMBOO, AND COFFEE.
YOU ALWAYS GET THE SAME THING, PANDA-KUN.
LIKE A CAFFE LATTE, OR A CAPPUCCINO. THERE'S SO MUCH TO CHOOSE FROM!
IT'S NEW YEAR'S. TRY SOMETHING NEW.
WHA...
WELL, I DON'T REALLY UNDER-STAND ALL THIS.

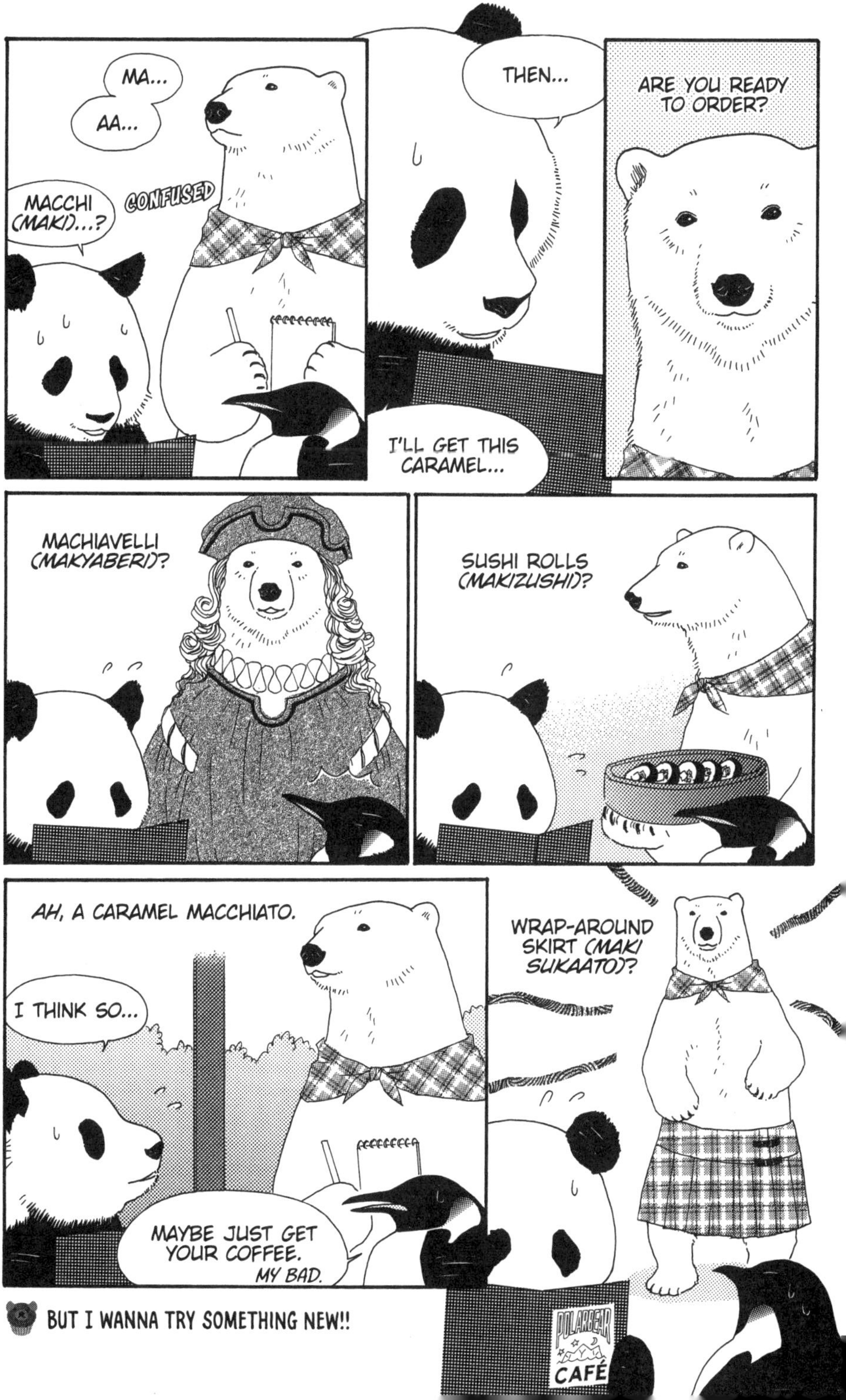
ARE YOU READY TO ORDER?
THEN...
I'LL GET THIS CARAMEL...
MA...
AA...
MACCHI (MAKI)...?
CONFUSED
SUSHI ROLLS (MAKIZUSHI)?
MACHIAVELLI (MAKYABERI)?
WRAP-AROUND SKIRT (MAKI SUKAATO)?
POLARBEAR CAFÉ
AH, A CARAMEL MACCHIATO.
I THINK SO...
MAYBE JUST GET YOUR COFFEE.
MY BAD.

BUT I WANNA TRY SOMETHING NEW!!

POLAR BEAR RECIPE ① BREWING COFFEE

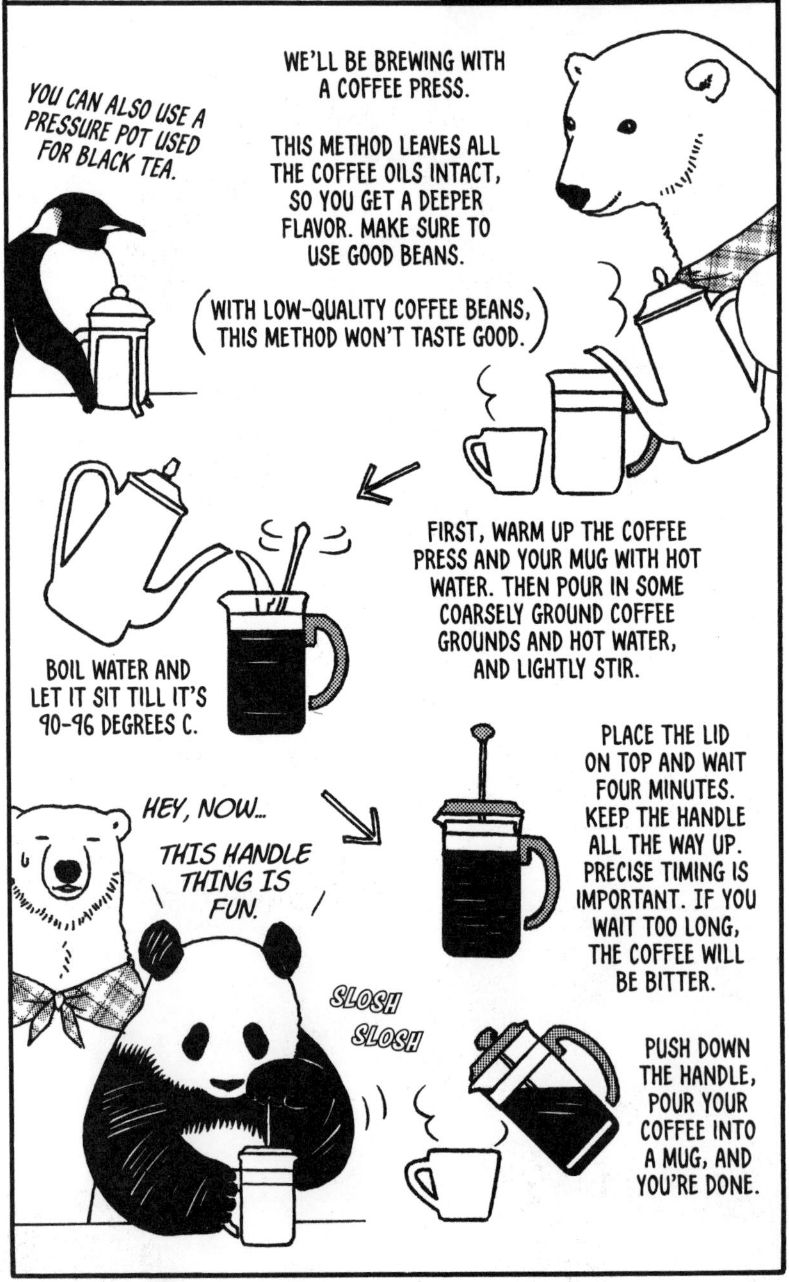
WE'LL BE BREWING WITH A COFFEE PRESS.
THIS METHOD LEAVES ALL THE COFFEE OILS INTACT, SO YOU GET A DEEPER FLAVOR. MAKE SURE TO USE GOOD BEANS.
(WITH LOW-QUALITY COFFEE BEANS, THIS METHOD WON'T TASTE GOOD.)
YOU CAN ALSO USE A PRESSURE POT USED FOR BLACK TEA.
FIRST, WARM UP THE COFFEE PRESS AND YOUR MUG WITH HOT WATER. THEN POUR IN SOME COARSELY GROUND COFFEE GROUNDS AND HOT WATER, AND LIGHTLY STIR.
BOIL WATER AND LET IT SIT TILL IT'S 90–96 DEGREES C.
PLACE THE LID ON TOP AND WAIT FOUR MINUTES. KEEP THE HANDLE ALL THE WAY UP. PRECISE TIMING IS IMPORTANT. IF YOU WAIT TOO LONG, THE COFFEE WILL BE BITTER.
HEY, NOW...
THIS HANDLE THING IS FUN.
PUSH DOWN THE HANDLE, POUR YOUR COFFEE INTO A MUG, AND YOU'RE DONE.
SLOSH
SLOSH

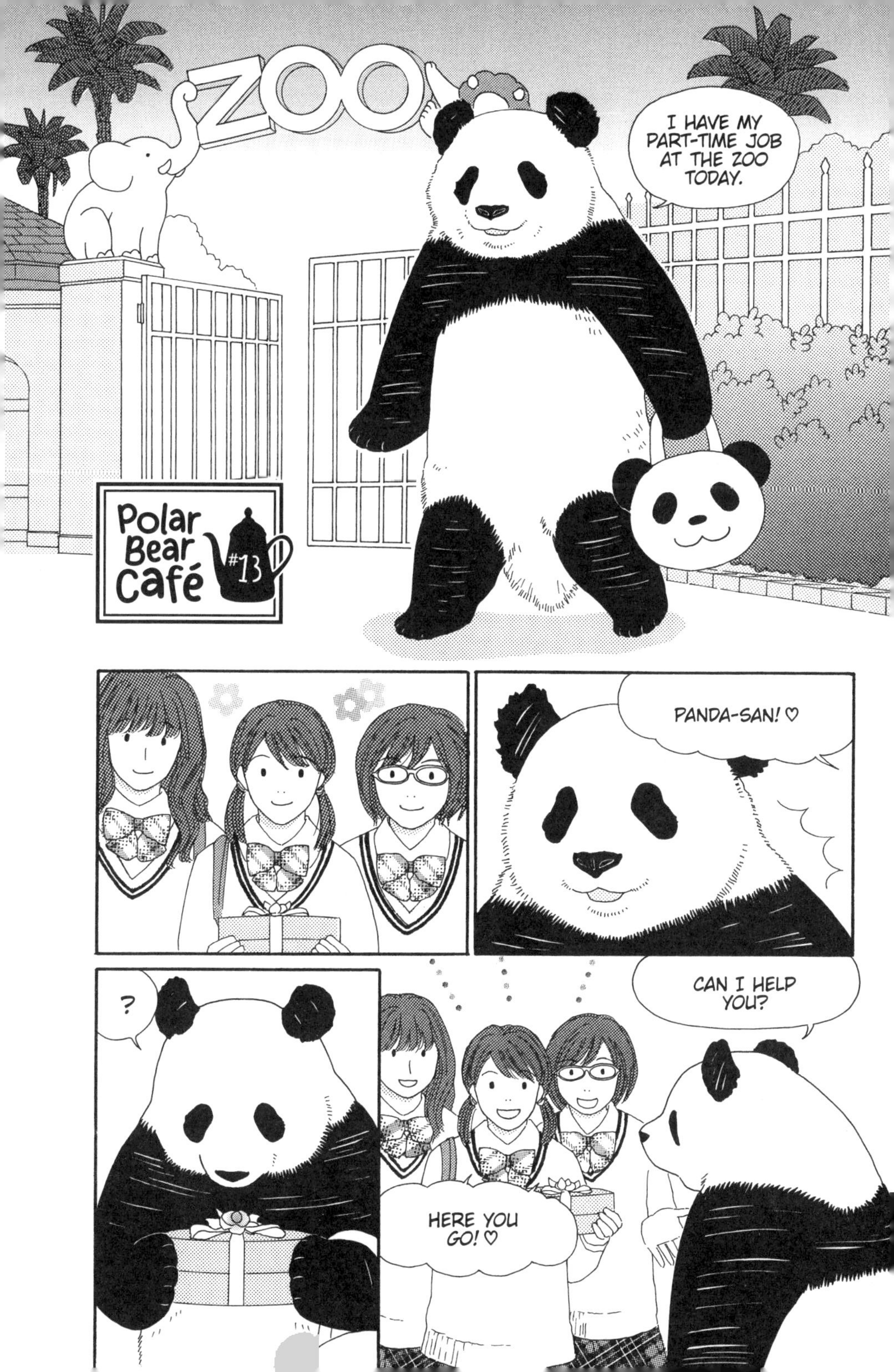
ZOO
I HAVE MY PART-TIME JOB AT THE ZOO TODAY.
Polar Bear Café
#13
PANDA-SAN! ♡
CAN I HELP YOU?
HERE YOU GO! ♡
?

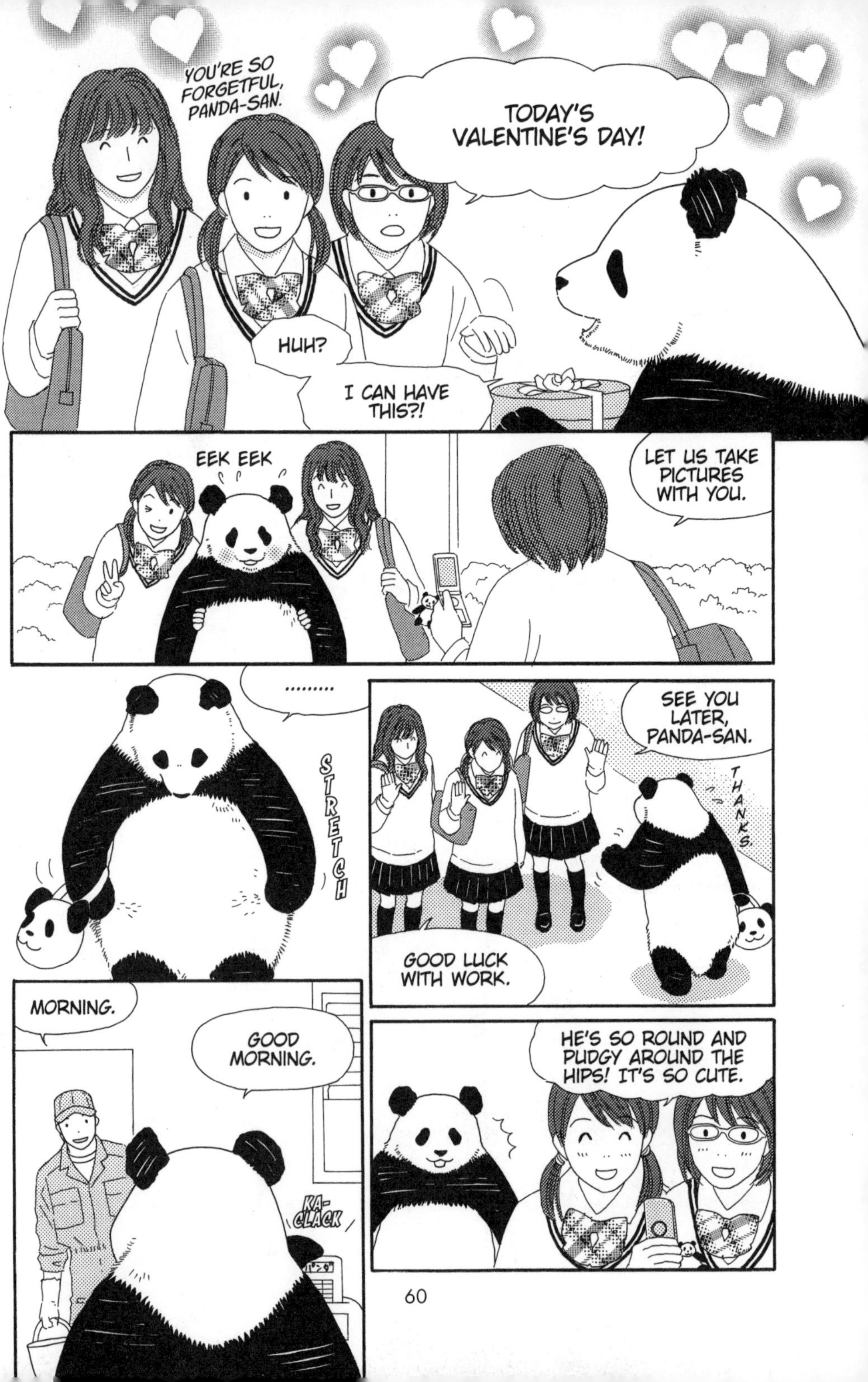
TODAY'S VALENTINE'S DAY!
YOU'RE SO FORGETFUL, PANDA-SAN.
HUH?
I CAN HAVE THIS?!
LET US TAKE PICTURES WITH YOU.
EEK EEK
SEE YOU LATER, PANDA-SAN.
THANKS
GOOD LUCK WITH WORK.
....
STRETCH
HE'S SO ROUND AND PUDGY AROUND THE HIPS! IT'S SO CUTE.
MORNING.
GOOD MORNING.
KA-CLACK

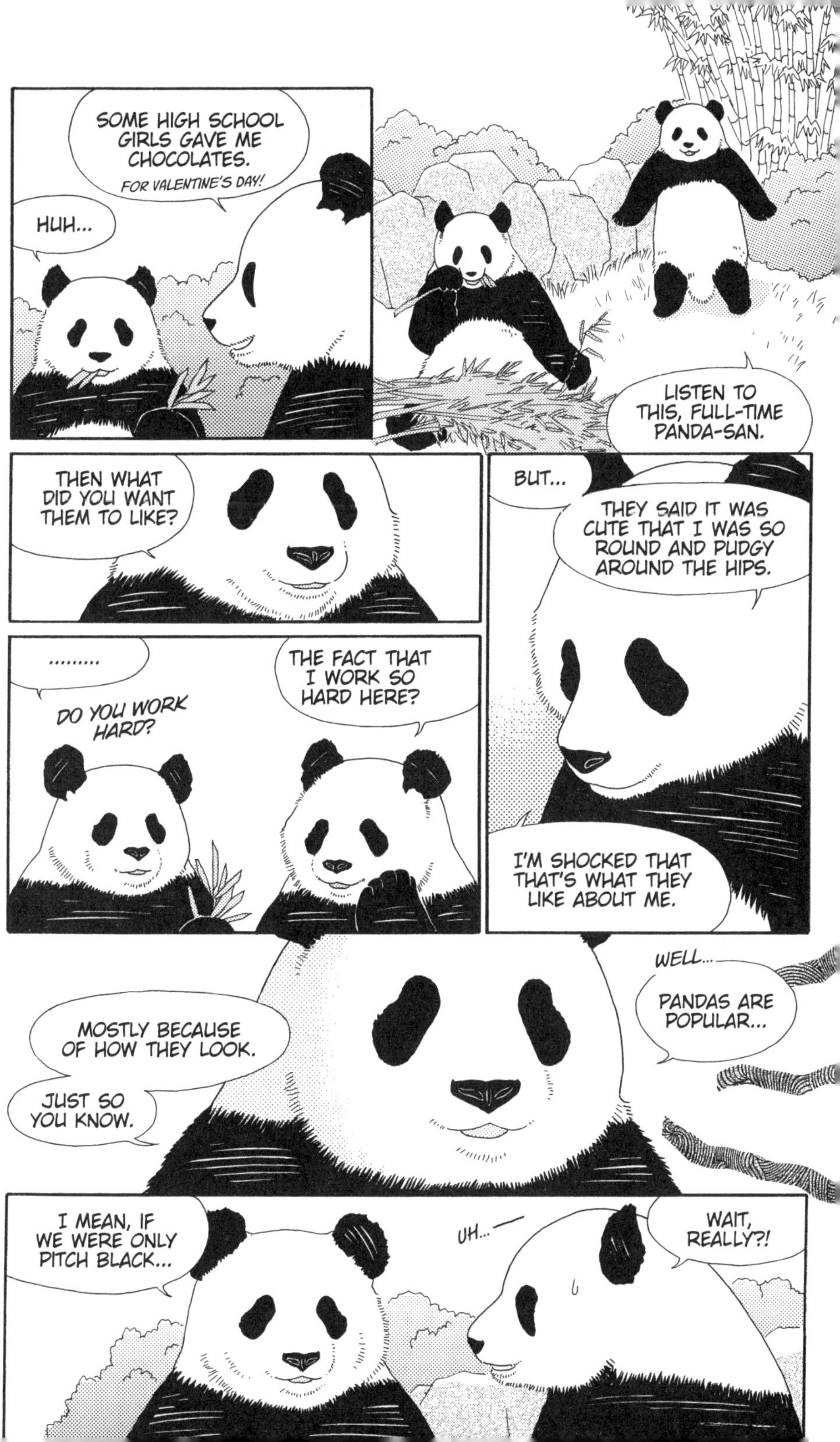
LISTEN TO THIS, FULL-TIME PANDA-SAN.
SOME HIGH SCHOOL GIRLS GAVE ME CHOCOLATES.
FOR VALENTINE'S DAY!
HUH...
BUT...
THEY SAID IT WAS CUTE THAT I WAS SO ROUND AND PUDGY AROUND THE HIPS.
I'M SHOCKED THAT THAT'S WHAT THEY LIKE ABOUT ME.
THEN WHAT DID YOU WANT THEM TO LIKE?
THE FACT THAT I WORK SO HARD HERE?
....
DO YOU WORK HARD?
WELL...
PANDAS ARE POPULAR...
MOSTLY BECAUSE OF HOW THEY LOOK.
JUST SO YOU KNOW.
WAIT, REALLY?!
UH...—
I MEAN, IF WE WERE ONLY PITCH BLACK...

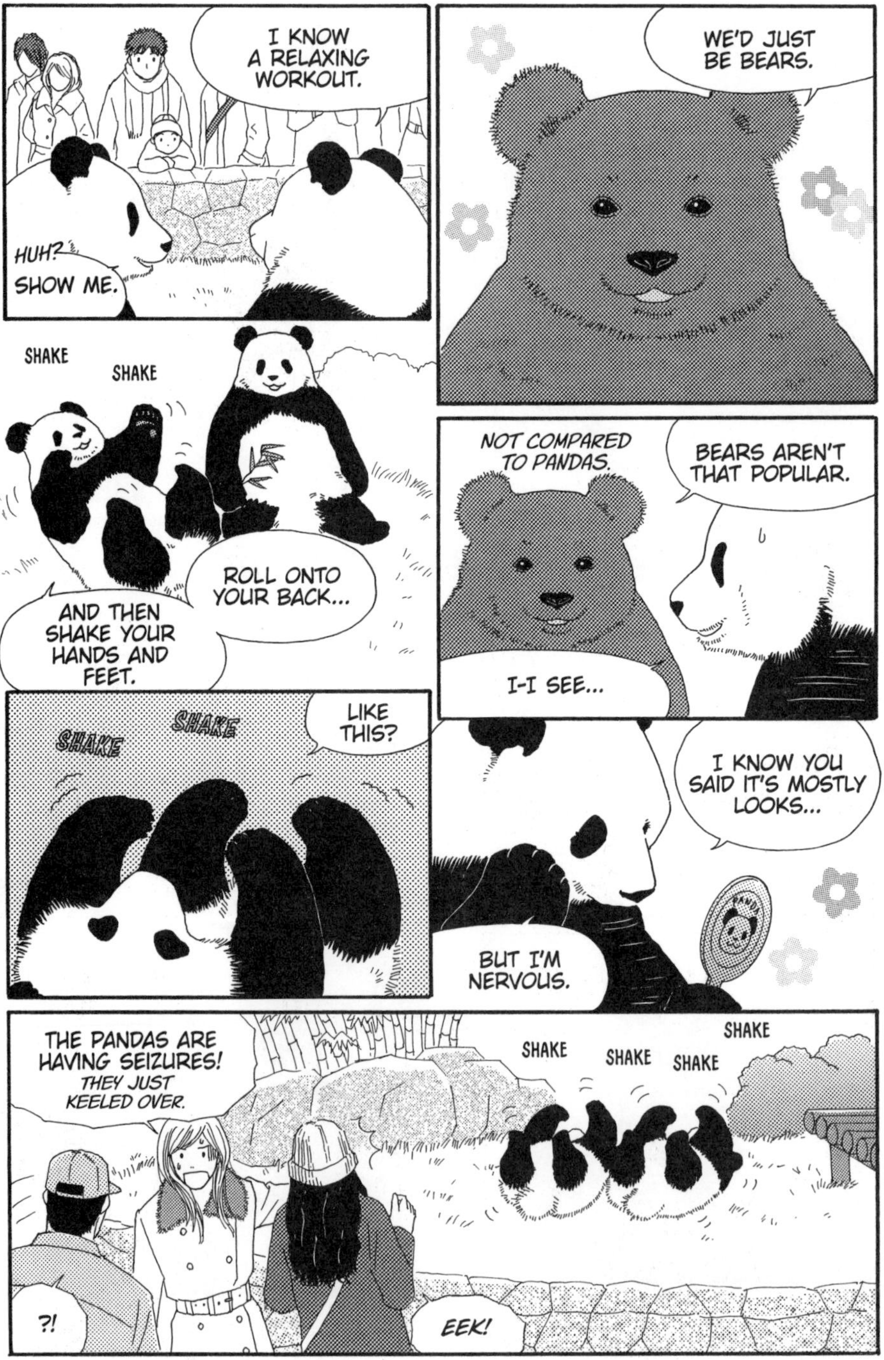
WE'D JUST BE BEARS.
BEARS AREN'T THAT POPULAR.
NOT COMPARED TO PANDAS.
I-I SEE...
I KNOW YOU SAID IT'S MOSTLY LOOKS...
BUT I'M NERVOUS.
I KNOW A RELAXING WORKOUT.
HUH?
SHOW ME.
SHAKE
SHAKE
ROLL ONTO YOUR BACK...
AND THEN SHAKE YOUR HANDS AND FEET.
LIKE THIS?
SHAKE
SHAKE
SHAKE
SHAKE
SHAKE
SHAKE
THE PANDAS ARE HAVING SEIZURES!
THEY JUST KEELED OVER.
EEK!
?!

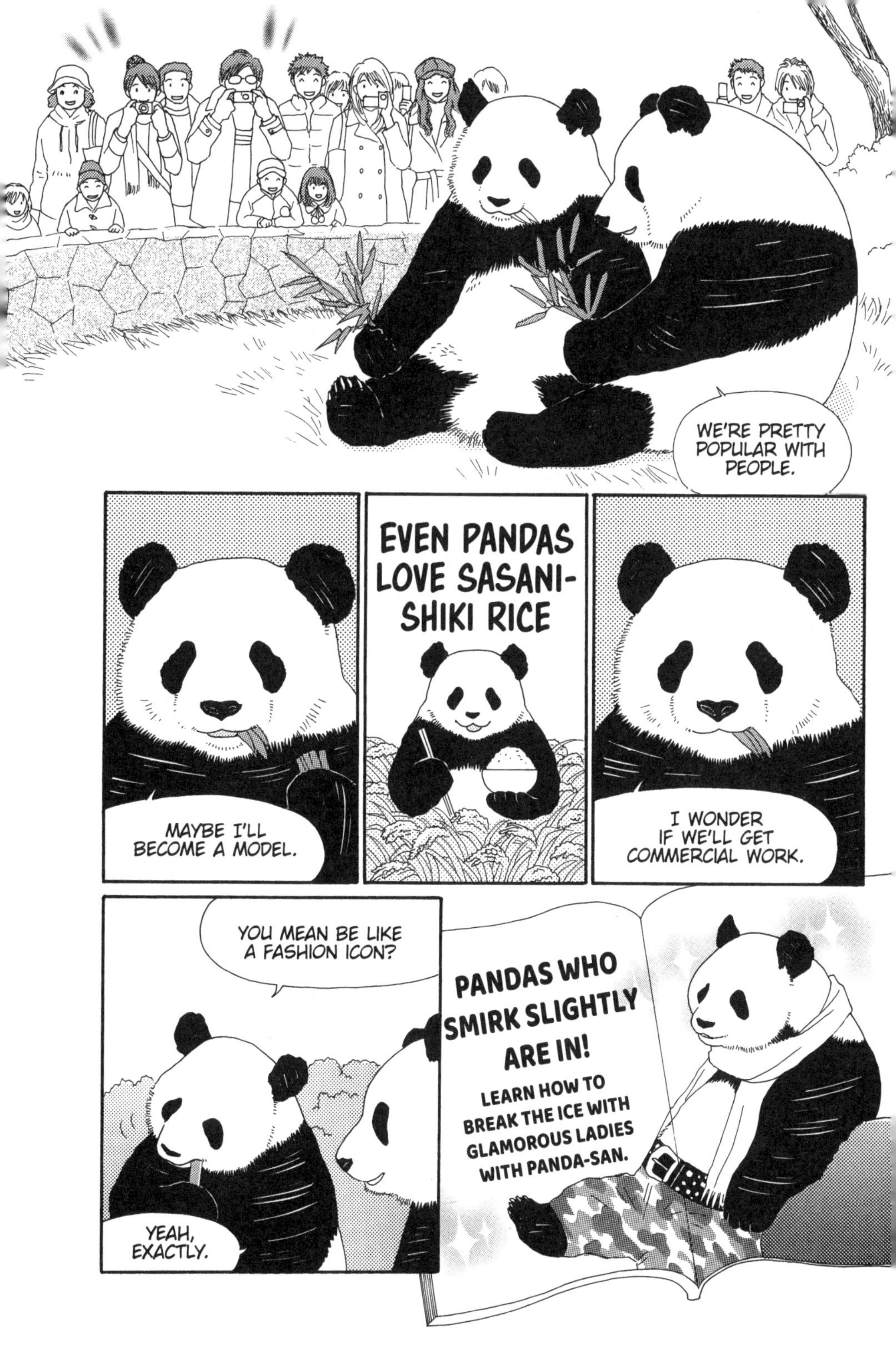
WE'RE PRETTY POPULAR WITH PEOPLE.
I WONDER IF WE'LL GET COMMERCIAL WORK.
EVEN PANDAS LOVE SASANI-SHIKI RICE
MAYBE I'LL BECOME A MODEL.
PANDAS WHO SMIRK SLIGHTLY ARE IN!
LEARN HOW TO BREAK THE ICE WITH GLAMOROUS LADIES WITH PANDA-SAN.
YOU MEAN BE LIKE A FASHION ICON?
YEAH, EXACTLY.

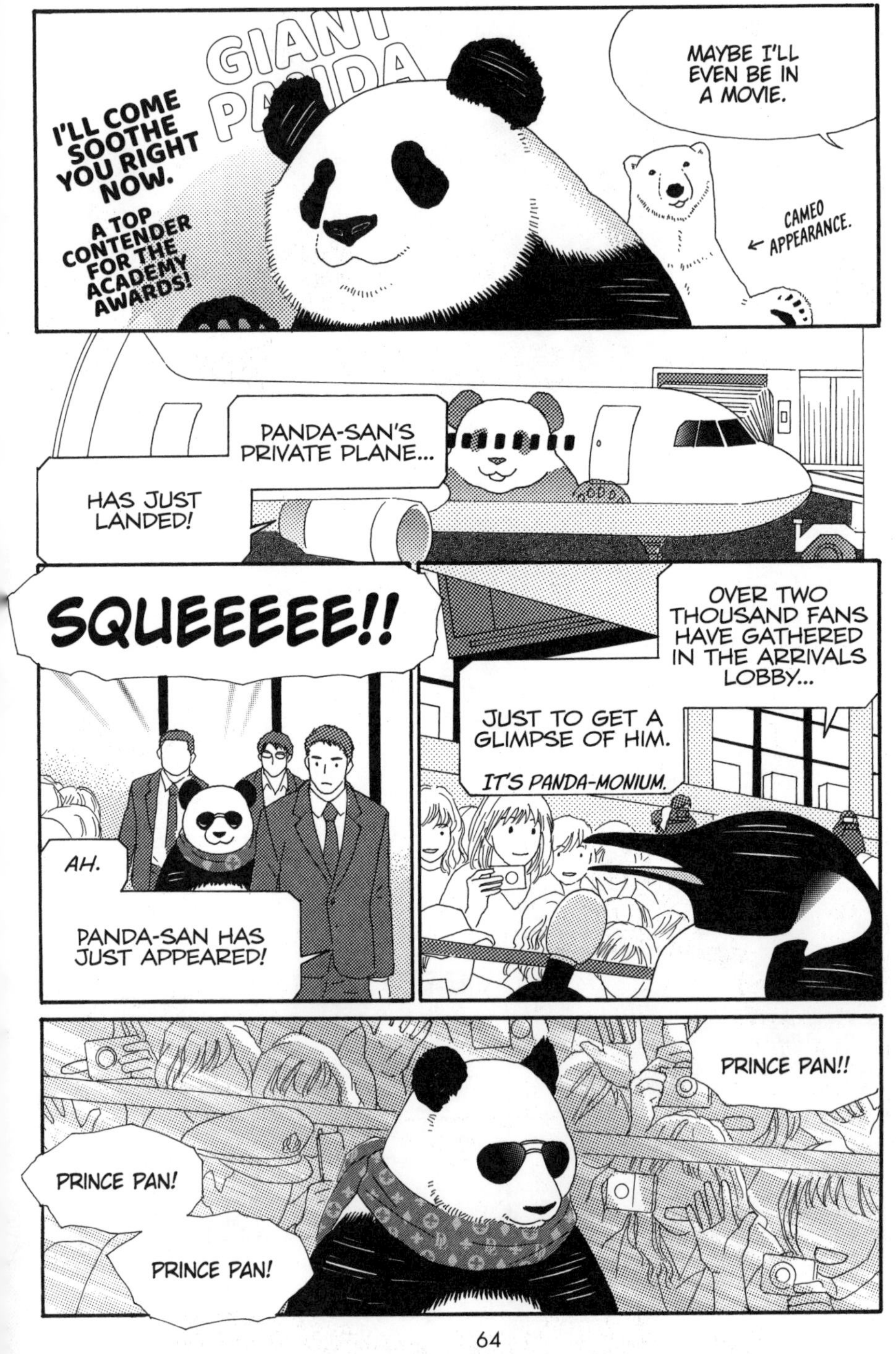
MAYBE I'LL EVEN BE IN A MOVIE.
GIANT PANDA
I'LL COME SOOTHE YOU RIGHT NOW.
A TOP CONTENDER FOR THE ACADEMY AWARDS!
← CAMEO APPEARANCE.
PANDA-SAN'S PRIVATE PLANE...
HAS JUST LANDED!
OVER TWO THOUSAND FANS HAVE GATHERED IN THE ARRIVALS LOBBY...
JUST TO GET A GLIMPSE OF HIM.
IT'S PANDA-MONIUM.
SQUEEEEEE!!
AH.
PANDA-SAN HAS JUST APPEARED!
PRINCE PAN!!
PRINCE PAN!
PRINCE PAN!

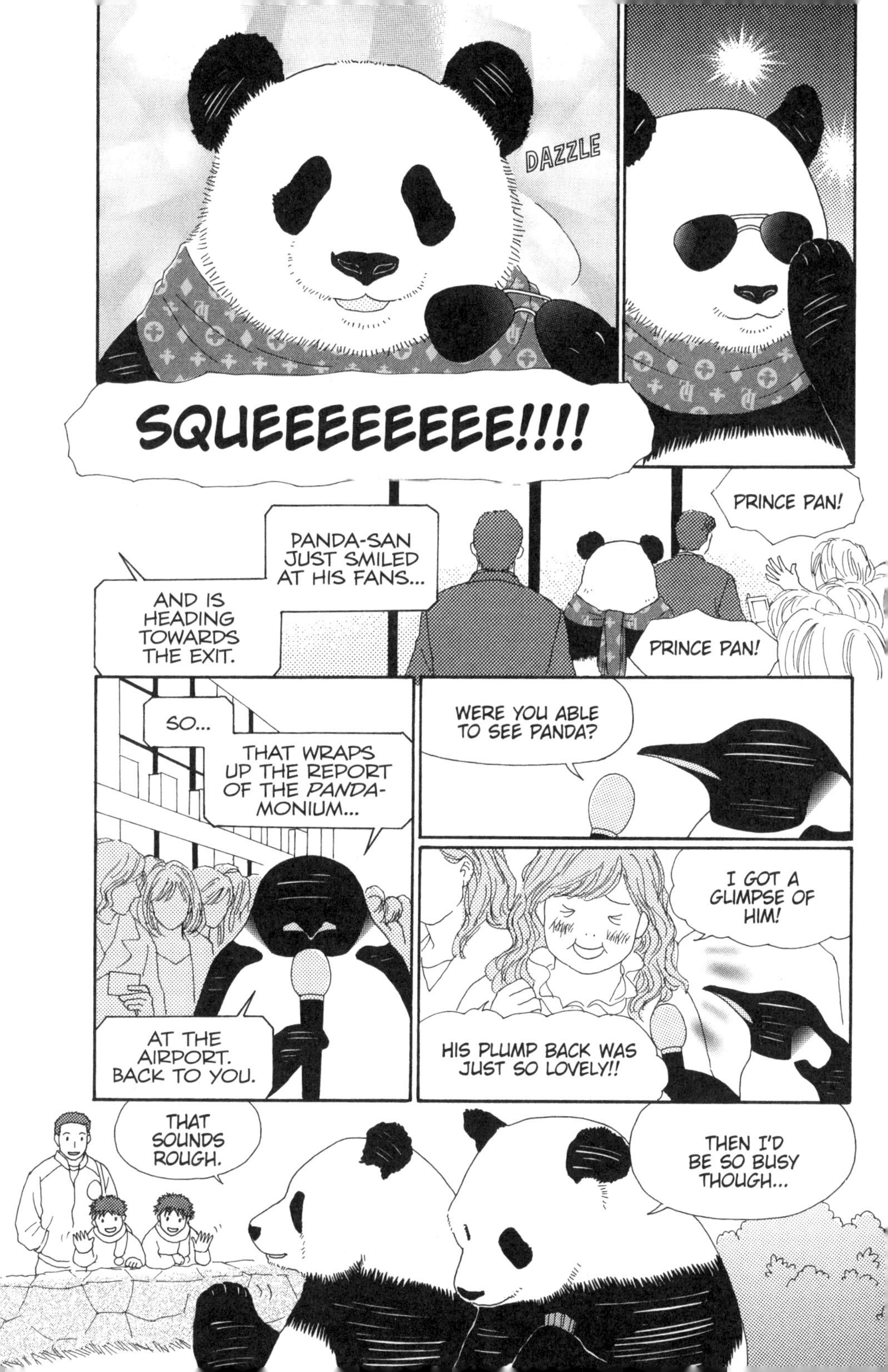
DAZZLE
SQUEEEEEEEEE!!!!
PRINCE PAN!
PRINCE PAN!
PANDA-SAN JUST SMILED AT HIS FANS...
AND IS HEADING TOWARDS THE EXIT.
WERE YOU ABLE TO SEE PANDA?
I GOT A GLIMPSE OF HIM!
HIS PLUMP BACK WAS JUST SO LOVELY!!
SO...
THAT WRAPS UP THE REPORT OF THE *PANDA*-MONIUM...
AT THE AIRPORT. BACK TO YOU.
THEN I'D BE SO BUSY THOUGH...
THAT SOUNDS ROUGH.

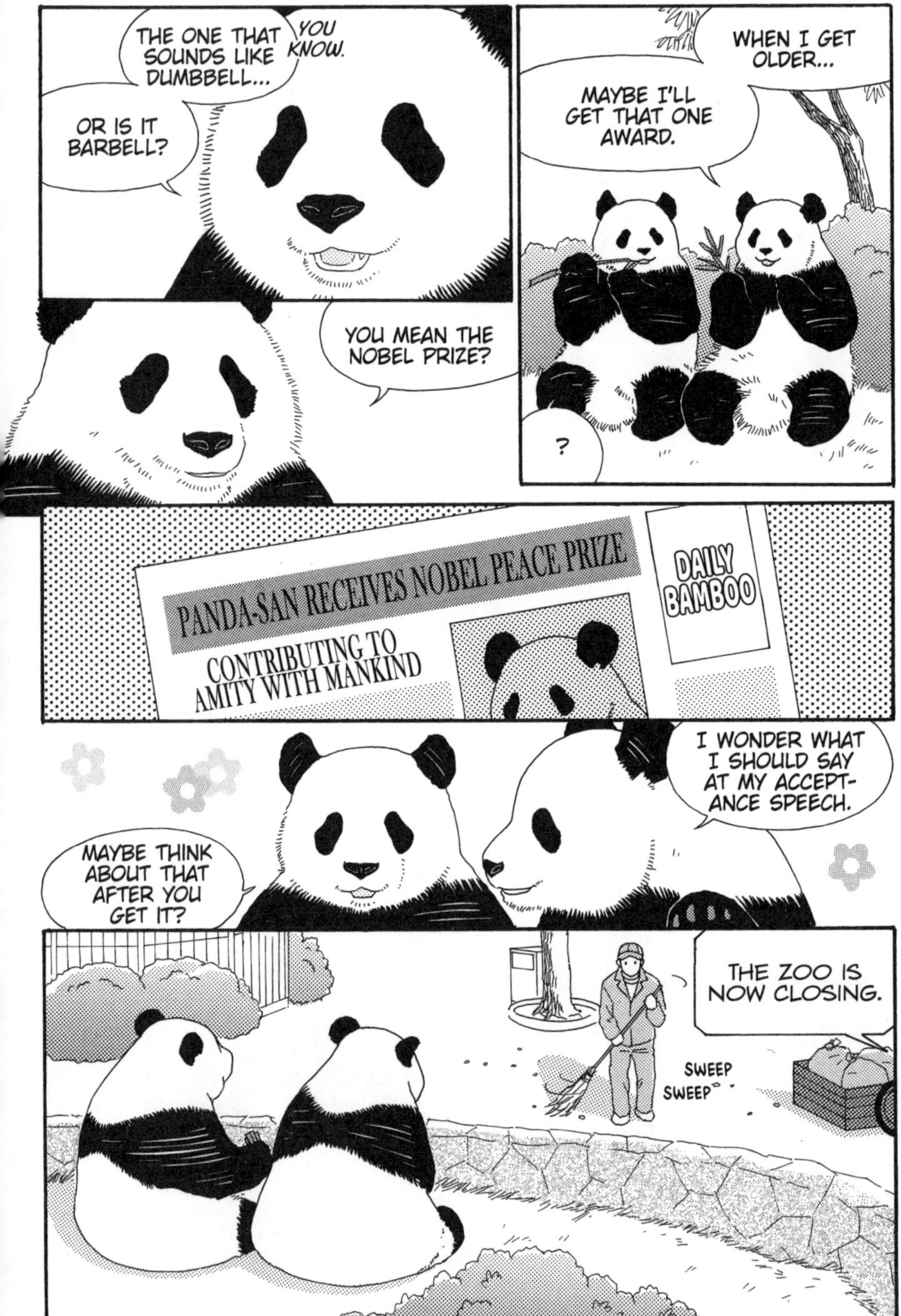
WHEN I GET OLDER...
MAYBE I'LL GET THAT ONE AWARD.
?
YOU KNOW.
THE ONE THAT SOUNDS LIKE DUMBBELL...
OR IS IT BARBELL?
YOU MEAN THE NOBEL PRIZE?
DAILY BAMBOO
PANDA-SAN RECEIVES NOBEL PEACE PRIZE
CONTRIBUTING TO AMITY WITH MANKIND
I WONDER WHAT I SHOULD SAY AT MY ACCEPTANCE SPEECH.
MAYBE THINK ABOUT THAT AFTER YOU GET IT?
THE ZOO IS NOW CLOSING.
SWEEP
SWEEP

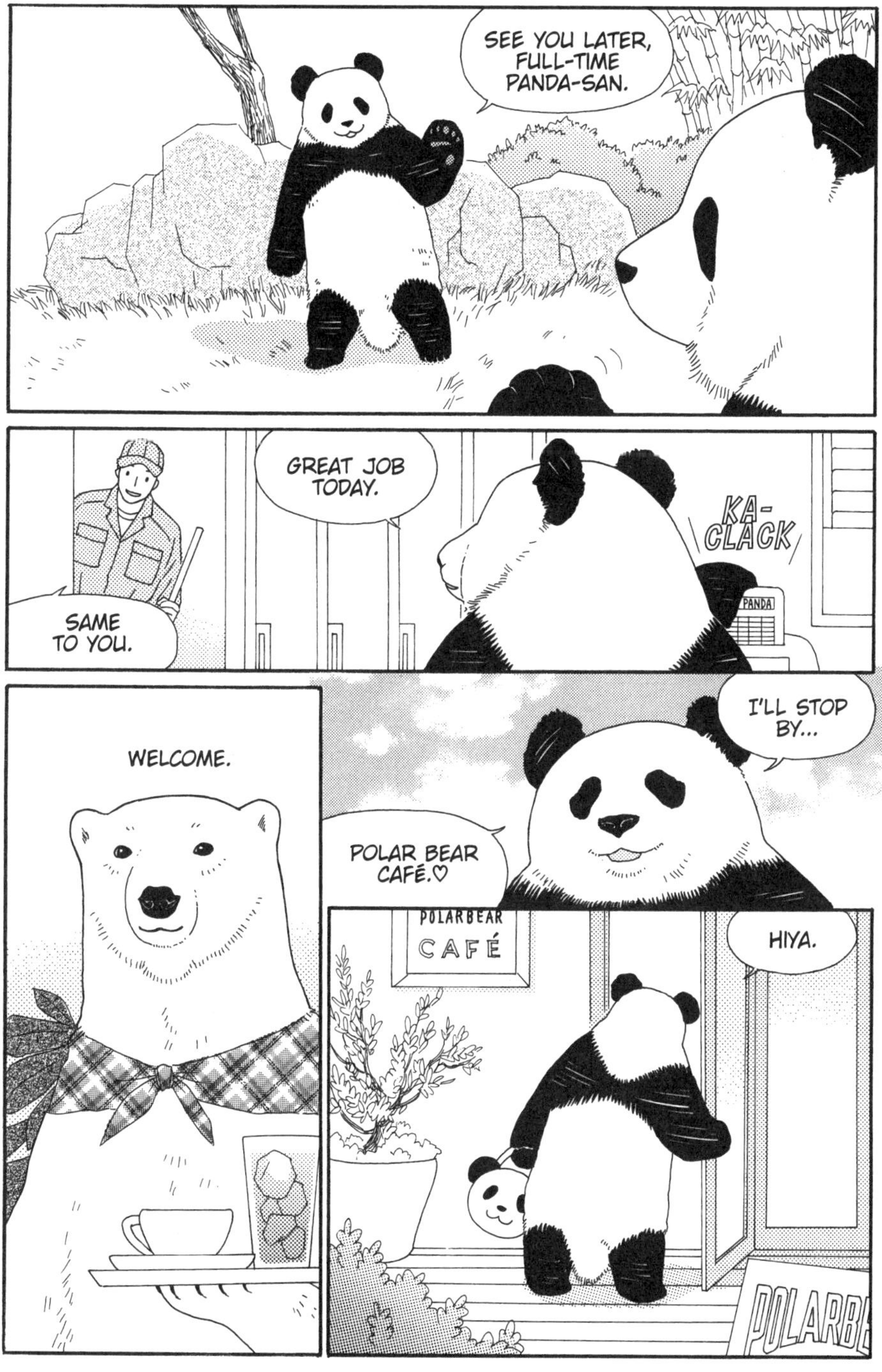
SEE YOU LATER, FULL-TIME PANDA-SAN.
GREAT JOB TODAY.
KA-CLACK
PANDA
SAME TO YOU.
I'LL STOP BY...
POLAR BEAR CAFÉ.♡
HIYA.
POLARBEAR CAFÉ
POLARBE
WELCOME.

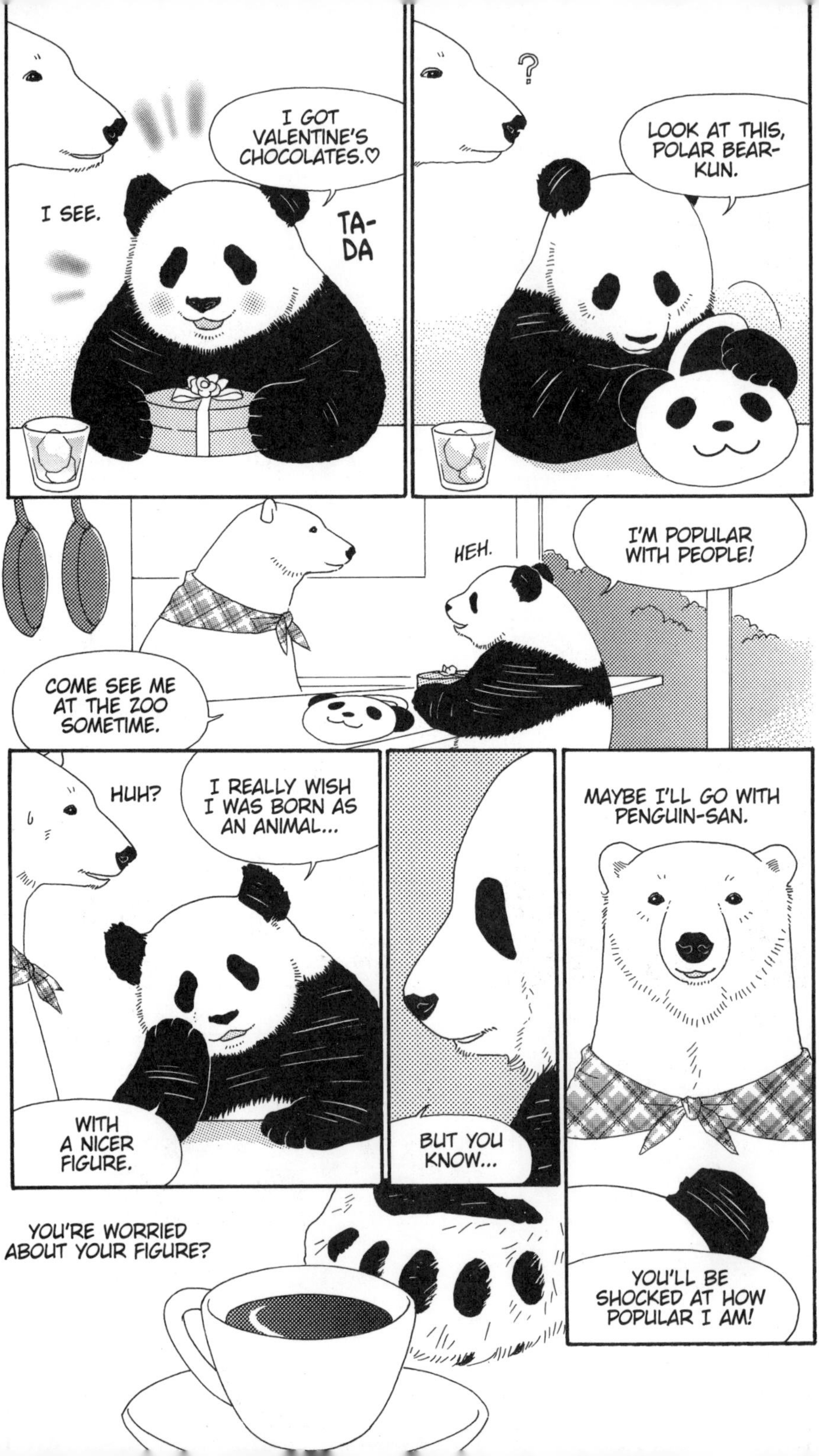
LOOK AT THIS, POLAR BEAR-KUN.
I GOT VALENTINE'S CHOCOLATES.♡
TA-DA
I SEE.
I'M POPULAR WITH PEOPLE!
HEH.
COME SEE ME AT THE ZOO SOMETIME.
MAYBE I'LL GO WITH PENGUIN-SAN.
YOU'LL BE SHOCKED AT HOW POPULAR I AM!
BUT YOU KNOW...
I REALLY WISH I WAS BORN AS AN ANIMAL...
HUH?
WITH A NICER FIGURE.
YOU'RE WORRIED ABOUT YOUR FIGURE?

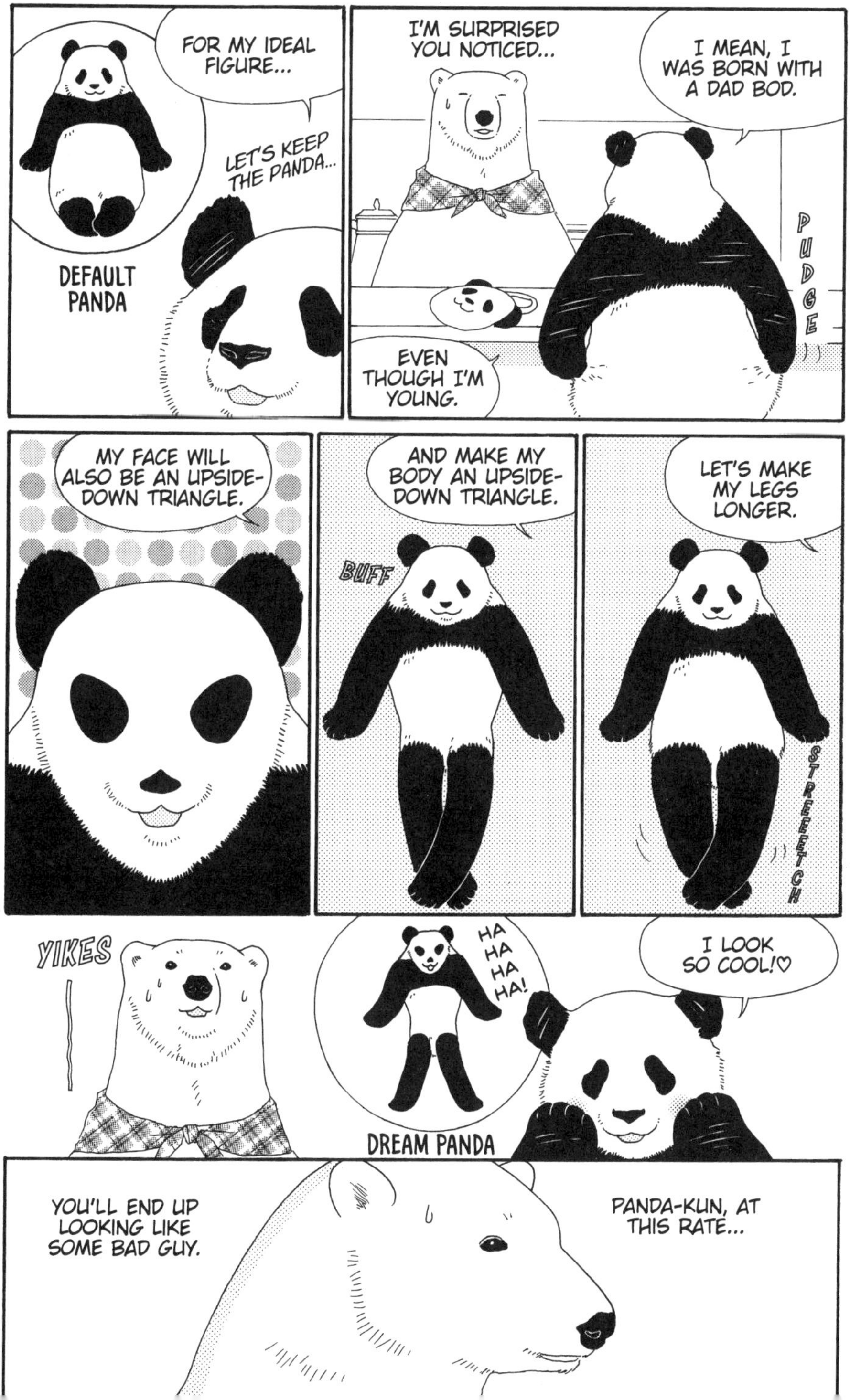

I MEAN, I WAS BORN WITH A DAD BOD.
I'M SURPRISED YOU NOTICED...
PUDGE
EVEN THOUGH I'M YOUNG.
FOR MY IDEAL FIGURE...
LET'S KEEP THE PANDA...
DEFAULT PANDA
LET'S MAKE MY LEGS LONGER.
STREEETCH
AND MAKE MY BODY AN UPSIDE-DOWN TRIANGLE.
BUFF
MY FACE WILL ALSO BE AN UPSIDE-DOWN TRIANGLE.
I LOOK SO COOL!♡
HA HA HA HA!
DREAM PANDA
YIKES
PANDA-KUN, AT THIS RATE...
YOU'LL END UP LOOKING LIKE SOME BAD GUY.

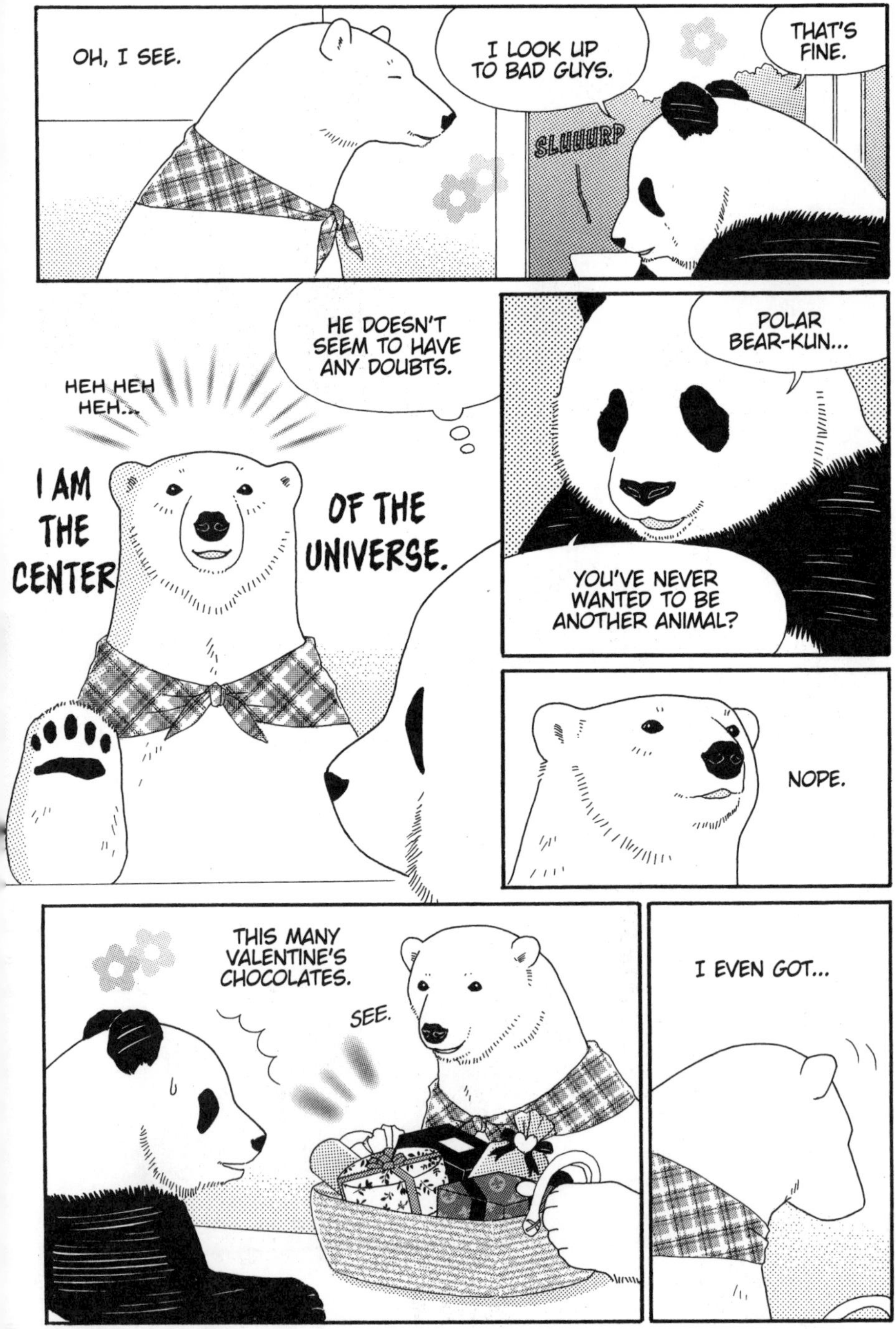
THAT'S FINE.
SLUUURP
I LOOK UP TO BAD GUYS.
OH, I SEE.
POLAR BEAR-KUN...
YOU'VE NEVER WANTED TO BE ANOTHER ANIMAL?
NOPE.
HE DOESN'T SEEM TO HAVE ANY DOUBTS.
HEH HEH HEH...
I AM THE CENTER OF THE UNIVERSE.
I EVEN GOT...
THIS MANY VALENTINE'S CHOCOLATES.
SEE.

A CONFIDENT GUY IS VERY CHARMING!!

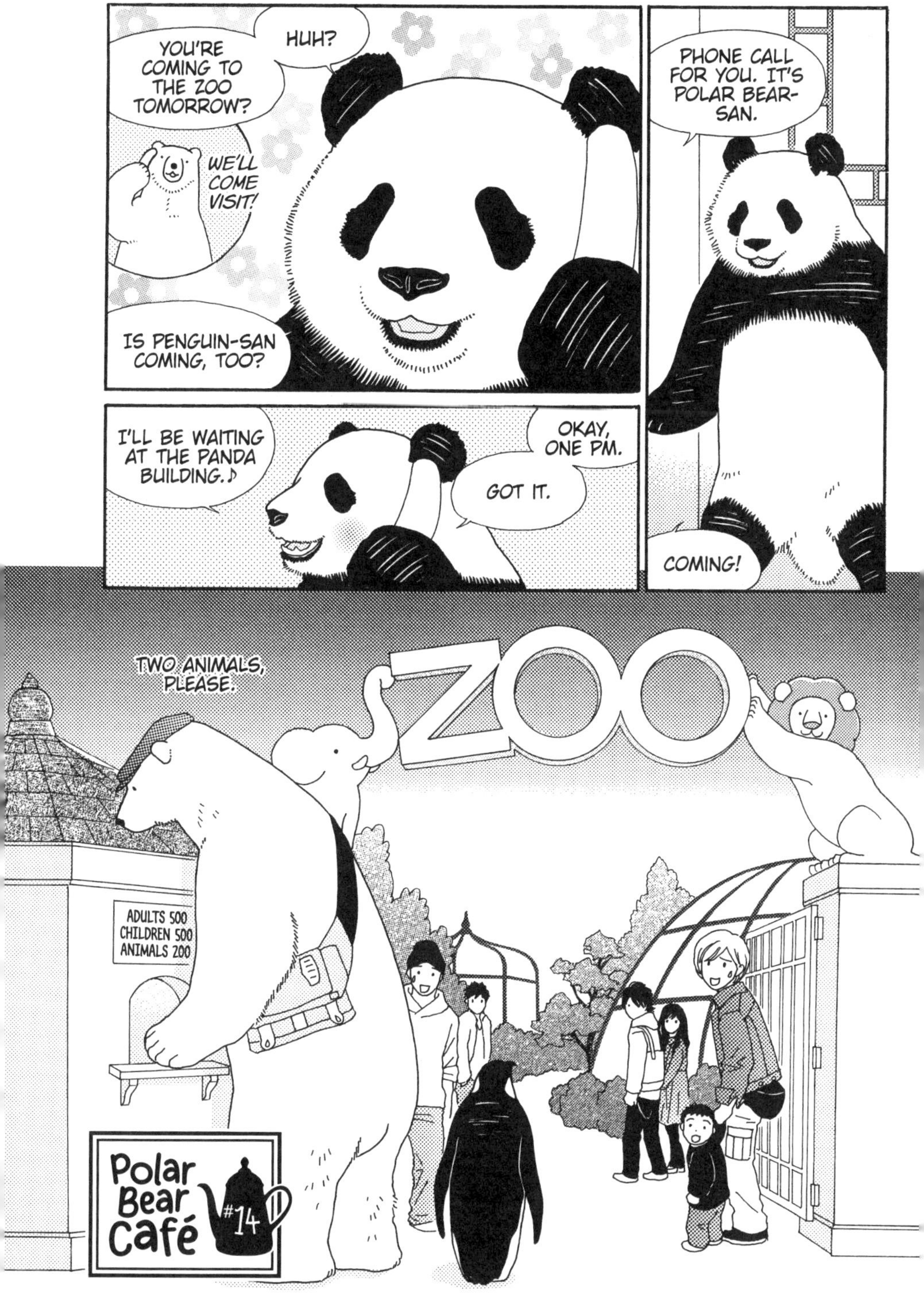
PHONE CALL FOR YOU. IT'S POLAR BEAR-SAN.
COMING!
HUH?
YOU'RE COMING TO THE ZOO TOMORROW?
WE'LL COME VISIT!
IS PENGUIN-SAN COMING, TOO?
OKAY, ONE PM.
GOT IT.
I'LL BE WAITING AT THE PANDA BUILDING.♪
ZOO
TWO ANIMALS, PLEASE.
ADULTS 500
CHILDREN 500
ANIMALS 200
Polar Bear Café
#14

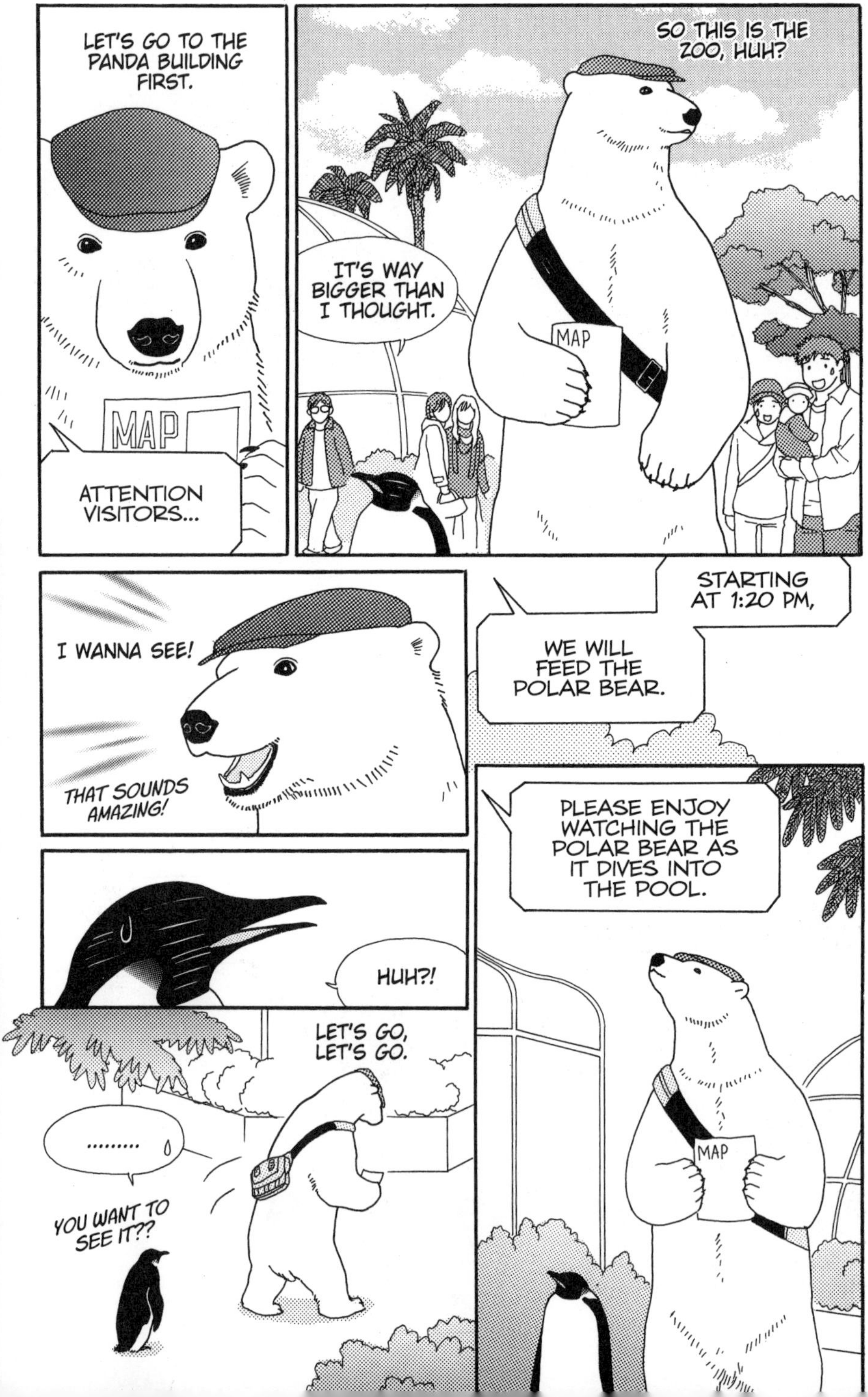
SO THIS IS THE ZOO, HUH?
IT'S WAY BIGGER THAN I THOUGHT.
MAP
LET'S GO TO THE PANDA BUILDING FIRST.
MAP
ATTENTION VISITORS...
STARTING AT 1:20 PM,
WE WILL FEED THE POLAR BEAR.
PLEASE ENJOY WATCHING THE POLAR BEAR AS IT DIVES INTO THE POOL.
MAP
I WANNA SEE!
THAT SOUNDS AMAZING!
HUH?!
LET'S GO, LET'S GO.
....
YOU WANT TO SEE IT??

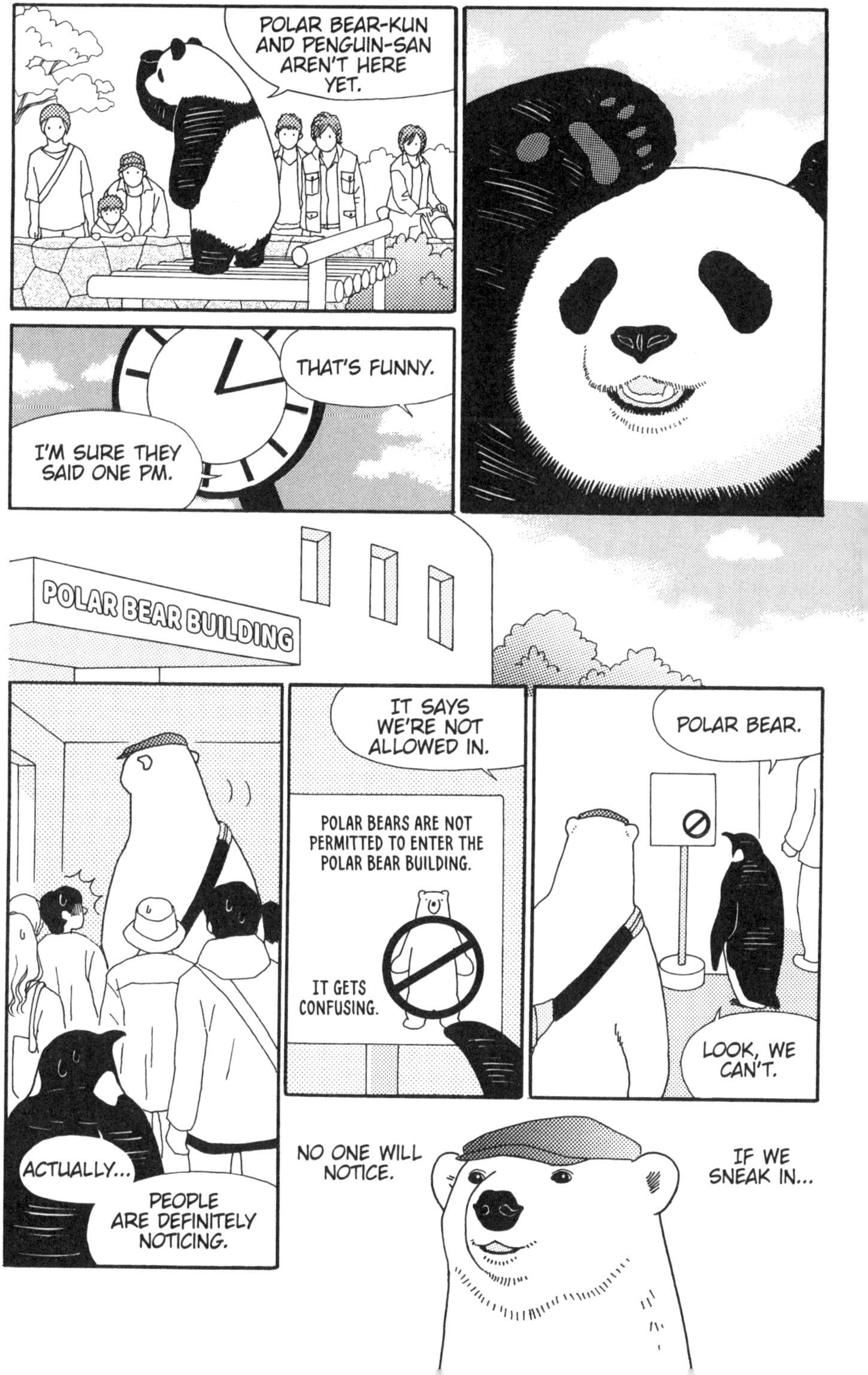

POLAR BEAR-KUN AND PENGUIN-SAN AREN'T HERE YET.
THAT'S FUNNY.
I'M SURE THEY SAID ONE PM.
POLAR BEAR BUILDING
POLAR BEAR.
LOOK, WE CAN'T.
IT SAYS WE'RE NOT ALLOWED IN.
POLAR BEARS ARE NOT PERMITTED TO ENTER THE POLAR BEAR BUILDING.
IT GETS CONFUSING.
IF WE SNEAK IN...
NO ONE WILL NOTICE.
ACTUALLY...
PEOPLE ARE DEFINITELY NOTICING.

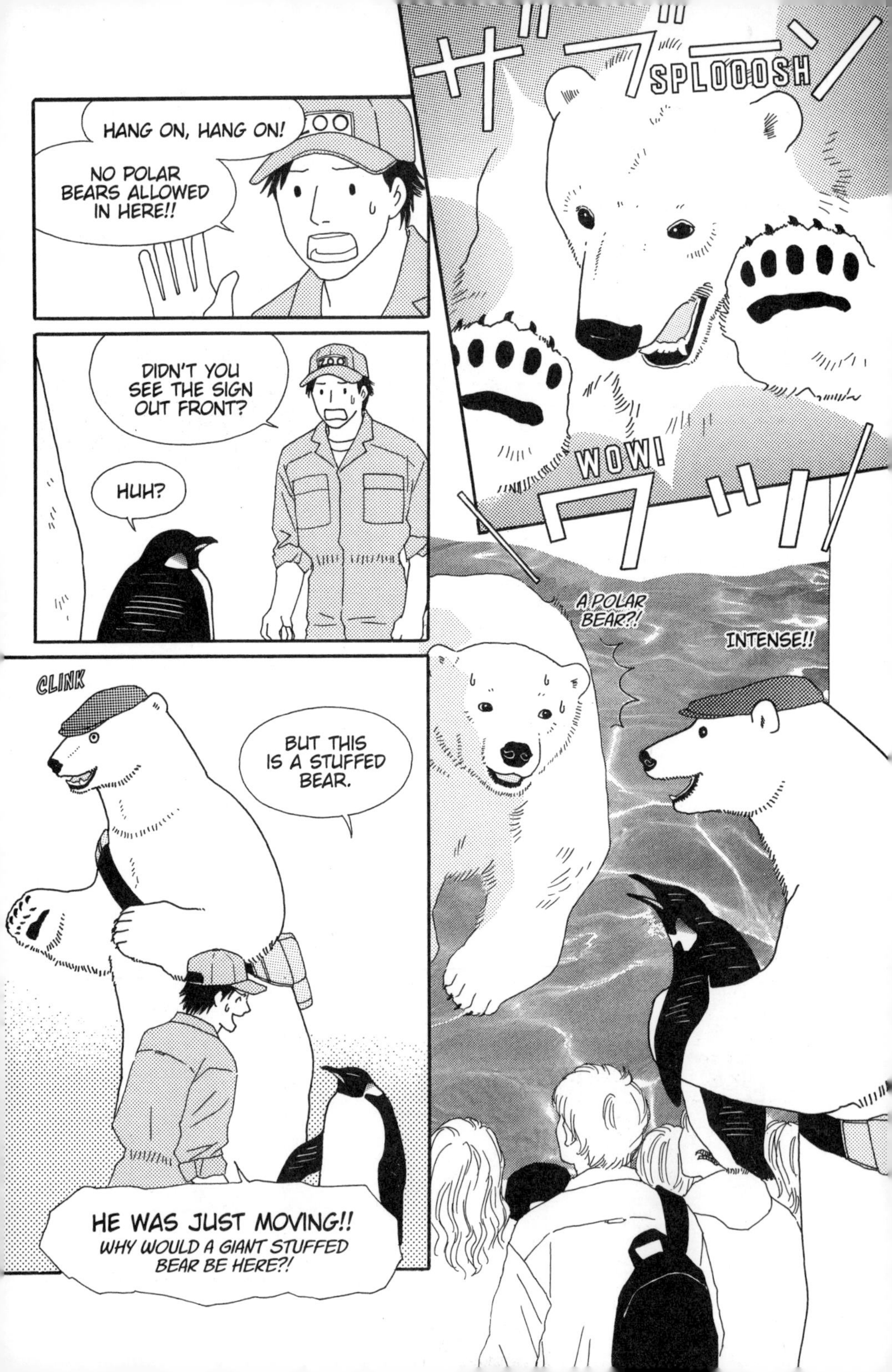
SPLOOOSH
WOW!
HANG ON, HANG ON!
NO POLAR BEARS ALLOWED IN HERE!!
DIDN'T YOU SEE THE SIGN OUT FRONT?
HUH?
A POLAR BEAR?!
INTENSE!!
CLINK
BUT THIS IS A STUFFED BEAR.
HE WAS JUST MOVING!!
WHY WOULD A GIANT STUFFED BEAR BE HERE?!

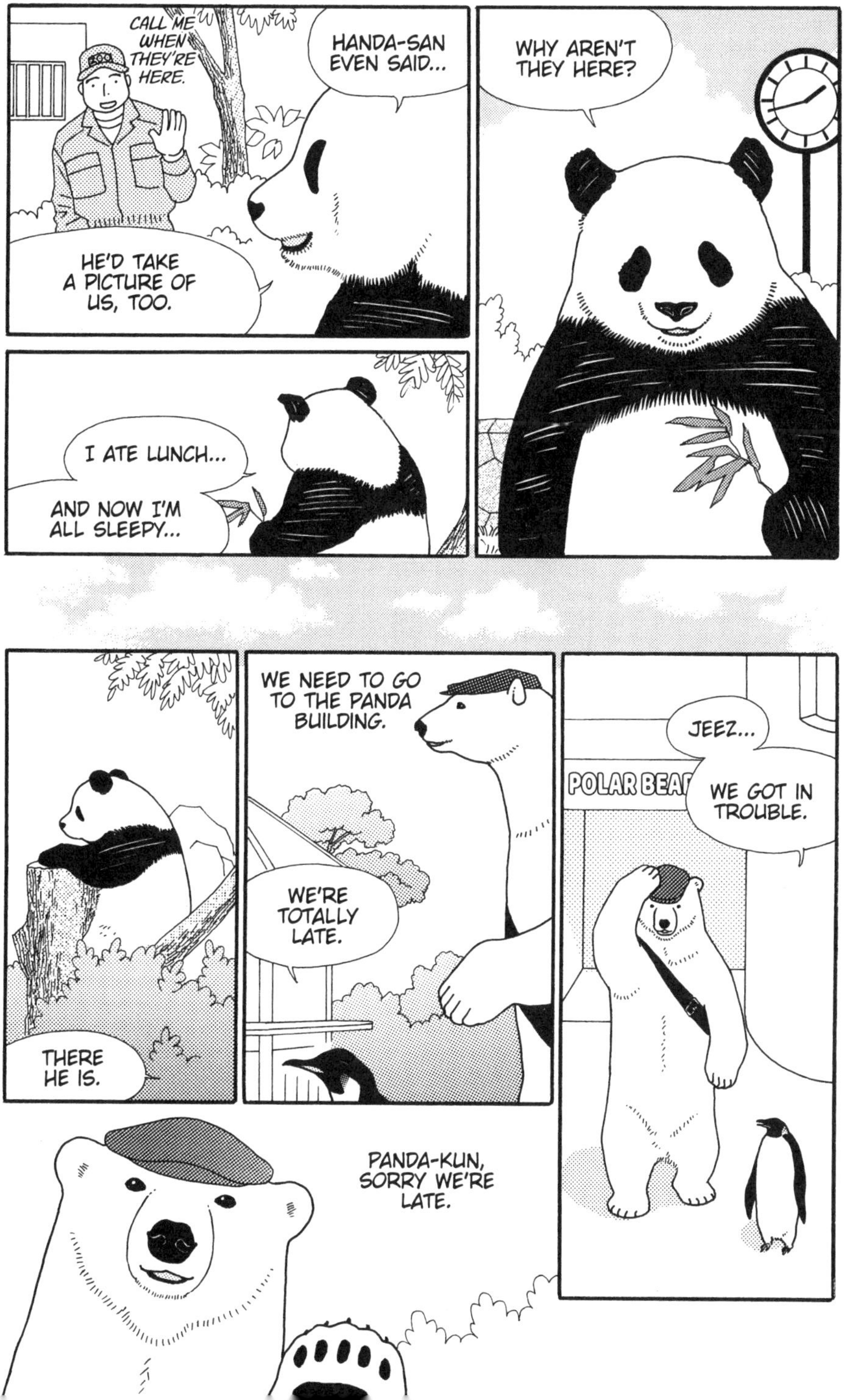
WHY AREN'T THEY HERE?
HANDA-SAN EVEN SAID...
ZOO
CALL ME WHEN THEY'RE HERE.
HE'D TAKE A PICTURE OF US, TOO.
I ATE LUNCH...
AND NOW I'M ALL SLEEPY...
JEEZ...
POLAR BEA
WE GOT IN TROUBLE.
WE NEED TO GO TO THE PANDA BUILDING.
WE'RE TOTALLY LATE.
THERE HE IS.
PANDA-KUN, SORRY WE'RE LATE.

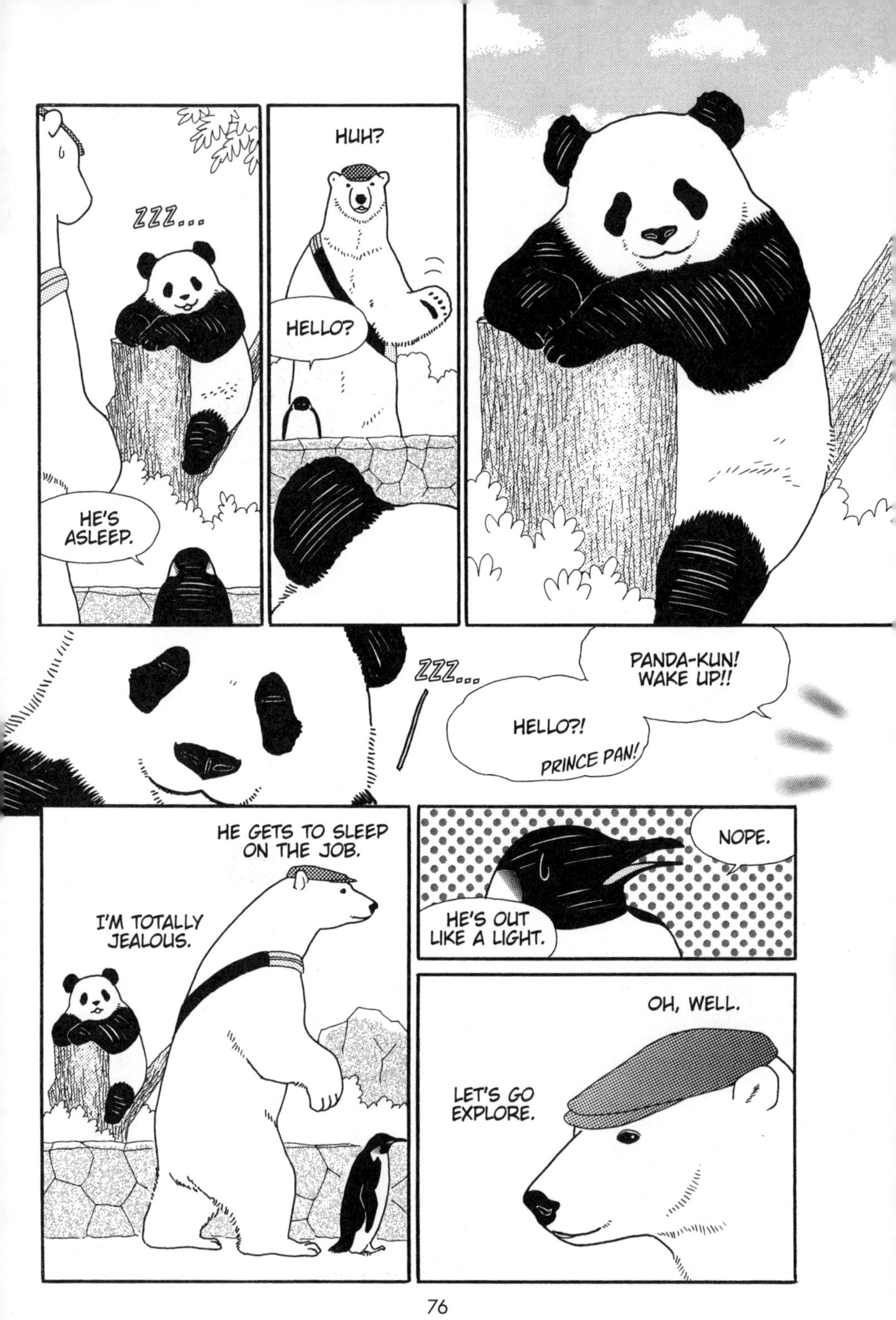
HUH?
HELLO?
ZZZ...
HE'S ASLEEP.
PANDA-KUN! WAKE UP!!
HELLO?!
PRINCE PAN!
ZZZ...
NOPE.
HE'S OUT LIKE A LIGHT.
OH, WELL.
LET'S GO EXPLORE.
HE GETS TO SLEEP ON THE JOB.
I'M TOTALLY JEALOUS.

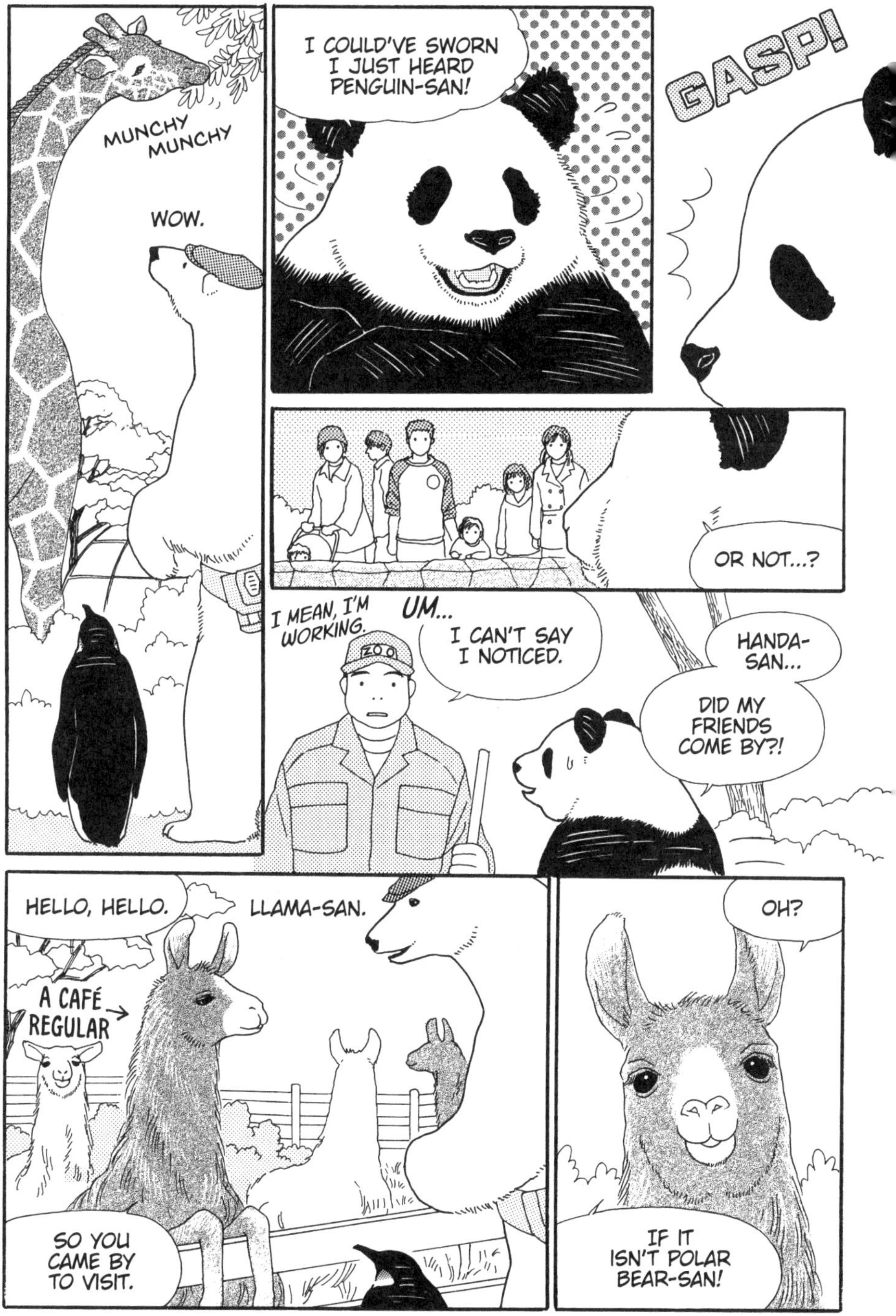
GASP!
I COULD'VE SWORN I JUST HEARD PENGUIN-SAN!
OR NOT...?
HANDA-SAN...
DID MY FRIENDS COME BY?!
UM...
I CAN'T SAY I NOTICED.
I MEAN, I'M WORKING.
ZOO
MUNCHY MUNCHY
WOW.
OH?
IF IT ISN'T POLAR BEAR-SAN!
LLAMA-SAN.
HELLO, HELLO.
A CAFÉ REGULAR
SO YOU CAME BY TO VISIT.

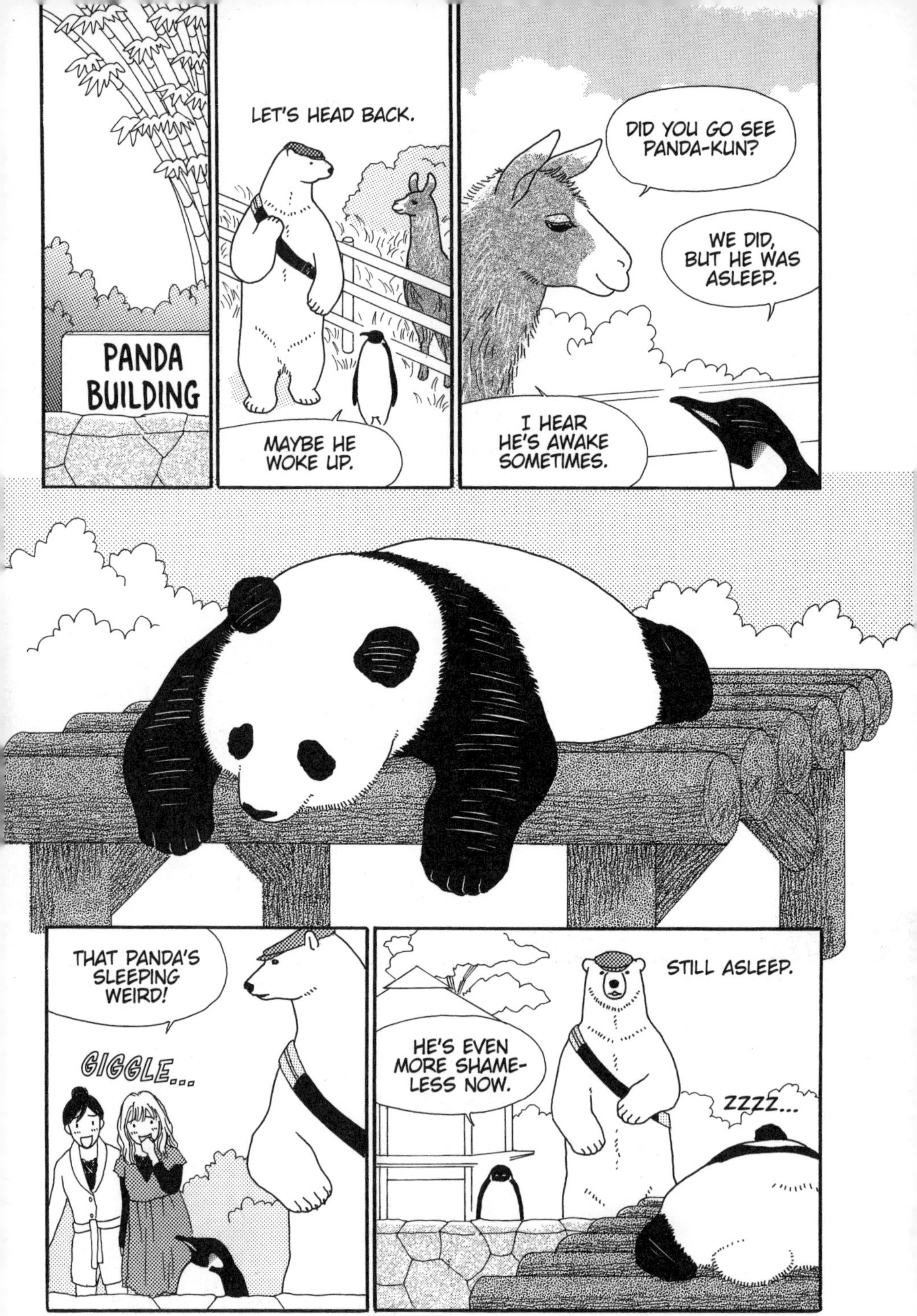
DID YOU GO SEE PANDA-KUN?
WE DID, BUT HE WAS ASLEEP.
I HEAR HE'S AWAKE SOMETIMES.
LET'S HEAD BACK.
MAYBE HE WOKE UP.
PANDA BUILDING
STILL ASLEEP.
HE'S EVEN MORE SHAME-LESS NOW.
ZZZZ...
THAT PANDA'S SLEEPING WEIRD!
GIGGLE...

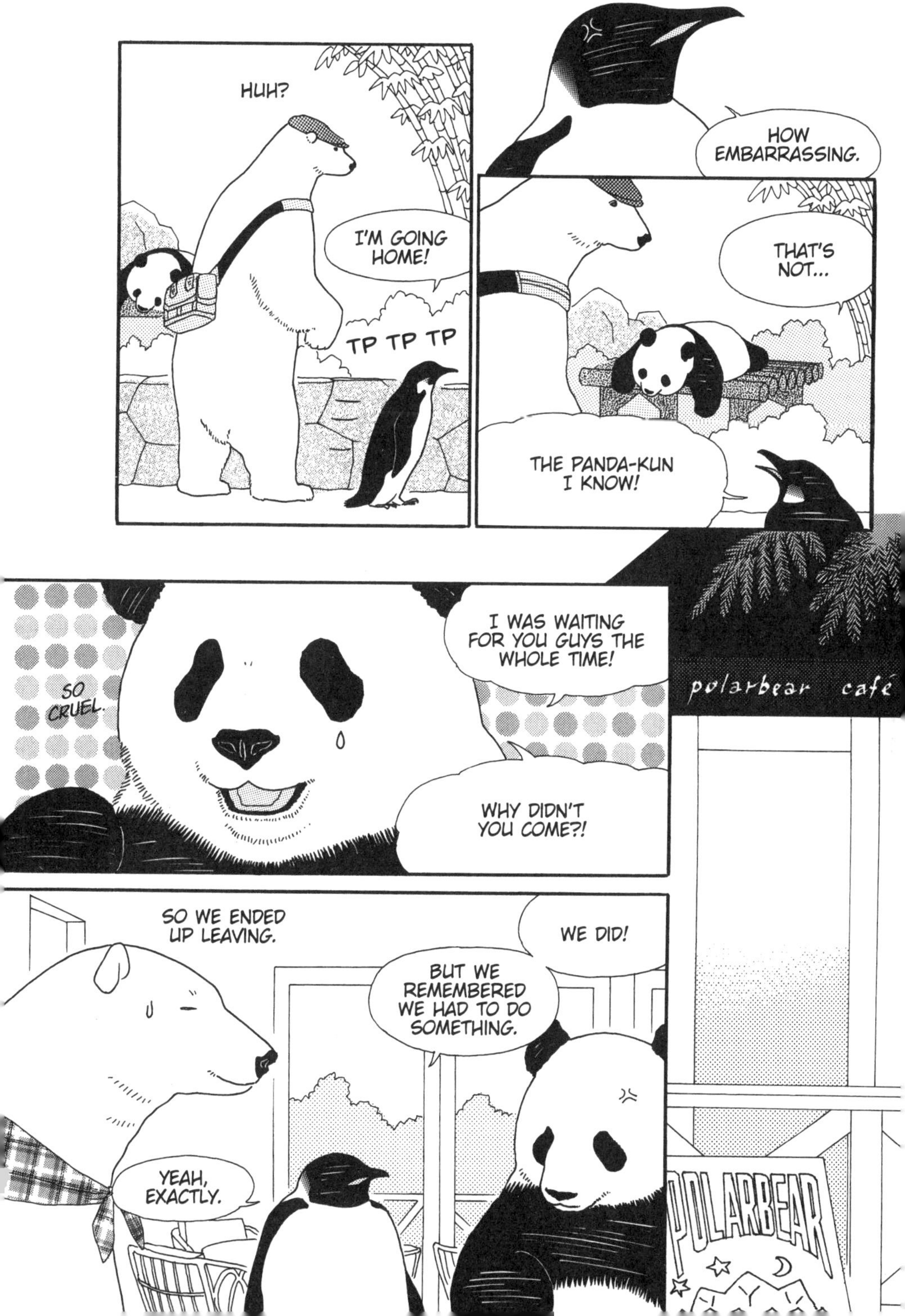

HOW EMBARRASSING.
THAT'S NOT...
THE PANDA-KUN I KNOW!
HUH?
I'M GOING HOME!
TP TP TP
polarbear café
POLARBEAR
I WAS WAITING FOR YOU GUYS THE WHOLE TIME!
WHY DIDN'T YOU COME?!
SO CRUEL.
WE DID!
SO WE ENDED UP LEAVING.
BUT WE REMEMBERED WE HAD TO DO SOMETHING.
YEAH, EXACTLY.

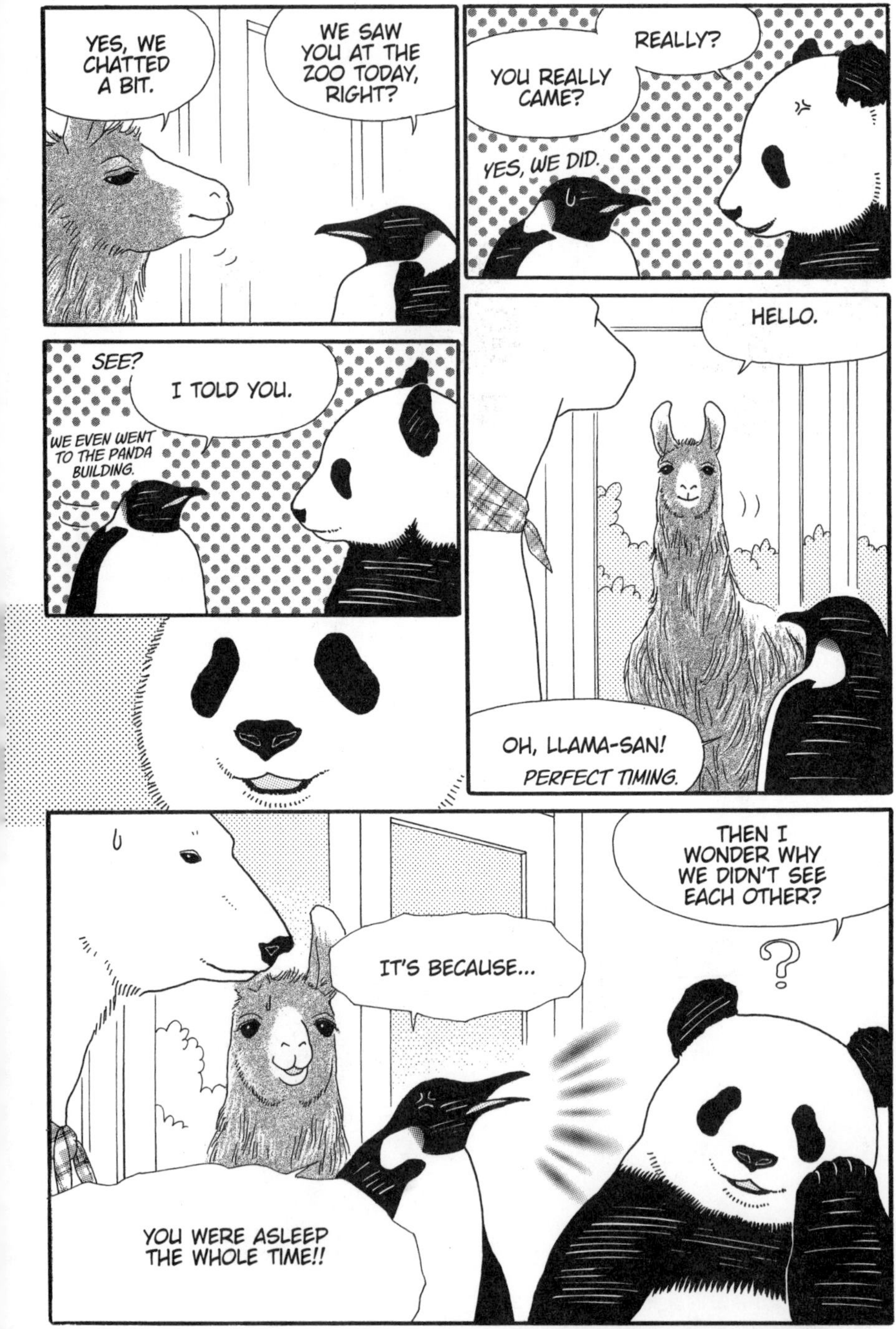
REALLY?
YOU REALLY CAME?
YES, WE DID.
WE SAW YOU AT THE ZOO TODAY, RIGHT?
YES, WE CHATTED A BIT.
HELLO.
OH, LLAMA-SAN!
PERFECT TIMING.
SEE?
I TOLD YOU.
WE EVEN WENT TO THE PANDA BUILDING.
THEN I WONDER WHY WE DIDN'T SEE EACH OTHER?
IT'S BECAUSE...
YOU WERE ASLEEP THE WHOLE TIME!!

IF YOU WANT TO RUN INTO PANDA WHEN HE'S AWAKE, MAYBE TRY IN THE MORNING!

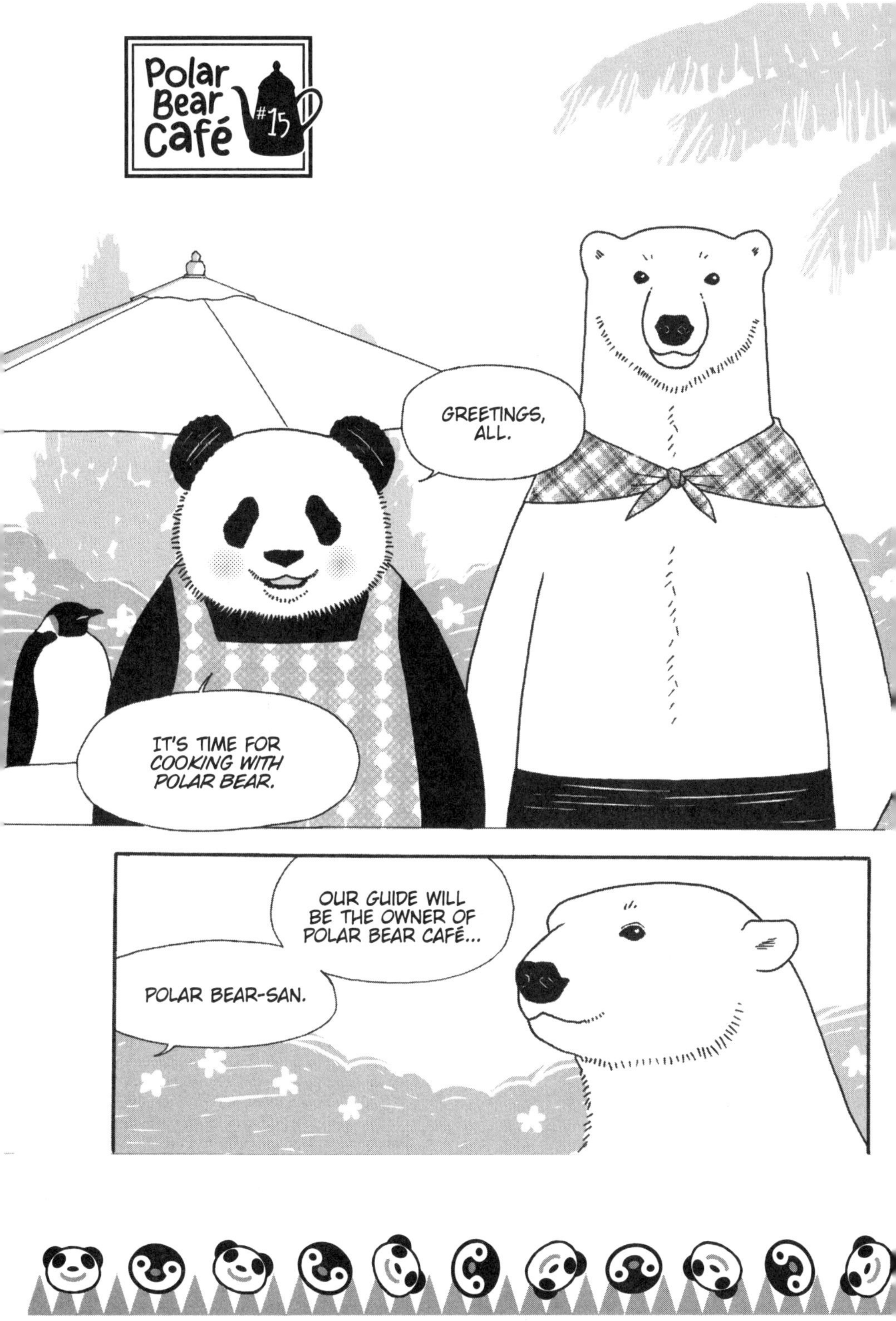
Polar Bear Café #15
GREETINGS, ALL.
IT'S TIME FOR COOKING WITH POLAR BEAR.
OUR GUIDE WILL BE THE OWNER OF POLAR BEAR CAFÉ...
POLAR BEAR-SAN.

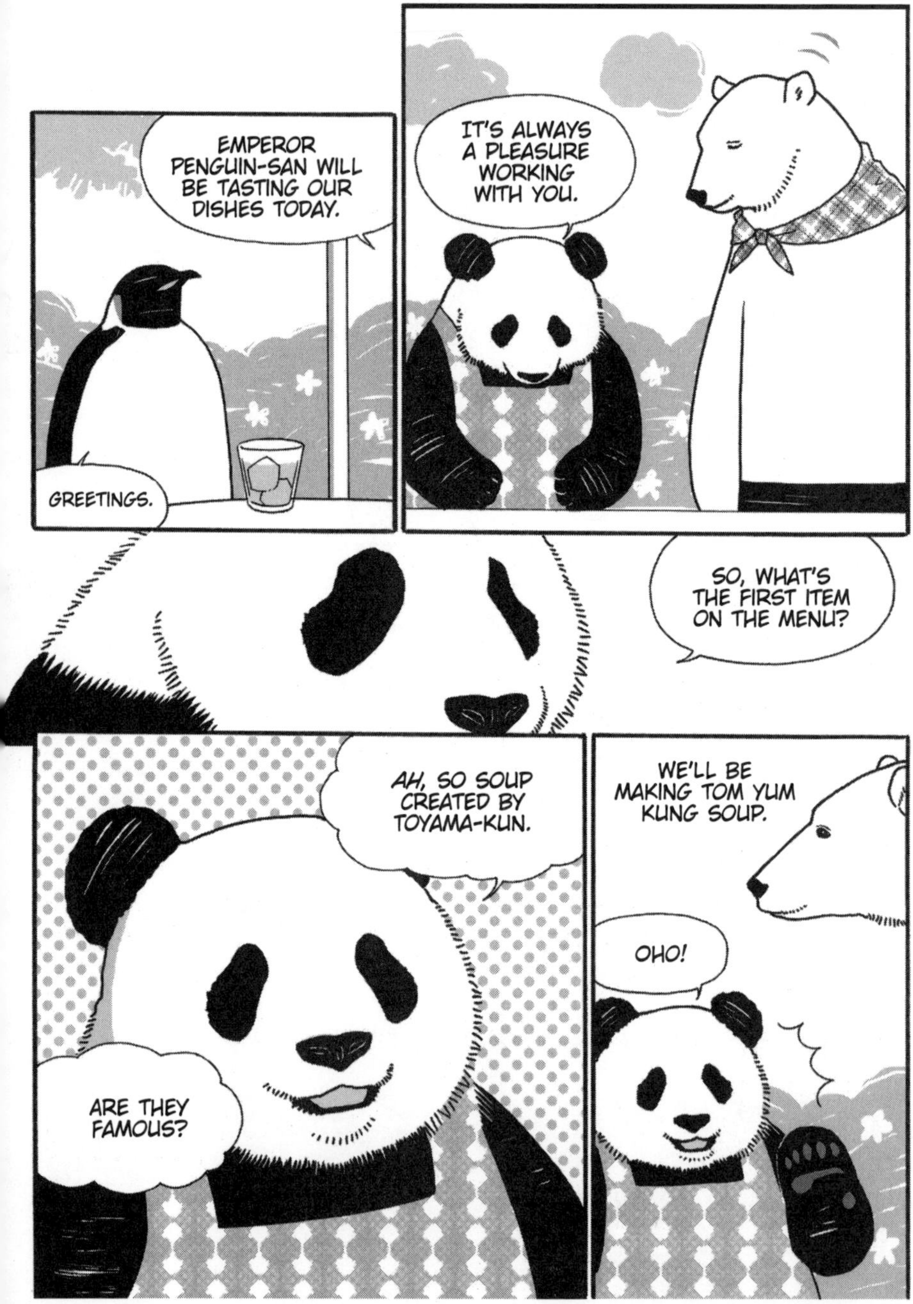
IT'S ALWAYS A PLEASURE WORKING WITH YOU.
EMPEROR PENGUIN-SAN WILL BE TASTING OUR DISHES TODAY.
GREETINGS.
SO, WHAT'S THE FIRST ITEM ON THE MENU?
WE'LL BE MAKING TOM YUM KUNG SOUP.
OHO!
AH, SO SOUP CREATED BY TOYAMA-KUN.
ARE THEY FAMOUS?

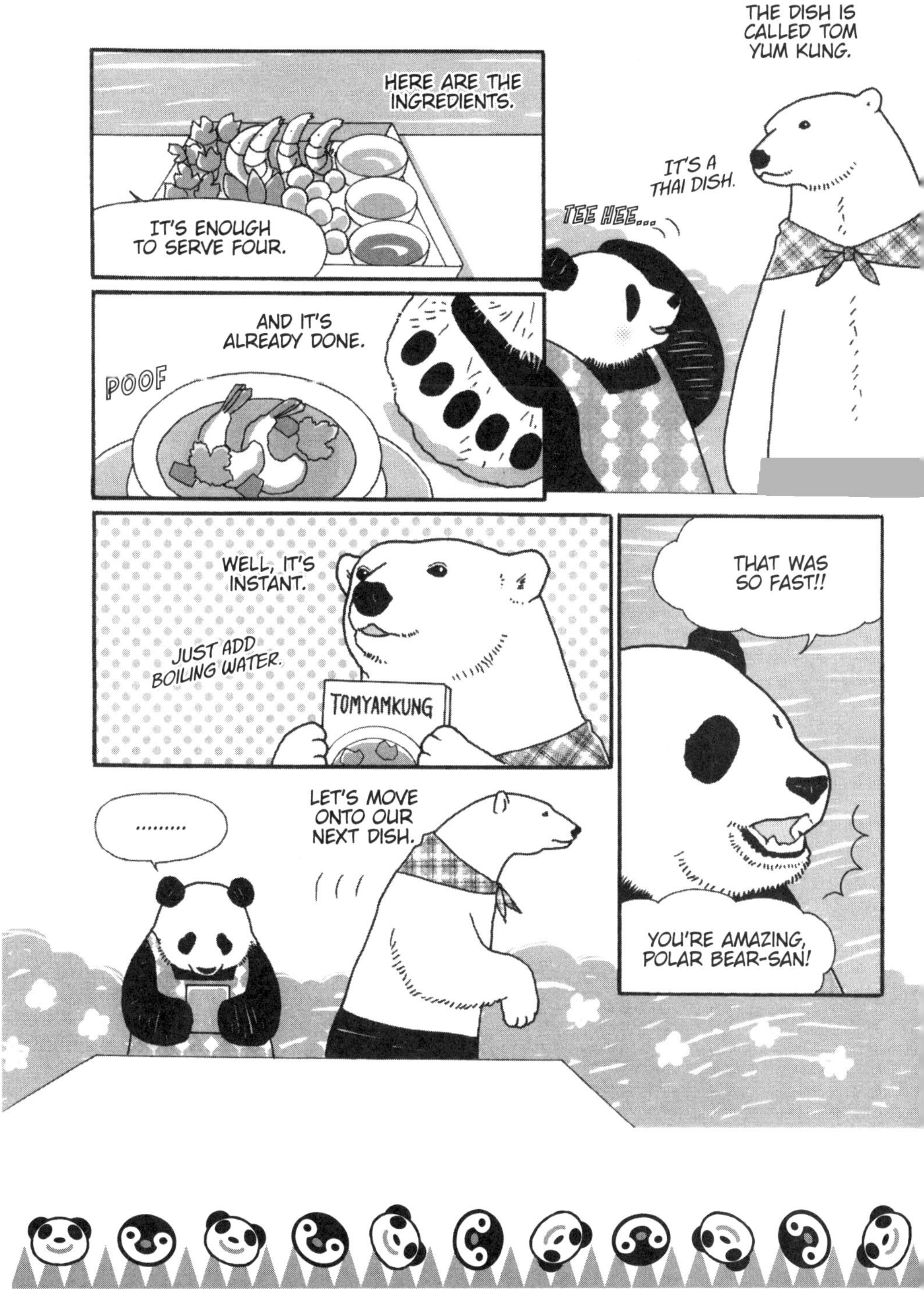
THE DISH IS CALLED TOM YUM KUNG.
IT'S A THAI DISH.
TEE HEE...
HERE ARE THE INGREDIENTS.
IT'S ENOUGH TO SERVE FOUR.
AND IT'S ALREADY DONE.
POOF
THAT WAS SO FAST!!
YOU'RE AMAZING, POLAR BEAR-SAN!
WELL, IT'S INSTANT.
JUST ADD BOILING WATER.
TOMYAMKUNG
LET'S MOVE ONTO OUR NEXT DISH.
....

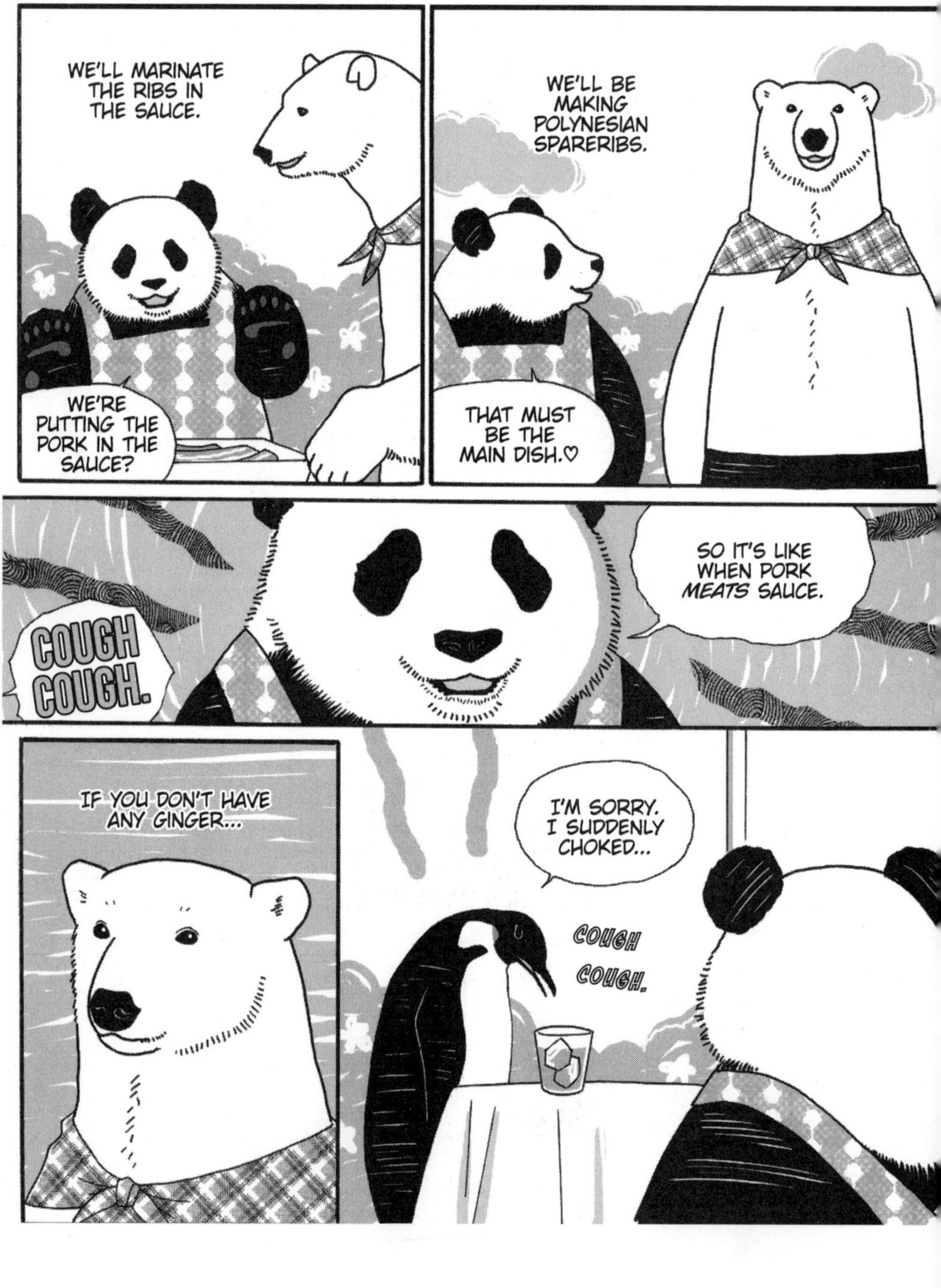
WE'LL BE MAKING POLYNESIAN SPARERIBS.
THAT MUST BE THE MAIN DISH.♡
WE'LL MARINATE THE RIBS IN THE SAUCE.
WE'RE PUTTING THE PORK IN THE SAUCE?
SO IT'S LIKE WHEN PORK *MEATS* SAUCE.
COUGH COUGH.
I'M SORRY. I SUDDENLY CHOKED...
COUGH COUGH.
IF YOU DON'T HAVE ANY GINGER...

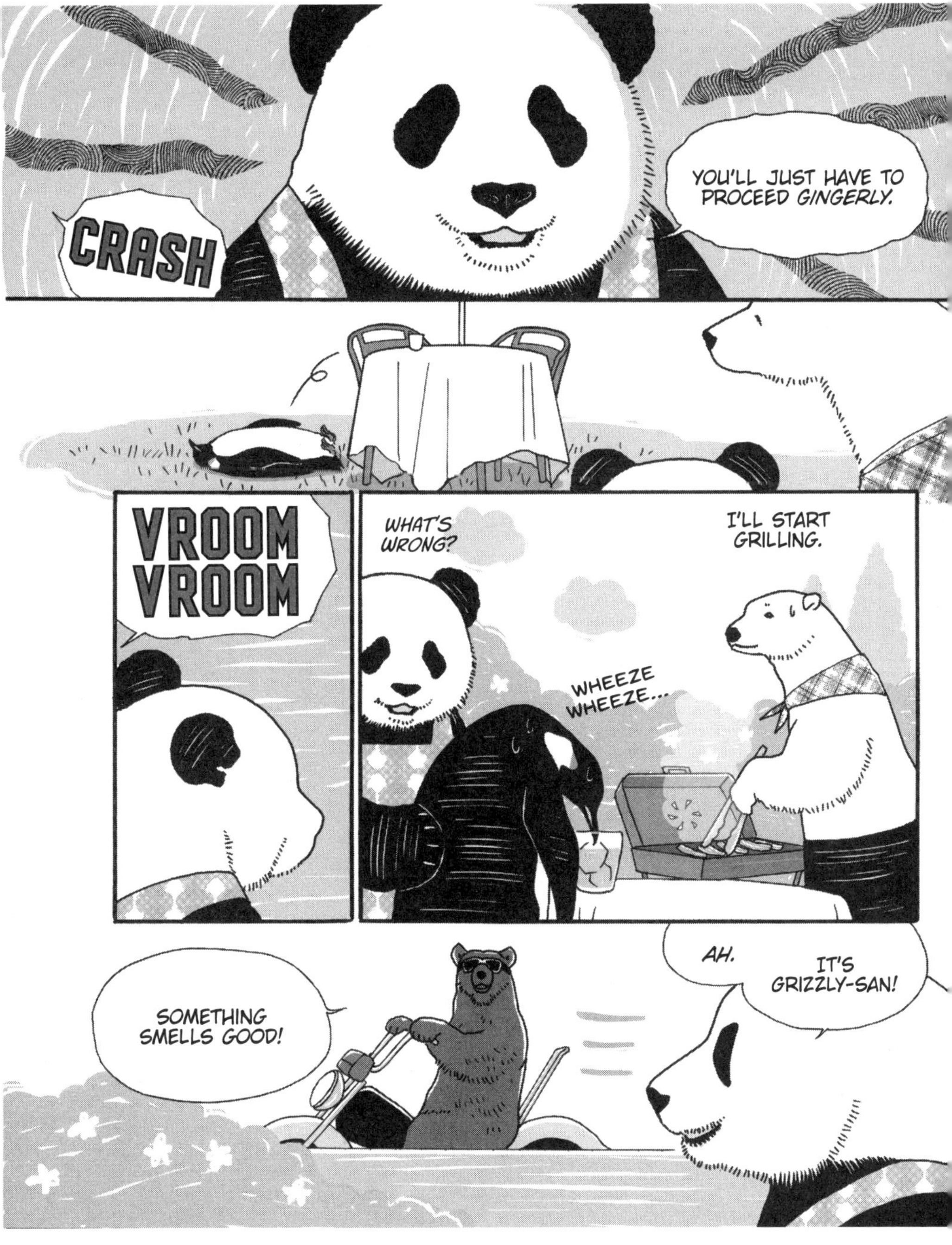
YOU'LL JUST HAVE TO PROCEED GINGERLY.
CRASH
I'LL START GRILLING.
WHAT'S WRONG?
WHEEZE WHEEZE...
VROOM VROOM
AH.
IT'S GRIZZLY-SAN!
SOMETHING SMELLS GOOD!

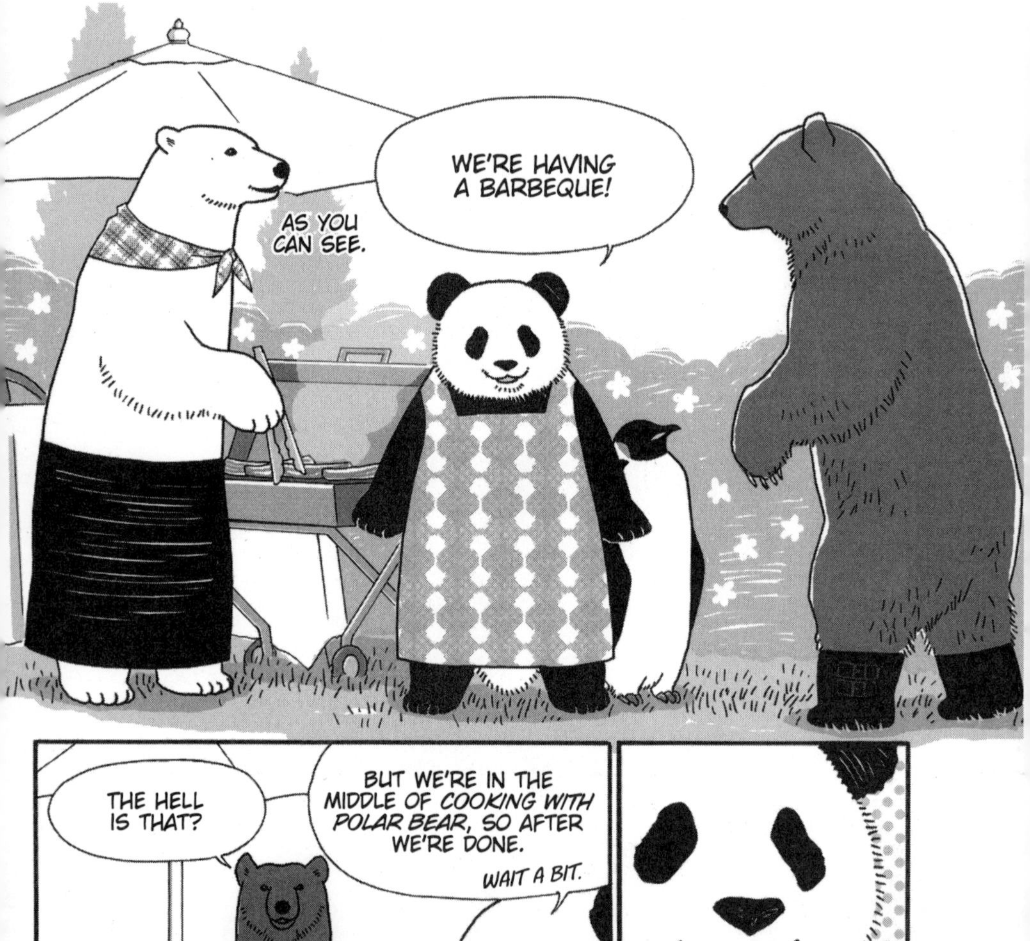
WE'RE HAVING A BARBEQUE!
AS YOU CAN SEE.
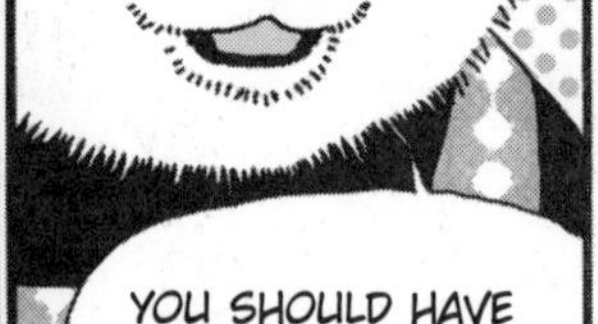
YOU SHOULD HAVE SOME, GRIZZLY-SAN.
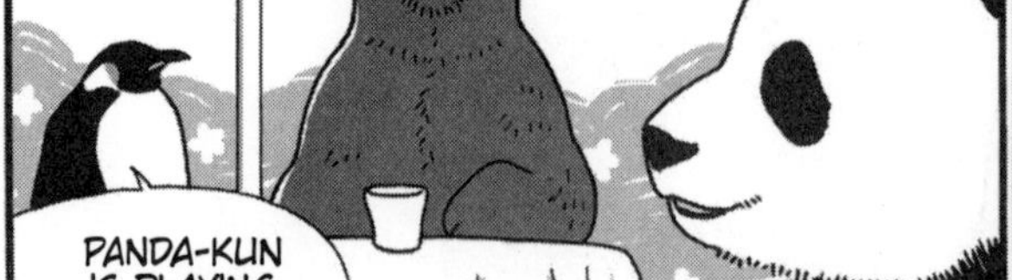
BUT WE'RE IN THE MIDDLE OF *COOKING WITH POLAR BEAR*, SO AFTER WE'RE DONE.
WAIT A BIT.
THE HELL IS THAT?
PANDA-KUN IS PLAYING MAKE-BELIEVE.

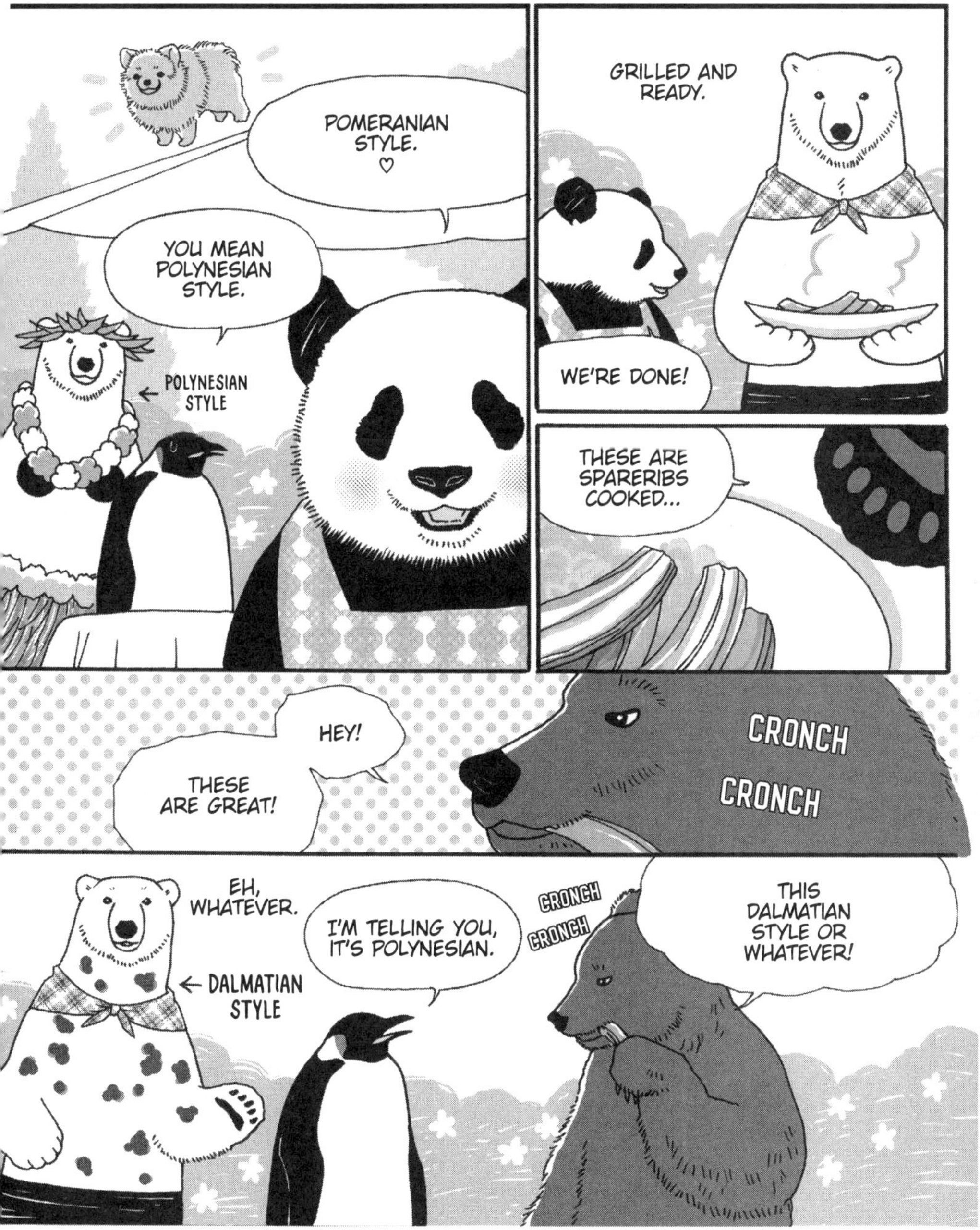
GRILLED AND READY.
WE'RE DONE!
THESE ARE SPARERIBS COOKED...
POMERANIAN STYLE. ♡
YOU MEAN POLYNESIAN STYLE.
POLYNESIAN STYLE
CRONCH
CRONCH
HEY!
THESE ARE GREAT!
THIS DALMATIAN STYLE OR WHATEVER!
CRONCH
CRONCH
I'M TELLING YOU, IT'S POLYNESIAN.
EH, WHATEVER.
DALMATIAN STYLE

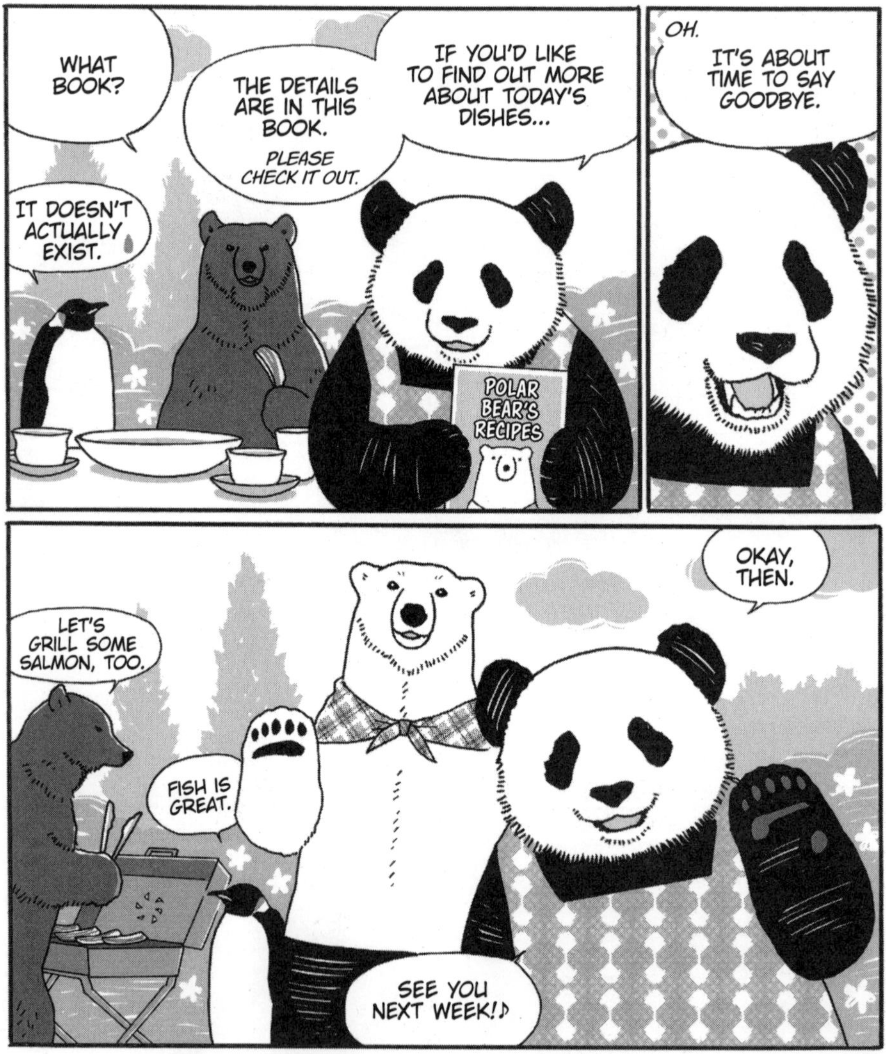
OH.
IT'S ABOUT TIME TO SAY GOODBYE.
IF YOU'D LIKE TO FIND OUT MORE ABOUT TODAY'S DISHES...
THE DETAILS ARE IN THIS BOOK.
PLEASE CHECK IT OUT.
WHAT BOOK?
POLAR BEAR'S RECIPES
IT DOESN'T ACTUALLY EXIST.
OKAY, THEN.
LET'S GRILL SOME SALMON, TOO.
FISH IS GREAT.
SEE YOU NEXT WEEK!♪

YOU CAN FIND OUT HOW TO MAKE POLYNESIAN SAUCE ON THE NEXT PAGE. ♡

POLAR BEAR RECIPE ② POLYNESIAN SAUCE

YOU CAN MARINATE PORK OR CHICKEN IN THIS SAUCE BEFORE GRILLING.

MARINATE FOR ONE TO TWO HOURS.

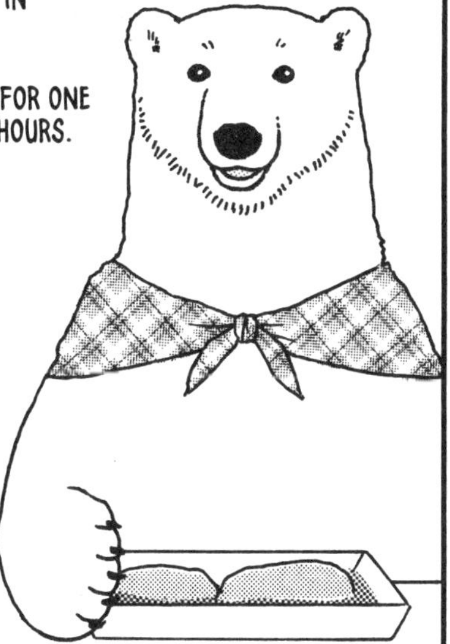

MAKES APPROXIMATELY 150CC

SOY SAUCE: 50CC
MIRIN: 50CC
SESAME OIL: 1 TABLESPOON
GRATED GARLIC: 1 CLOVE
GRATED GINGER: 1 TEASPOON
KETCHUP: 1 TABLESPOON
CURRY POWDER: 1-2 TABLESPOONS, TO TASTE

MIX ALL THE INGREDIENTS TOGETHER.

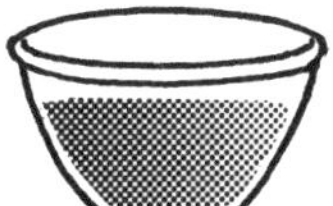

YOU CAN ADD WHITE SESAME, HOT SAUCE, OR HONEY IF YOU LIKE.

THIS SAUCE IS ALSO GOOD FOR VEGETABLE STIR-FRY OR FRIED RICE.

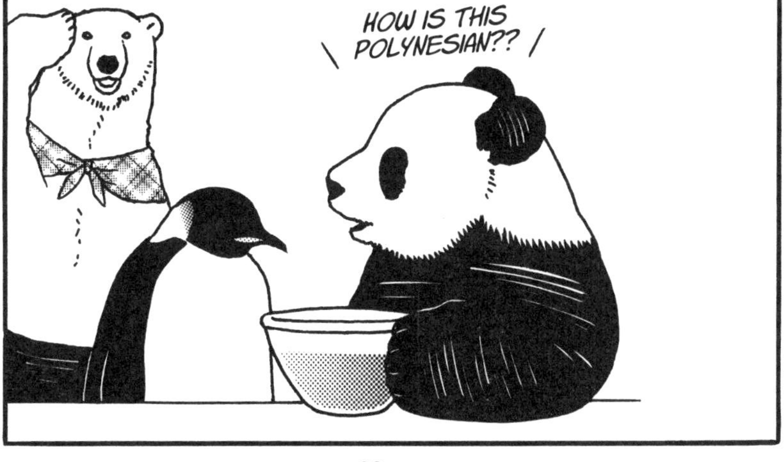
HOW IS THIS POLYNESIAN??
HM... PROBABLY THE SOY SAUCE...

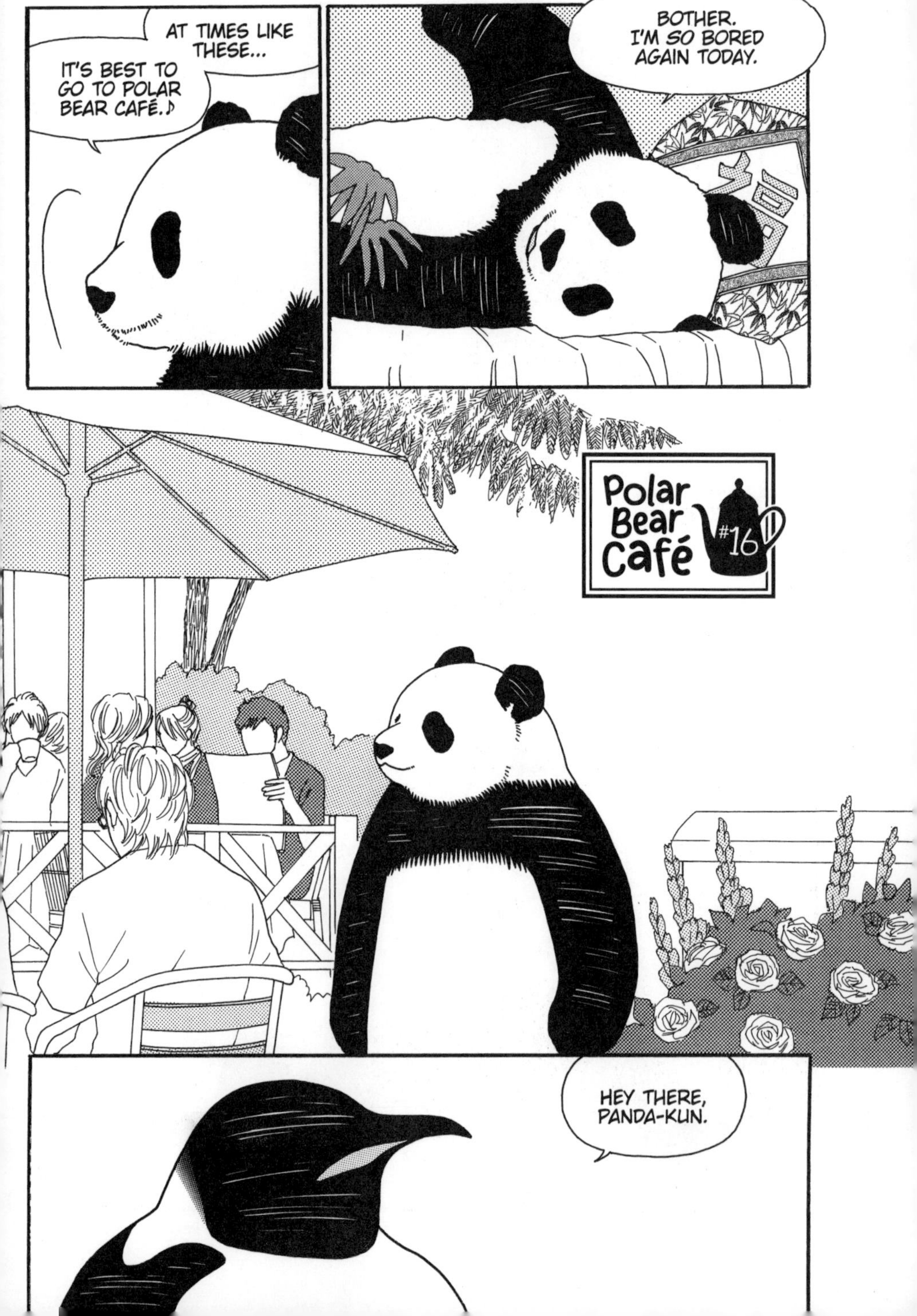
BOTHER. I'M SO BORED AGAIN TODAY.
AT TIMES LIKE THESE...
IT'S BEST TO GO TO POLAR BEAR CAFÉ.♪
Polar Bear Café
#16
HEY THERE, PANDA-KUN.

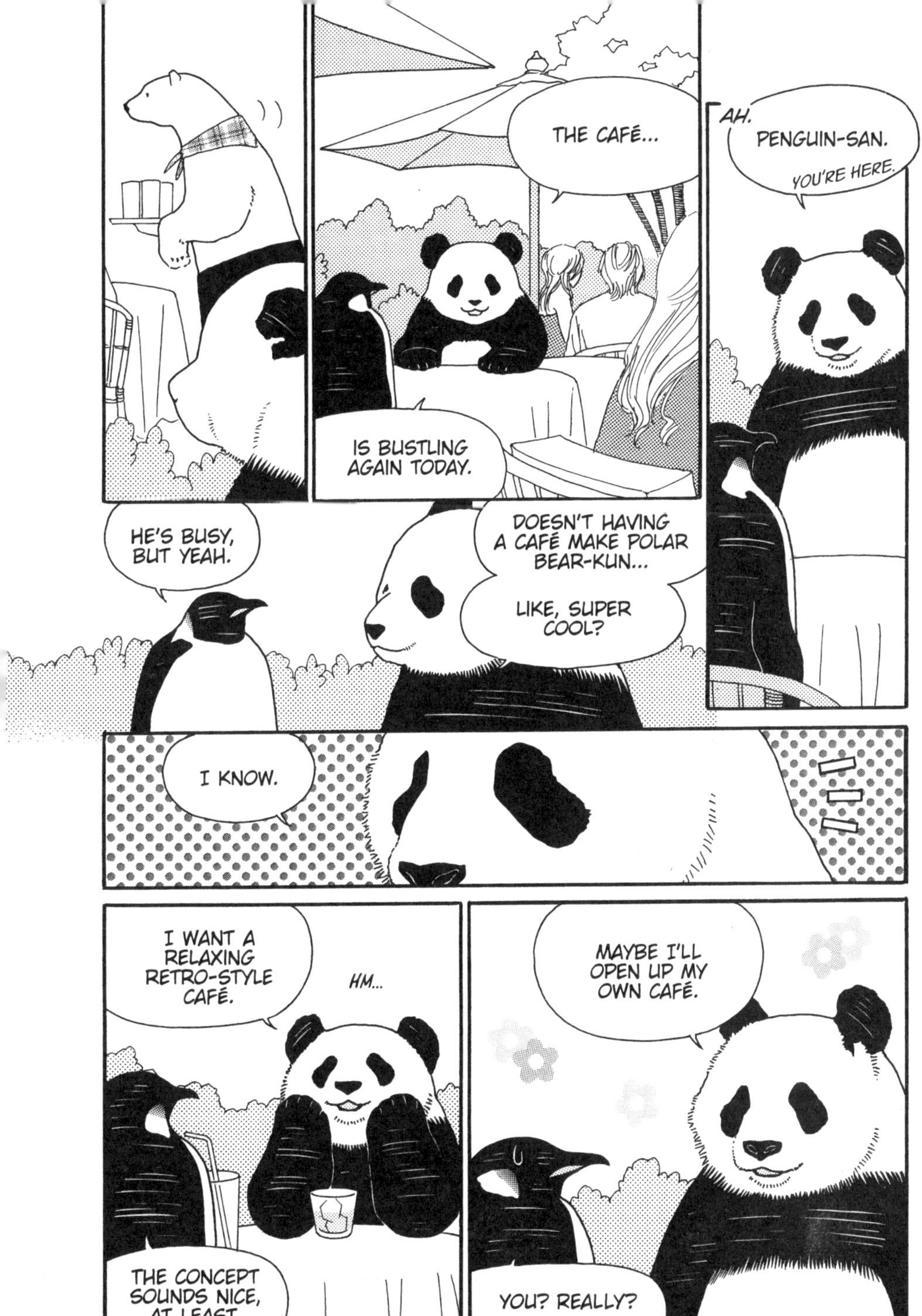
AH. PENGUIN-SAN. YOU'RE HERE.
THE CAFÉ...
IS BUSTLING AGAIN TODAY.
DOESN'T HAVING A CAFÉ MAKE POLAR BEAR-KUN...
LIKE, SUPER COOL?
HE'S BUSY, BUT YEAH.
I KNOW.
MAYBE I'LL OPEN UP MY OWN CAFÉ.
YOU? REALLY?
I WANT A RELAXING RETRO-STYLE CAFÉ.
HM...
THE CONCEPT SOUNDS NICE, AT LEAST.

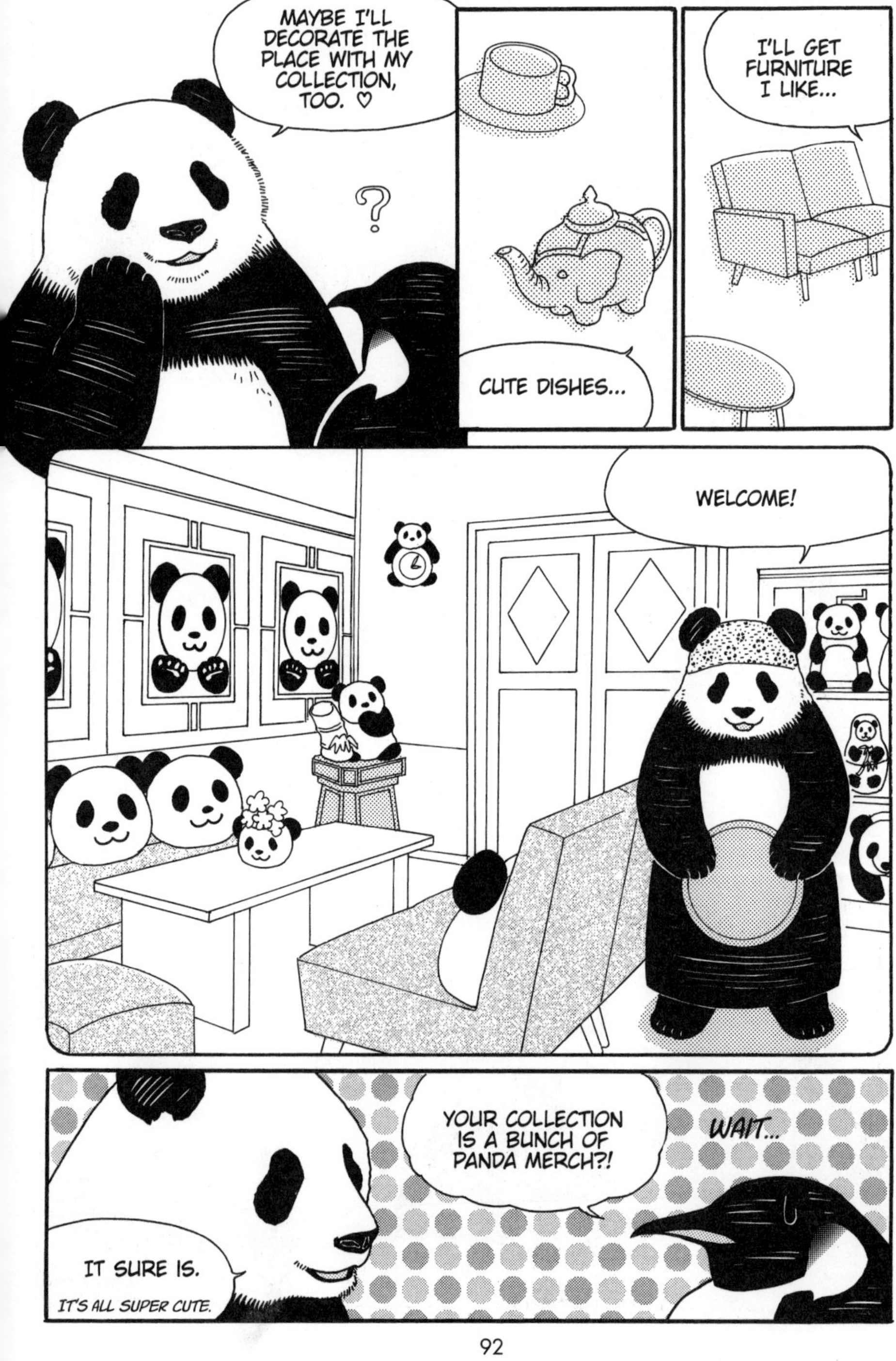
I'LL GET FURNITURE I LIKE...
CUTE DISHES...
MAYBE I'LL DECORATE THE PLACE WITH MY COLLECTION, TOO. ♡
?
WELCOME!
WAIT...
YOUR COLLECTION IS A BUNCH OF PANDA MERCH?!
IT SURE IS.
IT'S ALL SUPER CUTE.

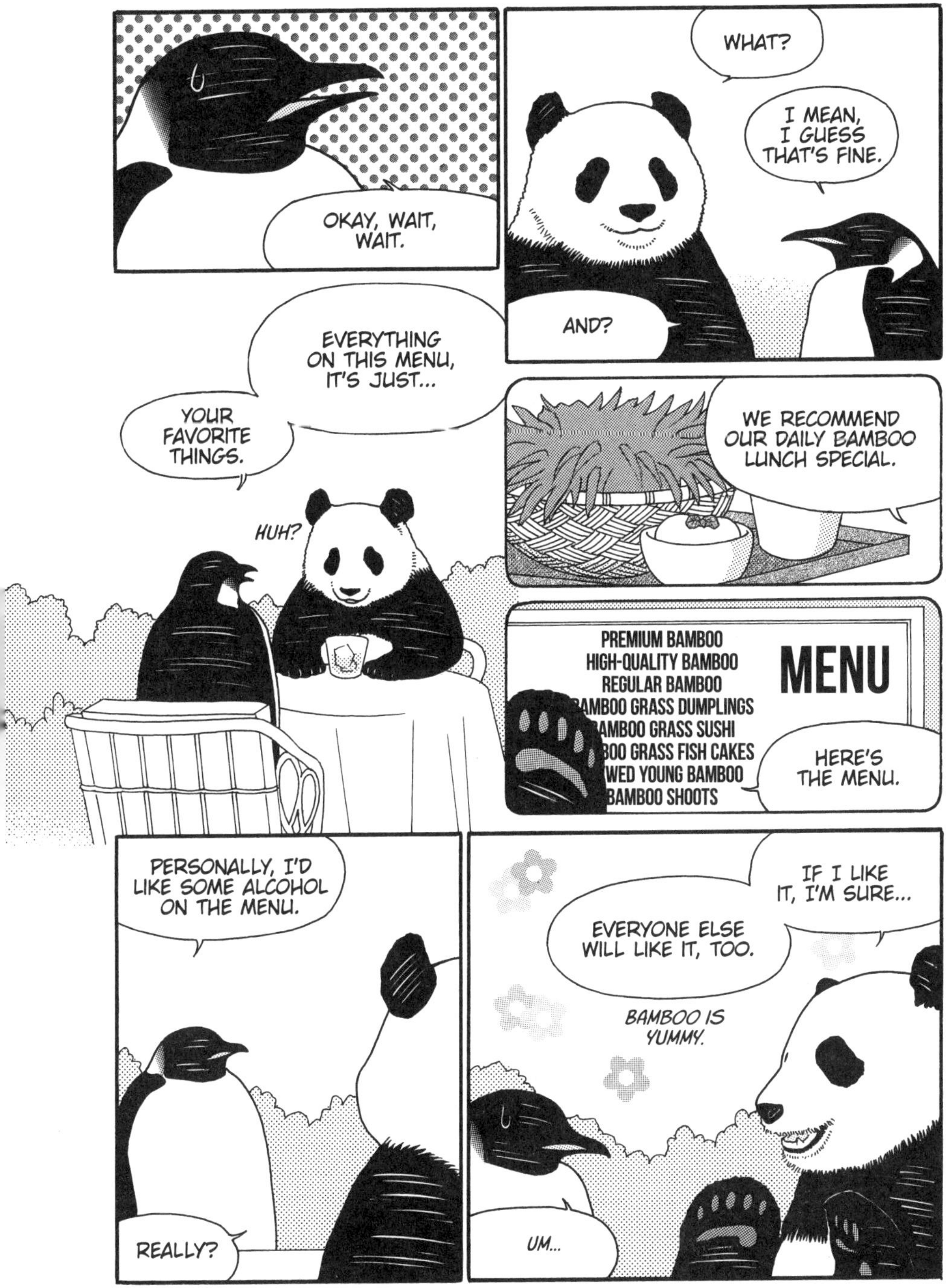
WHAT?
I MEAN, I GUESS THAT'S FINE.
AND?
OKAY, WAIT, WAIT.
WE RECOMMEND OUR DAILY BAMBOO LUNCH SPECIAL.
MENU
PREMIUM BAMBOO
HIGH-QUALITY BAMBOO
REGULAR BAMBOO
AMBOO GRASS DUMPLINGS
AMBOO GRASS SUSHI
BOO GRASS FISH CAKES
WED YOUNG BAMBOO
BAMBOO SHOOTS
HERE'S THE MENU.
EVERYTHING ON THIS MENU, IT'S JUST...
YOUR FAVORITE THINGS.
HUH?
IF I LIKE IT, I'M SURE...
EVERYONE ELSE WILL LIKE IT, TOO.
BAMBOO IS YUMMY.
UM...
PERSONALLY, I'D LIKE SOME ALCOHOL ON THE MENU.
REALLY?

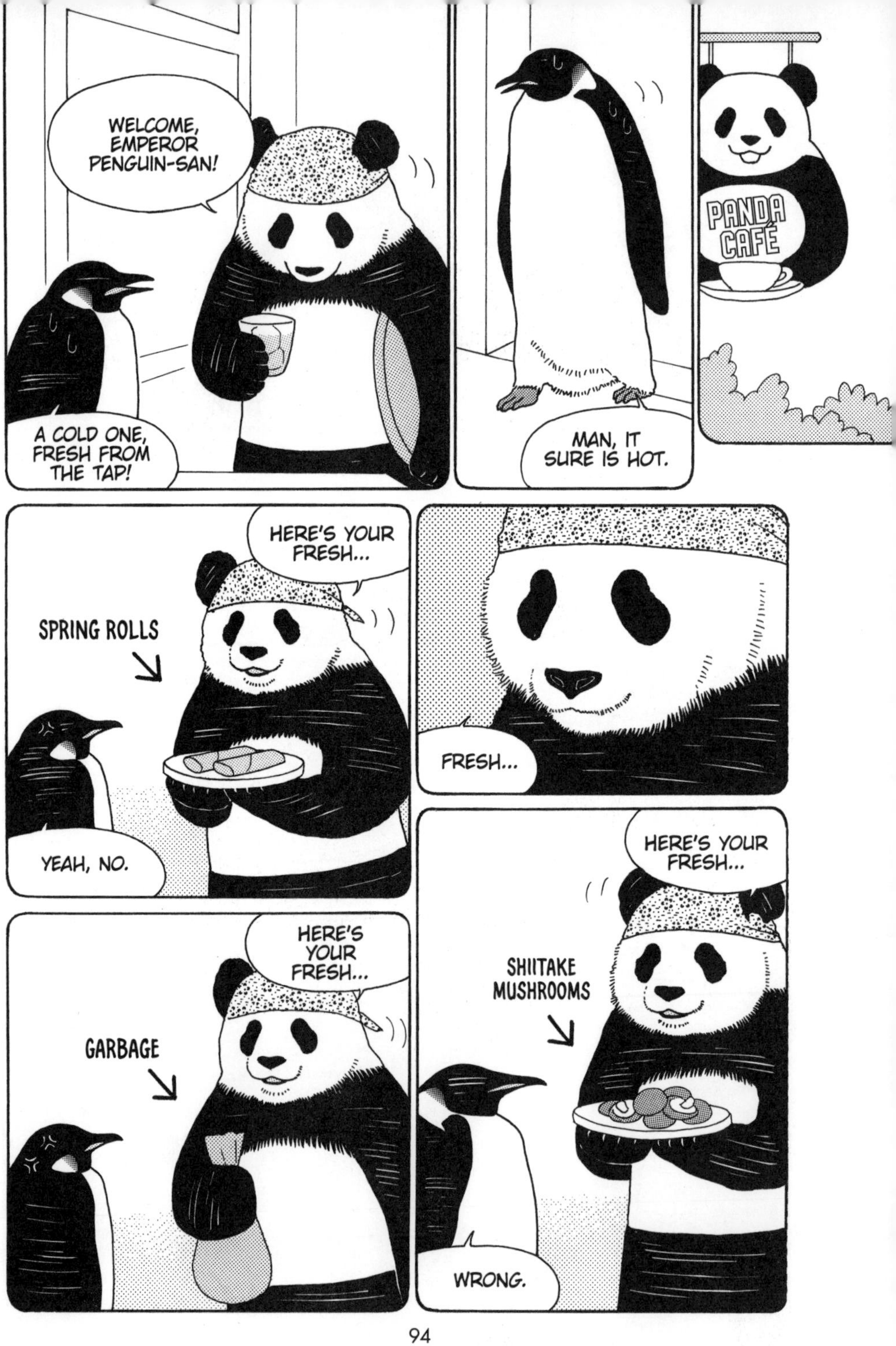
PANDA CAFÉ
MAN, IT SURE IS HOT.
WELCOME, EMPEROR PENGUIN-SAN!
A COLD ONE, FRESH FROM THE TAP!
FRESH...
HERE'S YOUR FRESH...
SPRING ROLLS
YEAH, NO.
HERE'S YOUR FRESH...
SHIITAKE MUSHROOMS
WRONG.
HERE'S YOUR FRESH...
GARBAGE

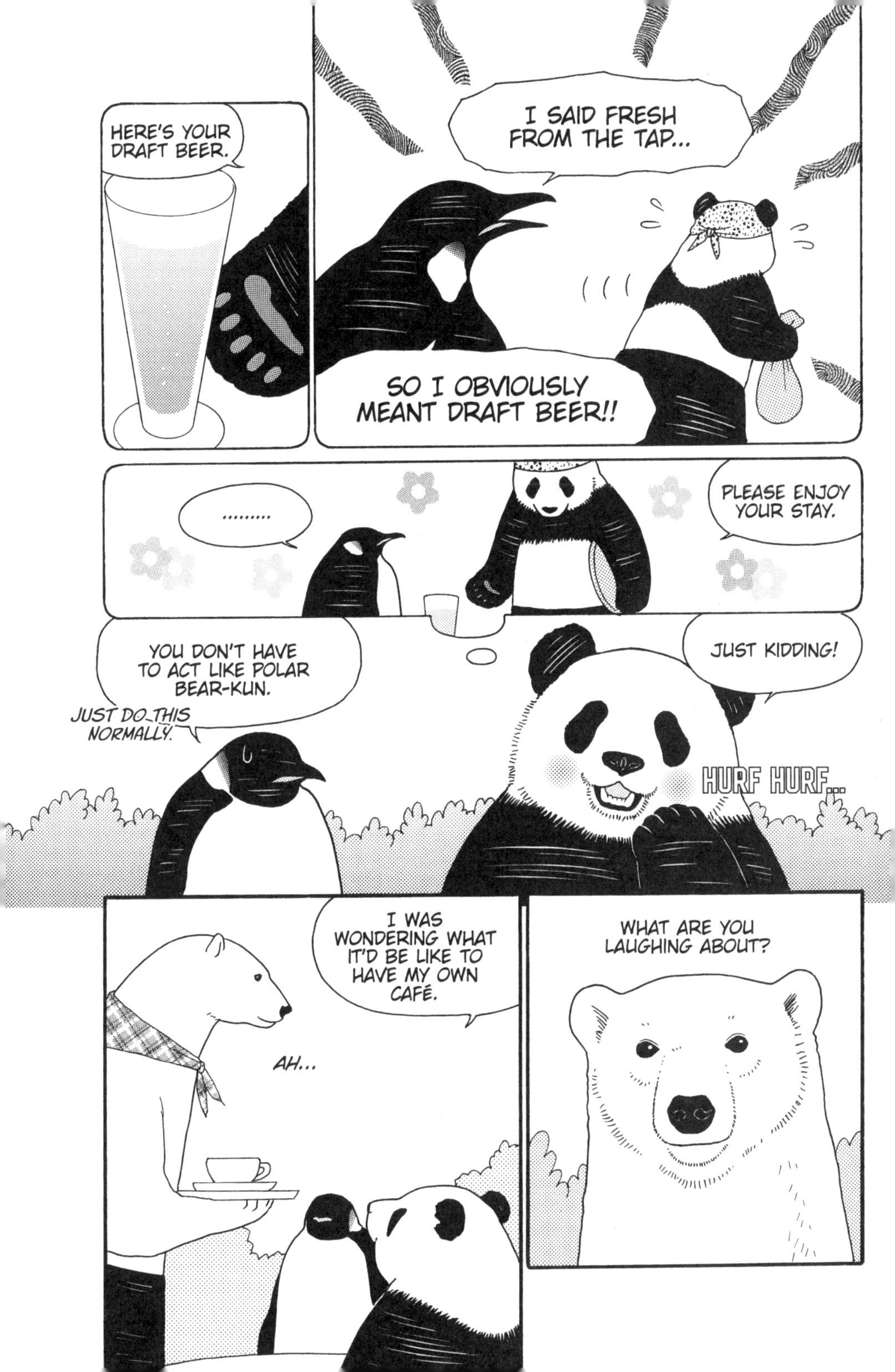
I SAID FRESH FROM THE TAP...
SO I OBVIOUSLY MEANT DRAFT BEER!!
HERE'S YOUR DRAFT BEER.
PLEASE ENJOY YOUR STAY.
....
JUST KIDDING!
HURF HURF...
YOU DON'T HAVE TO ACT LIKE POLAR BEAR-KUN.
JUST DO THIS NORMALLY.
WHAT ARE YOU LAUGHING ABOUT?
I WAS WONDERING WHAT IT'D BE LIKE TO HAVE MY OWN CAFÉ.
AH...

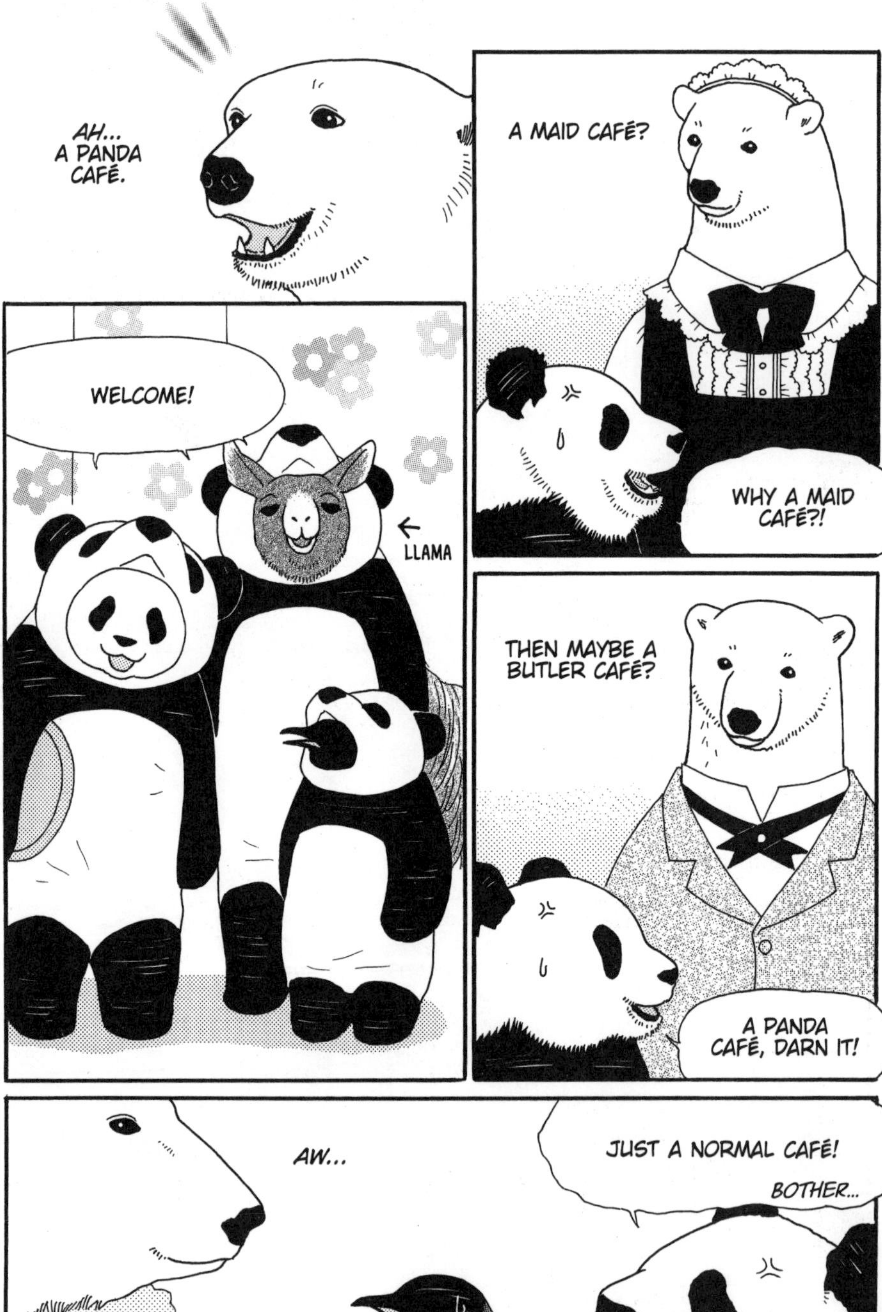
AH...
A PANDA
CAFÉ.
WELCOME!
← LLAMA
A MAID CAFÉ?
WHY A MAID
CAFÉ?!
THEN MAYBE A
BUTLER CAFÉ?
A PANDA
CAFÉ, DARN IT!
JUST A NORMAL CAFÉ!
BOTHER...
AW...

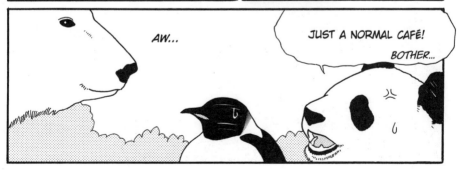

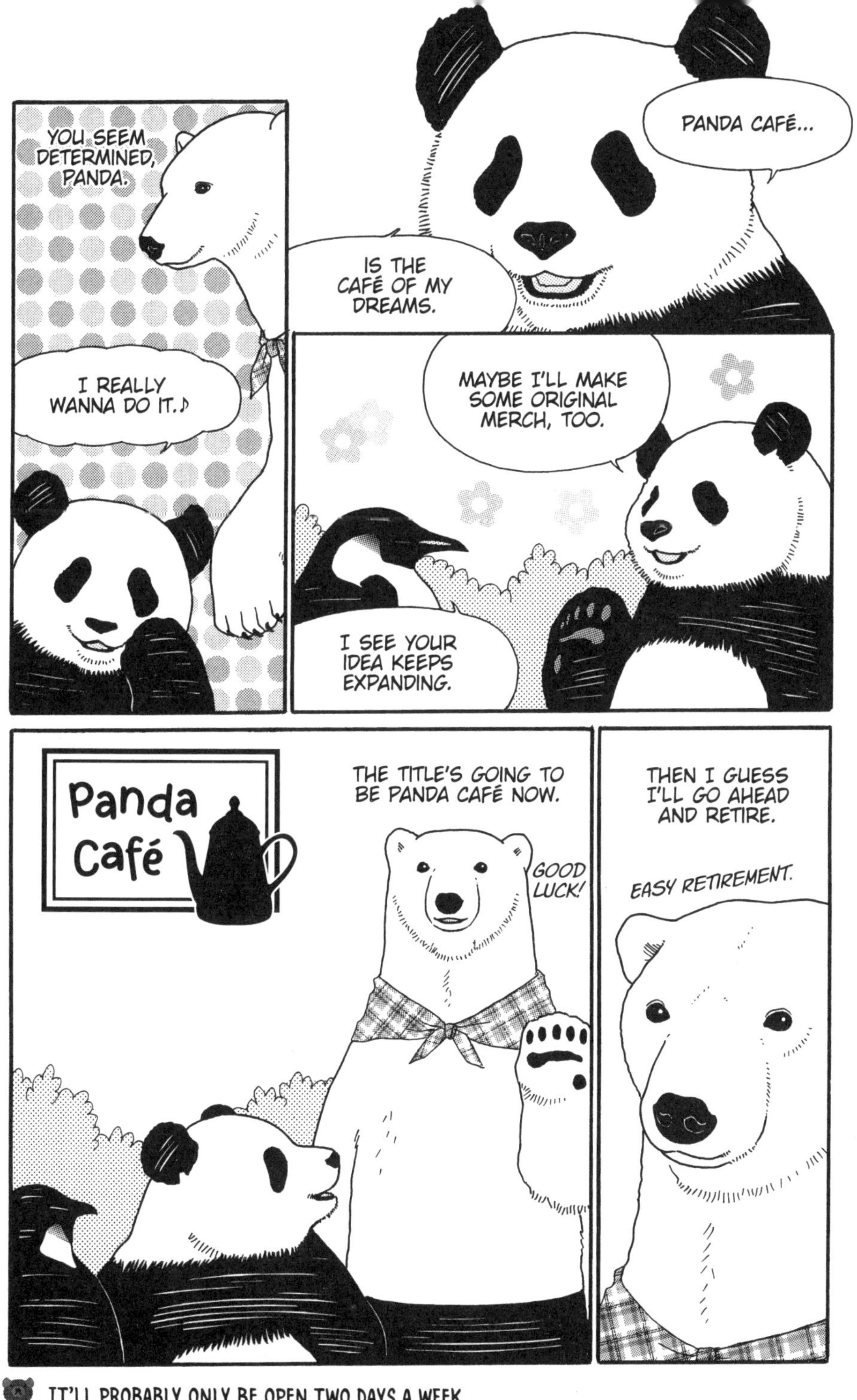
PANDA CAFÉ...
IS THE CAFÉ OF MY DREAMS.
MAYBE I'LL MAKE SOME ORIGINAL MERCH, TOO.
I SEE YOUR IDEA KEEPS EXPANDING.
YOU SEEM DETERMINED, PANDA.
I REALLY WANNA DO IT.♪
THEN I GUESS I'LL GO AHEAD AND RETIRE.
EASY RETIREMENT.
THE TITLE'S GOING TO BE PANDA CAFÉ NOW.
GOOD LUCK!
Panda Café

IT'LL PROBABLY ONLY BE OPEN TWO DAYS A WEEK...

POLAR BEAR RECIPE ③ BREWING BLACK TEA

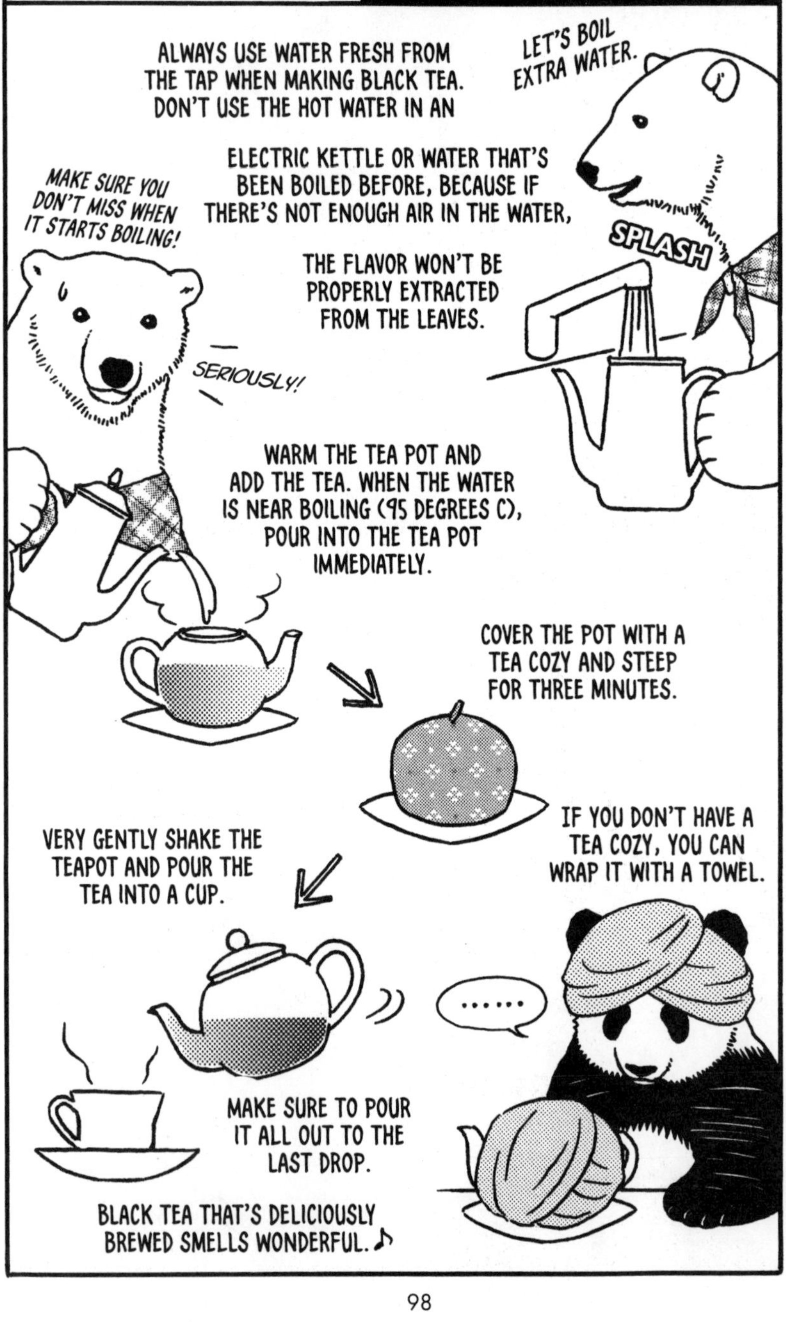
LET'S BOIL EXTRA WATER.
SPLASH
ALWAYS USE WATER FRESH FROM THE TAP WHEN MAKING BLACK TEA. DON'T USE THE HOT WATER IN AN
ELECTRIC KETTLE OR WATER THAT'S BEEN BOILED BEFORE, BECAUSE IF THERE'S NOT ENOUGH AIR IN THE WATER,
THE FLAVOR WON'T BE PROPERLY EXTRACTED FROM THE LEAVES.
MAKE SURE YOU DON'T MISS WHEN IT STARTS BOILING!
SERIOUSLY!
WARM THE TEA POT AND ADD THE TEA. WHEN THE WATER IS NEAR BOILING (95 DEGREES C), POUR INTO THE TEA POT IMMEDIATELY.
COVER THE POT WITH A TEA COZY AND STEEP FOR THREE MINUTES.
IF YOU DON'T HAVE A TEA COZY, YOU CAN WRAP IT WITH A TOWEL.
......
VERY GENTLY SHAKE THE TEAPOT AND POUR THE TEA INTO A CUP.
MAKE SURE TO POUR IT ALL OUT TO THE LAST DROP.
BLACK TEA THAT'S DELICIOUSLY BREWED SMELLS WONDERFUL.♪

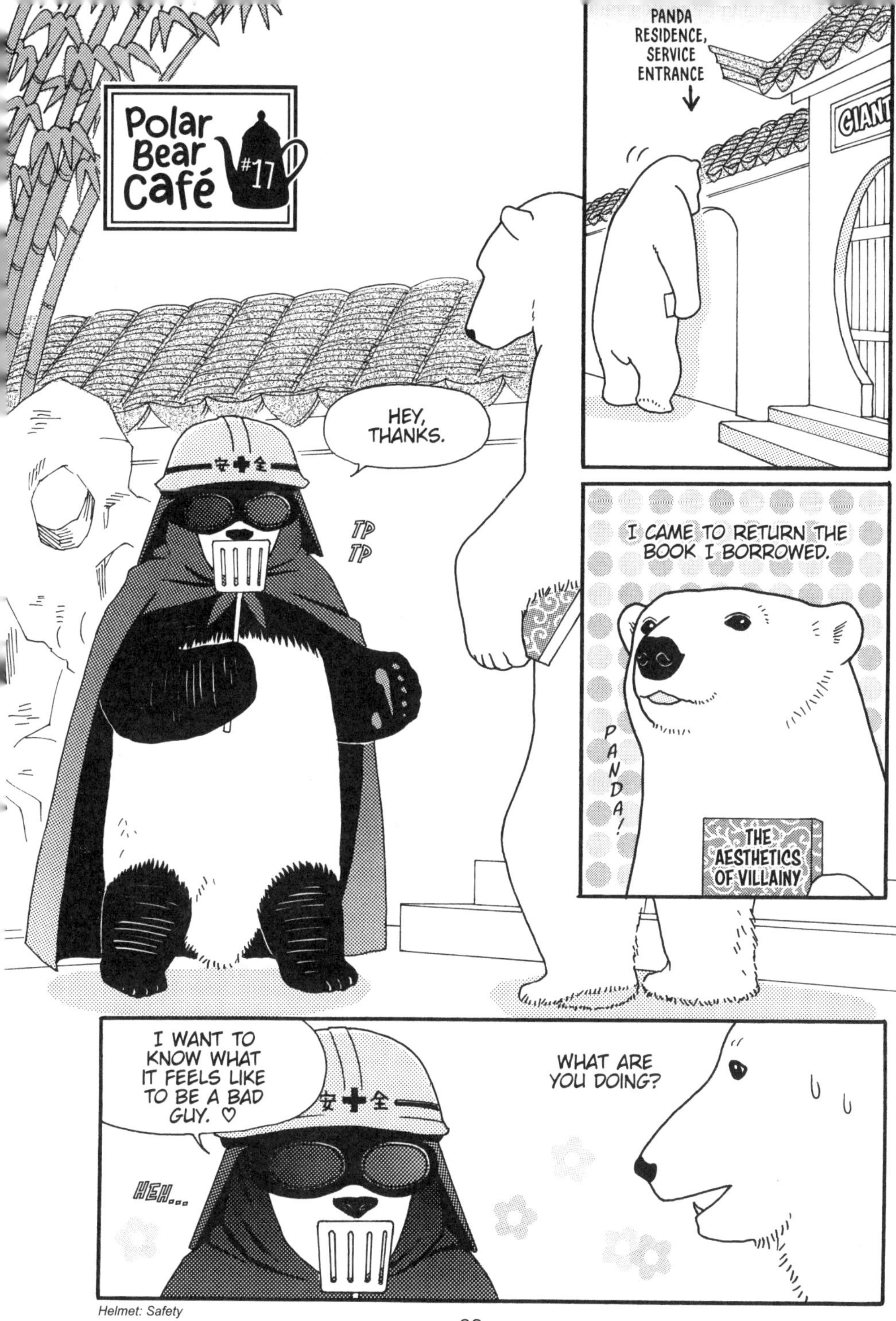

PANDA RESIDENCE, SERVICE ENTRANCE
GIANT
I CAME TO RETURN THE BOOK I BORROWED.
PANDA!
THE AESTHETICS OF VILLAINY
Polar Bear Café
#17
HEY, THANKS.
安全
TP TP
WHAT ARE YOU DOING?
I WANT TO KNOW WHAT IT FEELS LIKE TO BE A BAD GUY. ♡
安全
HEH...

Helmet: Safety

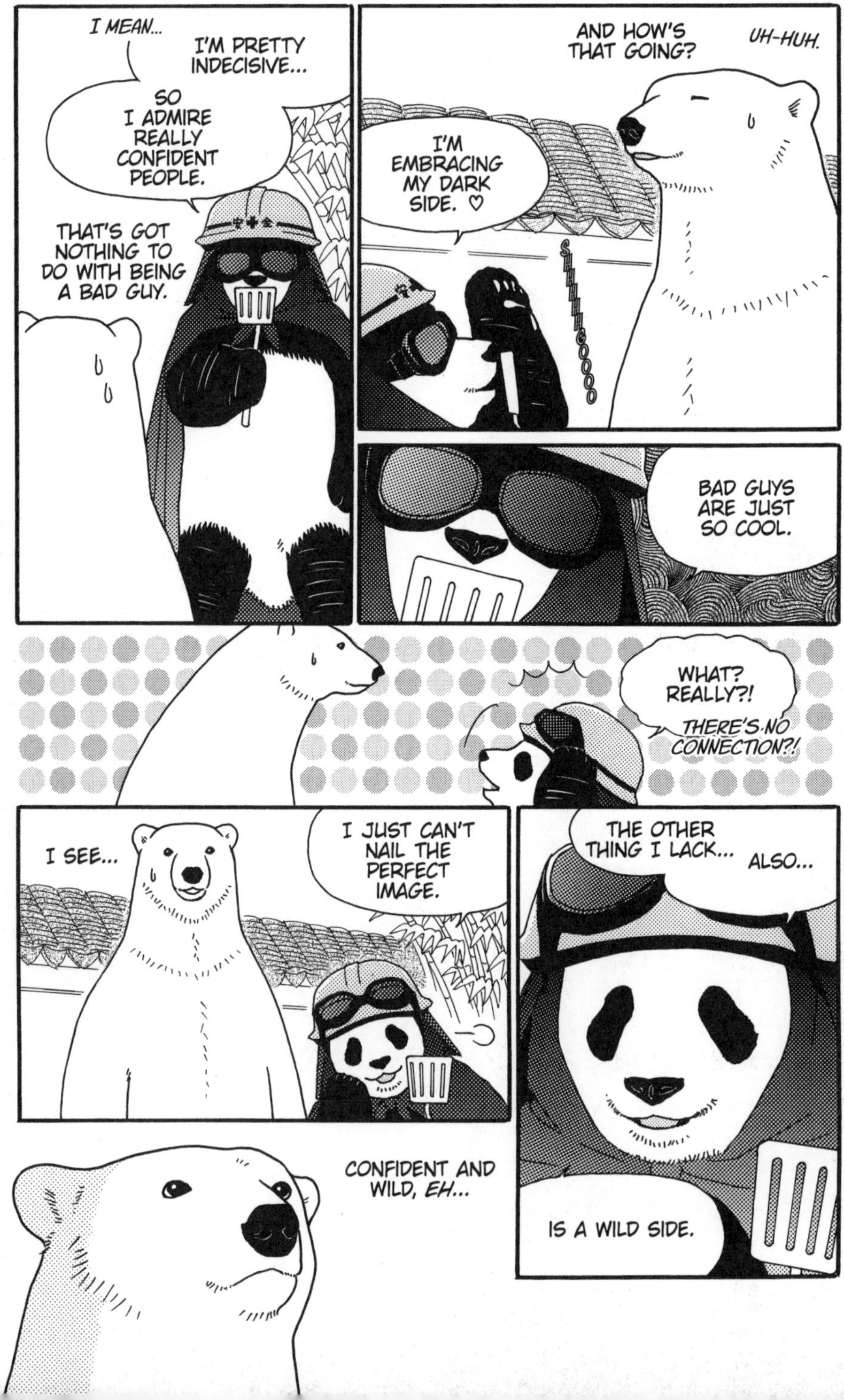
UH-HUH.
AND HOW'S THAT GOING?
I'M EMBRACING MY DARK SIDE. ♡
SHHHHGOOOO
BAD GUYS ARE JUST SO COOL.
I MEAN...
I'M PRETTY INDECISIVE...
SO I ADMIRE REALLY CONFIDENT PEOPLE.
THAT'S GOT NOTHING TO DO WITH BEING A BAD GUY.
WHAT? REALLY?!
THERE'S NO CONNECTION?!
ALSO...
THE OTHER THING I LACK...
IS A WILD SIDE.
I JUST CAN'T NAIL THE PERFECT IMAGE.
I SEE...
CONFIDENT AND WILD, EH...

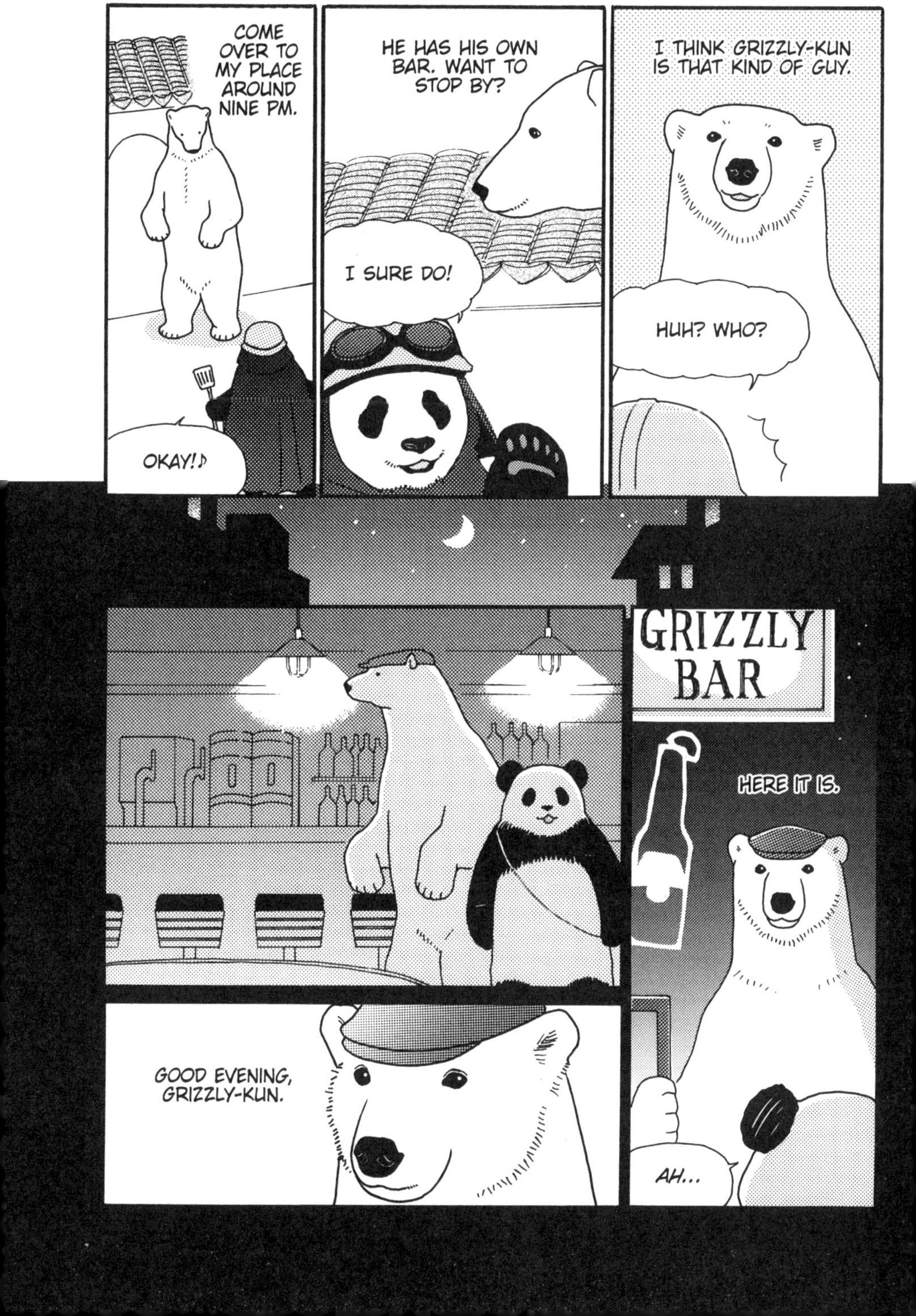
I THINK GRIZZLY-KUN IS THAT KIND OF GUY.
HUH? WHO?
HE HAS HIS OWN BAR. WANT TO STOP BY?
I SURE DO!
COME OVER TO MY PLACE AROUND NINE PM.
OKAY!♪
GRIZZLY BAR
HERE IT IS.
AH...
GOOD EVENING, GRIZZLY-KUN.

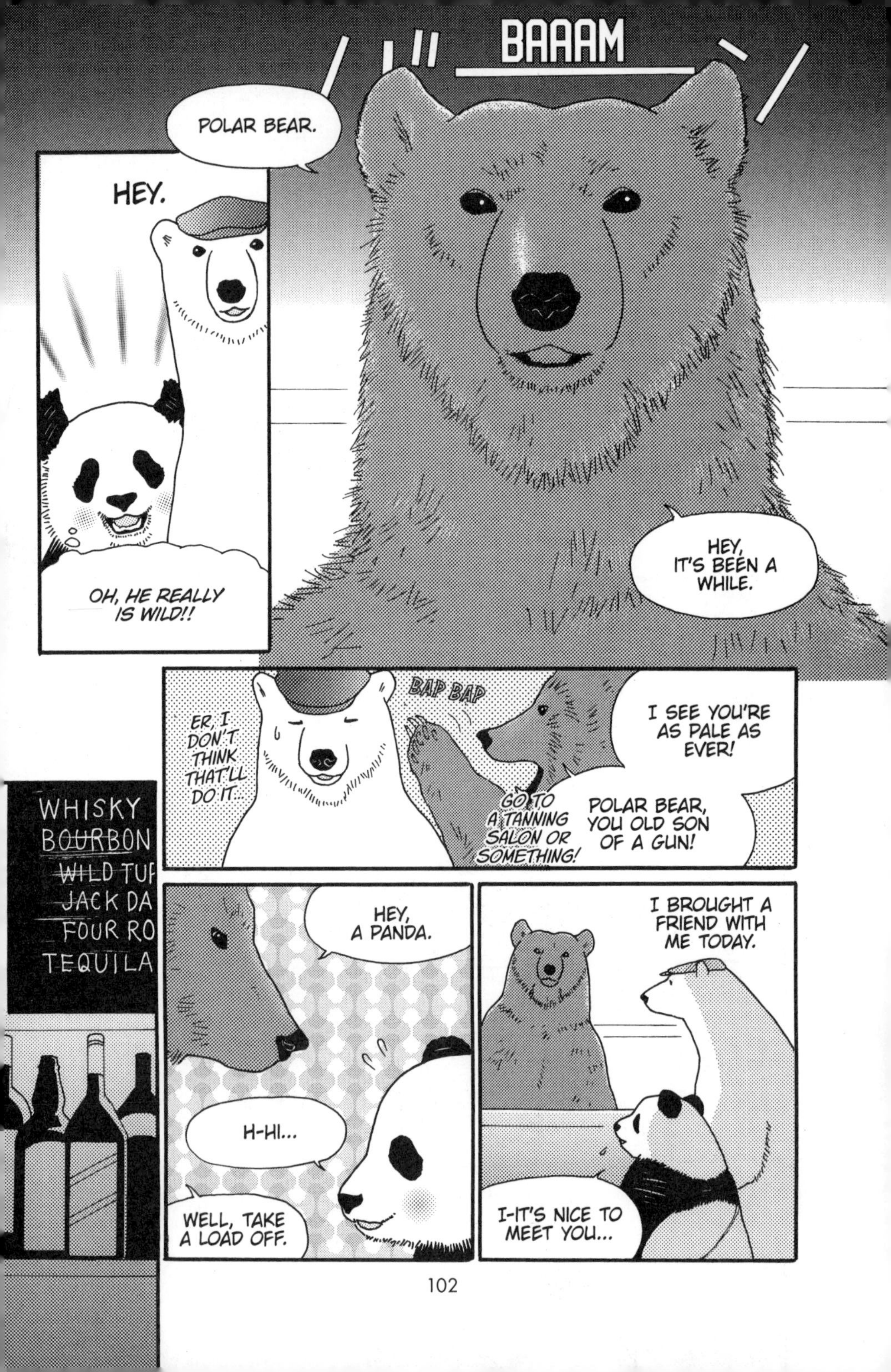
BAAAM
POLAR BEAR.
HEY, IT'S BEEN A WHILE.
HEY.
OH, HE REALLY IS WILD!!
I SEE YOU'RE AS PALE AS EVER!
BAP BAP
POLAR BEAR, YOU OLD SON OF A GUN!
GO TO A TANNING SALON OR SOMETHING!
ER, I DON'T THINK THAT'LL DO IT...
I BROUGHT A FRIEND WITH ME TODAY.
I-IT'S NICE TO MEET YOU...
HEY, A PANDA.
H-HI...
WELL, TAKE A LOAD OFF.
WHISKY
BOURBON
WILD TU
JACK DA
FOUR RO
TEQUILA

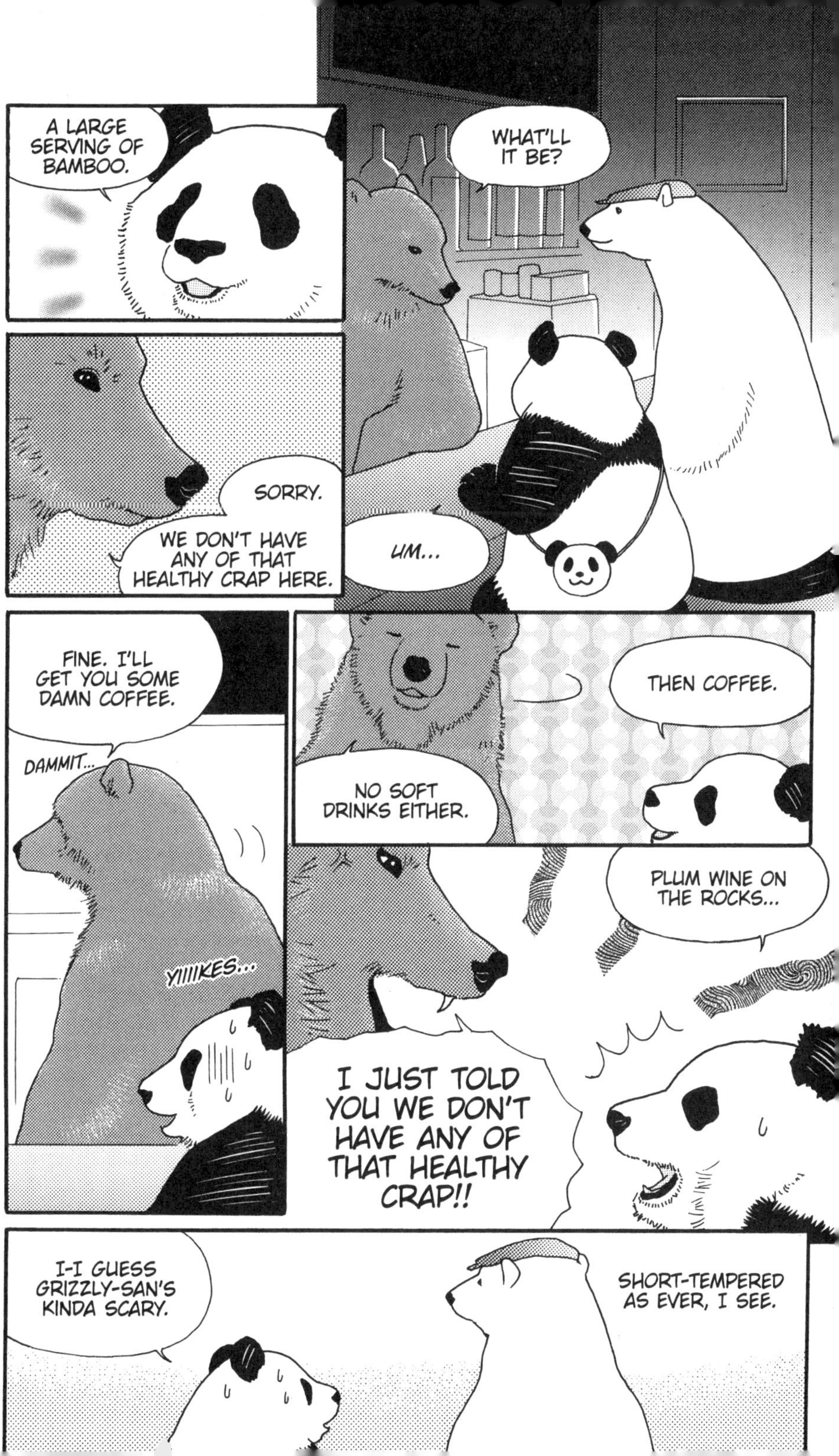
WHAT'LL IT BE?
UM...
A LARGE SERVING OF BAMBOO.
SORRY.
WE DON'T HAVE ANY OF THAT HEALTHY CRAP HERE.
THEN COFFEE.
NO SOFT DRINKS EITHER.
PLUM WINE ON THE ROCKS...
I JUST TOLD YOU WE DON'T HAVE ANY OF THAT HEALTHY CRAP!!
FINE. I'LL GET YOU SOME DAMN COFFEE.
DAMMIT...
YIIIIKES...
SHORT-TEMPERED AS EVER, I SEE.
I-I GUESS GRIZZLY-SAN'S KINDA SCARY.

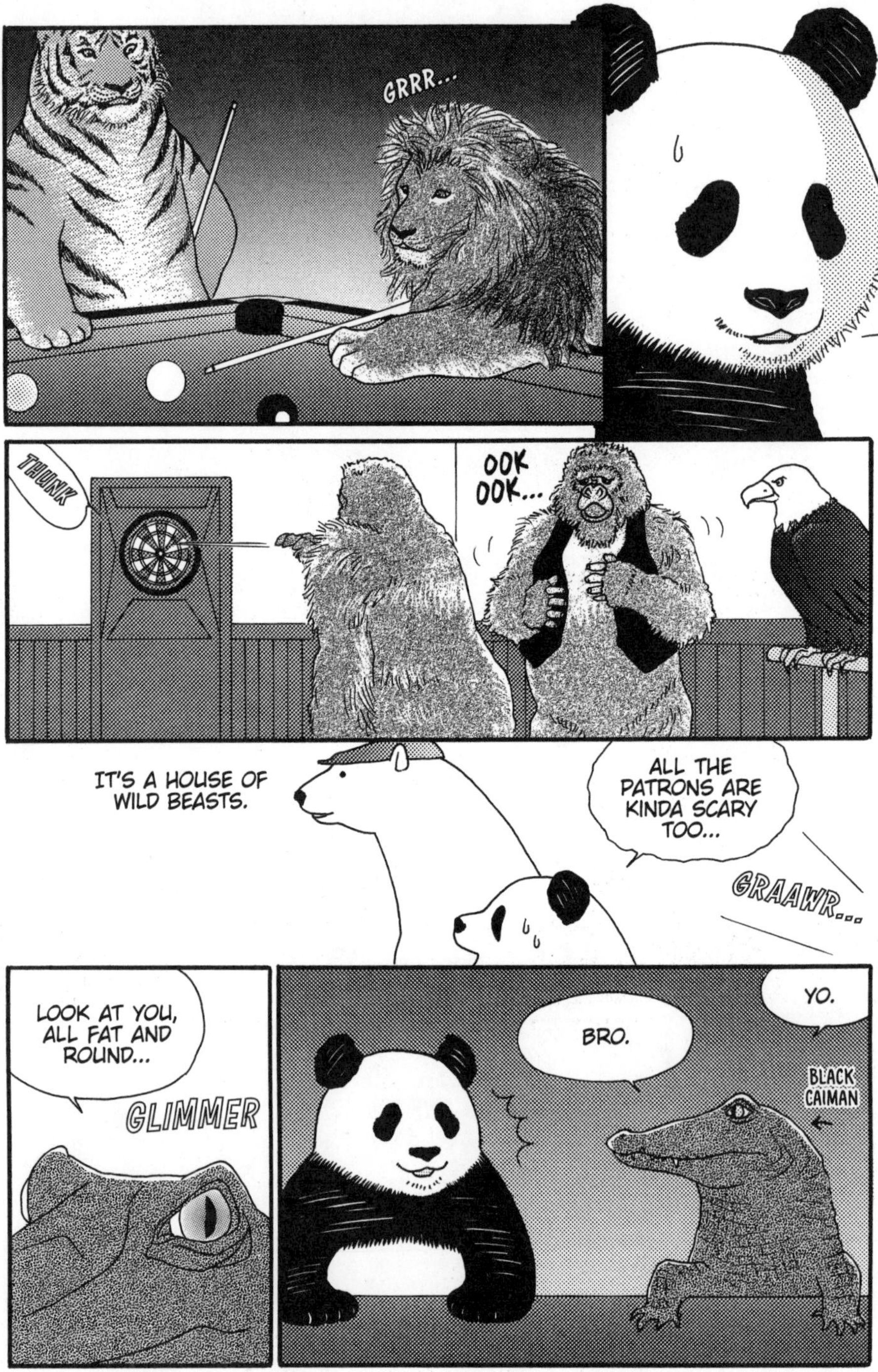
GRRR...
OOK OOK...
THUNK
ALL THE PATRONS ARE KINDA SCARY TOO...
GRAAWR...
IT'S A HOUSE OF WILD BEASTS.
YO.
BRO.
BLACK CAIMAN
LOOK AT YOU, ALL FAT AND ROUND...
GLIMMER

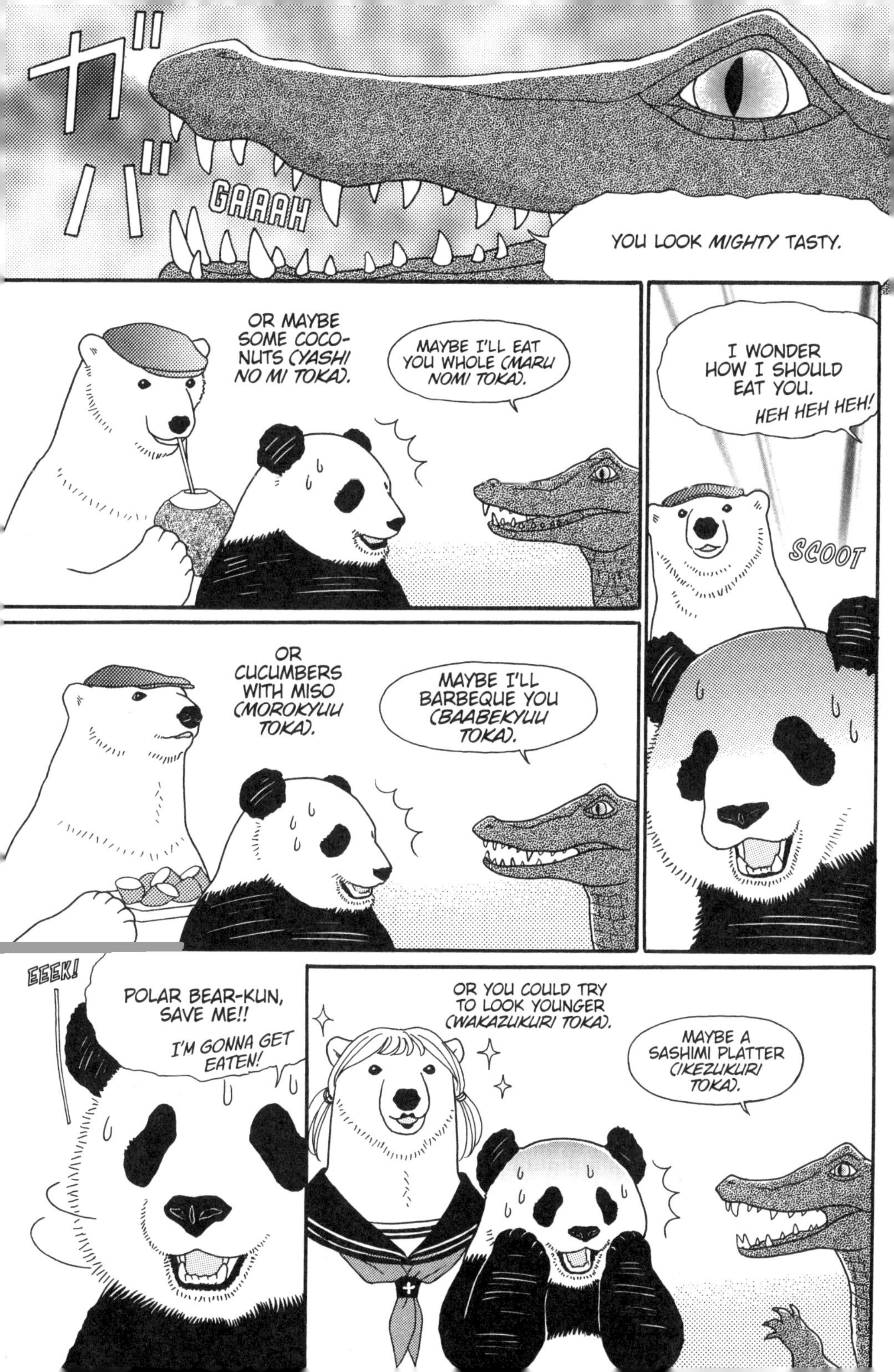

ガバ
GAAAH
YOU LOOK *MIGHTY* TASTY.
I WONDER HOW I SHOULD EAT YOU.
HEH HEH HEH!
SCOOT
MAYBE I'LL EAT YOU WHOLE (MARU NOMI TOKA).
OR MAYBE SOME COCONUTS (YASHI NO MI TOKA).
MAYBE I'LL BARBEQUE YOU (BAABEKYUU TOKA).
OR CUCUMBERS WITH MISO (MOROKYUU TOKA).
MAYBE A SASHIMI PLATTER (IKEZUKURI TOKA).
OR YOU COULD TRY TO LOOK YOUNGER (WAKAZUKURI TOKA).
EEEK!
POLAR BEAR-KUN, SAVE ME!!
I'M GONNA GET EATEN!

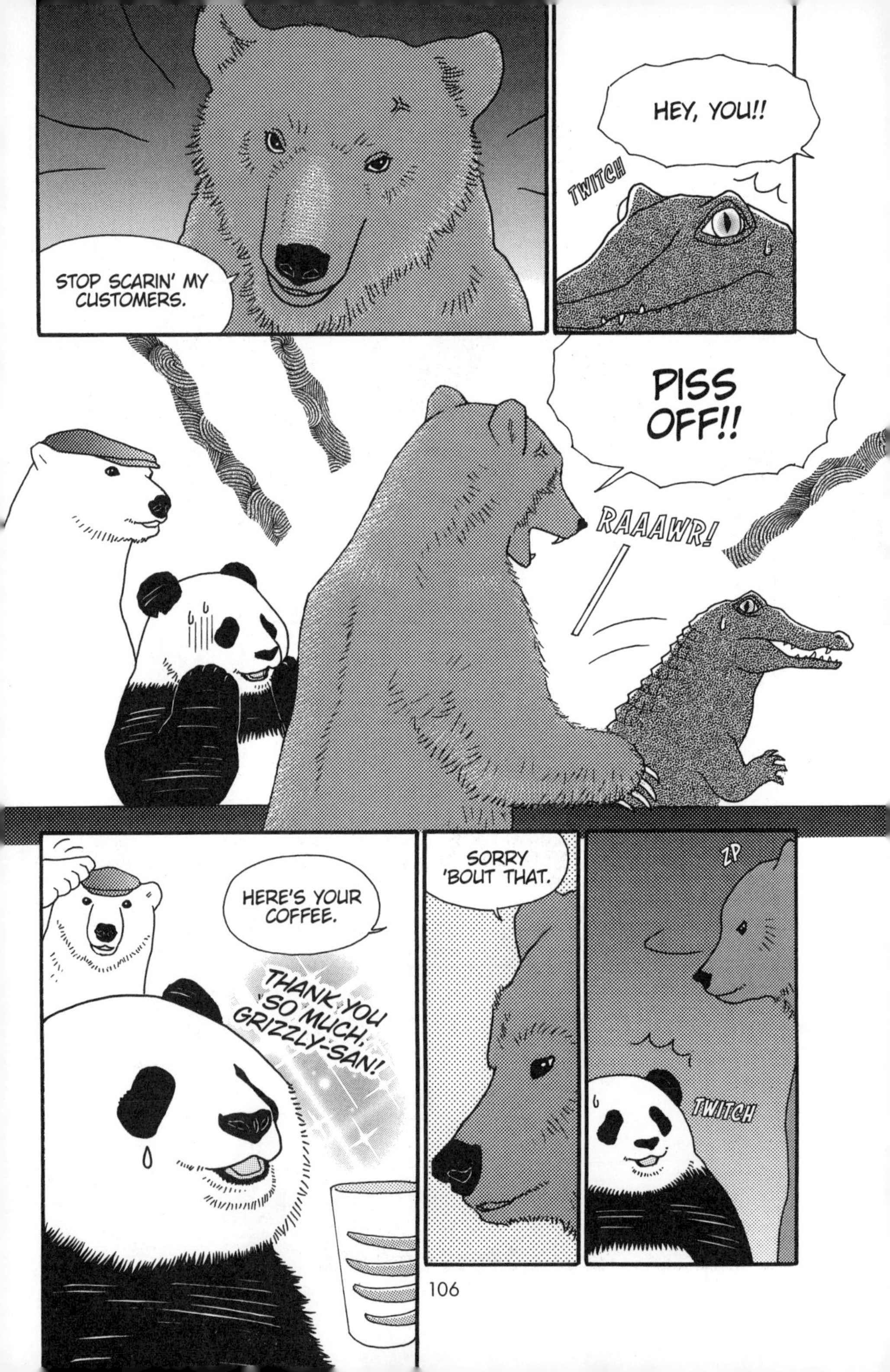
HEY, YOU!!
TWITCH
STOP SCARIN' MY CUSTOMERS.
PISS OFF!!
RAAAWR!
ZP
TWITCH
SORRY 'BOUT THAT.
HERE'S YOUR COFFEE.
THANK YOU SO MUCH, GRIZZLY-SAN!

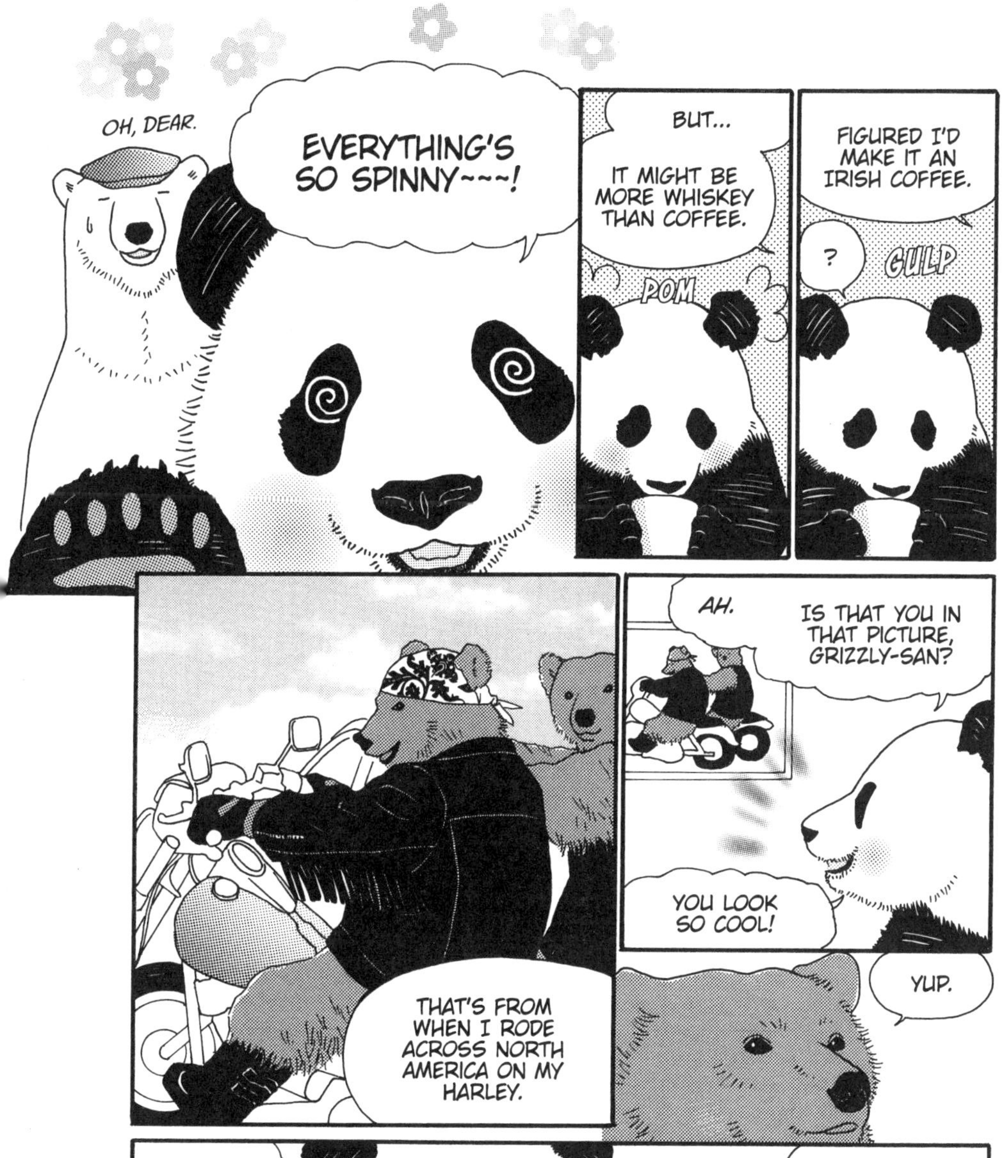
FIGURED I'D MAKE IT AN IRISH COFFEE.
?
GULP
BUT...
IT MIGHT BE MORE WHISKEY THAN COFFEE.
POM
EVERYTHING'S SO SPINNY~~~!
OH, DEAR.
AH.
IS THAT YOU IN THAT PICTURE, GRIZZLY-SAN?
YOU LOOK SO COOL!
YUP.
THAT'S FROM WHEN I RODE ACROSS NORTH AMERICA ON MY HARLEY.
IT WAS GREAT.
WE BASICALLY BLASTED THROUGH A ROAD THAT LED TO THE HORIZON.
NOT TO·MENTION, ALL THE SALMON I COULD CATCH.
WOW... I'M STAR-STRUCK!

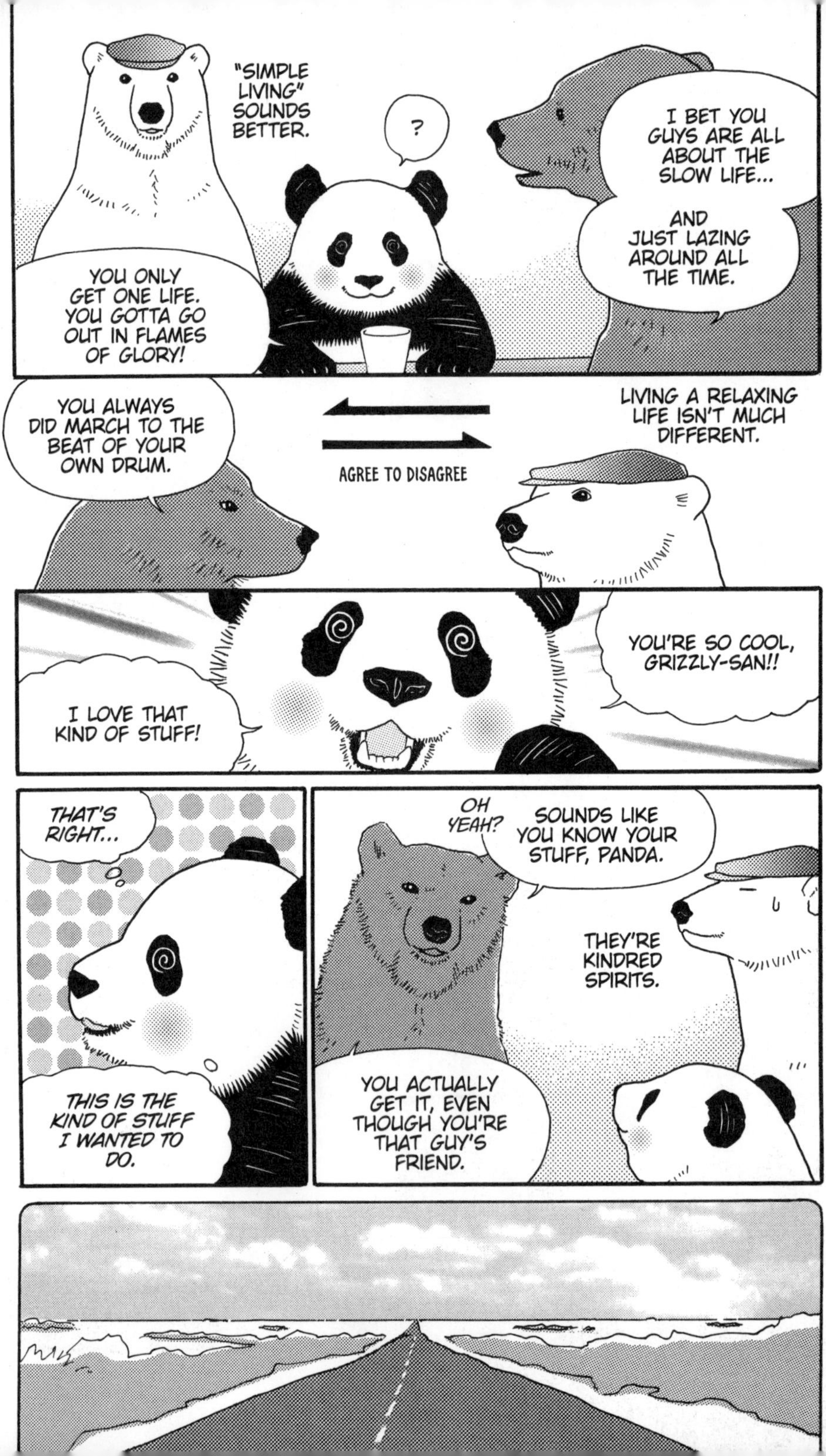
I BET YOU GUYS ARE ALL ABOUT THE SLOW LIFE...
AND JUST LAZING AROUND ALL THE TIME.
?
"SIMPLE LIVING" SOUNDS BETTER.
YOU ONLY GET ONE LIFE. YOU GOTTA GO OUT IN FLAMES OF GLORY!
LIVING A RELAXING LIFE ISN'T MUCH DIFFERENT.
AGREE TO DISAGREE
YOU ALWAYS DID MARCH TO THE BEAT OF YOUR OWN DRUM.
YOU'RE SO COOL, GRIZZLY-SAN!!
I LOVE THAT KIND OF STUFF!
SOUNDS LIKE YOU KNOW YOUR STUFF, PANDA.
OH YEAH?
THEY'RE KINDRED SPIRITS.
YOU ACTUALLY GET IT, EVEN THOUGH YOU'RE THAT GUY'S FRIEND.
THAT'S RIGHT...
THIS IS THE KIND OF STUFF I WANTED TO DO.

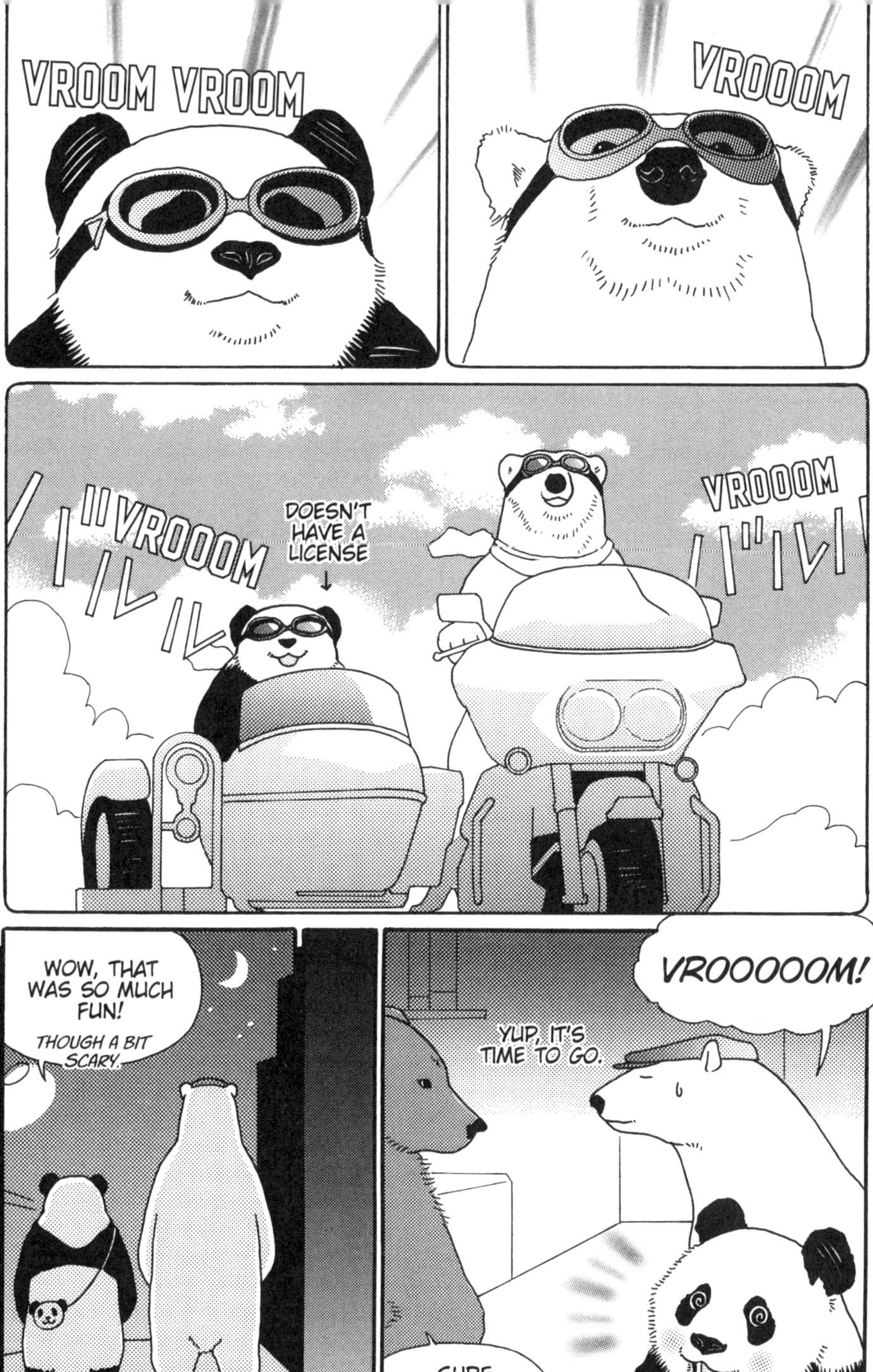
VROOOM
VROOM VROOM
VROOOM
DOESN'T HAVE A LICENSE
VROOOM
VROOOOOM!
YUP, IT'S TIME TO GO.
SURE. STOP BY ANYTIME.
WOW, THAT WAS SO MUCH FUN!
THOUGH A BIT SCARY.

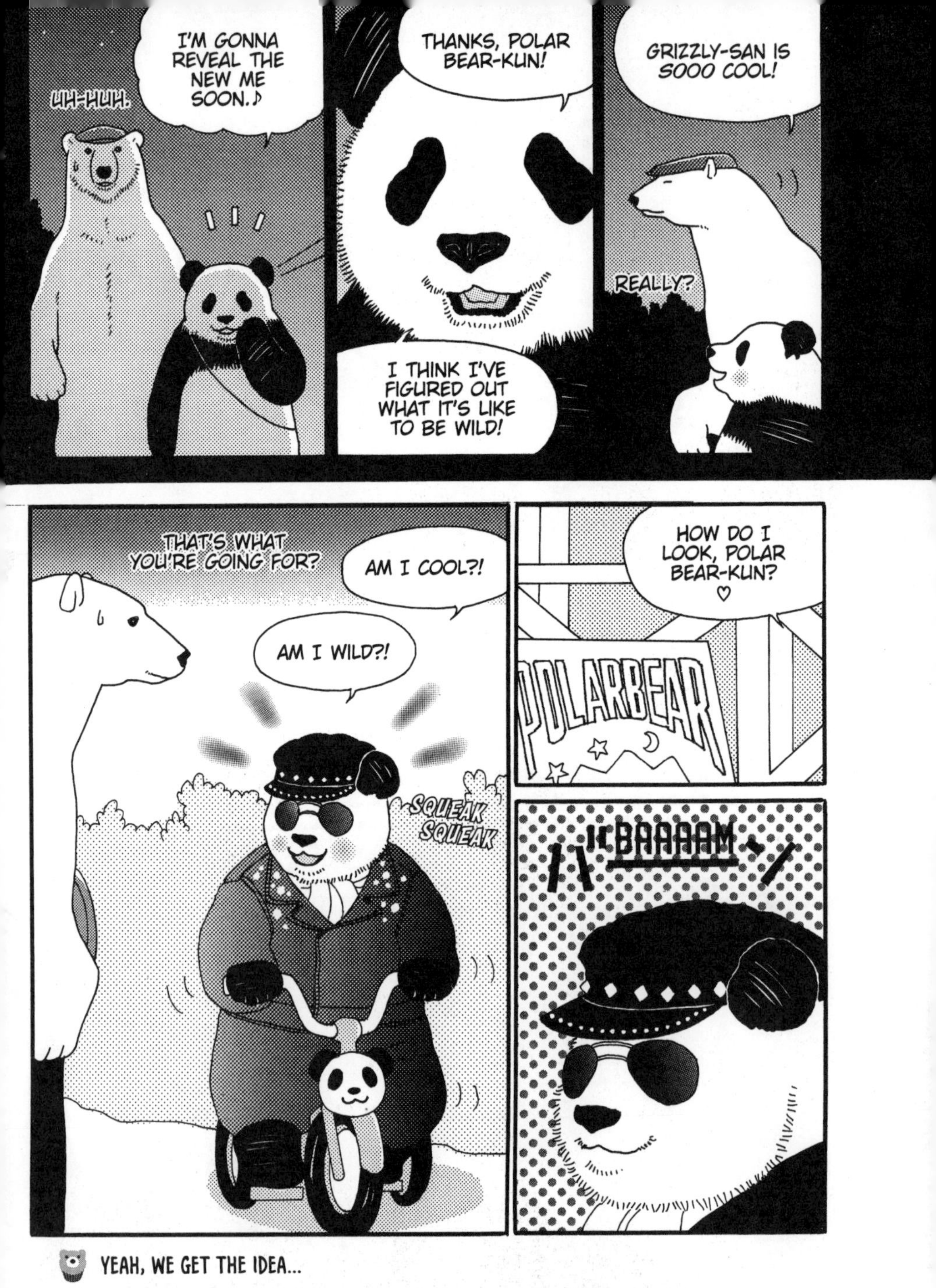
GRIZZLY-SAN IS SOOO COOL!
REALLY?
THANKS, POLAR BEAR-KUN!
I THINK I'VE FIGURED OUT WHAT IT'S LIKE TO BE WILD!
I'M GONNA REVEAL THE NEW ME SOON.♪
UH-HUH.
HOW DO I LOOK, POLAR BEAR-KUN? ♡
POLARBEAR
BAAAAM
AM I COOL?!
THAT'S WHAT YOU'RE GOING FOR?
AM I WILD?!
SQUEAK SQUEAK

YEAH, WE GET THE IDEA...

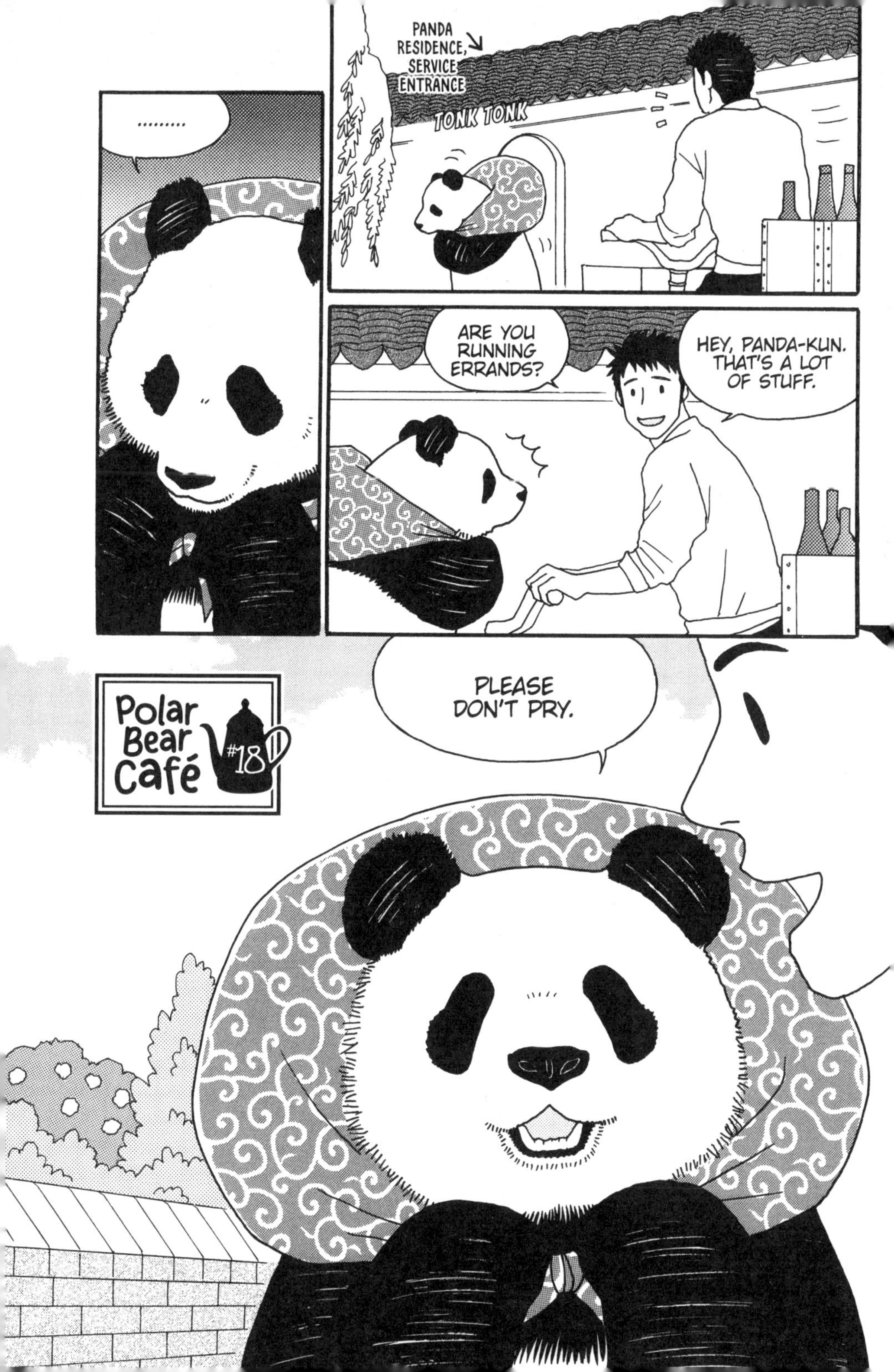
PANDA RESIDENCE, SERVICE ENTRANCE
TONK TONK
HEY, PANDA-KUN. THAT'S A LOT OF STUFF.
ARE YOU RUNNING ERRANDS?
....
PLEASE DON'T PRY.
Polar Bear Café
#18

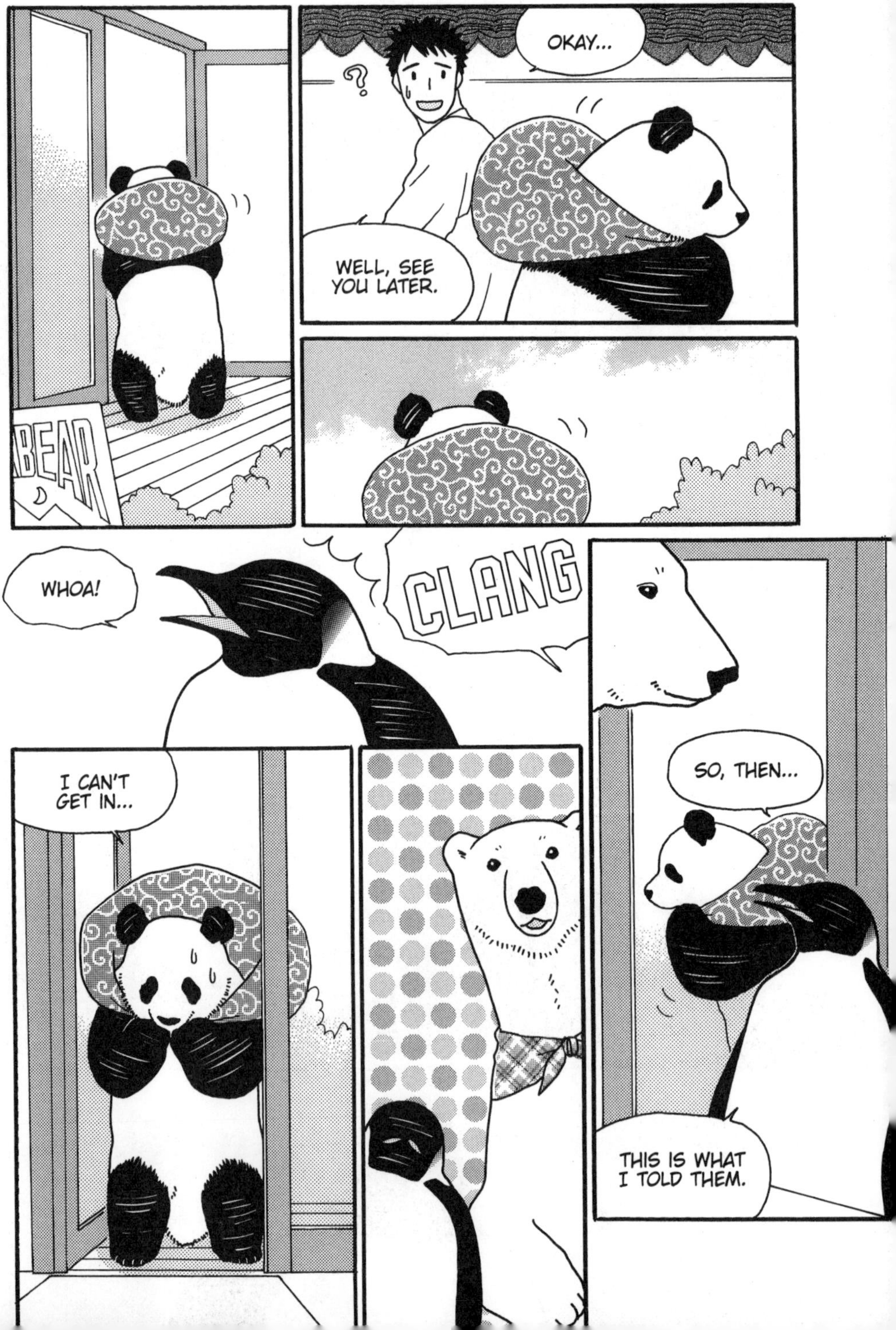
OKAY...
WELL, SEE YOU LATER.
CLANG
WHOA!
SO, THEN...
THIS IS WHAT I TOLD THEM.
I CAN'T GET IN...

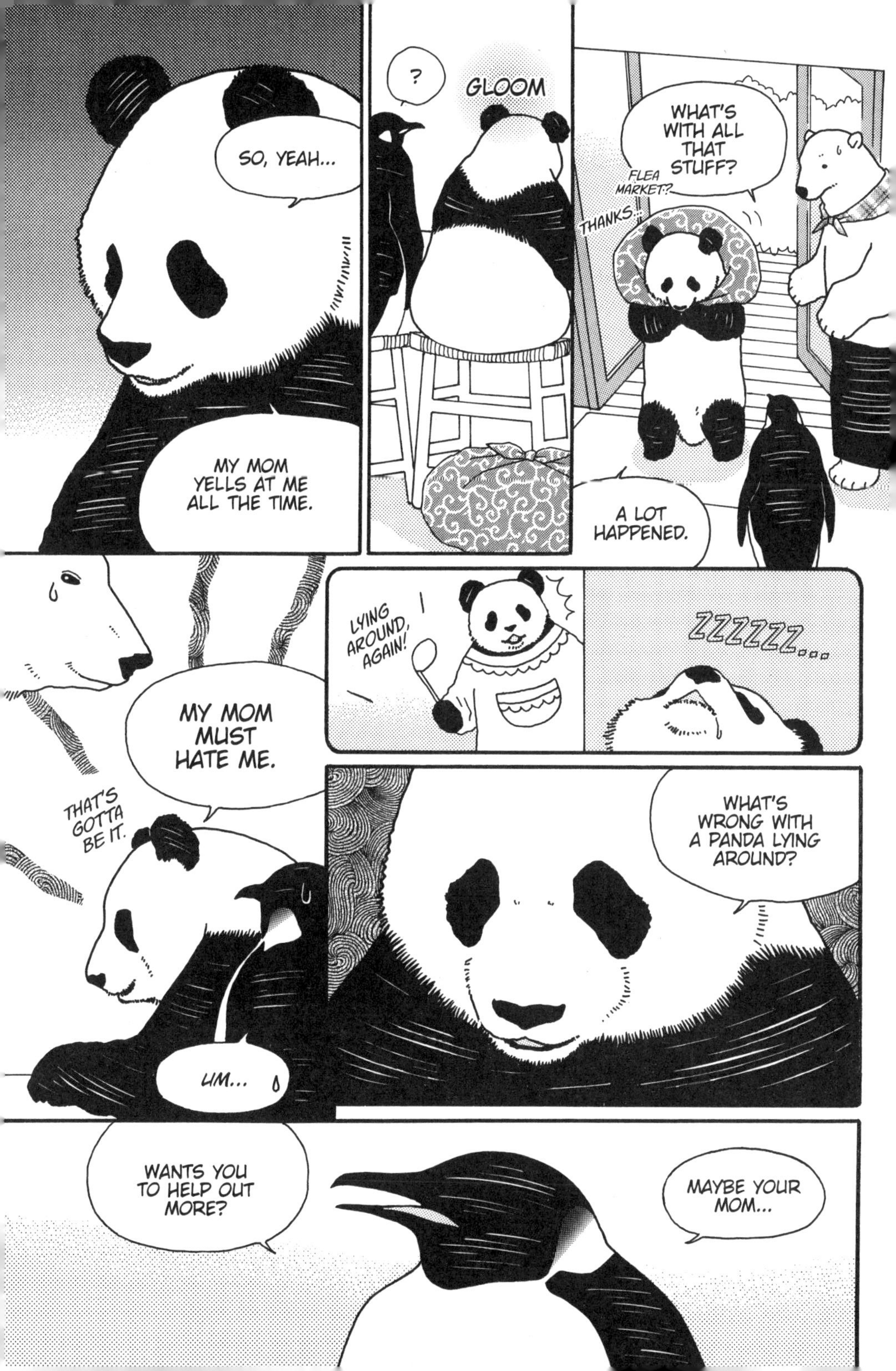
WHAT'S WITH ALL THAT STUFF?
FLEA MARKET?
THANKS...
A LOT HAPPENED.
?
GLOOM
SO, YEAH...
MY MOM YELLS AT ME ALL THE TIME.
ZZZZZZ...
LYING AROUND, AGAIN!
WHAT'S WRONG WITH A PANDA LYING AROUND?
MY MOM MUST HATE ME.
THAT'S GOTTA BE IT.
UM...
MAYBE YOUR MOM...
WANTS YOU TO HELP OUT MORE?

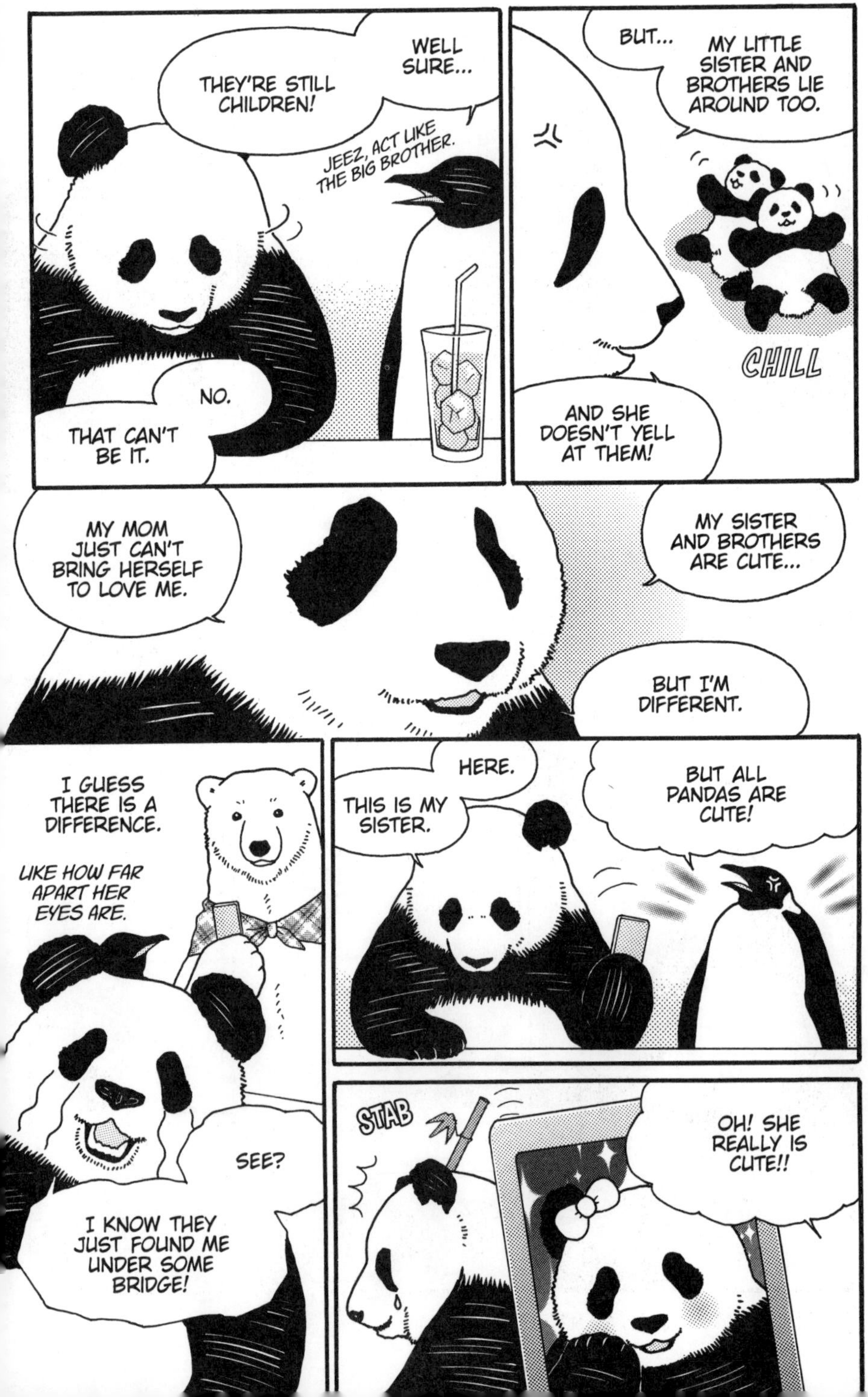
BUT... MY LITTLE SISTER AND BROTHERS LIE AROUND TOO.
CHILL
AND SHE DOESN'T YELL AT THEM!
WELL SURE... THEY'RE STILL CHILDREN!
JEEZ, ACT LIKE THE BIG BROTHER.
NO.
THAT CAN'T BE IT.
MY SISTER AND BROTHERS ARE CUTE...
BUT I'M DIFFERENT.
MY MOM JUST CAN'T BRING HERSELF TO LOVE ME.
BUT ALL PANDAS ARE CUTE!
HERE.
THIS IS MY SISTER.
OH! SHE REALLY IS CUTE!!
STAB
I GUESS THERE IS A DIFFERENCE.
LIKE HOW FAR APART HER EYES ARE.
SEE?
I KNOW THEY JUST FOUND ME UNDER SOME BRIDGE!

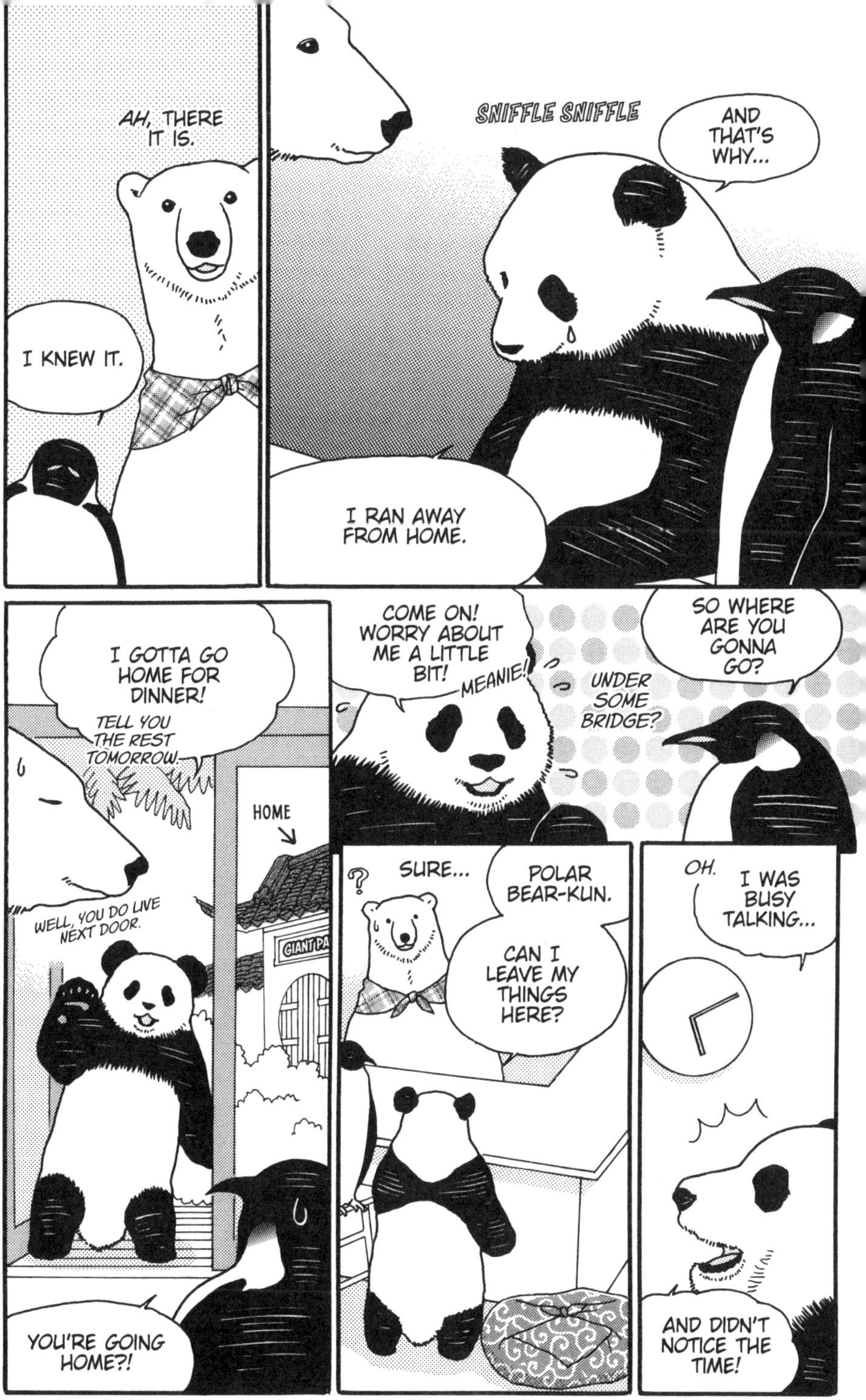
SNIFFLE SNIFFLE
AND THAT'S WHY...
I RAN AWAY FROM HOME.
AH, THERE IT IS.
I KNEW IT.
SO WHERE ARE YOU GONNA GO?
UNDER SOME BRIDGE?
COME ON! WORRY ABOUT ME A LITTLE BIT!
MEANIE!
OH.
I WAS BUSY TALKING...
AND DIDN'T NOTICE THE TIME!
POLAR BEAR-KUN.
CAN I LEAVE MY THINGS HERE?
SURE...
I GOTTA GO HOME FOR DINNER!
TELL YOU THE REST TOMORROW.
HOME
GIANT PA
WELL, YOU DO LIVE NEXT DOOR.
YOU'RE GOING HOME?!

HE CAN'T MISS A MEAL, NO MATTER WHAT.

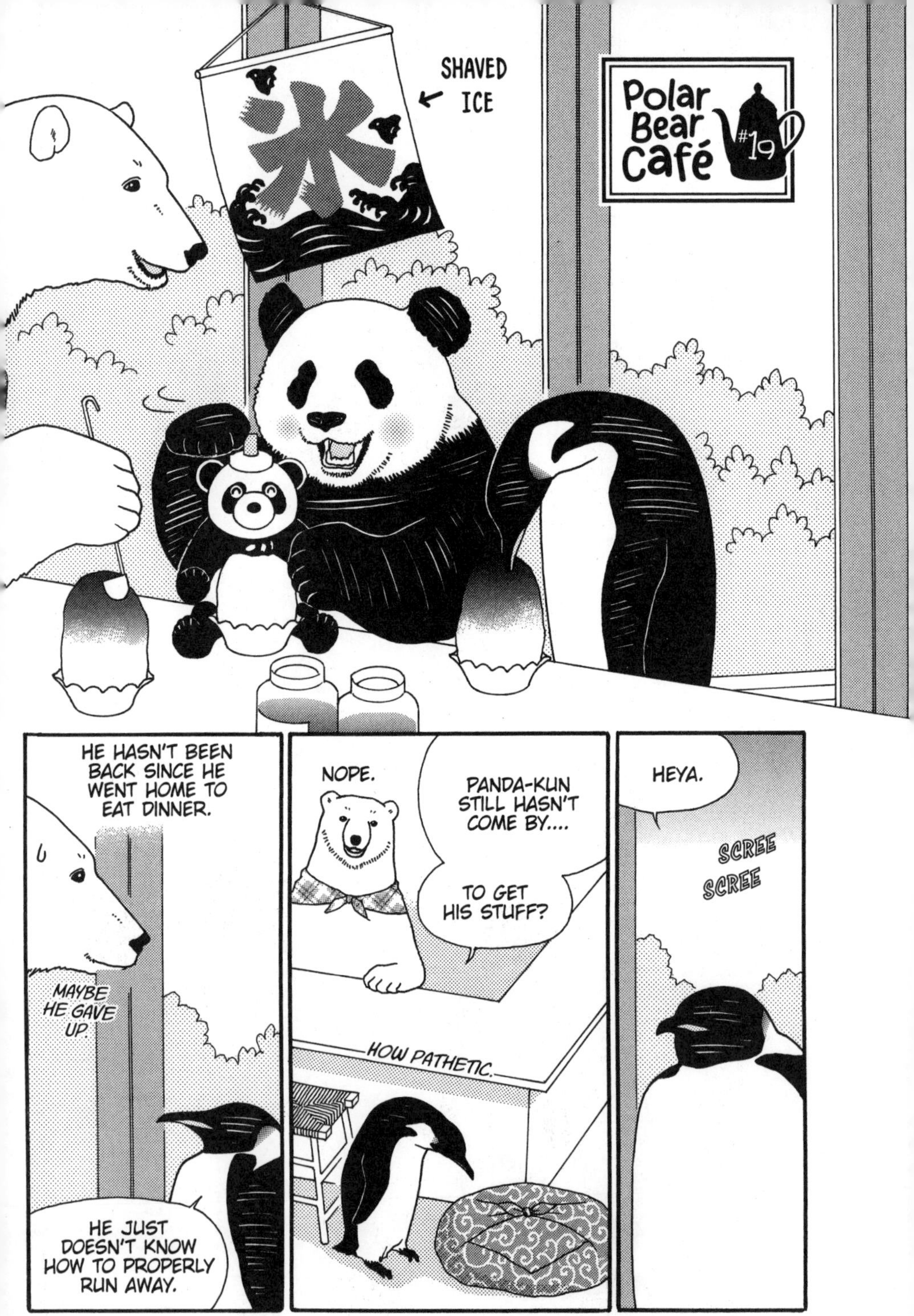
Polar Bear Café #19
SHAVED ICE
HEYA.
SCREE SCREE
PANDA-KUN STILL HASN'T COME BY....
TO GET HIS STUFF?
NOPE.
HOW PATHETIC.
HE HASN'T BEEN BACK SINCE HE WENT HOME TO EAT DINNER.
MAYBE HE GAVE UP.
HE JUST DOESN'T KNOW HOW TO PROPERLY RUN AWAY.

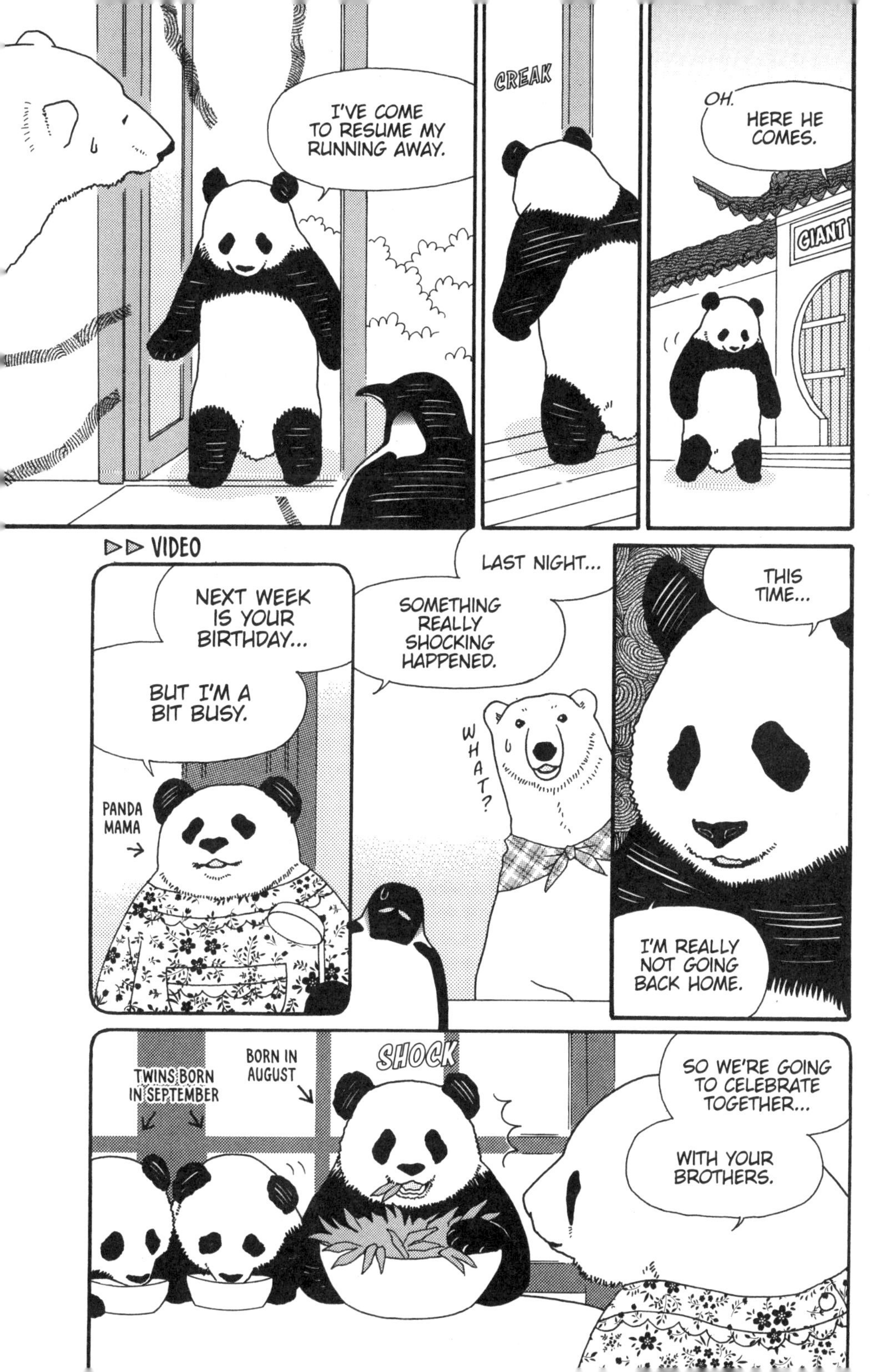
OH.
HERE HE COMES.
GIANT
CREAK
I'VE COME TO RESUME MY RUNNING AWAY.
THIS TIME...
I'M REALLY NOT GOING BACK HOME.
LAST NIGHT...
SOMETHING REALLY SHOCKING HAPPENED.
WHAT?
▷▷ VIDEO
NEXT WEEK IS YOUR BIRTHDAY...
BUT I'M A BIT BUSY.
PANDA MAMA
SO WE'RE GOING TO CELEBRATE TOGETHER...
WITH YOUR BROTHERS.
SHOCK
BORN IN AUGUST
TWINS BORN IN SEPTEMBER

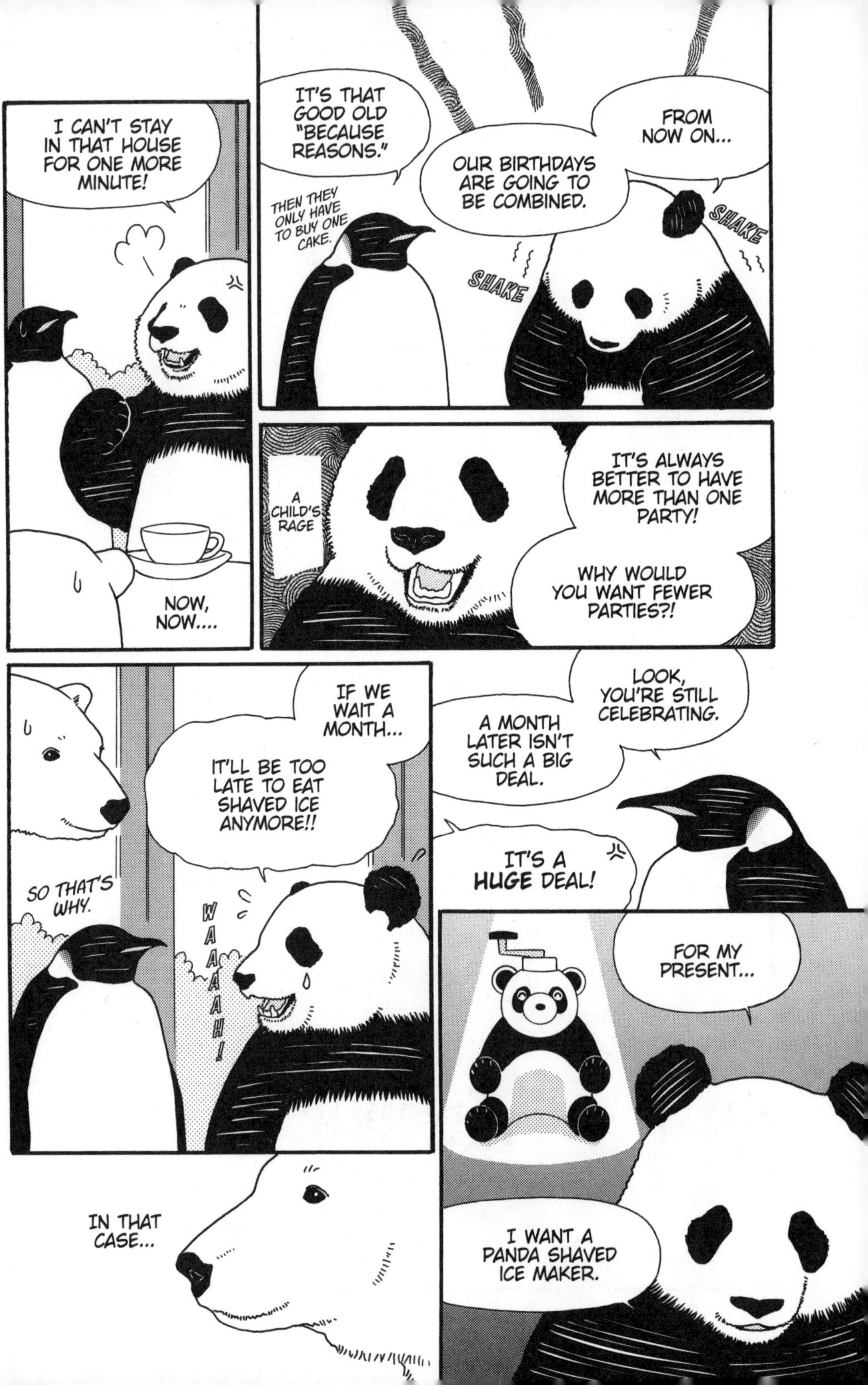

FROM NOW ON...
OUR BIRTHDAYS ARE GOING TO BE COMBINED.
SHAKE
SHAKE
IT'S THAT GOOD OLD "BECAUSE REASONS."
THEN THEY ONLY HAVE TO BUY ONE CAKE.
IT'S ALWAYS BETTER TO HAVE MORE THAN ONE PARTY!
WHY WOULD YOU WANT FEWER PARTIES?!
A CHILD'S RAGE
I CAN'T STAY IN THAT HOUSE FOR ONE MORE MINUTE!
NOW, NOW....
LOOK, YOU'RE STILL CELEBRATING.
A MONTH LATER ISN'T SUCH A BIG DEAL.
IT'S A **HUGE** DEAL!
IF WE WAIT A MONTH...
IT'LL BE TOO LATE TO EAT SHAVED ICE ANYMORE!!
WAAAAAH!
SO THAT'S WHY.
FOR MY PRESENT...
I WANT A PANDA SHAVED ICE MAKER.
IN THAT CASE...

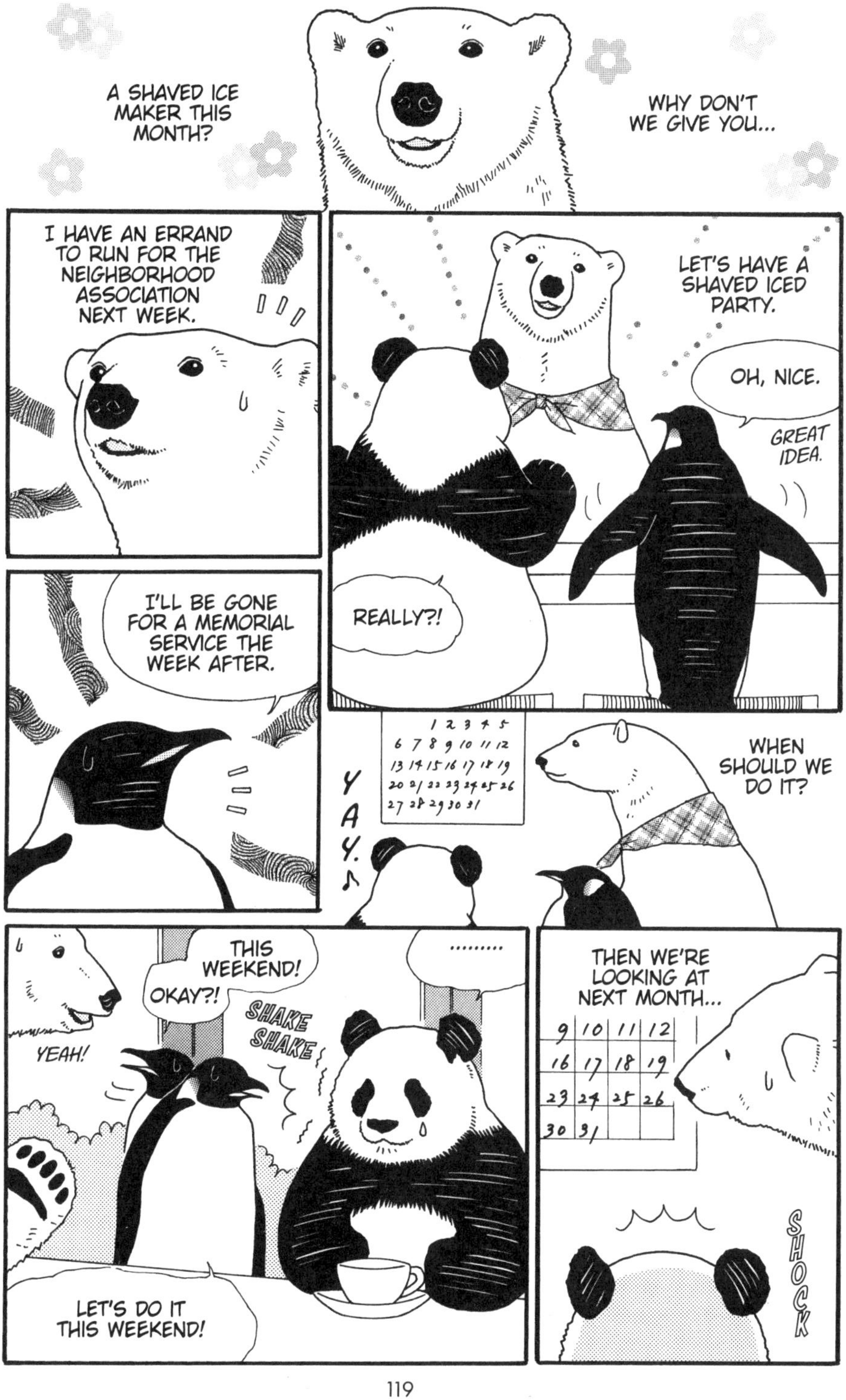

WHY DON'T WE GIVE YOU...
A SHAVED ICE MAKER THIS MONTH?
LET'S HAVE A SHAVED ICED PARTY.
OH, NICE.
GREAT IDEA.
REALLY?!
WHEN SHOULD WE DO IT?
YAY.♪
I HAVE AN ERRAND TO RUN FOR THE NEIGHBORHOOD ASSOCIATION NEXT WEEK.
I'LL BE GONE FOR A MEMORIAL SERVICE THE WEEK AFTER.
THEN WE'RE LOOKING AT NEXT MONTH...
SHOCK
....
THIS WEEKEND!
OKAY?!
SHAKE SHAKE
YEAH!
LET'S DO IT THIS WEEKEND!

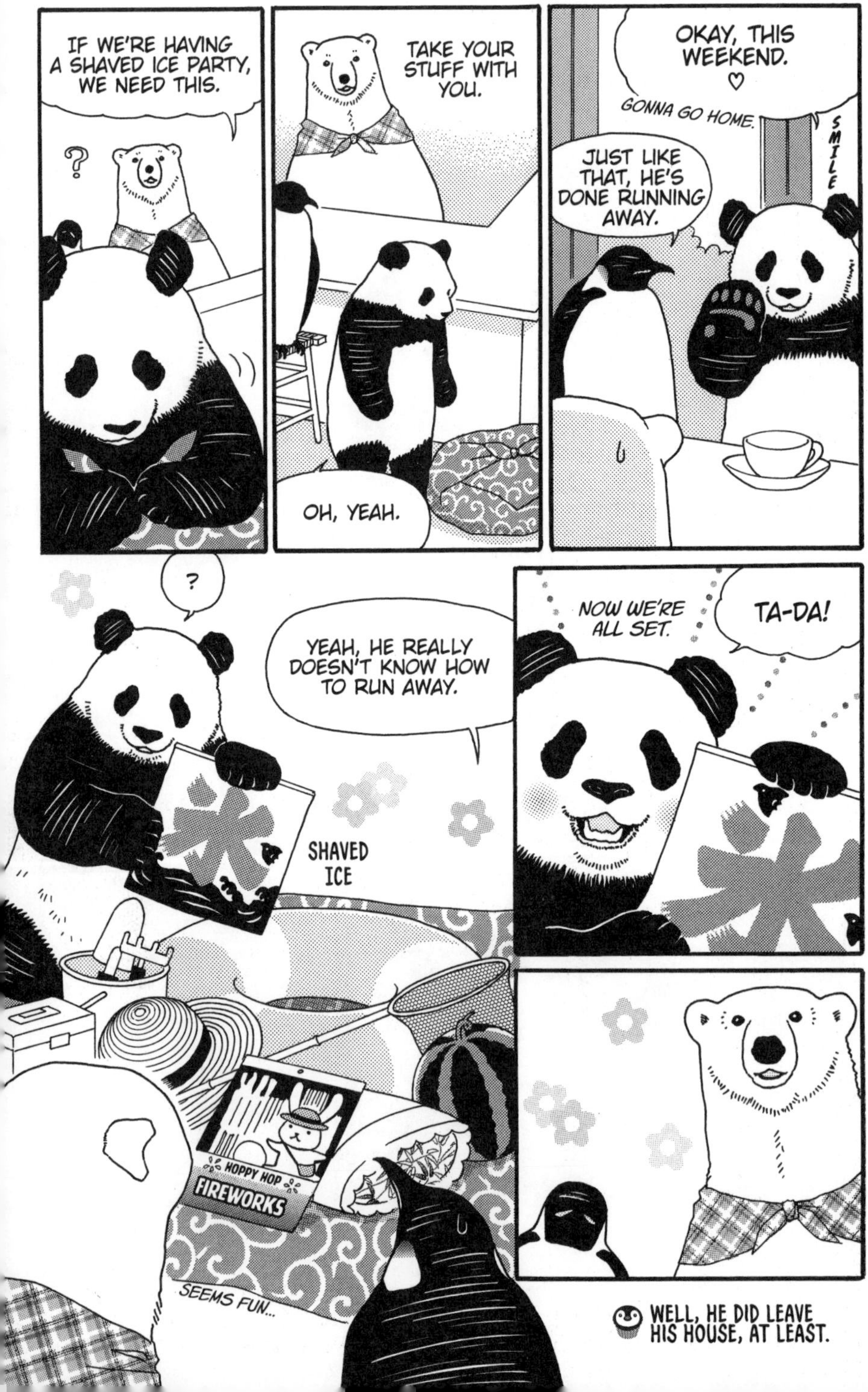
OKAY, THIS WEEKEND. ♡
GONNA GO HOME.
SMILE
JUST LIKE THAT, HE'S DONE RUNNING AWAY.
TAKE YOUR STUFF WITH YOU.
OH, YEAH.
IF WE'RE HAVING A SHAVED ICE PARTY, WE NEED THIS.
?
TA-DA!
NOW WE'RE ALL SET.
?
YEAH, HE REALLY DOESN'T KNOW HOW TO RUN AWAY.
SHAVED ICE
HOPPY HOP
FIREWORKS
SEEMS FUN...

WELL, HE DID LEAVE HIS HOUSE, AT LEAST.

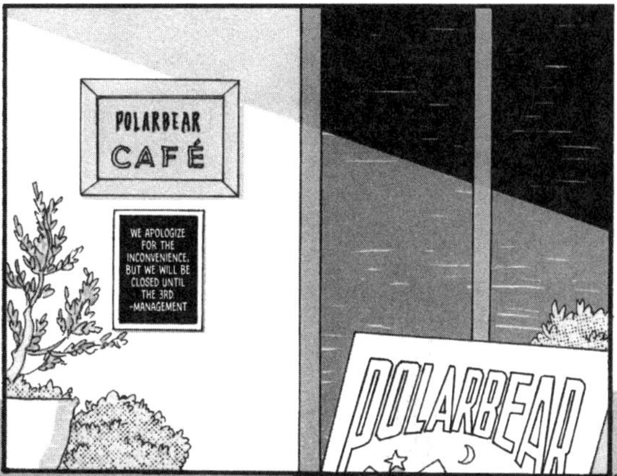
POLARBEAR CAFÉ
WE APOLOGIZE FOR THE INCONVENIENCE, BUT WE WILL BE CLOSED UNTIL THE 3RD. -MANAGEMENT
POLARBEAR

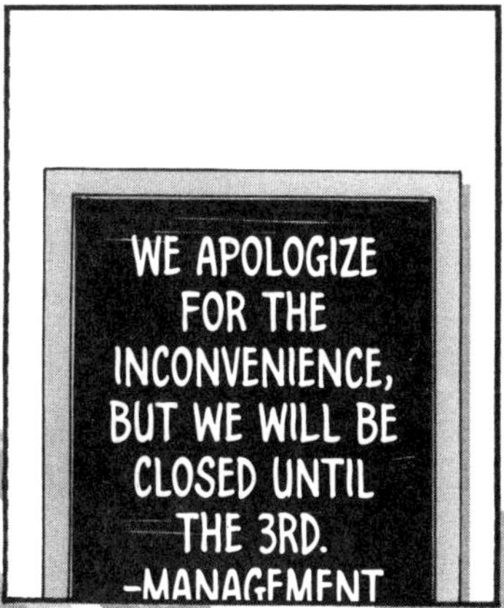
WE APOLOGIZE FOR THE INCONVENIENCE, BUT WE WILL BE CLOSED UNTIL THE 3RD. -MANAGEMENT

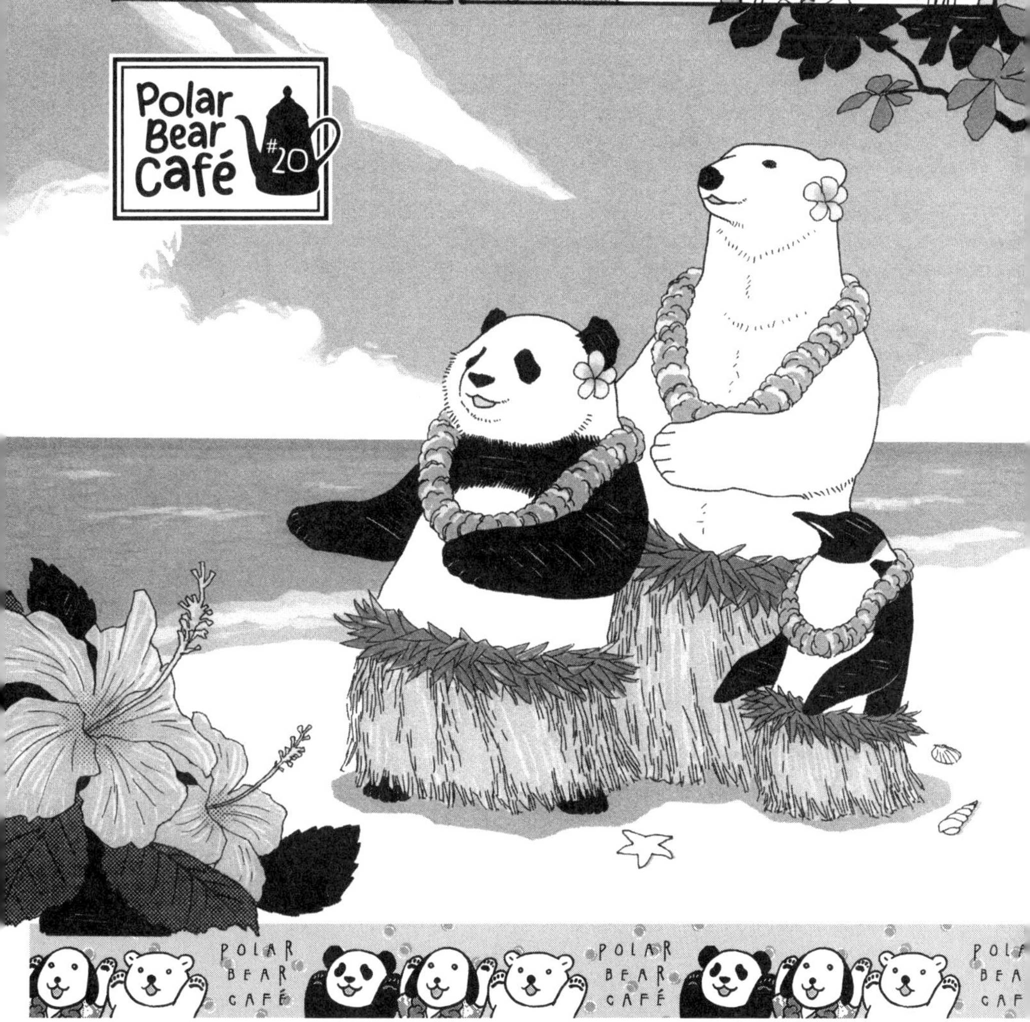
Polar Bear Café #20
POLAR BEAR CAFÉ
POLAR BEAR CAFÉ

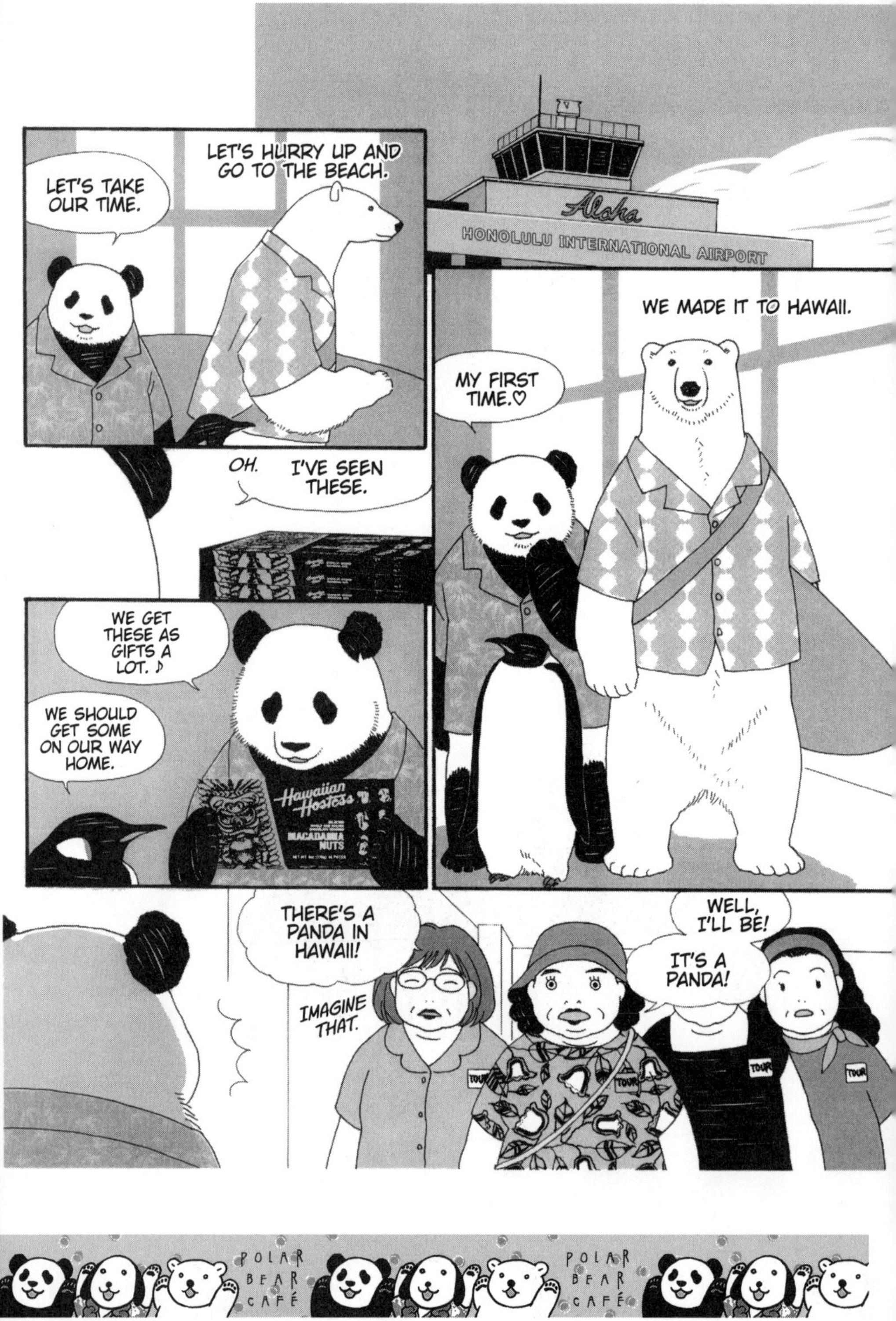
Aloha
HONOLULU INTERNATIONAL AIRPORT
WE MADE IT TO HAWAII.
MY FIRST TIME.♡
LET'S HURRY UP AND GO TO THE BEACH.
LET'S TAKE OUR TIME.
OH.
I'VE SEEN THESE.
WE GET THESE AS GIFTS A LOT. ♪
WE SHOULD GET SOME ON OUR WAY HOME.
Hawaiian Host
MACADAMIA NUTS
WELL, I'LL BE!
IT'S A PANDA!
THERE'S A PANDA IN HAWAII!
IMAGINE THAT.
TOUR
TOUR
TOUR
TOUR
POLAR BEAR CAFÉ
POLAR BEAR CAFÉ

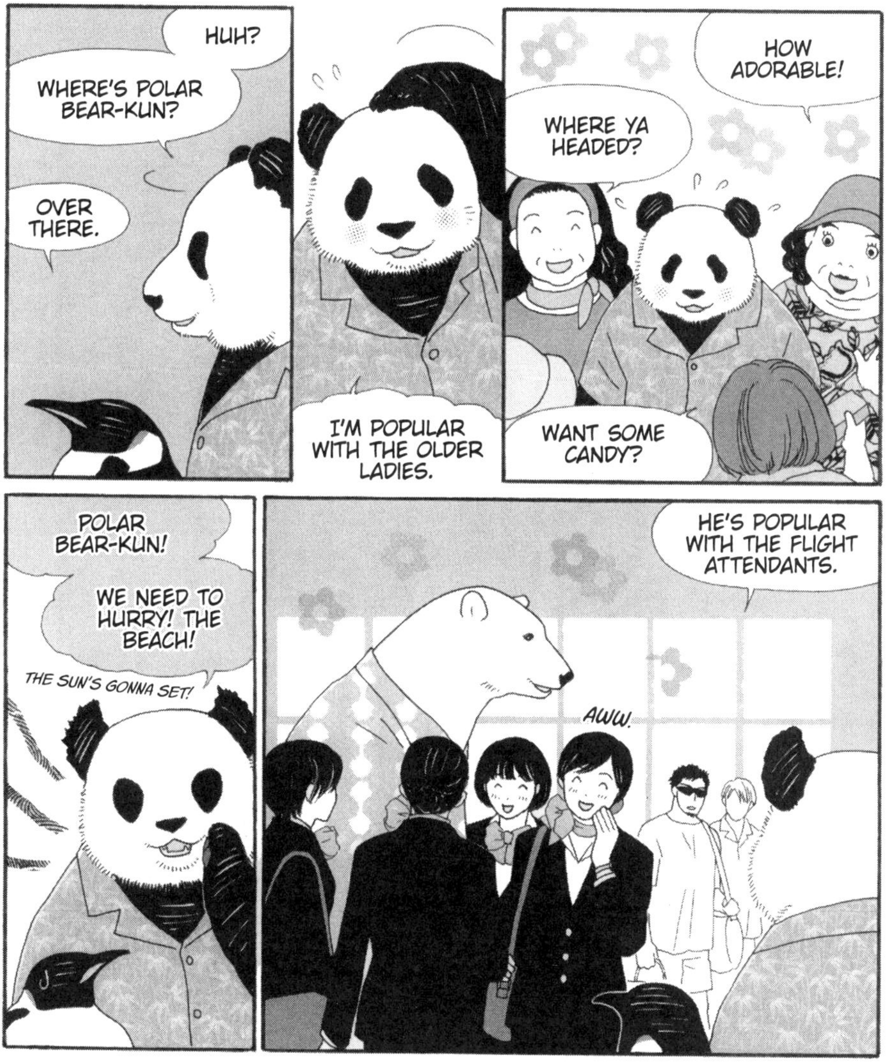
HOW ADORABLE!
WHERE YA HEADED?
WANT SOME CANDY?
I'M POPULAR WITH THE OLDER LADIES.
HUH?
WHERE'S POLAR BEAR-KUN?
OVER THERE.
HE'S POPULAR WITH THE FLIGHT ATTENDANTS.
AWW.
POLAR BEAR-KUN!
WE NEED TO HURRY! THE BEACH!
THE SUN'S GONNA SET!

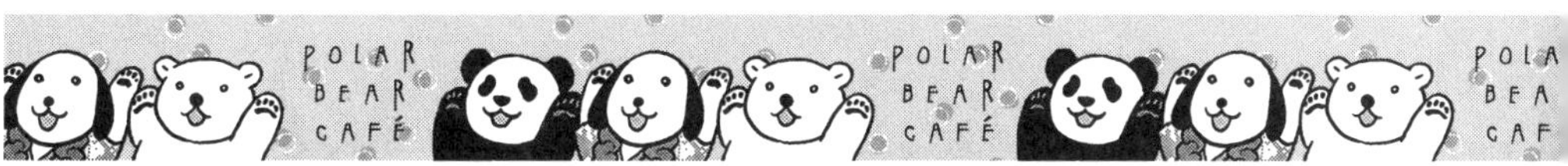
POLAR BEAR CAFÉ
POLAR BEAR CAFÉ

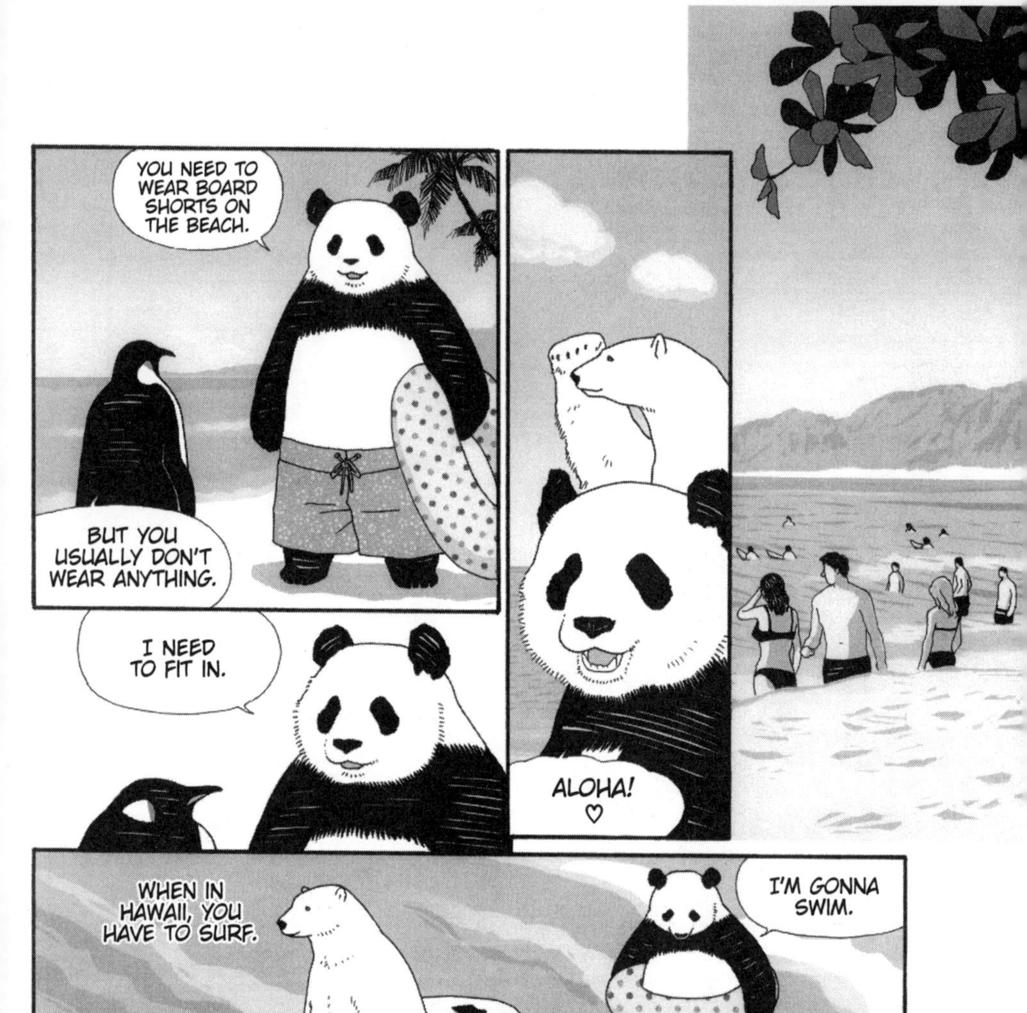
ALOHA! ♡
YOU NEED TO WEAR BOARD SHORTS ON THE BEACH.
BUT YOU USUALLY DON'T WEAR ANYTHING.
I NEED TO FIT IN.
I'M GONNA SWIM.
WHEN IN HAWAII, YOU HAVE TO SURF.
I'M GONNA FISH.

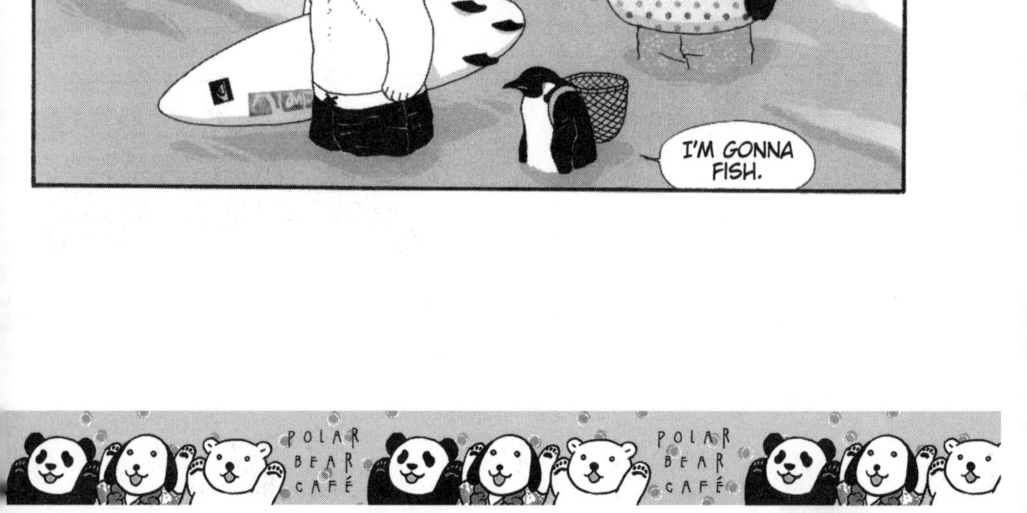
POLAR BEAR CAFÉ
POLAR BEAR CAFÉ

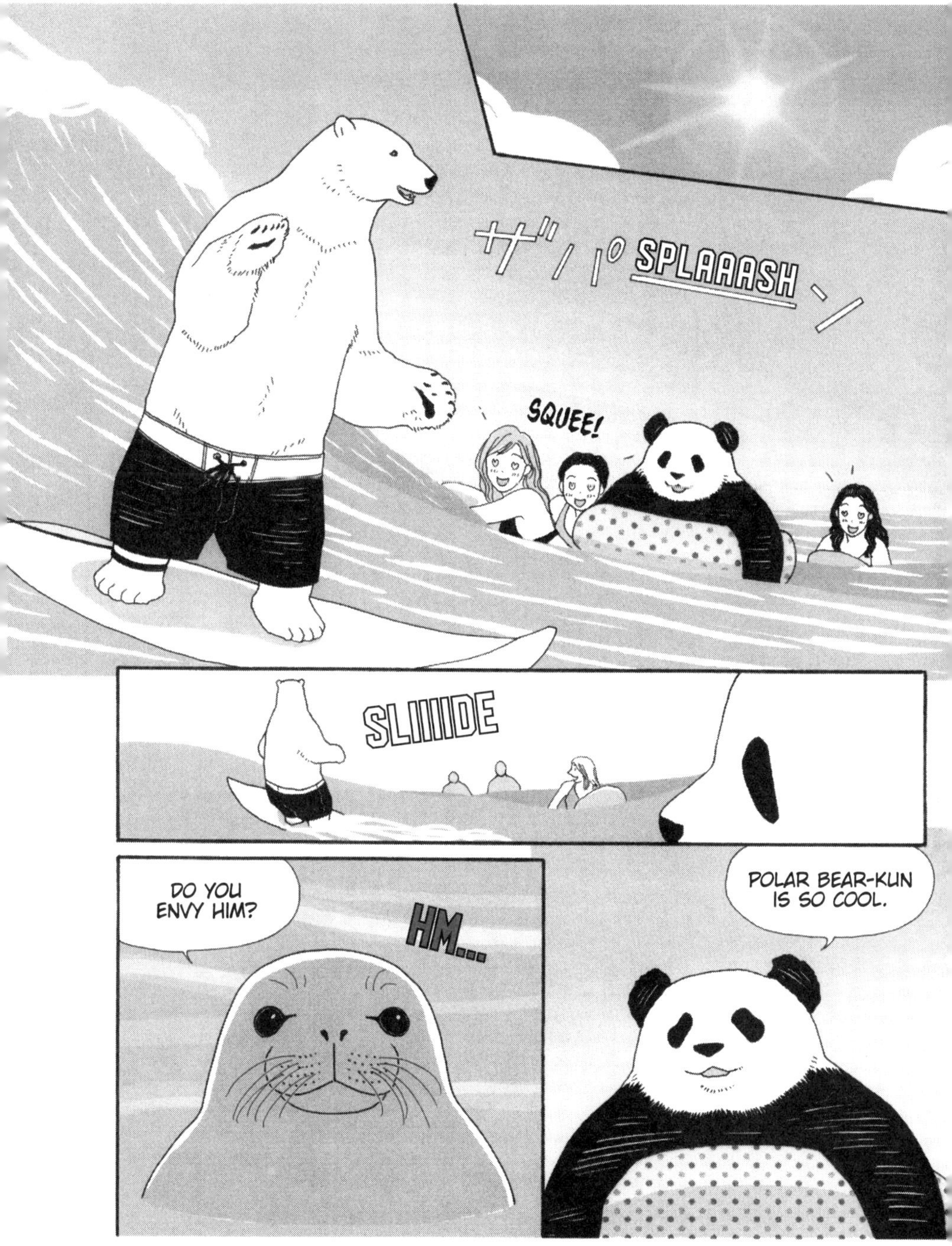
SPLAAASH
SQUEE!
SLIIIIDE
POLAR BEAR-KUN IS SO COOL.
DO YOU ENVY HIM?
HM...

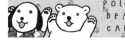

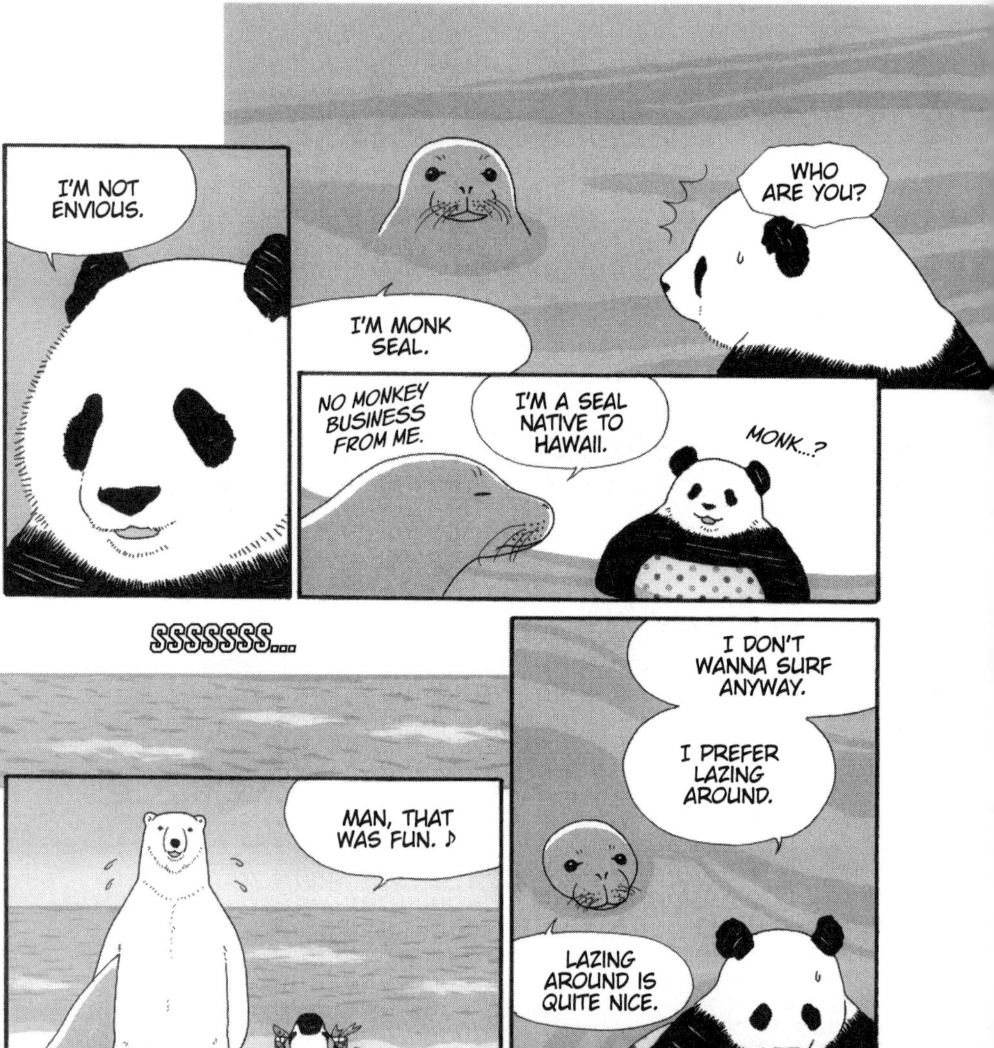
WHO ARE YOU?
I'M MONK SEAL.
MONK...?
I'M A SEAL NATIVE TO HAWAII.
NO MONKEY BUSINESS FROM ME.
I'M NOT ENVIOUS.
I DON'T WANNA SURF ANYWAY.
I PREFER LAZING AROUND.
LAZING AROUND IS QUITE NICE.
SSSSSSS...
MAN, THAT WAS FUN. ♪

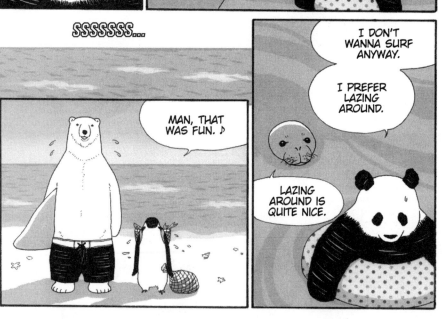

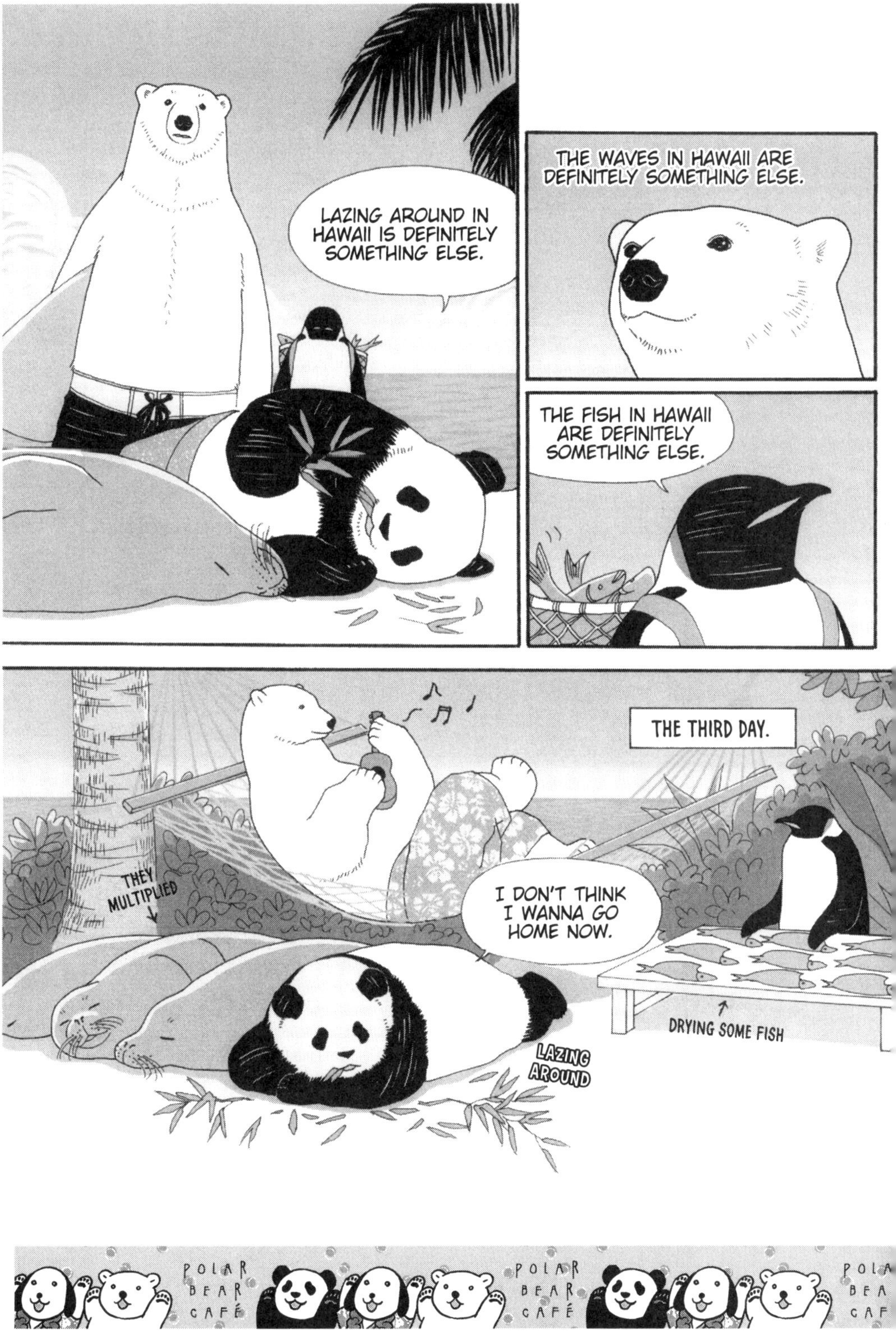
THE WAVES IN HAWAII ARE DEFINITELY SOMETHING ELSE.
THE FISH IN HAWAII ARE DEFINITELY SOMETHING ELSE.
LAZING AROUND IN HAWAII IS DEFINITELY SOMETHING ELSE.
THE THIRD DAY.
I DON'T THINK I WANNA GO HOME NOW.
THEY MULTIPLIED
DRYING SOME FISH
LAZING AROUND
POLAR BEAR CAFÉ

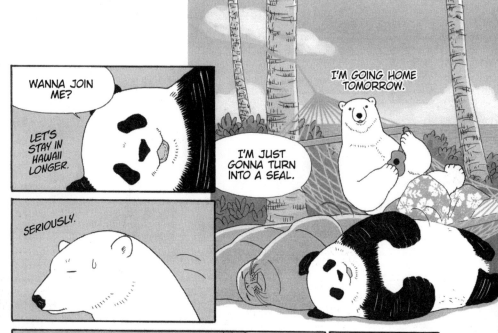

I'M GOING HOME TOMORROW.
I'M JUST GONNA TURN INTO A SEAL.
WANNA JOIN ME?
LET'S STAY IN HAWAII LONGER.
SERIOUSLY.
GRAB
BECOME...
A SEAL WITH ME!

I'M PRETTY SURE PANDA'S THE SAME WAY AT HOME...

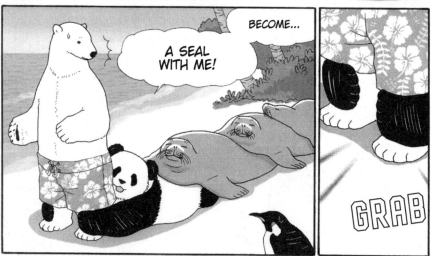

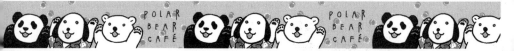

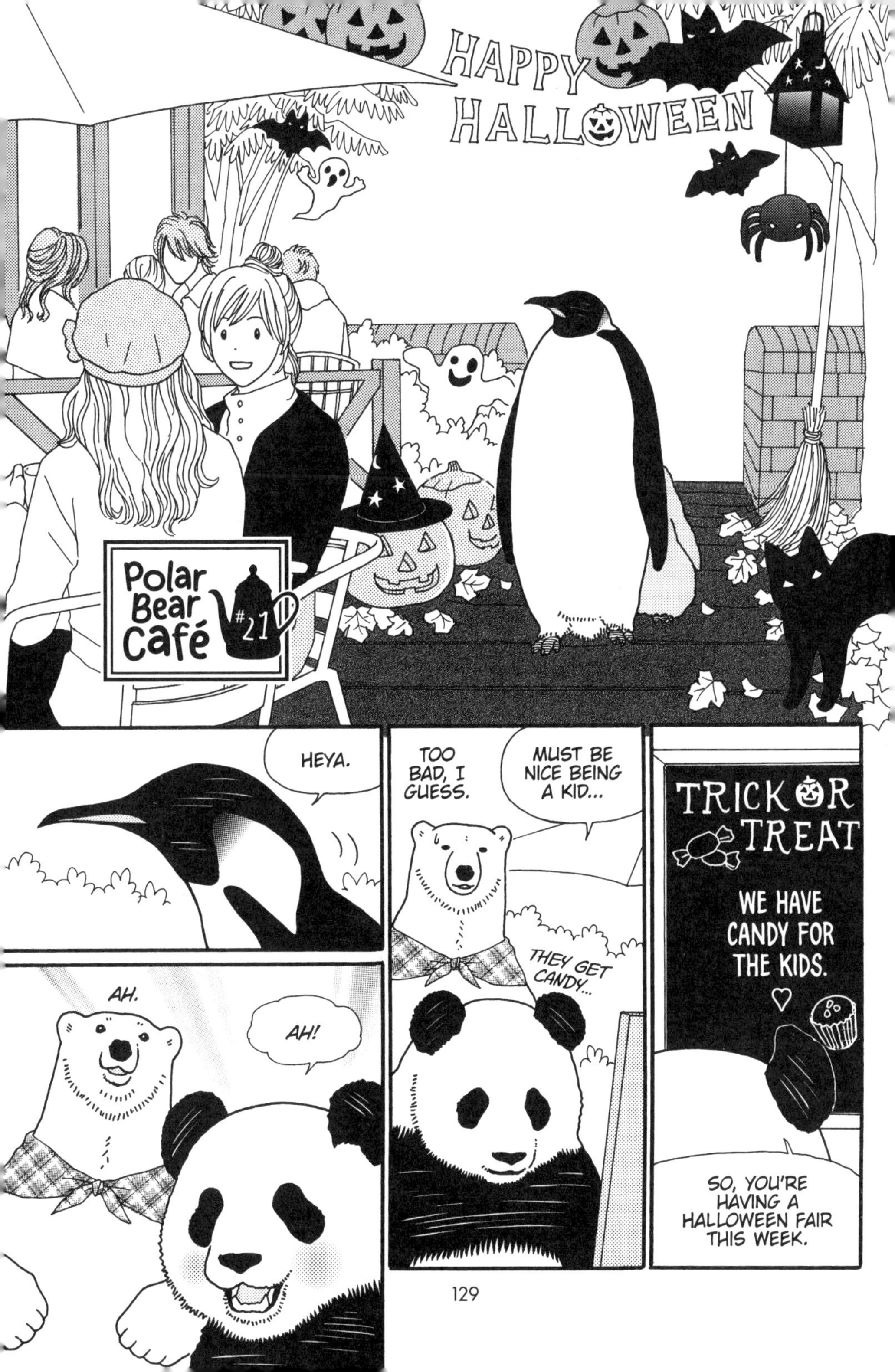
HAPPY HALLOWEEN
Polar Bear Café #21
TRICK OR TREAT
WE HAVE CANDY FOR THE KIDS.
SO, YOU'RE HAVING A HALLOWEEN FAIR THIS WEEK.
MUST BE NICE BEING A KID...
TOO BAD, I GUESS.
THEY GET CANDY...
HEYA.
AH!
AH.

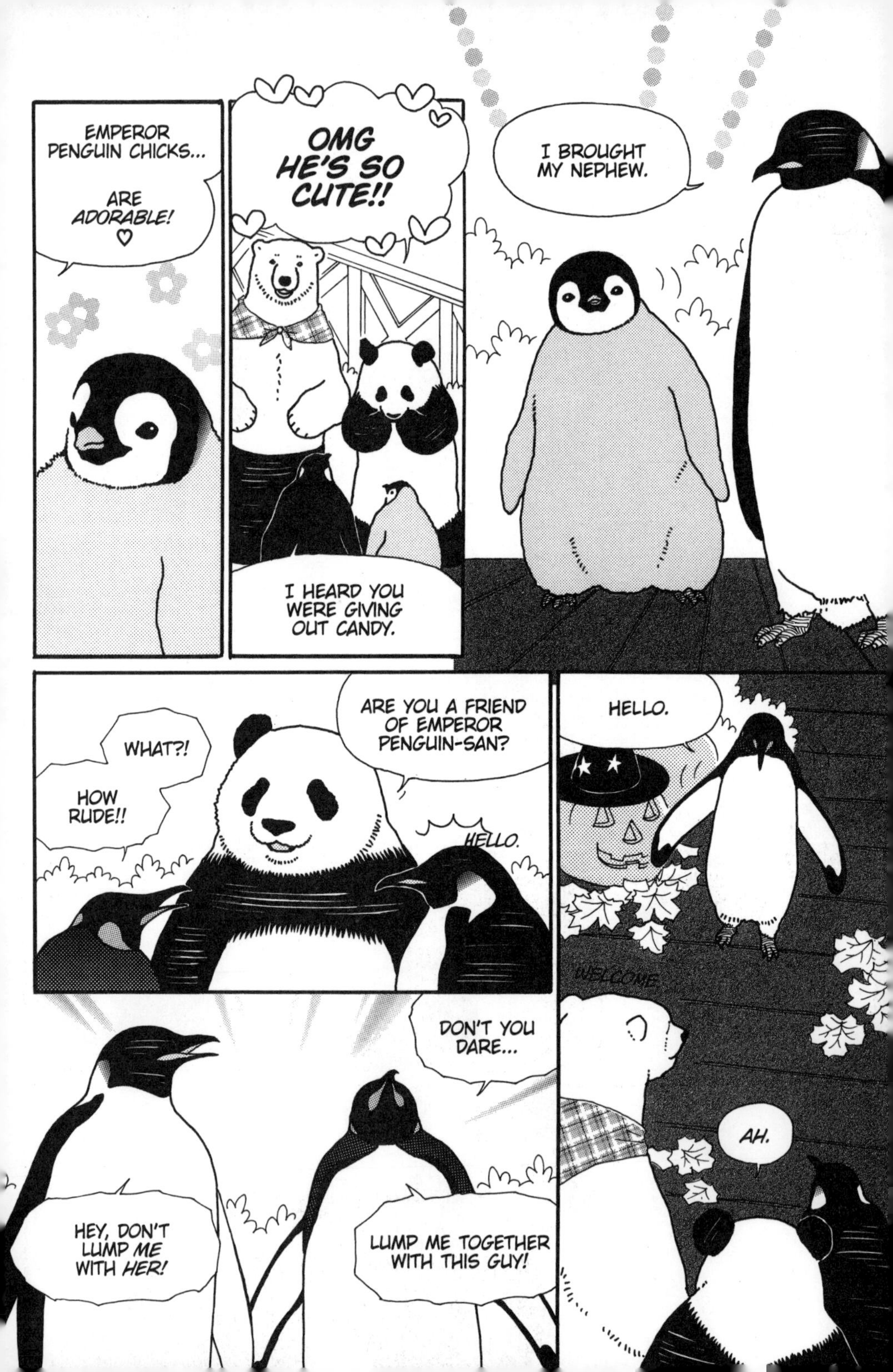
I BROUGHT MY NEPHEW.
OMG HE'S SO CUTE!!
I HEARD YOU WERE GIVING OUT CANDY.
EMPEROR PENGUIN CHICKS...
ARE *ADORABLE!* ♡
HELLO.
WELCOME
AH.
ARE YOU A FRIEND OF EMPEROR PENGUIN-SAN?
HELLO.
WHAT?!
HOW RUDE!!
DON'T YOU DARE...
LUMP ME TOGETHER WITH THIS GUY!
HEY, DON'T LUMP *ME* WITH *HER!*

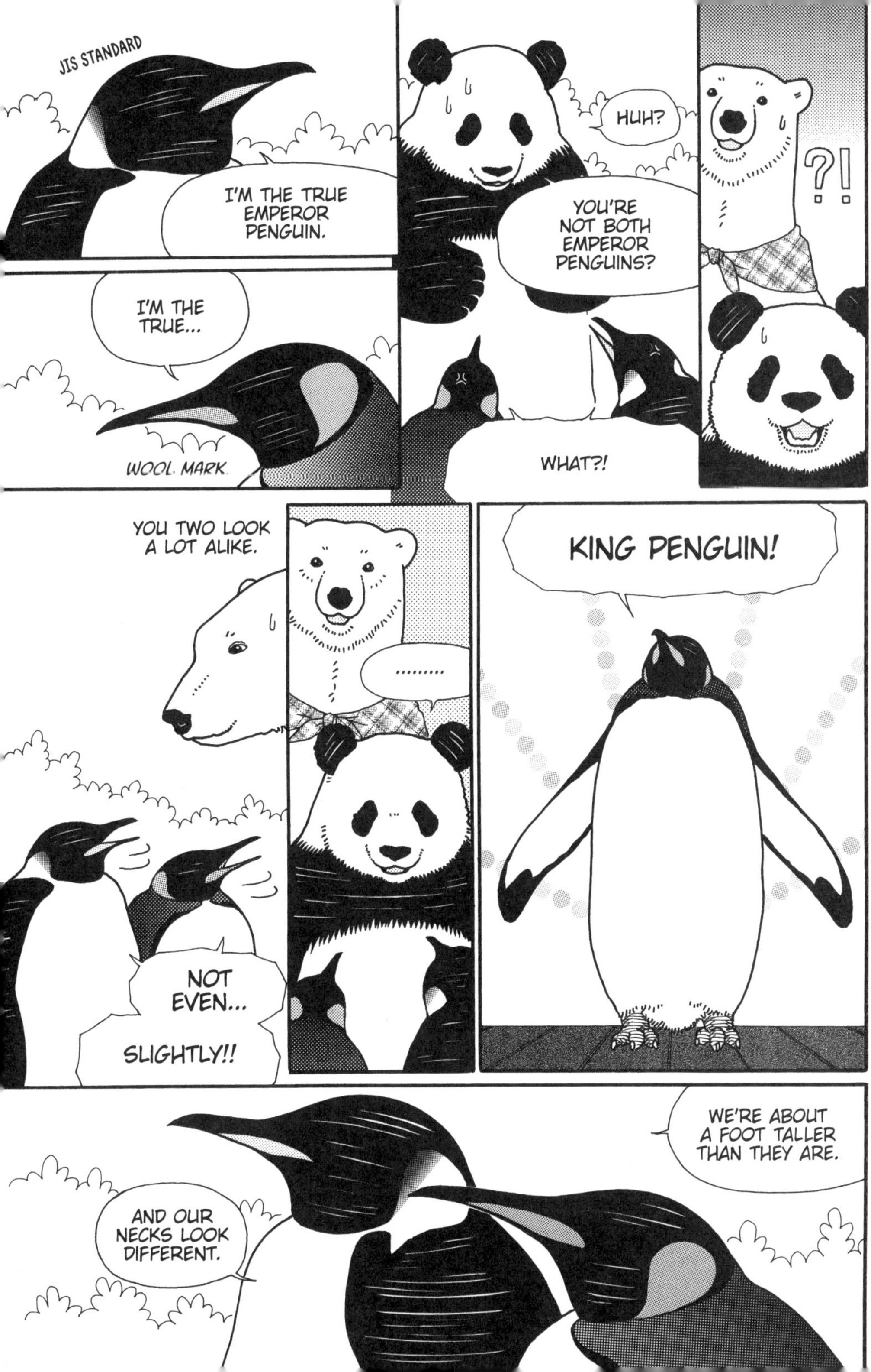
?!
HUH?
YOU'RE NOT BOTH EMPEROR PENGUINS?
WHAT?!
JIS STANDARD
I'M THE TRUE EMPEROR PENGUIN.
I'M THE TRUE...
WOOL MARK.
KING PENGUIN!
....
YOU TWO LOOK A LOT ALIKE.
NOT EVEN...
SLIGHTLY!!
WE'RE ABOUT A FOOT TALLER THAN THEY ARE.
AND OUR NECKS LOOK DIFFERENT.

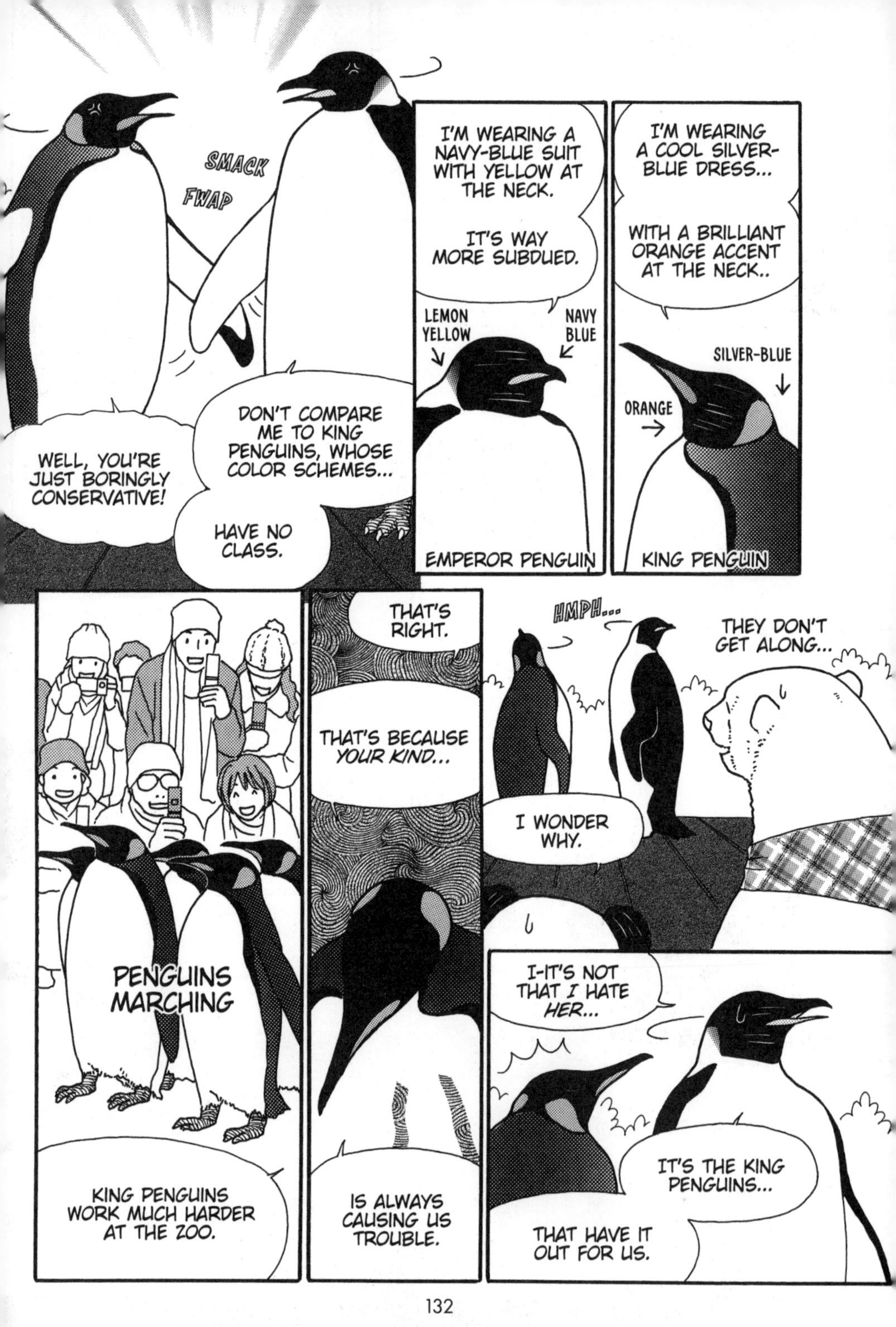
I'M WEARING A COOL SILVER-BLUE DRESS...
WITH A BRILLIANT ORANGE ACCENT AT THE NECK..
SILVER-BLUE
ORANGE
KING PENGUIN
I'M WEARING A NAVY-BLUE SUIT WITH YELLOW AT THE NECK.
IT'S WAY MORE SUBDUED.
LEMON YELLOW
NAVY BLUE
EMPEROR PENGUIN
SMACK
FWAP
DON'T COMPARE ME TO KING PENGUINS, WHOSE COLOR SCHEMES...
HAVE NO CLASS.
WELL, YOU'RE JUST BORINGLY CONSERVATIVE!
THEY DON'T GET ALONG...
HMPH...
I WONDER WHY.
I-IT'S NOT THAT I HATE HER...
IT'S THE KING PENGUINS...
THAT HAVE IT OUT FOR US.
THAT'S RIGHT.
THAT'S BECAUSE YOUR KIND...
IS ALWAYS CAUSING US TROUBLE.
PENGUINS MARCHING
KING PENGUINS WORK MUCH HARDER AT THE ZOO.

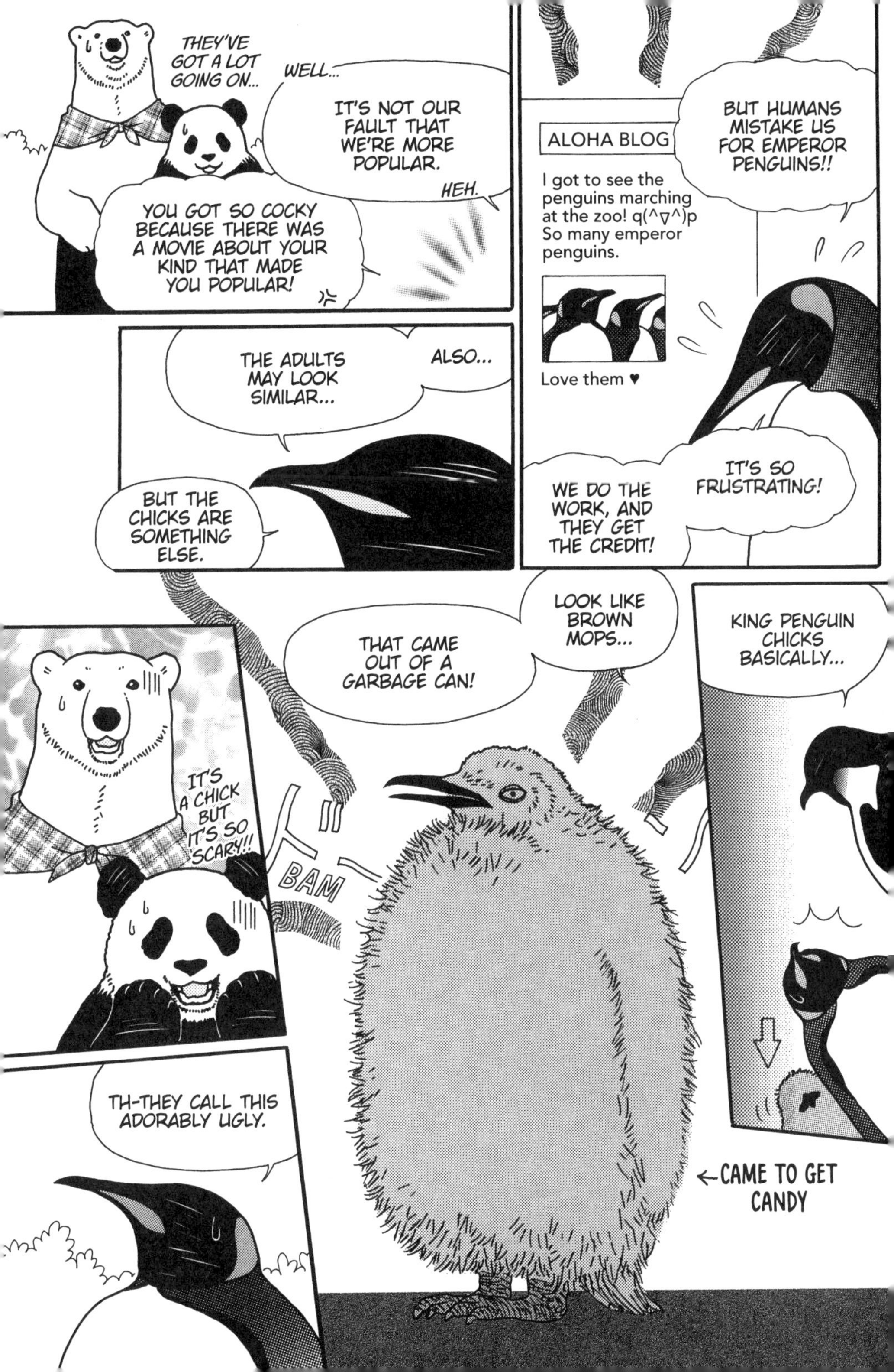
BUT HUMANS MISTAKE US FOR EMPEROR PENGUINS!!
ALOHA BLOG
I got to see the penguins marching at the zoo! q(^▽^)p So many emperor penguins.
Love them ♥
IT'S SO FRUSTRATING!
WE DO THE WORK, AND THEY GET THE CREDIT!
WELL...
IT'S NOT OUR FAULT THAT WE'RE MORE POPULAR.
HEH.
THEY'VE GOT A LOT GOING ON...
YOU GOT SO COCKY BECAUSE THERE WAS A MOVIE ABOUT YOUR KIND THAT MADE YOU POPULAR!
ALSO...
THE ADULTS MAY LOOK SIMILAR...
BUT THE CHICKS ARE SOMETHING ELSE.
KING PENGUIN CHICKS BASICALLY...
LOOK LIKE BROWN MOPS...
THAT CAME OUT OF A GARBAGE CAN!
BAM
←CAME TO GET CANDY
IT'S A CHICK BUT IT'S SO SCARY!!
TH-THEY CALL THIS ADORABLY UGLY.

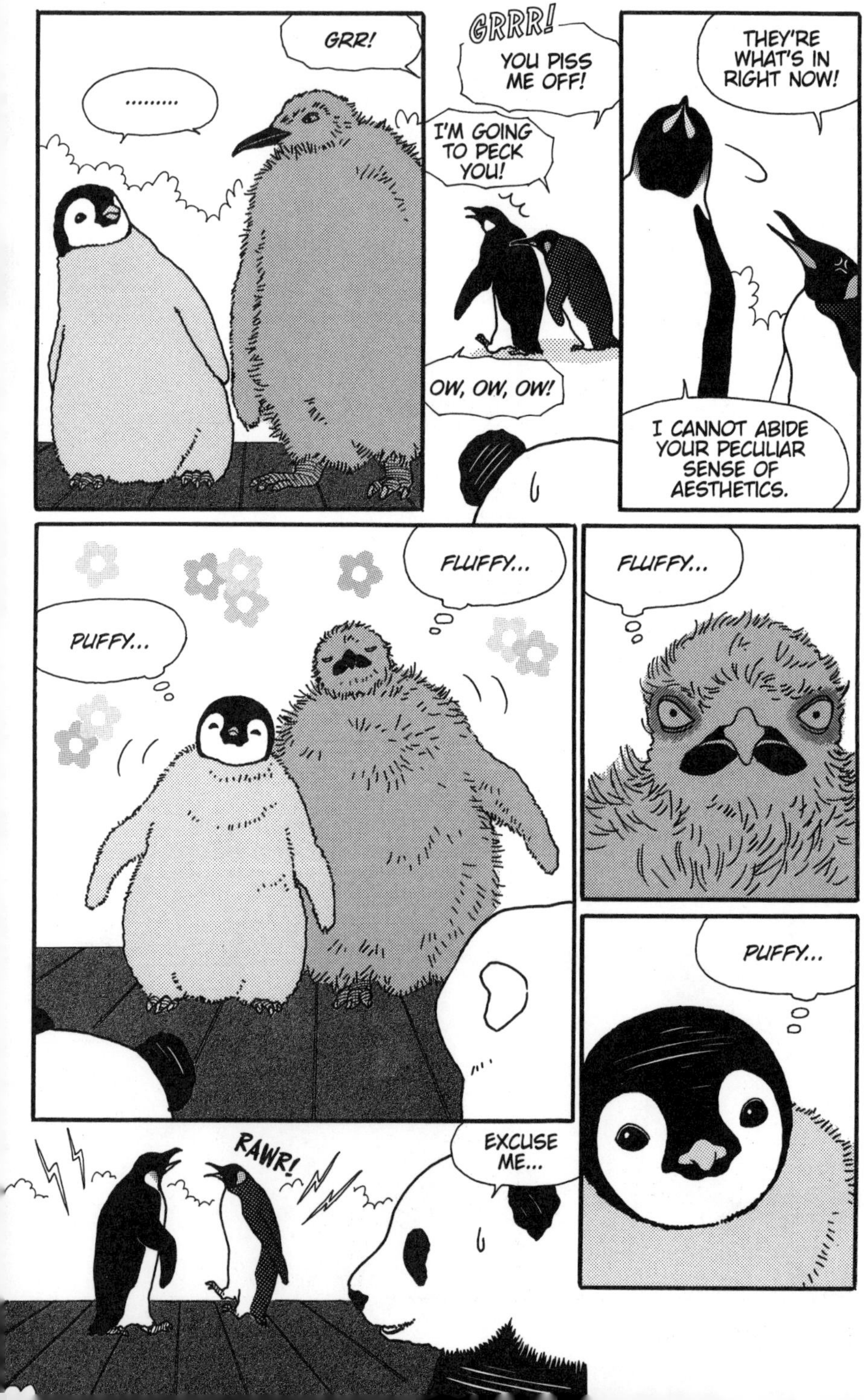
THEY'RE WHAT'S IN RIGHT NOW!
I CANNOT ABIDE YOUR PECULIAR SENSE OF AESTHETICS.
GRRR!
YOU PISS ME OFF!
I'M GOING TO PECK YOU!
OW, OW, OW!
GRR!
....
FLUFFY...
PUFFY...
FLUFFY...
PUFFY...
EXCUSE ME...
RAWR!

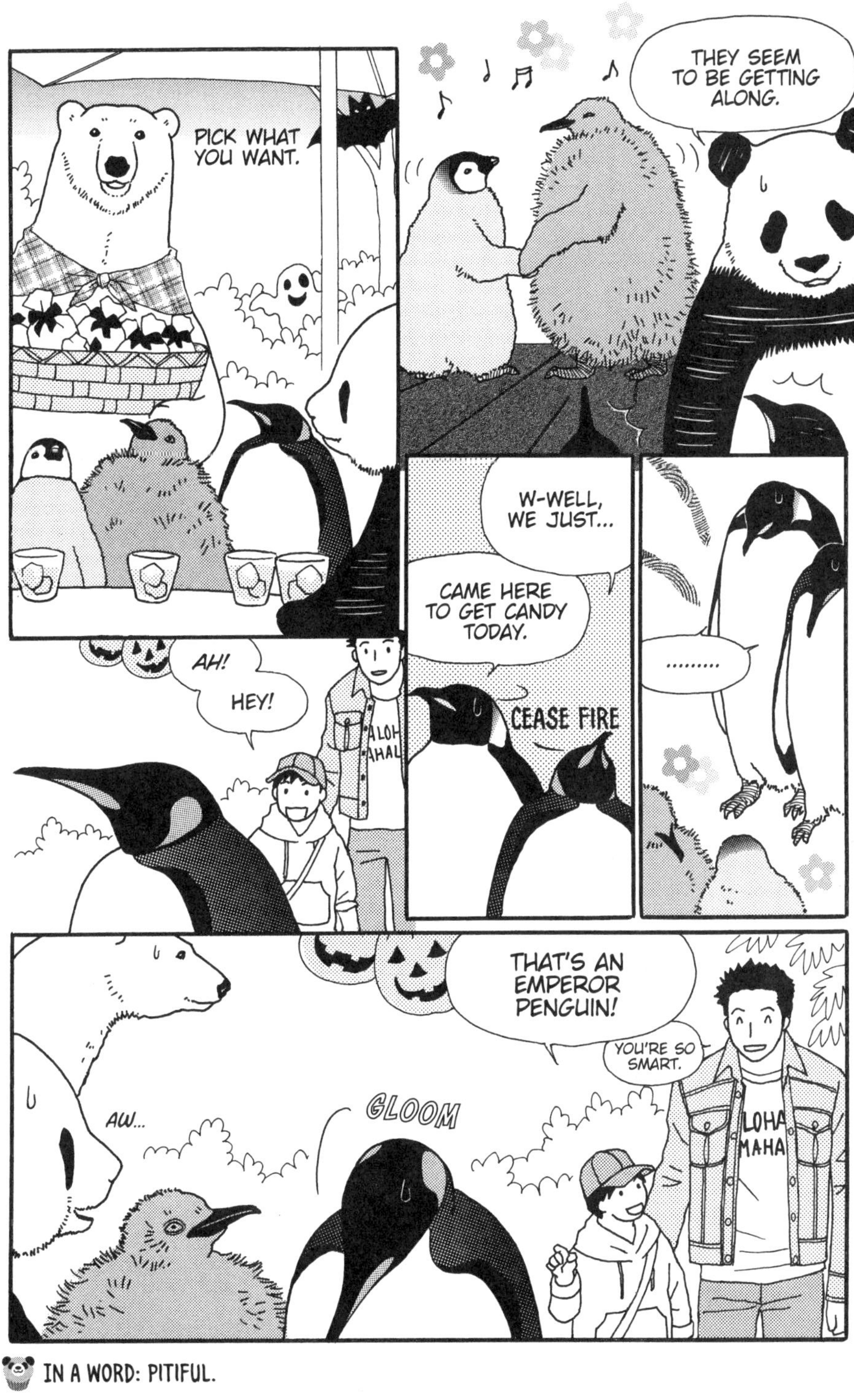
THEY SEEM TO BE GETTING ALONG.
PICK WHAT YOU WANT.
....
W-WELL, WE JUST...
CAME HERE TO GET CANDY TODAY.
CEASE FIRE
ALOHA MAHAL
AH!
HEY!
THAT'S AN EMPEROR PENGUIN!
YOU'RE SO SMART.
ALOHA MAHA
GLOOM
AW...

IN A WORD: PITIFUL.

DOSUKOI!

Polar Bear Café

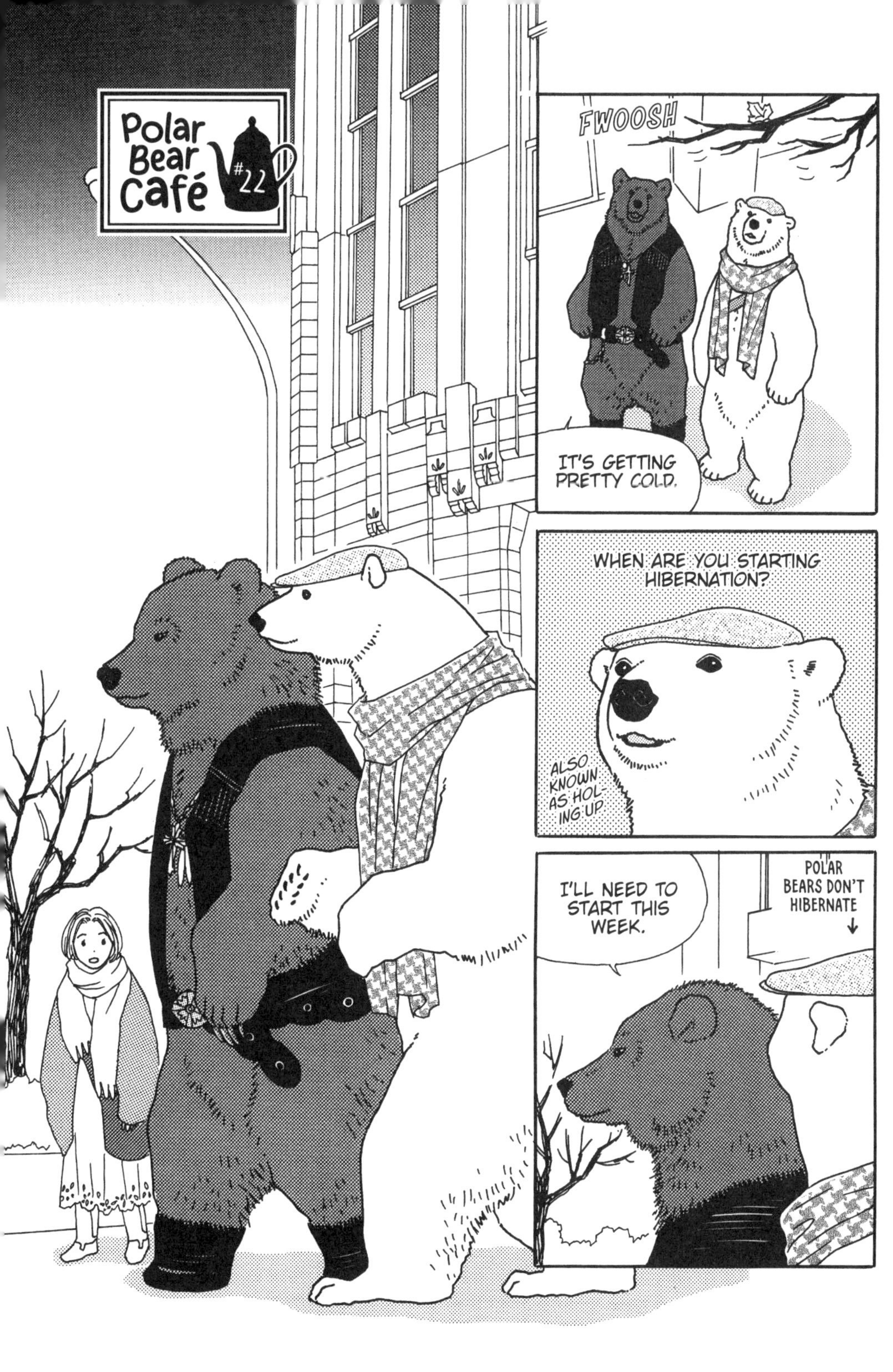
FWOOSH
IT'S GETTING PRETTY COLD.
WHEN ARE YOU STARTING HIBERNATION?
ALSO KNOWN AS HOL-ING UP
I'LL NEED TO START THIS WEEK.
POLAR BEARS DON'T HIBERNATE ↓
Polar Bear Café
#22

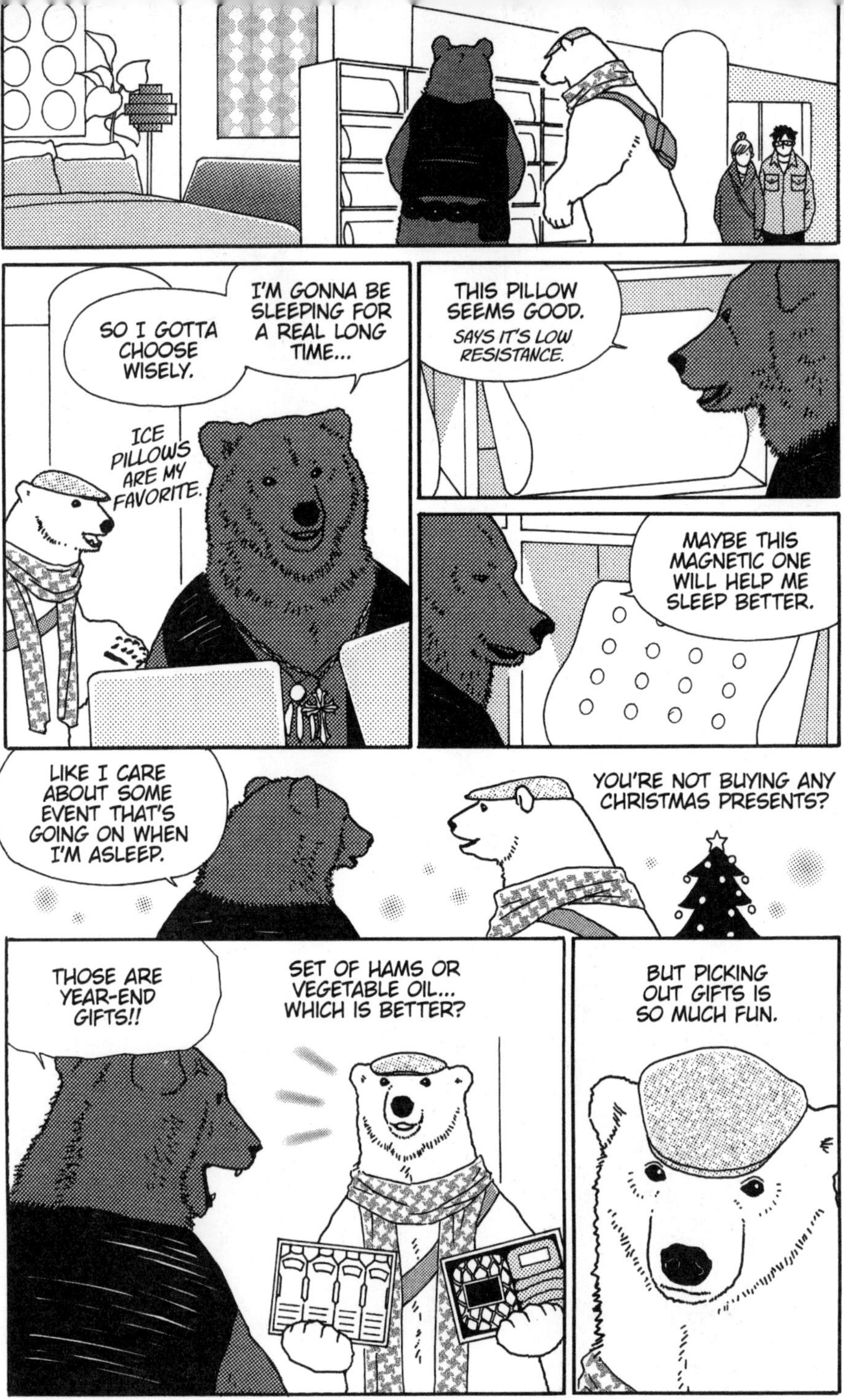
THIS PILLOW SEEMS GOOD.
SAYS IT'S LOW RESISTANCE.
MAYBE THIS MAGNETIC ONE WILL HELP ME SLEEP BETTER.
I'M GONNA BE SLEEPING FOR A REAL LONG TIME...
SO I GOTTA CHOOSE WISELY.
ICE PILLOWS ARE MY FAVORITE.
YOU'RE NOT BUYING ANY CHRISTMAS PRESENTS?
LIKE I CARE ABOUT SOME EVENT THAT'S GOING ON WHEN I'M ASLEEP.
BUT PICKING OUT GIFTS IS SO MUCH FUN.
SET OF HAMS OR VEGETABLE OIL... WHICH IS BETTER?
THOSE ARE YEAR-END GIFTS!!

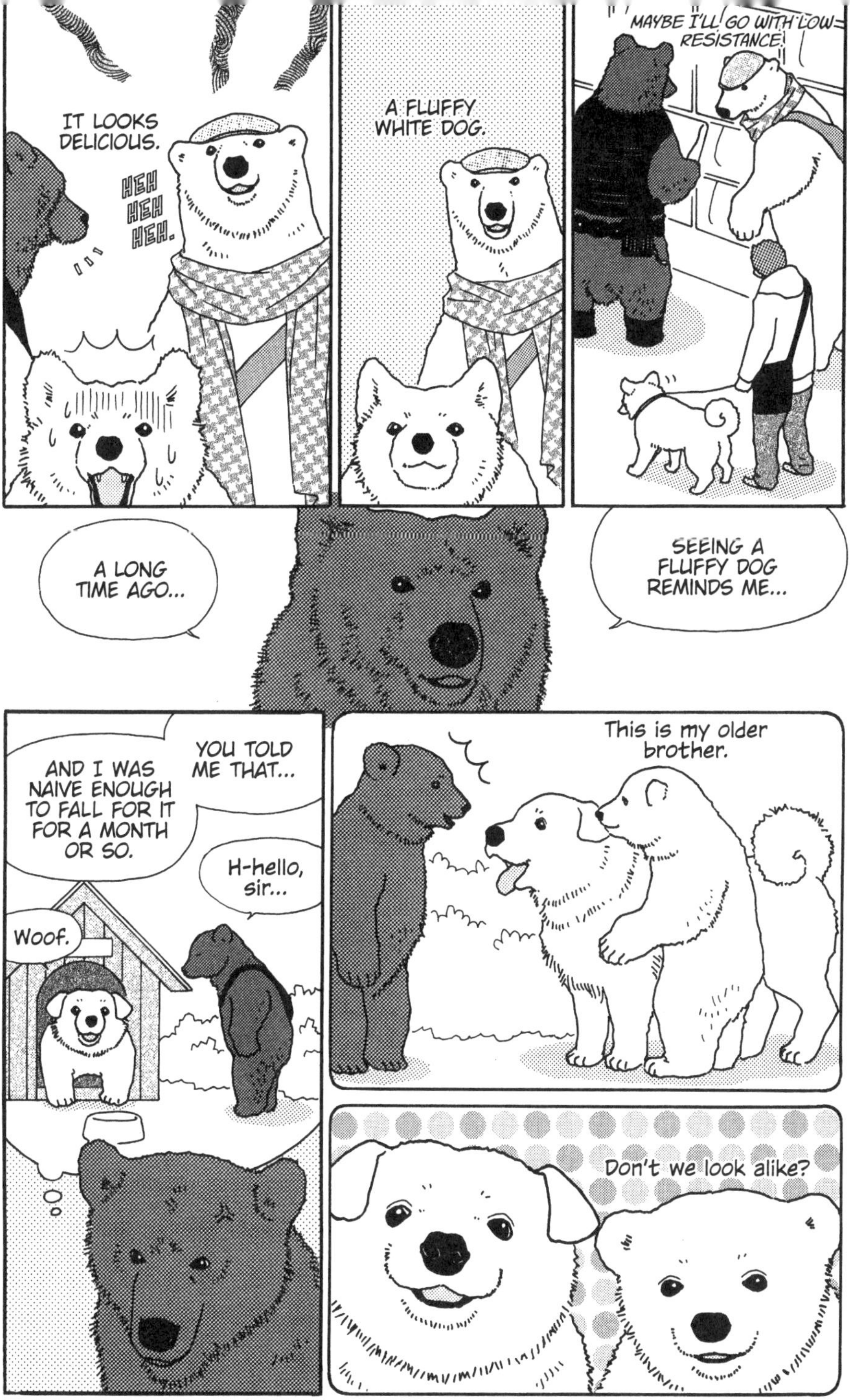
MAYBE I'LL GO WITH LOW-RESISTANCE.
A FLUFFY WHITE DOG.
IT LOOKS DELICIOUS.
HEH HEH HEH.
SEEING A FLUFFY DOG REMINDS ME...
A LONG TIME AGO...
This is my older brother.
Don't we look alike?
YOU TOLD ME THAT...
AND I WAS NAIVE ENOUGH TO FALL FOR IT FOR A MONTH OR SO.
H-hello, sir...
Woof.

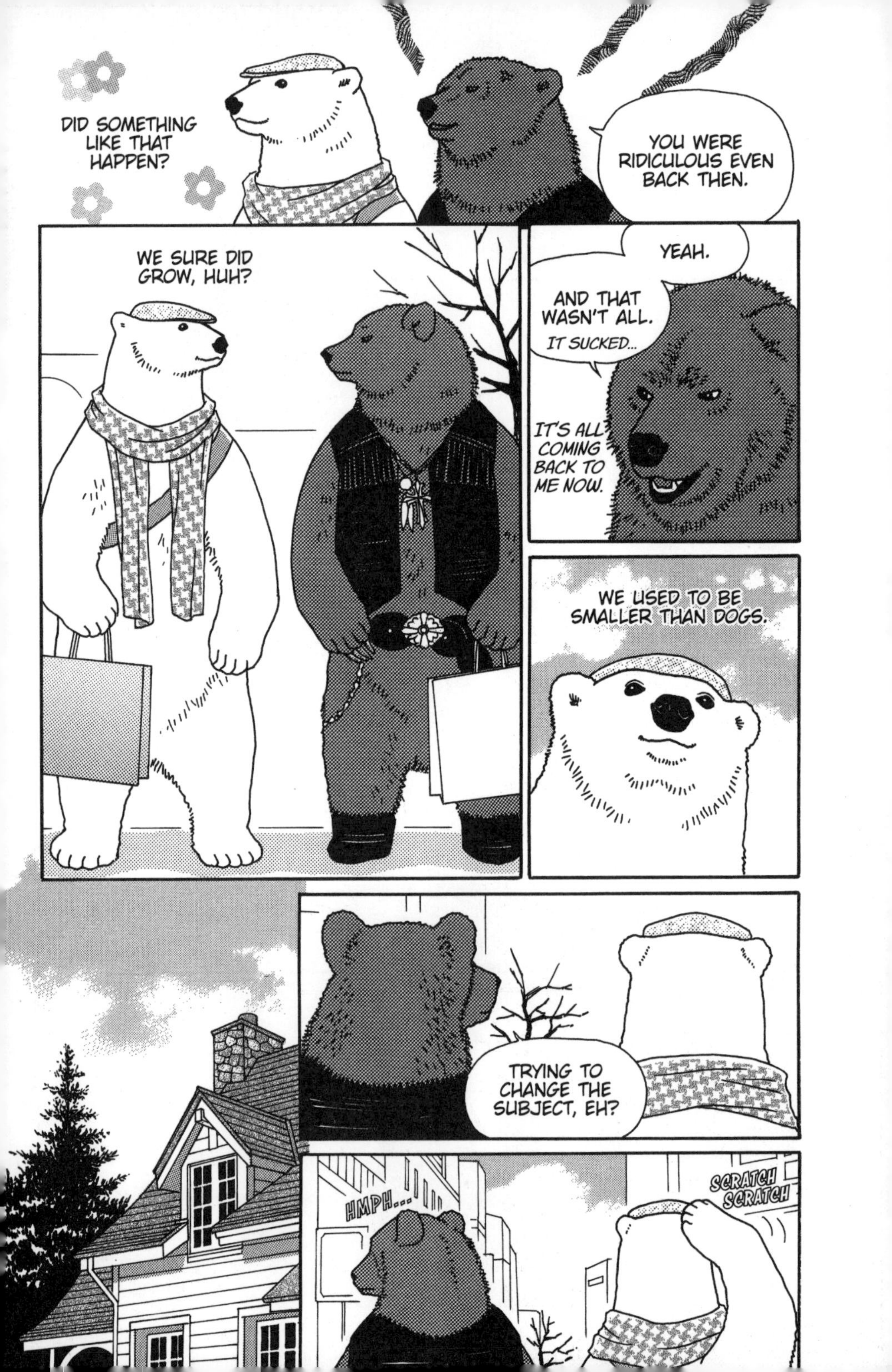
YOU WERE RIDICULOUS EVEN BACK THEN.
DID SOMETHING LIKE THAT HAPPEN?
YEAH.
AND THAT WASN'T ALL. IT SUCKED...
IT'S ALL COMING BACK TO ME NOW.
WE USED TO BE SMALLER THAN DOGS.
WE SURE DID GROW, HUH?
TRYING TO CHANGE THE SUBJECT, EH?
SCRATCH SCRATCH
HMPH...

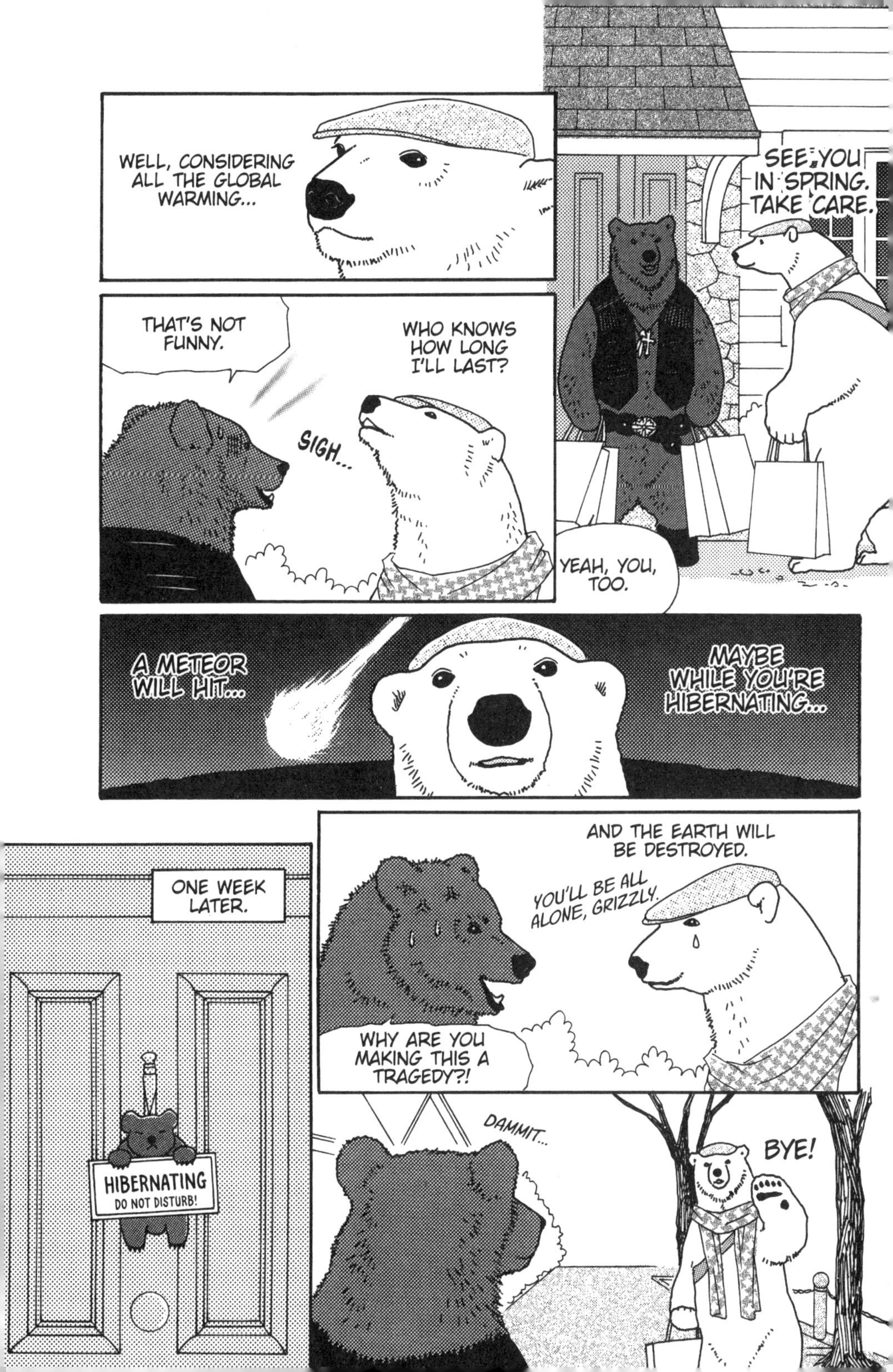
SEE YOU IN SPRING. TAKE CARE.
YEAH, YOU, TOO.
WELL, CONSIDERING ALL THE GLOBAL WARMING...
WHO KNOWS HOW LONG I'LL LAST?
SIGH...
THAT'S NOT FUNNY.
MAYBE WHILE YOU'RE HIBERNATING...
A METEOR WILL HIT...
AND THE EARTH WILL BE DESTROYED.
YOU'LL BE ALL ALONE, GRIZZLY.
WHY ARE YOU MAKING THIS A TRAGEDY?!
BYE!
DAMMIT...
ONE WEEK LATER.
HIBERNATING
DO NOT DISTURB!

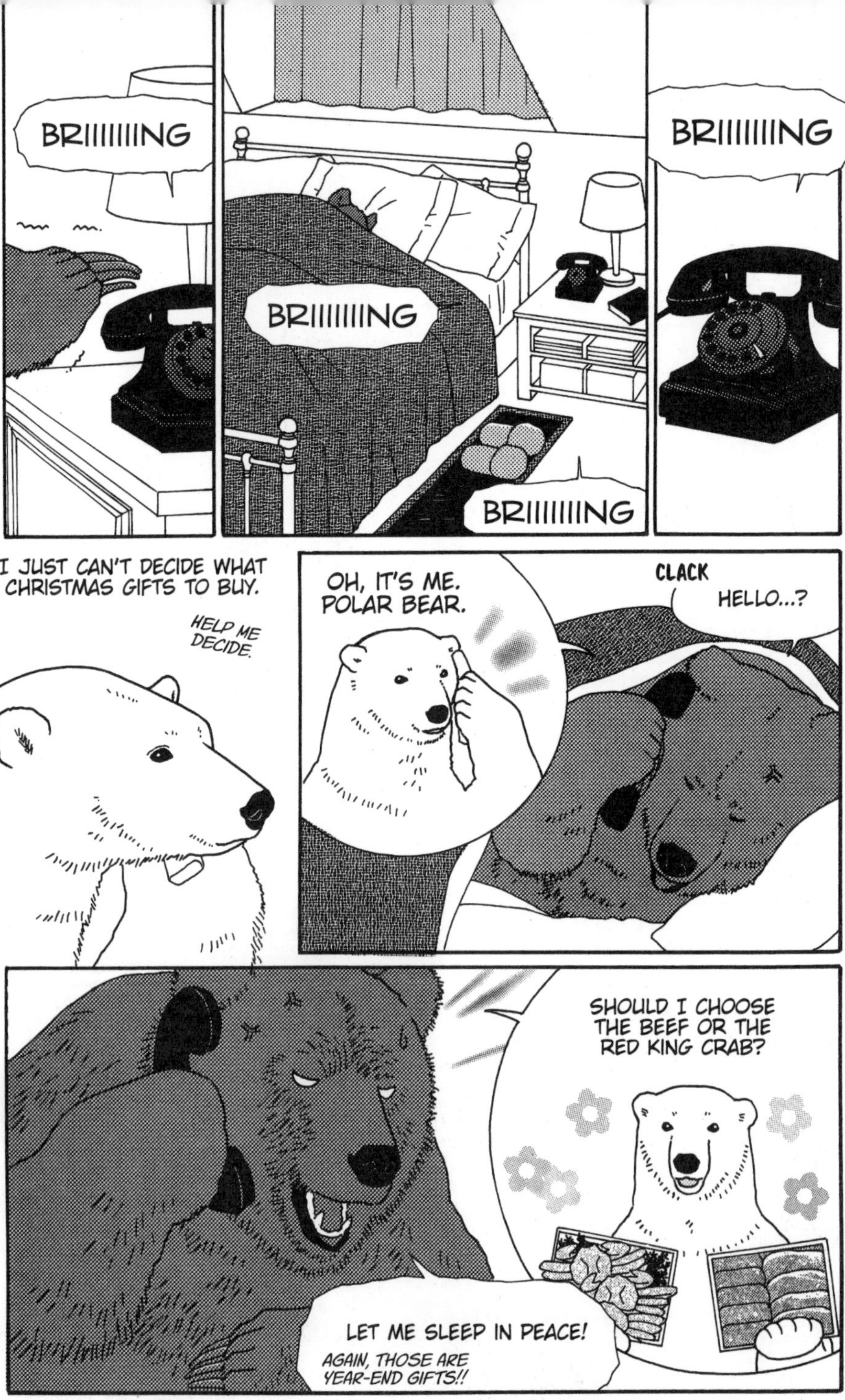
BRIIIIIIING
BRIIIIIIING
BRIIIIIIING
BRIIIIIIING
CLACK
HELLO...?
OH, IT'S ME. POLAR BEAR.
I JUST CAN'T DECIDE WHAT CHRISTMAS GIFTS TO BUY.
HELP ME DECIDE.
SHOULD I CHOOSE THE BEEF OR THE RED KING CRAB?
LET ME SLEEP IN PEACE!
AGAIN, THOSE ARE YEAR-END GIFTS!!

HE JUST LOVES GRIZZLY-SAN SO MUCH...♡

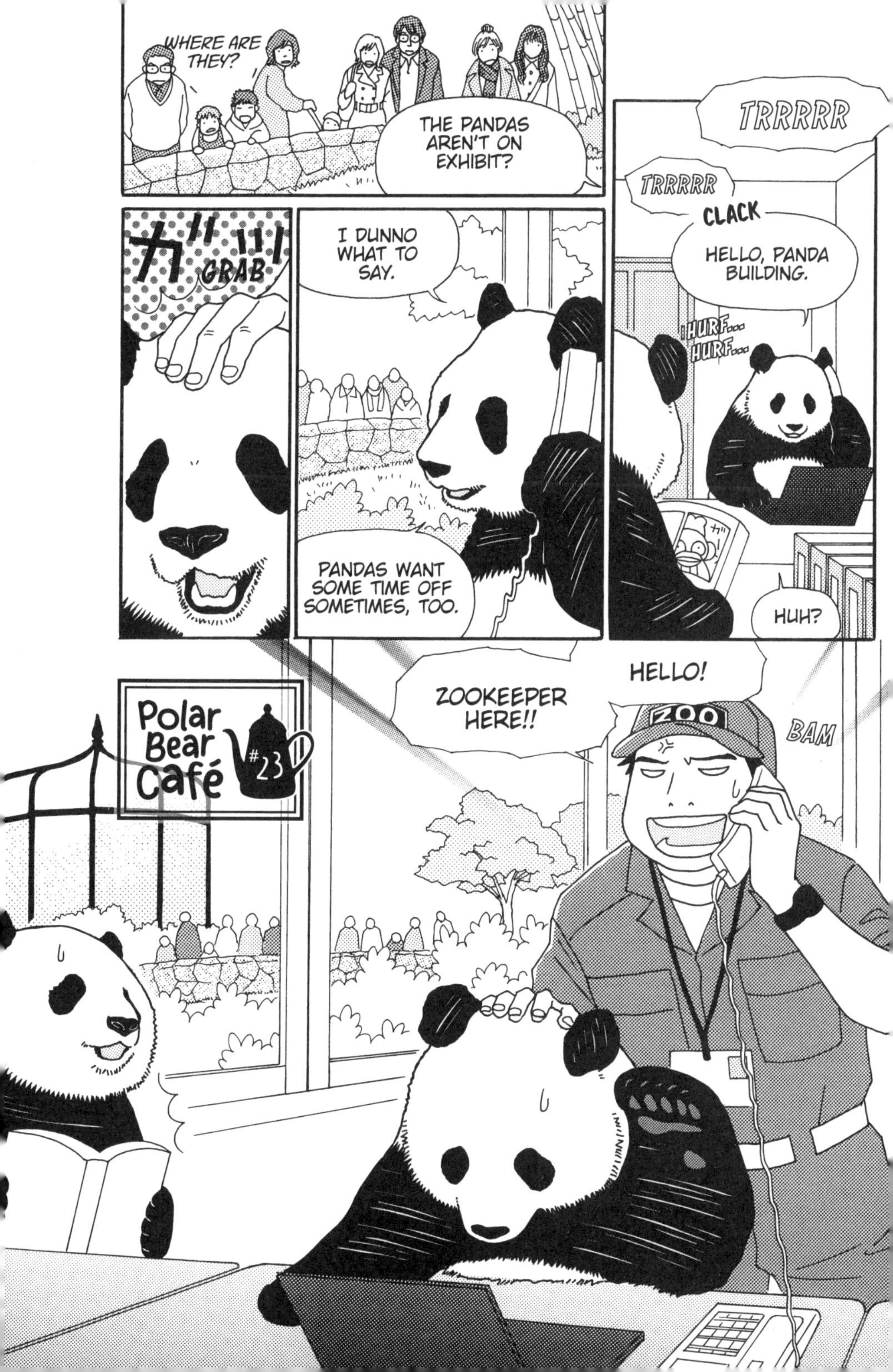
WHERE ARE THEY?
THE PANDAS AREN'T ON EXHIBIT?
TRRRRR
TRRRRR
CLACK
HELLO, PANDA BUILDING.
HURF... HURF...
HUH?
I DUNNO WHAT TO SAY.
PANDAS WANT SOME TIME OFF SOMETIMES, TOO.
カ゛ッ
GRAB
Polar Bear Café #23
HELLO!
ZOOKEEPER HERE!!
ZOO
BAM

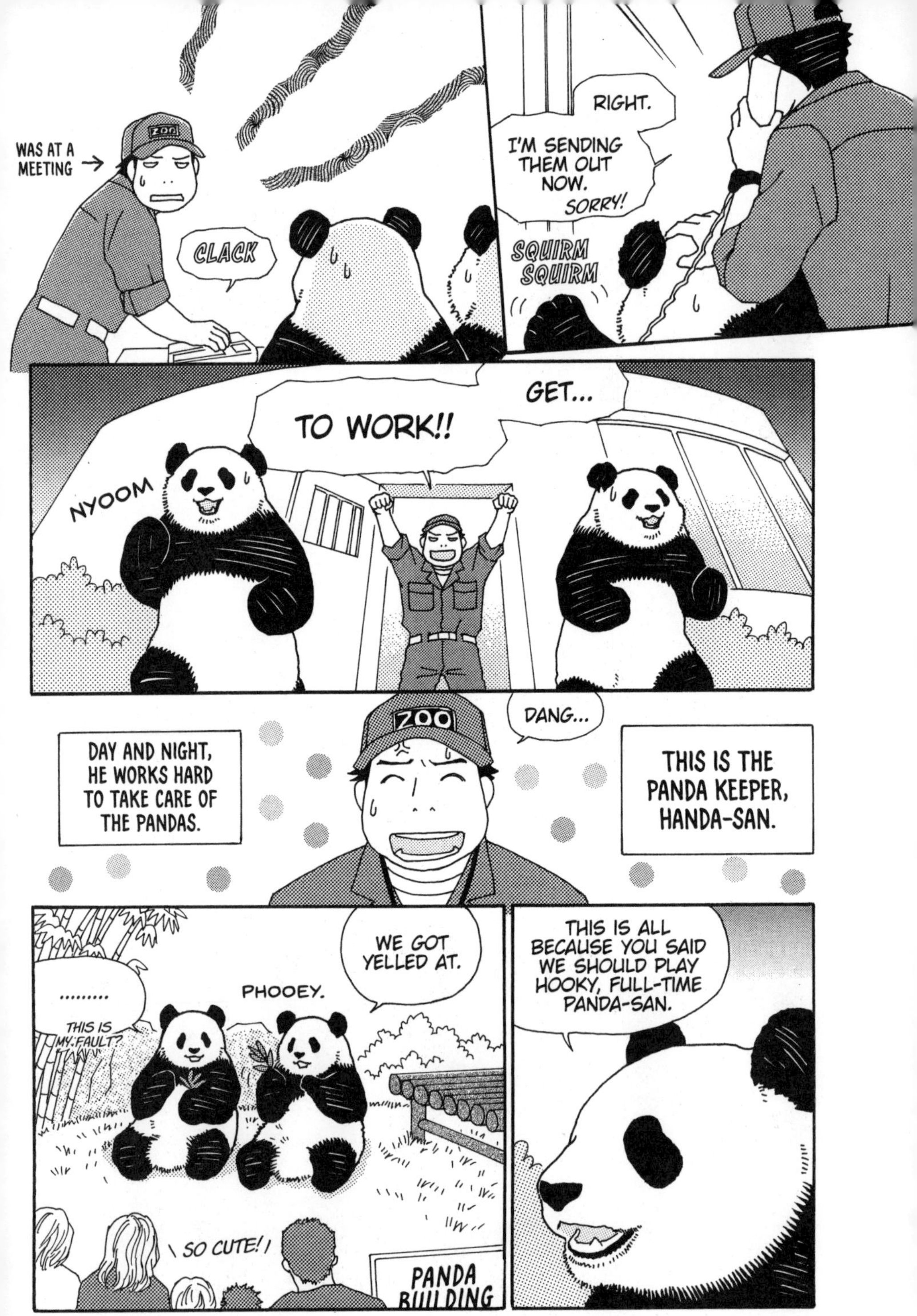
RIGHT.
I'M SENDING THEM OUT NOW.
SORRY!
SQUIRM SQUIRM
WAS AT A MEETING →
CLACK
GET...
TO WORK!!
NYOOM
DANG...
THIS IS THE PANDA KEEPER, HANDA-SAN.
DAY AND NIGHT, HE WORKS HARD TO TAKE CARE OF THE PANDAS.
THIS IS ALL BECAUSE YOU SAID WE SHOULD PLAY HOOKY, FULL-TIME PANDA-SAN.
WE GOT YELLED AT.
PHOOEY.
....
THIS IS MY FAULT?
SO CUTE!
PANDA BUILDING

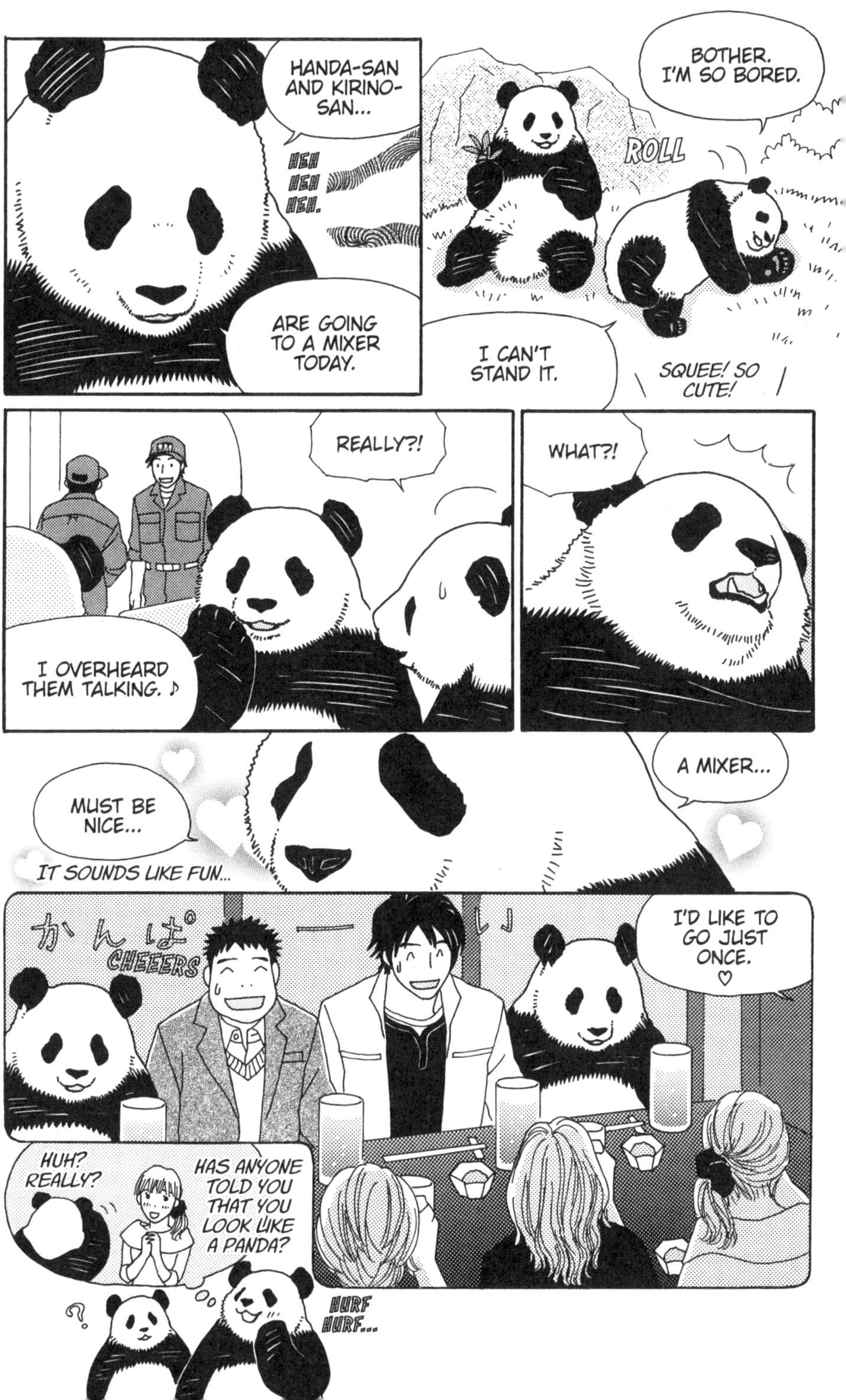
BOTHER. I'M SO BORED.
ROLL
I CAN'T STAND IT.
SQUEE! SO CUTE!
HANDA-SAN AND KIRINO-SAN...
HEH HEH HEH.
ARE GOING TO A MIXER TODAY.
WHAT?!
REALLY?!
I OVERHEARD THEM TALKING. ♪
A MIXER...
MUST BE NICE...
IT SOUNDS LIKE FUN...
I'D LIKE TO GO JUST ONCE. ♡
かんぱーーい
CHEEERS
HAS ANYONE TOLD YOU THAT YOU LOOK LIKE A PANDA?
HUH? REALLY?
HURF HURF...
?

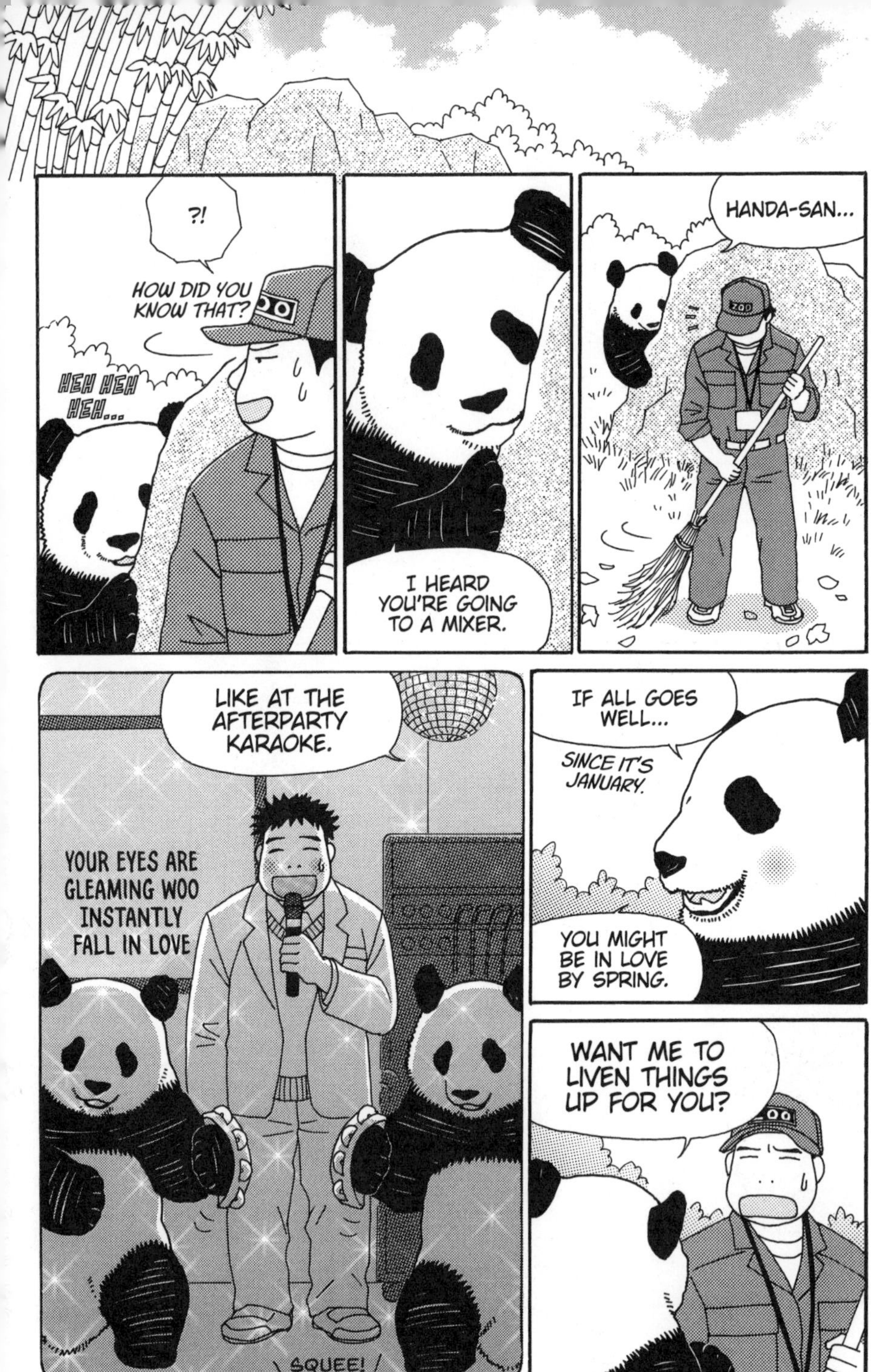
HANDA-SAN...
I HEARD YOU'RE GOING TO A MIXER.
?!
HOW DID YOU KNOW THAT?
HEH HEH HEH...
IF ALL GOES WELL...
SINCE IT'S JANUARY.
YOU MIGHT BE IN LOVE BY SPRING.
WANT ME TO LIVEN THINGS UP FOR YOU?
LIKE AT THE AFTERPARTY KARAOKE.
YOUR EYES ARE GLEAMING WOO INSTANTLY FALL IN LOVE
SQUEE!

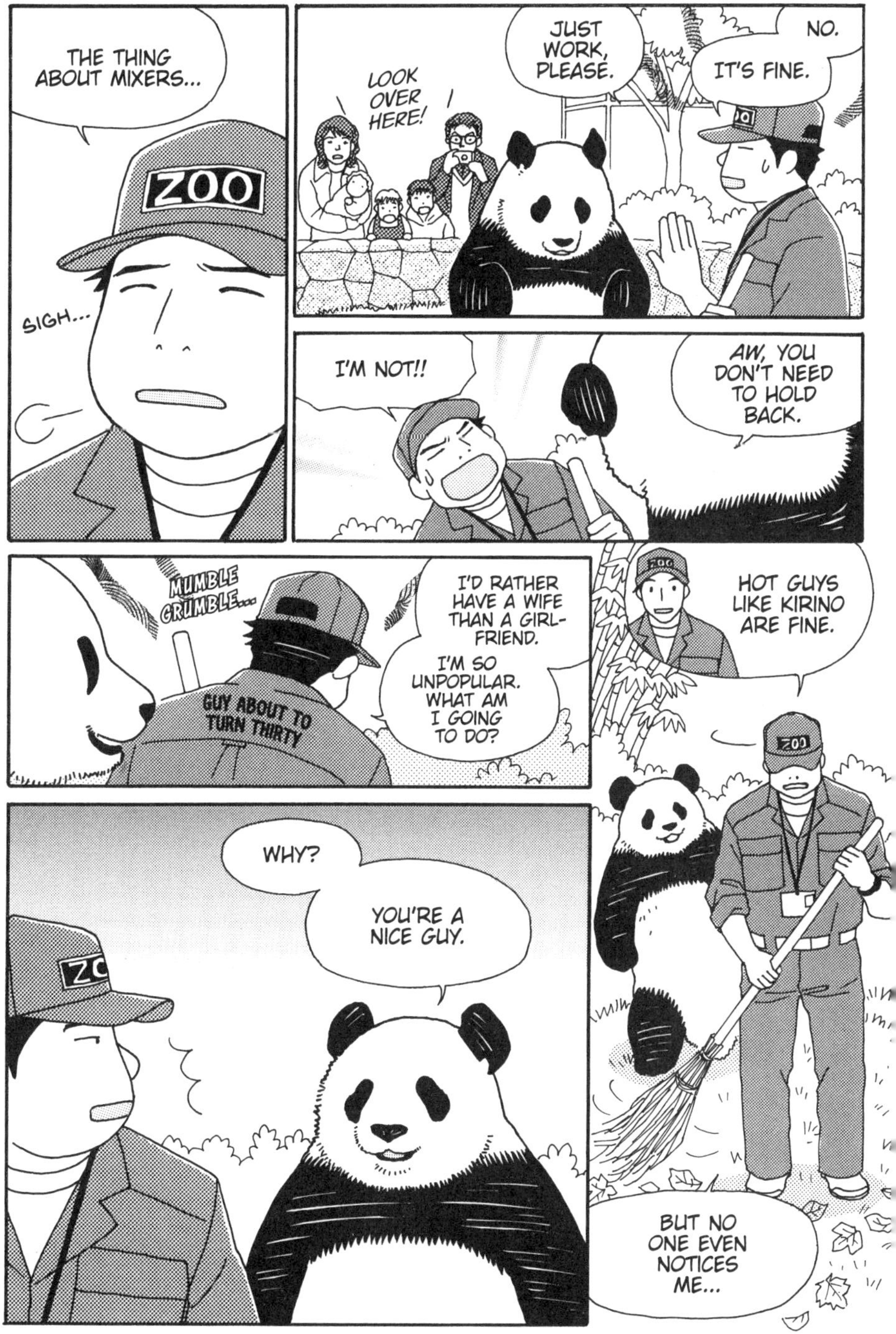
NO.
IT'S FINE.
JUST WORK, PLEASE.
LOOK OVER HERE!
AW, YOU DON'T NEED TO HOLD BACK.
I'M NOT!!
THE THING ABOUT MIXERS...
SIGH...
HOT GUYS LIKE KIRINO ARE FINE.
BUT NO ONE EVEN NOTICES ME...
I'D RATHER HAVE A WIFE THAN A GIRL-FRIEND.
I'M SO UNPOPULAR. WHAT AM I GOING TO DO?
MUMBLE GRUMBLE...
GUY ABOUT TO TURN THIRTY
WHY?
YOU'RE A NICE GUY.

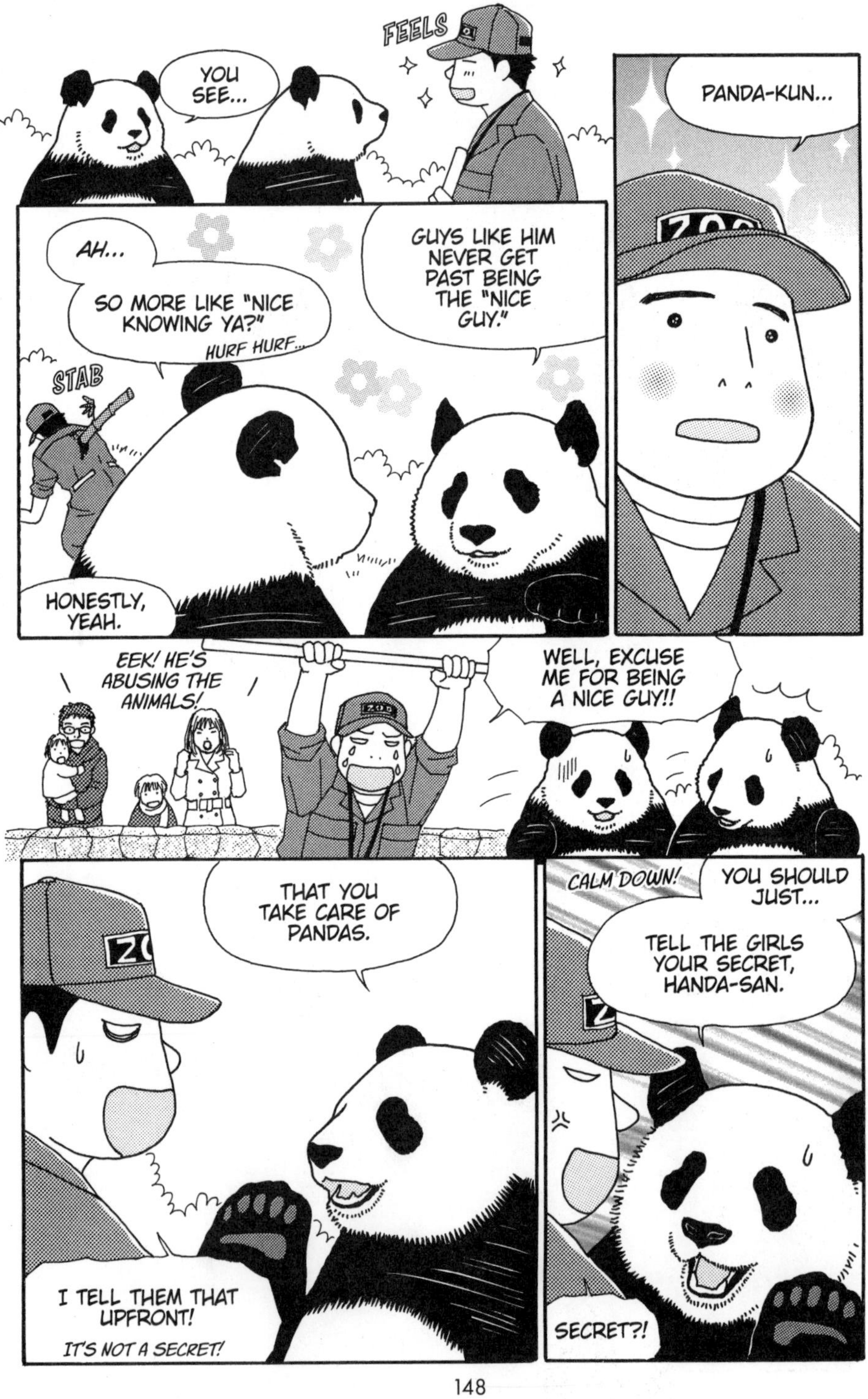
PANDA-KUN...
YOU SEE...
FEELS
GUYS LIKE HIM NEVER GET PAST BEING THE "NICE GUY."
AH...
SO MORE LIKE "NICE KNOWING YA?"
HURF HURF...
STAB
HONESTLY, YEAH.
WELL, EXCUSE ME FOR BEING A NICE GUY!!
EEK! HE'S ABUSING THE ANIMALS!
YOU SHOULD JUST...
CALM DOWN!
TELL THE GIRLS YOUR SECRET, HANDA-SAN.
SECRET?!
THAT YOU TAKE CARE OF PANDAS.
I TELL THEM THAT UPFRONT!
IT'S NOT A SECRET!

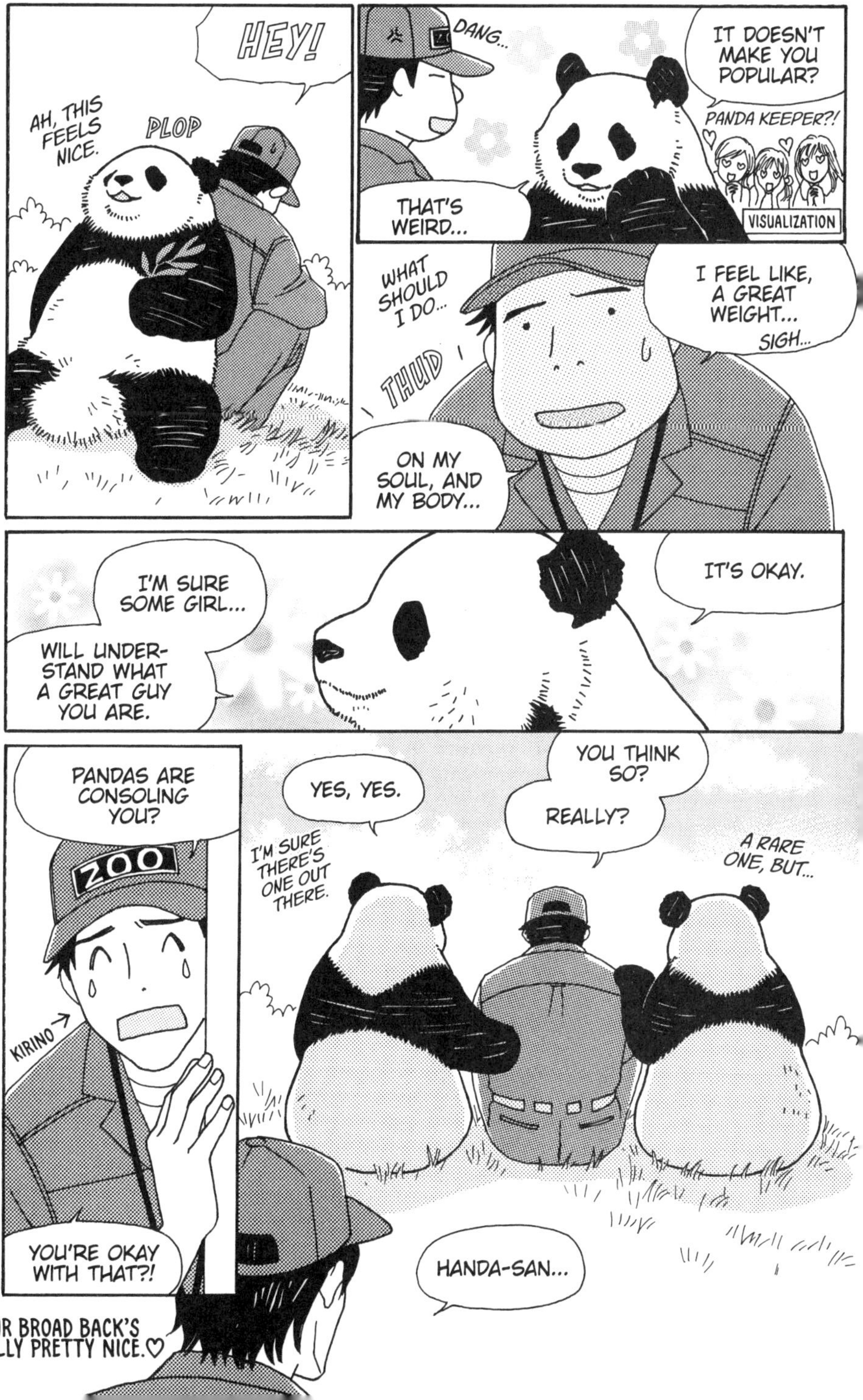
IT DOESN'T MAKE YOU POPULAR?
PANDA KEEPER?!
VISUALIZATION
DANG...
THAT'S WEIRD...
I FEEL LIKE, A GREAT WEIGHT...
SIGH...
WHAT SHOULD I DO...
THUD
ON MY SOUL, AND MY BODY...
HEY!
PLOP
AH, THIS FEELS NICE.
IT'S OKAY.
I'M SURE SOME GIRL...
WILL UNDER-STAND WHAT A GREAT GUY YOU ARE.
YOU THINK SO?
REALLY?
A RARE ONE, BUT...
YES, YES.
I'M SURE THERE'S ONE OUT THERE.
HANDA-SAN...
PANDAS ARE CONSOLING YOU?
ZOO
KIRINO→
YOU'RE OKAY WITH THAT?!

YOUR BROAD BACK'S ACTUALLY PRETTY NICE.♡

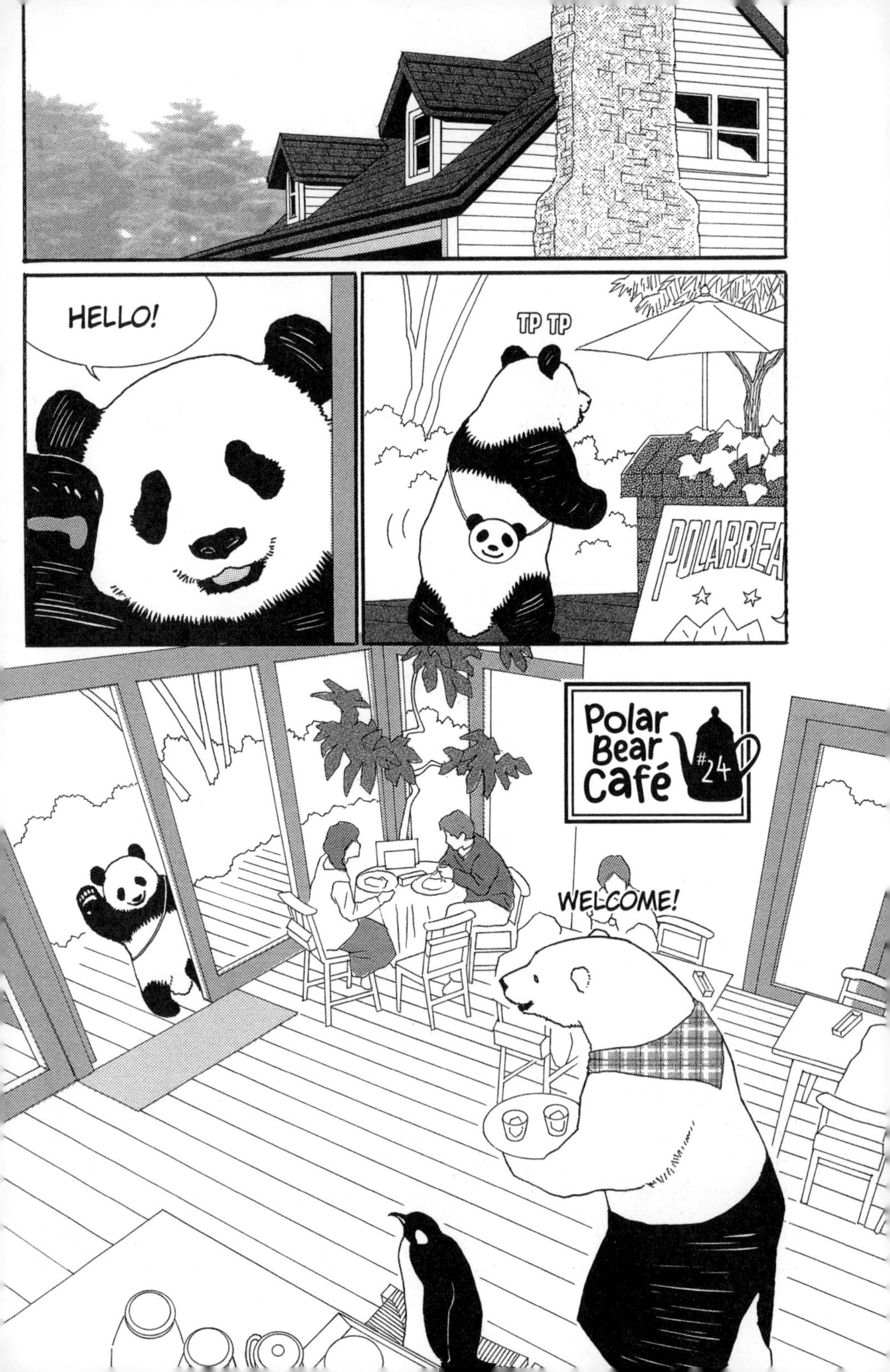
TP TP
HELLO!
Polar Bear Café
#24
WELCOME!

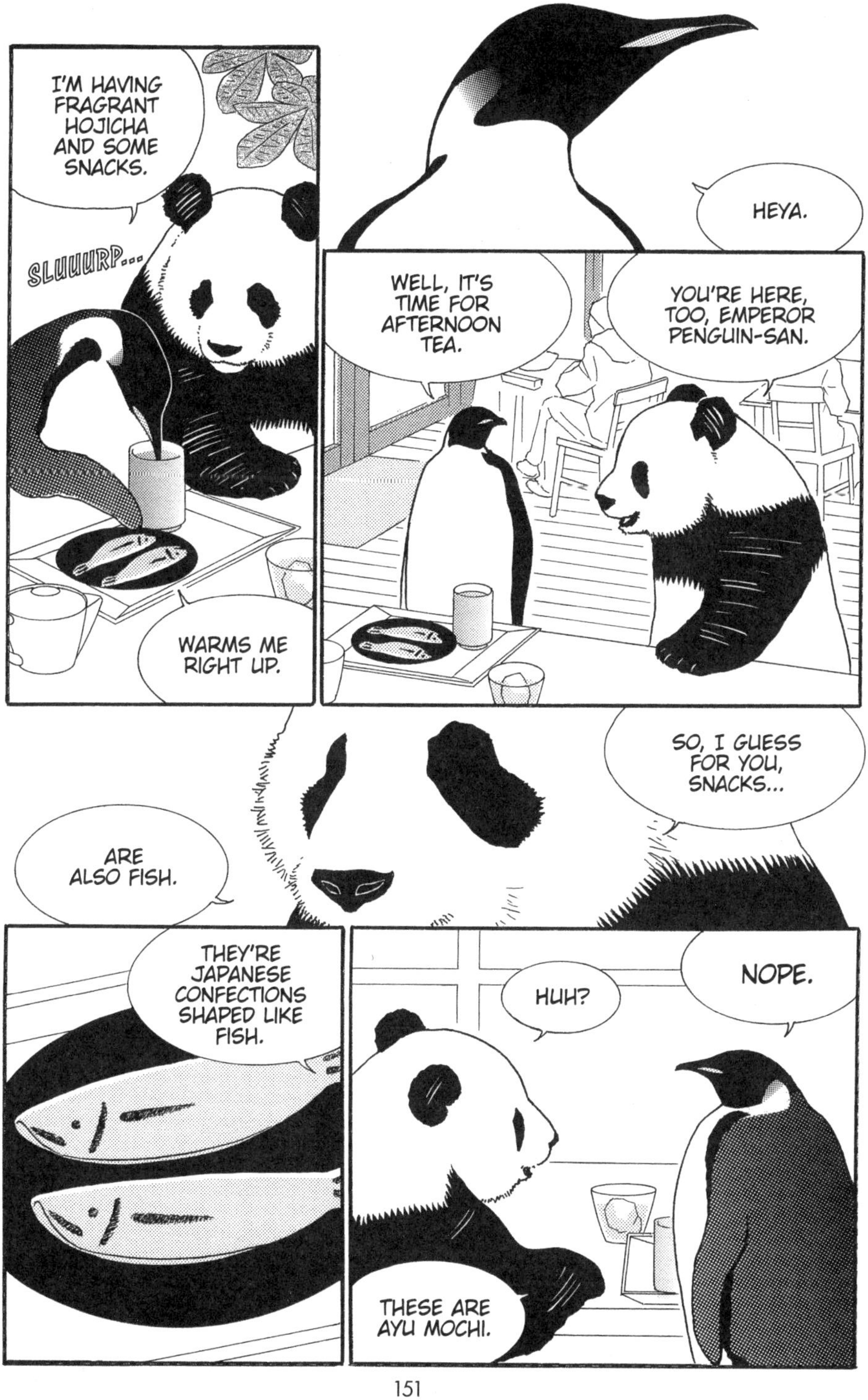
HEYA.
YOU'RE HERE, TOO, EMPEROR PENGUIN-SAN.
WELL, IT'S TIME FOR AFTERNOON TEA.
I'M HAVING FRAGRANT HOJICHA AND SOME SNACKS.
SLUUURP...
WARMS ME RIGHT UP.
SO, I GUESS FOR YOU, SNACKS...
ARE ALSO FISH.
NOPE.
HUH?
THESE ARE AYU MOCHI.
THEY'RE JAPANESE CONFECTIONS SHAPED LIKE FISH.

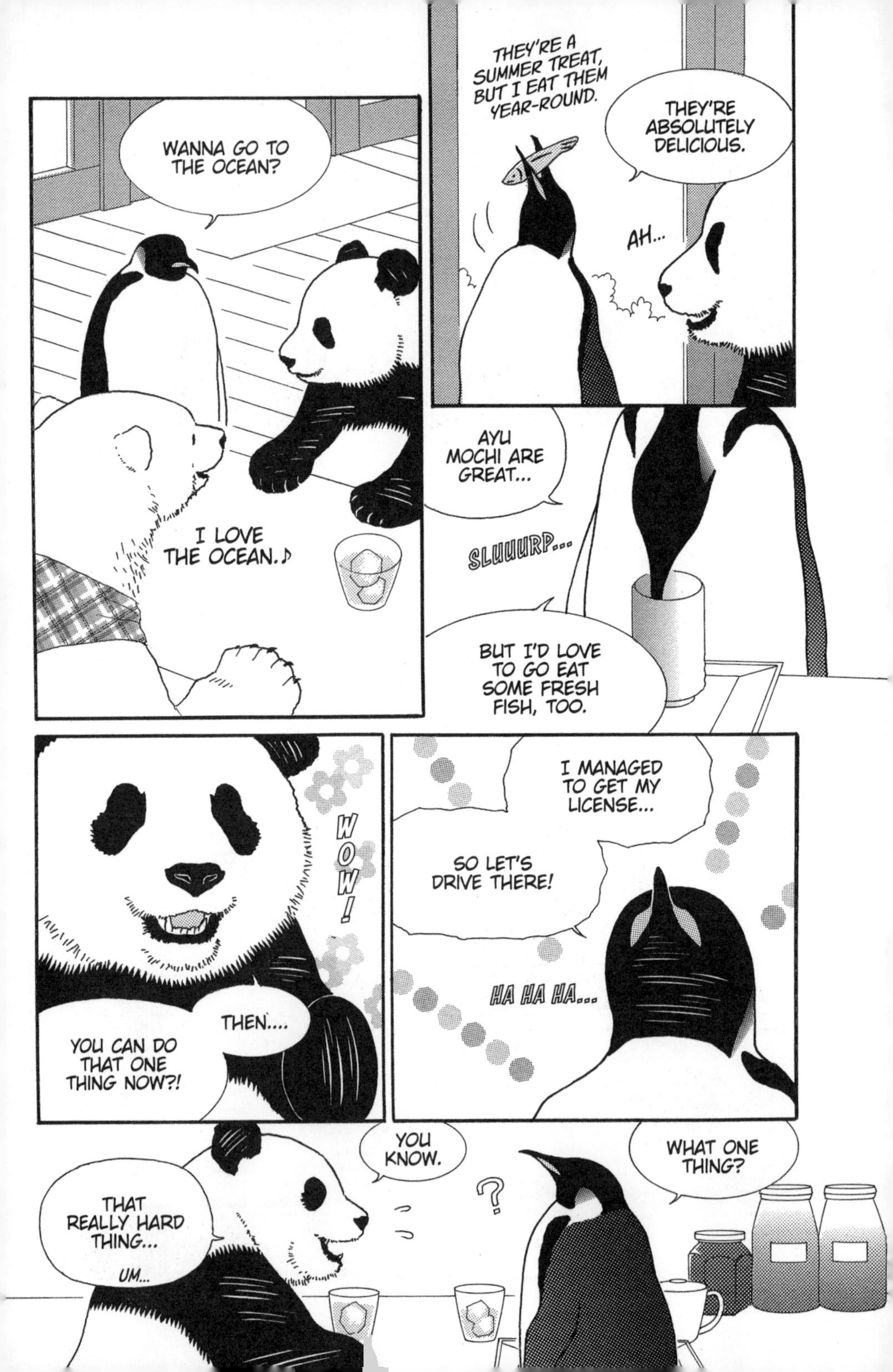
THEY'RE ABSOLUTELY DELICIOUS.
THEY'RE A SUMMER TREAT, BUT I EAT THEM YEAR-ROUND.
AH...
AYU MOCHI ARE GREAT...
SLUUURP...
BUT I'D LOVE TO GO EAT SOME FRESH FISH, TOO.
WANNA GO TO THE OCEAN?
I LOVE THE OCEAN.♪
I MANAGED TO GET MY LICENSE...
SO LET'S DRIVE THERE!
HA HA HA...
WOW!
THEN....
YOU CAN DO THAT ONE THING NOW?!
WHAT ONE THING?
?
YOU KNOW.
THAT REALLY HARD THING...
UM...

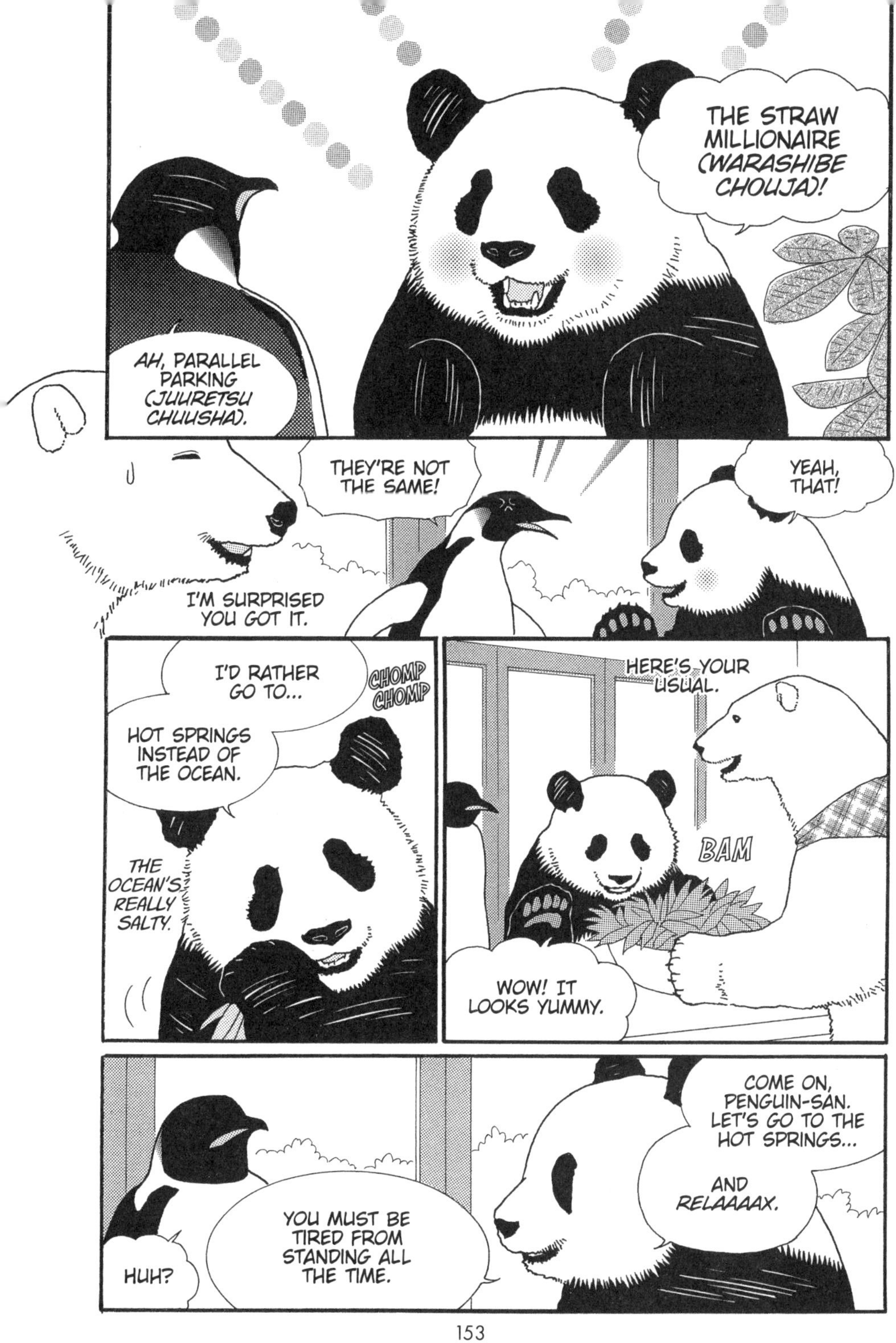
THE STRAW MILLIONAIRE (WARASHIBE CHOUJA)!
AH, PARALLEL PARKING (JUURETSU CHUUSHA).
YEAH, THAT!
THEY'RE NOT THE SAME!
I'M SURPRISED YOU GOT IT.
HERE'S YOUR USUAL.
BAM
WOW! IT LOOKS YUMMY.
CHOMP CHOMP
I'D RATHER GO TO...
HOT SPRINGS INSTEAD OF THE OCEAN.
THE OCEAN'S REALLY SALTY.
COME ON, PENGUIN-SAN. LET'S GO TO THE HOT SPRINGS...
AND RELAAAAX.
YOU MUST BE TIRED FROM STANDING ALL THE TIME.
HUH?

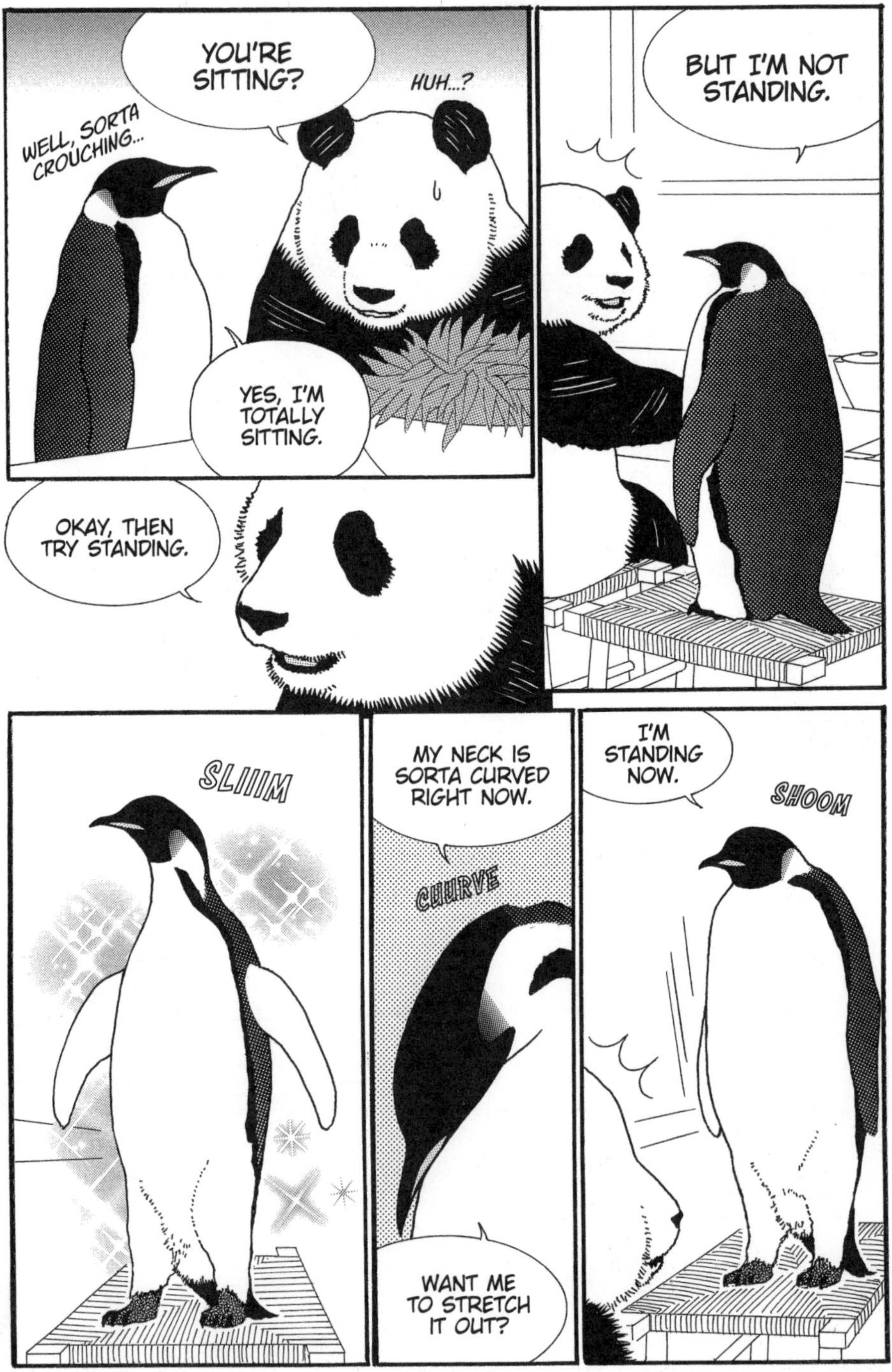
BUT I'M NOT STANDING.
YOU'RE SITTING?
HUH...?
WELL, SORTA CROUCHING...
YES, I'M TOTALLY SITTING.
OKAY, THEN TRY STANDING.
I'M STANDING NOW.
SHOOM
MY NECK IS SORTA CURVED RIGHT NOW.
CUURVE
WANT ME TO STRETCH IT OUT?
SLIIIM

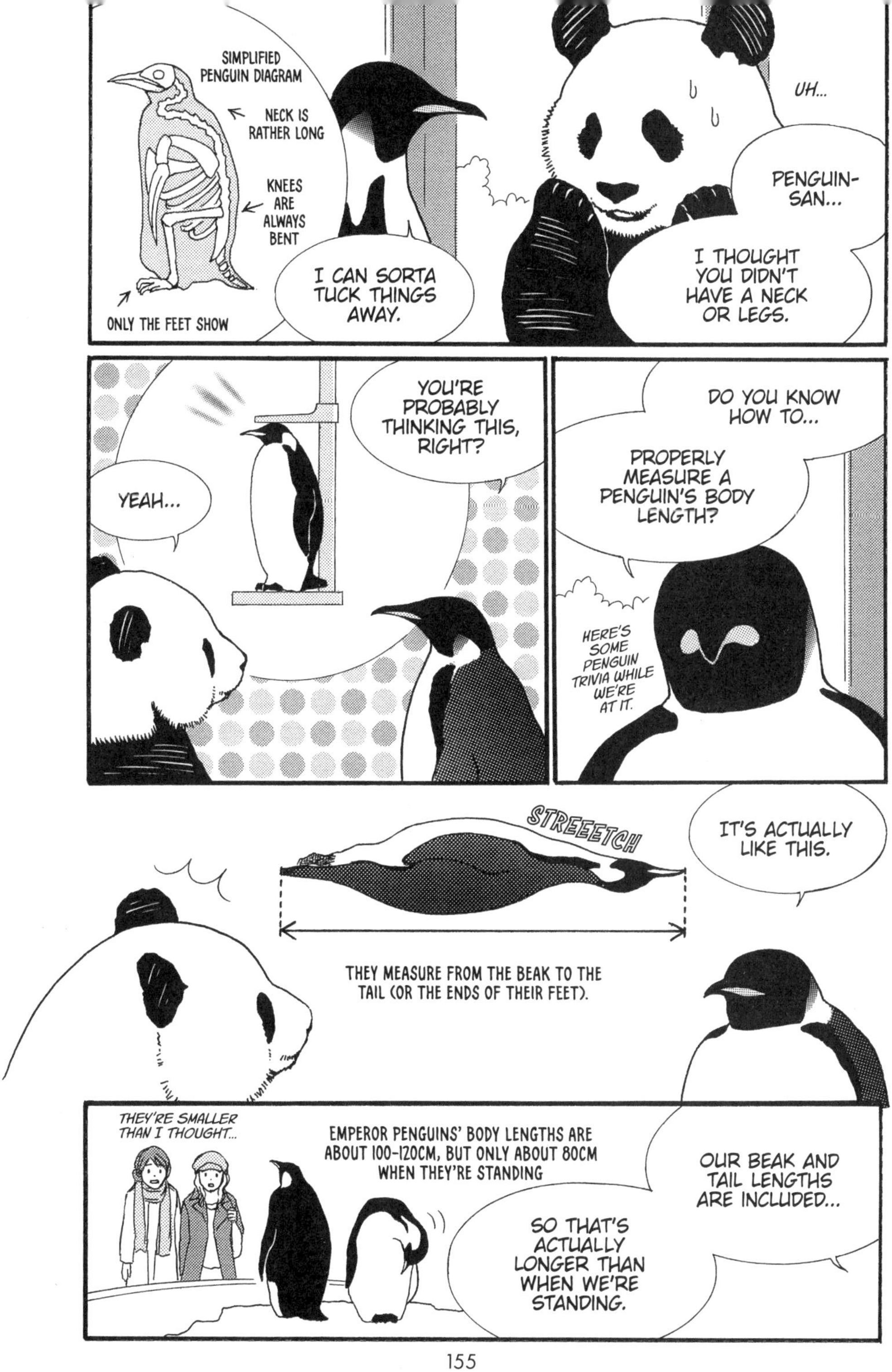
UH...
PENGUIN-SAN...
I THOUGHT YOU DIDN'T HAVE A NECK OR LEGS.
I CAN SORTA TUCK THINGS AWAY.
SIMPLIFIED PENGUIN DIAGRAM
NECK IS RATHER LONG
KNEES ARE ALWAYS BENT
ONLY THE FEET SHOW
DO YOU KNOW HOW TO...
PROPERLY MEASURE A PENGUIN'S BODY LENGTH?
HERE'S SOME PENGUIN TRIVIA WHILE WE'RE AT IT.
YOU'RE PROBABLY THINKING THIS, RIGHT?
YEAH...
IT'S ACTUALLY LIKE THIS.
STREEEETCH
THEY MEASURE FROM THE BEAK TO THE TAIL (OR THE ENDS OF THEIR FEET).
OUR BEAK AND TAIL LENGTHS ARE INCLUDED...
SO THAT'S ACTUALLY LONGER THAN WHEN WE'RE STANDING.
EMPEROR PENGUINS' BODY LENGTHS ARE ABOUT 100-120CM, BUT ONLY ABOUT 80CM WHEN THEY'RE STANDING
THEY'RE SMALLER THAN I THOUGHT...

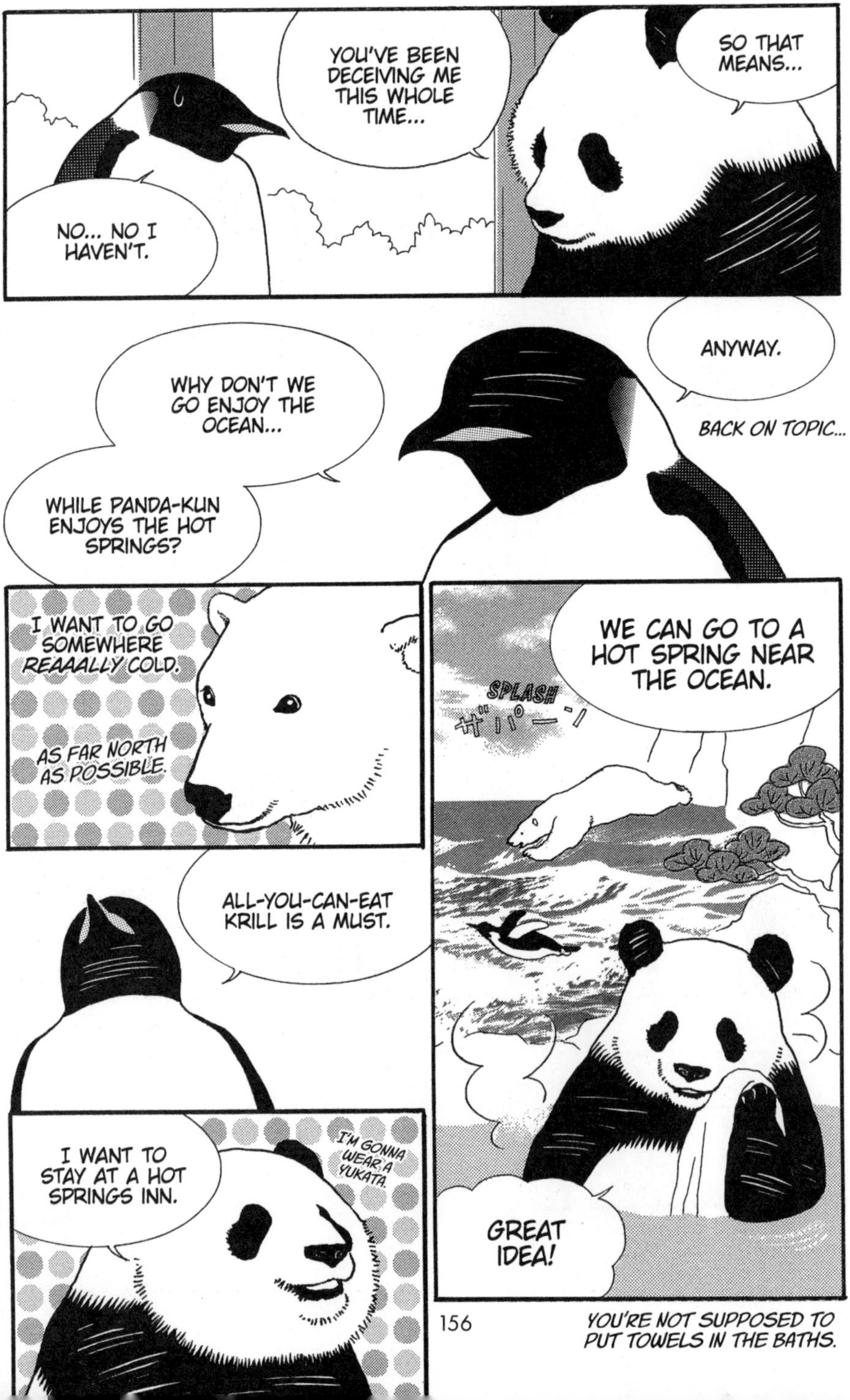
SO THAT MEANS...
YOU'VE BEEN DECEIVING ME THIS WHOLE TIME...
NO... NO I HAVEN'T.
ANYWAY.
WHY DON'T WE GO ENJOY THE OCEAN...
WHILE PANDA-KUN ENJOYS THE HOT SPRINGS?
BACK ON TOPIC...
WE CAN GO TO A HOT SPRING NEAR THE OCEAN.
SPLASH
ザパーン
GREAT IDEA!
I WANT TO GO SOMEWHERE REAAALLY COLD.
AS FAR NORTH AS POSSIBLE.
ALL-YOU-CAN-EAT KRILL IS A MUST.
I WANT TO STAY AT A HOT SPRINGS INN.
I'M GONNA WEAR A YUKATA.
YOU'RE NOT SUPPOSED TO PUT TOWELS IN THE BATHS.

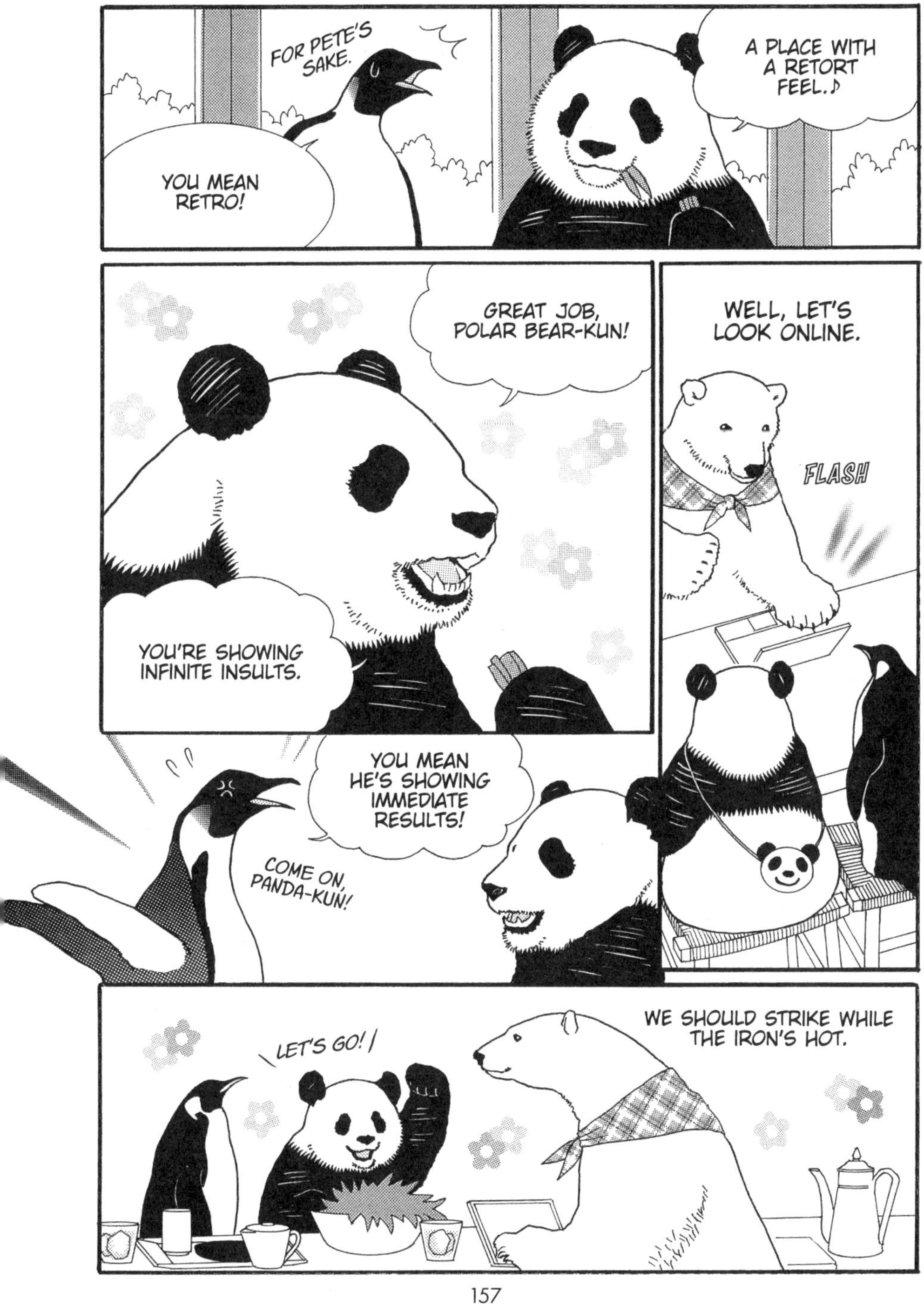

A PLACE WITH A RETORT FEEL.♪
FOR PETE'S SAKE.
YOU MEAN RETRO!
WELL, LET'S LOOK ONLINE.
FLASH
GREAT JOB, POLAR BEAR-KUN!
YOU'RE SHOWING INFINITE INSULTS.
YOU MEAN HE'S SHOWING IMMEDIATE RESULTS!
COME ON, PANDA-KUN!
WE SHOULD STRIKE WHILE THE IRON'S HOT.
LET'S GO!

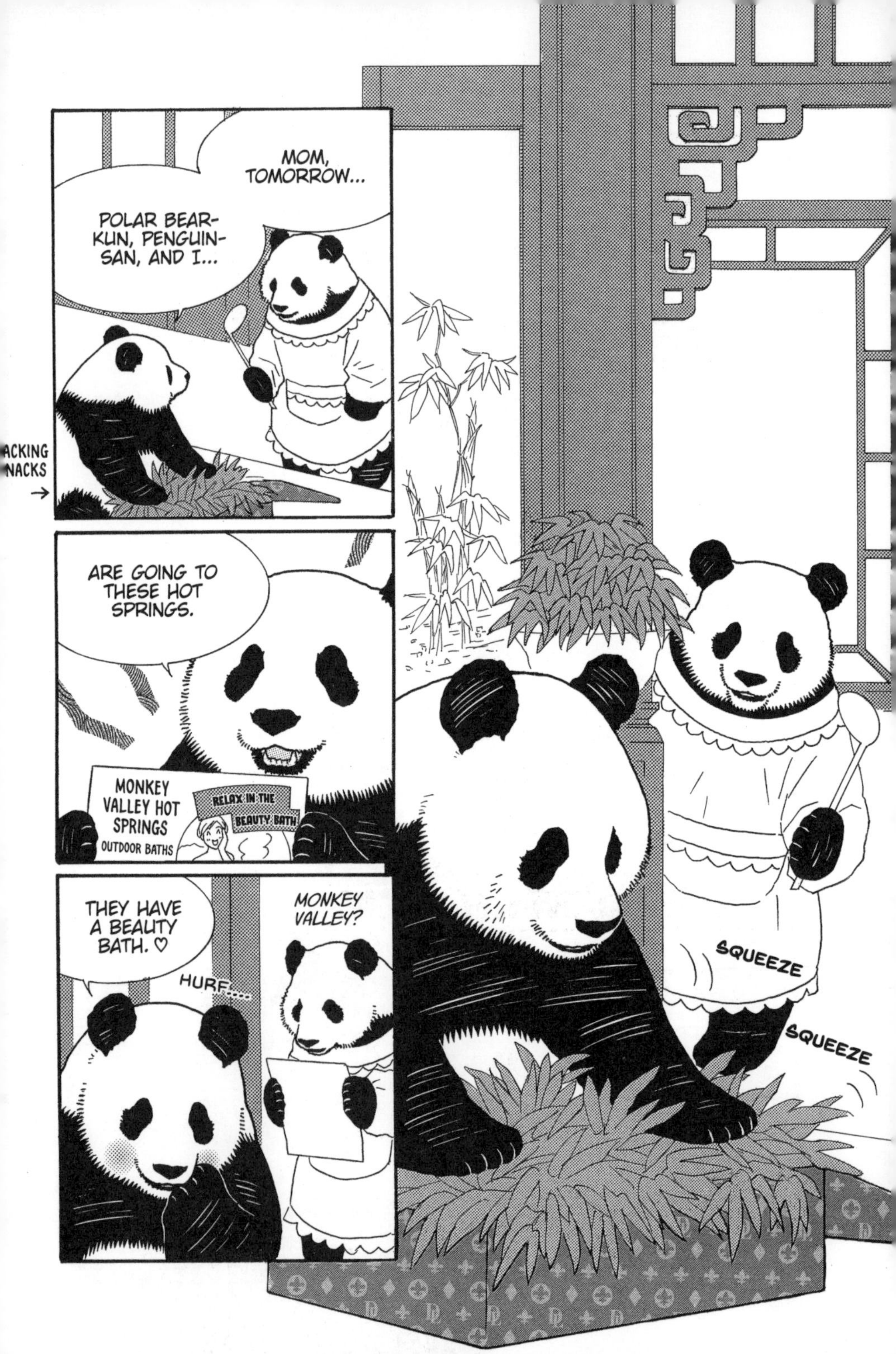
SQUEEZE
SQUEEZE
MOM, TOMORROW...
POLAR BEAR-KUN, PENGUIN-SAN, AND I...
ACKING NACKS →
ARE GOING TO THESE HOT SPRINGS.
MONKEY VALLEY HOT SPRINGS
OUTDOOR BATHS
RELAX IN THE BEAUTY BATH
MONKEY VALLEY?
THEY HAVE A BEAUTY BATH. ♡
HURF....

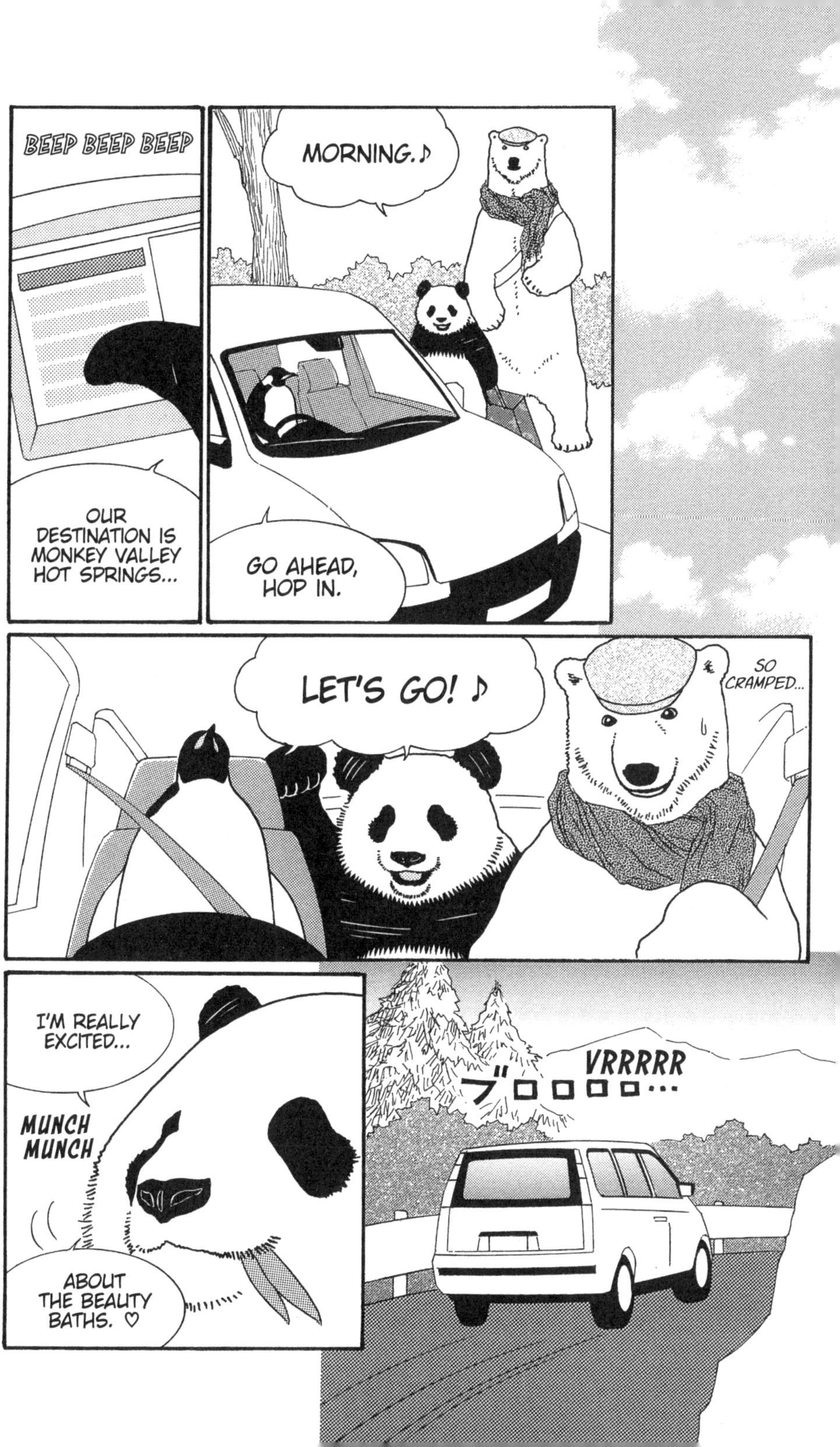
MORNING. ♪
GO AHEAD, HOP IN.
BEEP BEEP BEEP
OUR DESTINATION IS MONKEY VALLEY HOT SPRINGS...
SO CRAMPED...
LET'S GO! ♪
VRRRRR
ブロロロロ…
I'M REALLY EXCITED...
MUNCH MUNCH
ABOUT THE BEAUTY BATHS. ♡

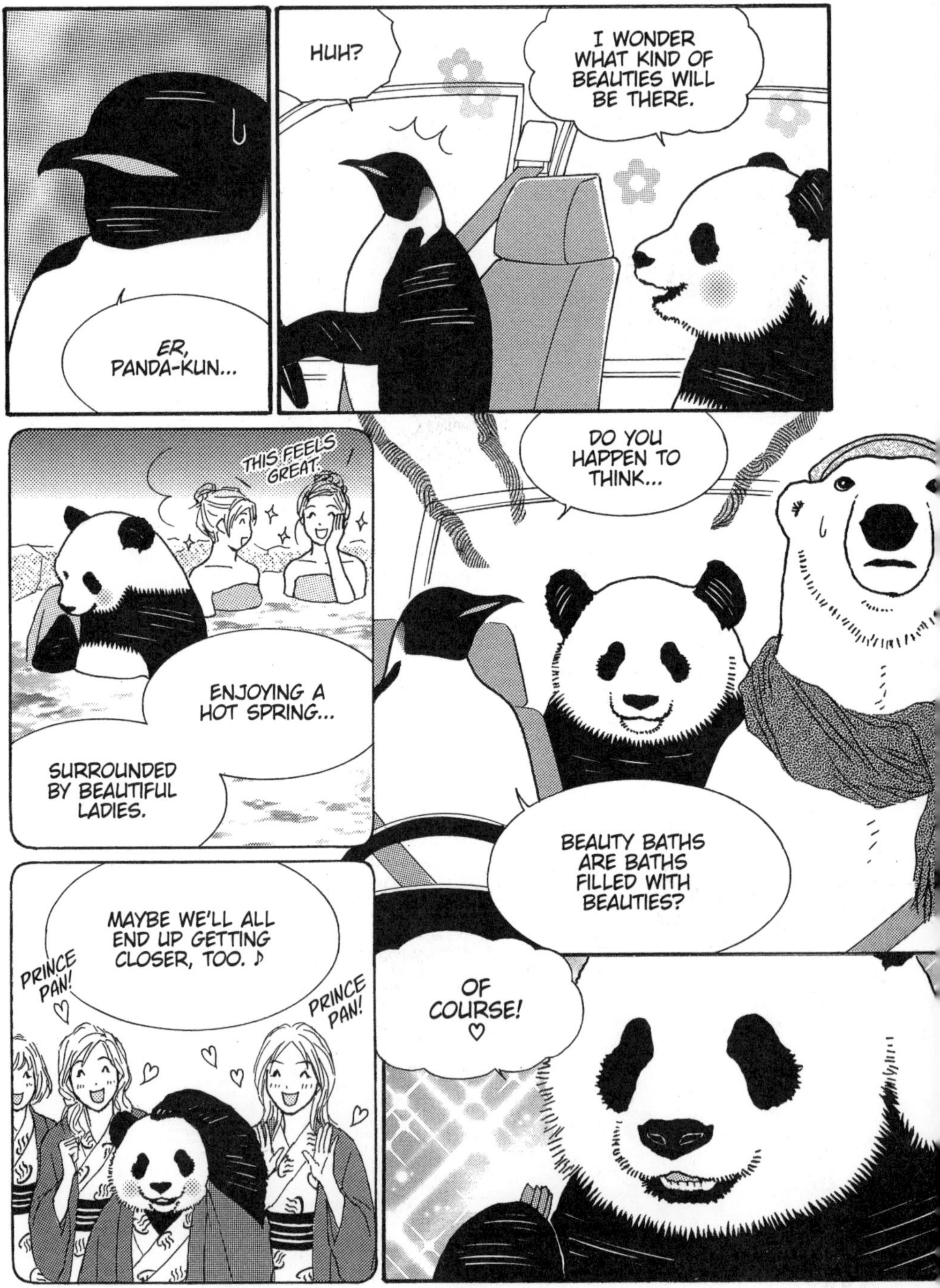
I WONDER WHAT KIND OF BEAUTIES WILL BE THERE.
HUH?
ER, PANDA-KUN...
DO YOU HAPPEN TO THINK...
BEAUTY BATHS ARE BATHS FILLED WITH BEAUTIES?
OF COURSE! ♡
THIS FEELS GREAT.
ENJOYING A HOT SPRING...
SURROUNDED BY BEAUTIFUL LADIES.
MAYBE WE'LL ALL END UP GETTING CLOSER, TOO. ♪
PRINCE PAN! ♡
PRINCE PAN!

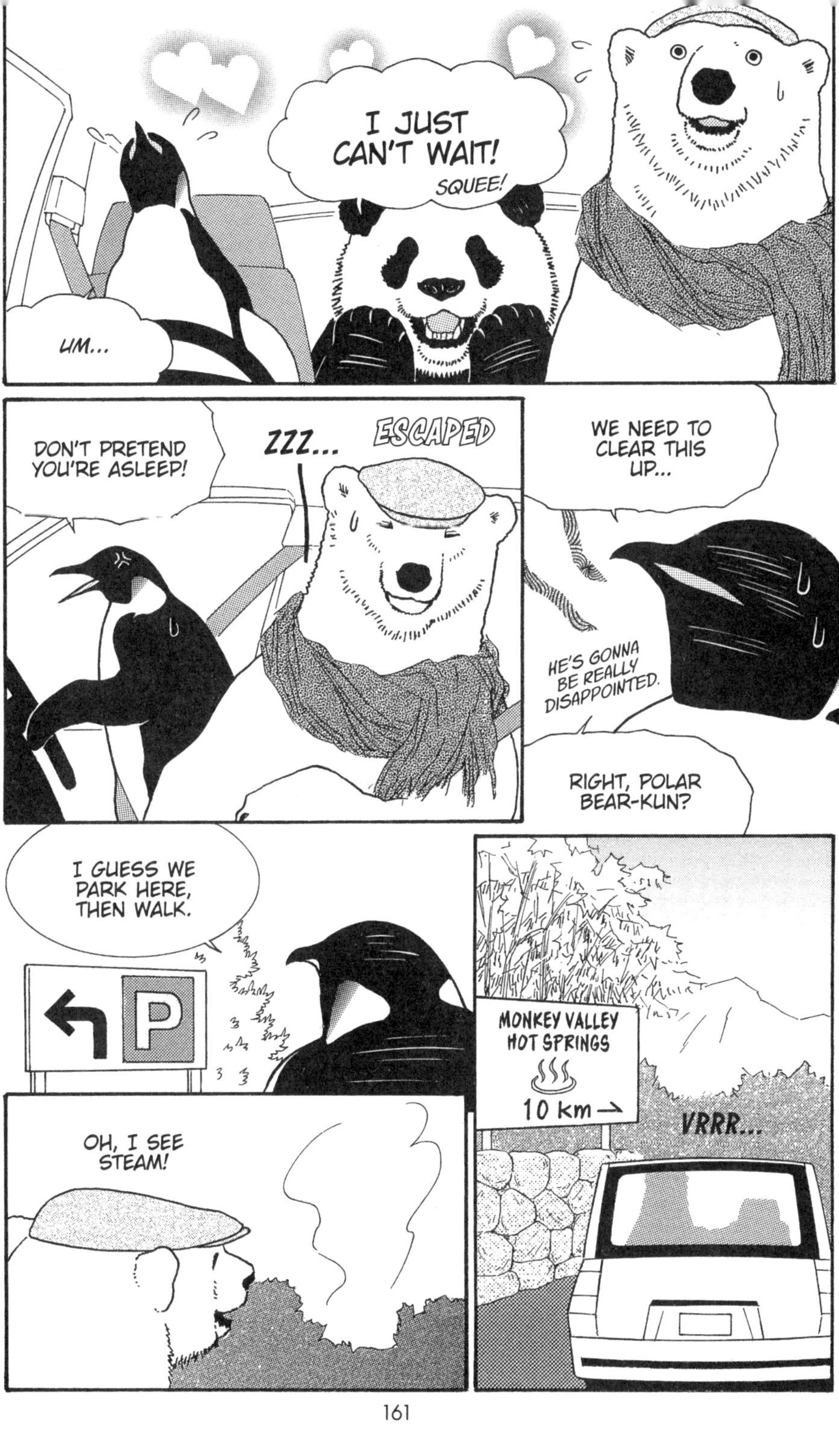
I JUST CAN'T WAIT!
SQUEE!
UM...
WE NEED TO CLEAR THIS UP...
HE'S GONNA BE REALLY DISAPPOINTED.
RIGHT, POLAR BEAR-KUN?
ESCAPED
ZZZ...
DON'T PRETEND YOU'RE ASLEEP!
MONKEY VALLEY HOT SPRINGS
10 km →
VRRR...
I GUESS WE PARK HERE, THEN WALK.
OH, I SEE STEAM!

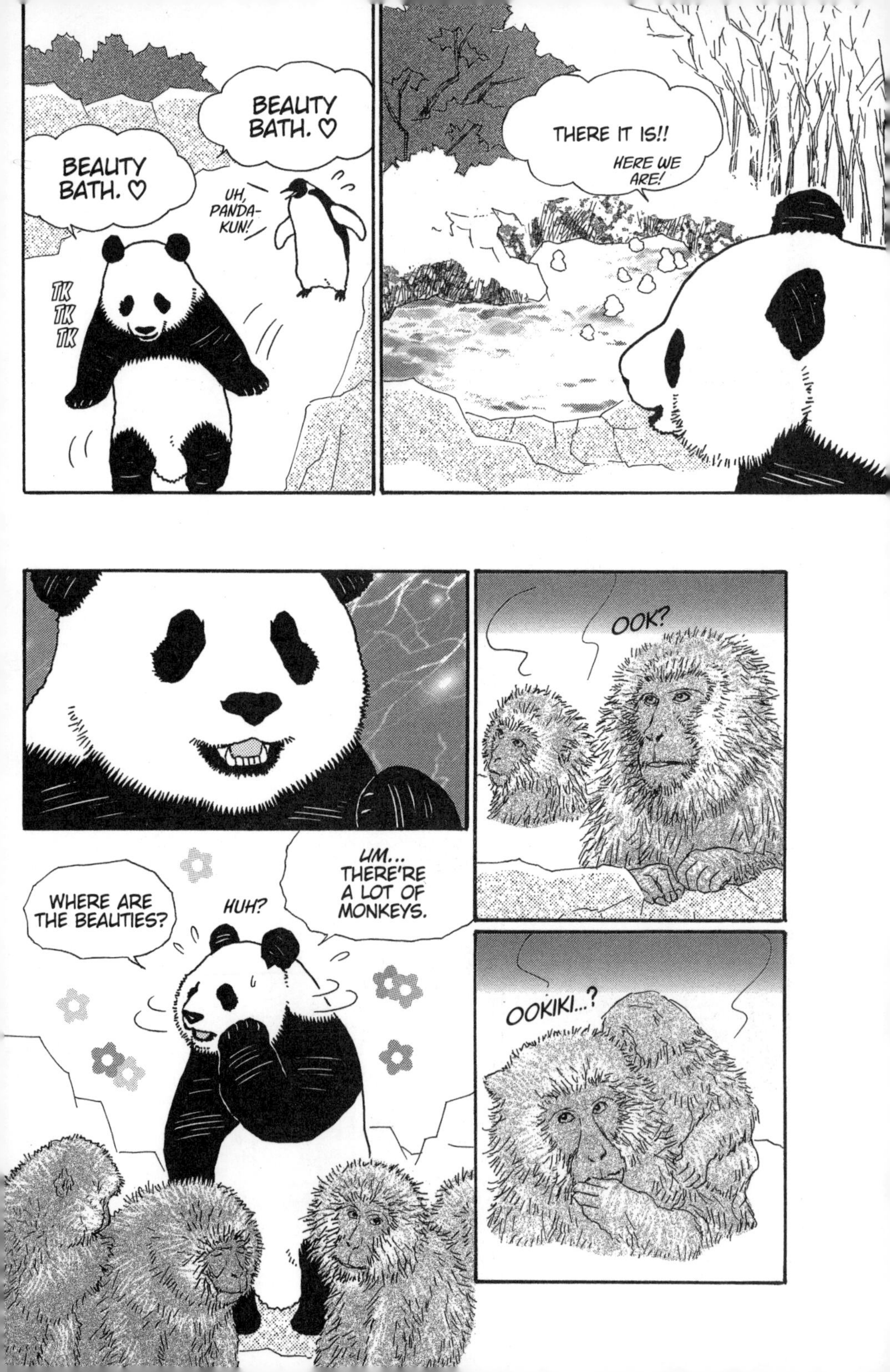
THERE IT IS!!
HERE WE ARE!
BEAUTY BATH. ♡
BEAUTY BATH. ♡
UH, PANDA-KUN!
TK TK TK
OOK?
OOKIKI...?
UM... THERE'RE A LOT OF MONKEYS.
HUH?
WHERE ARE THE BEAUTIES?

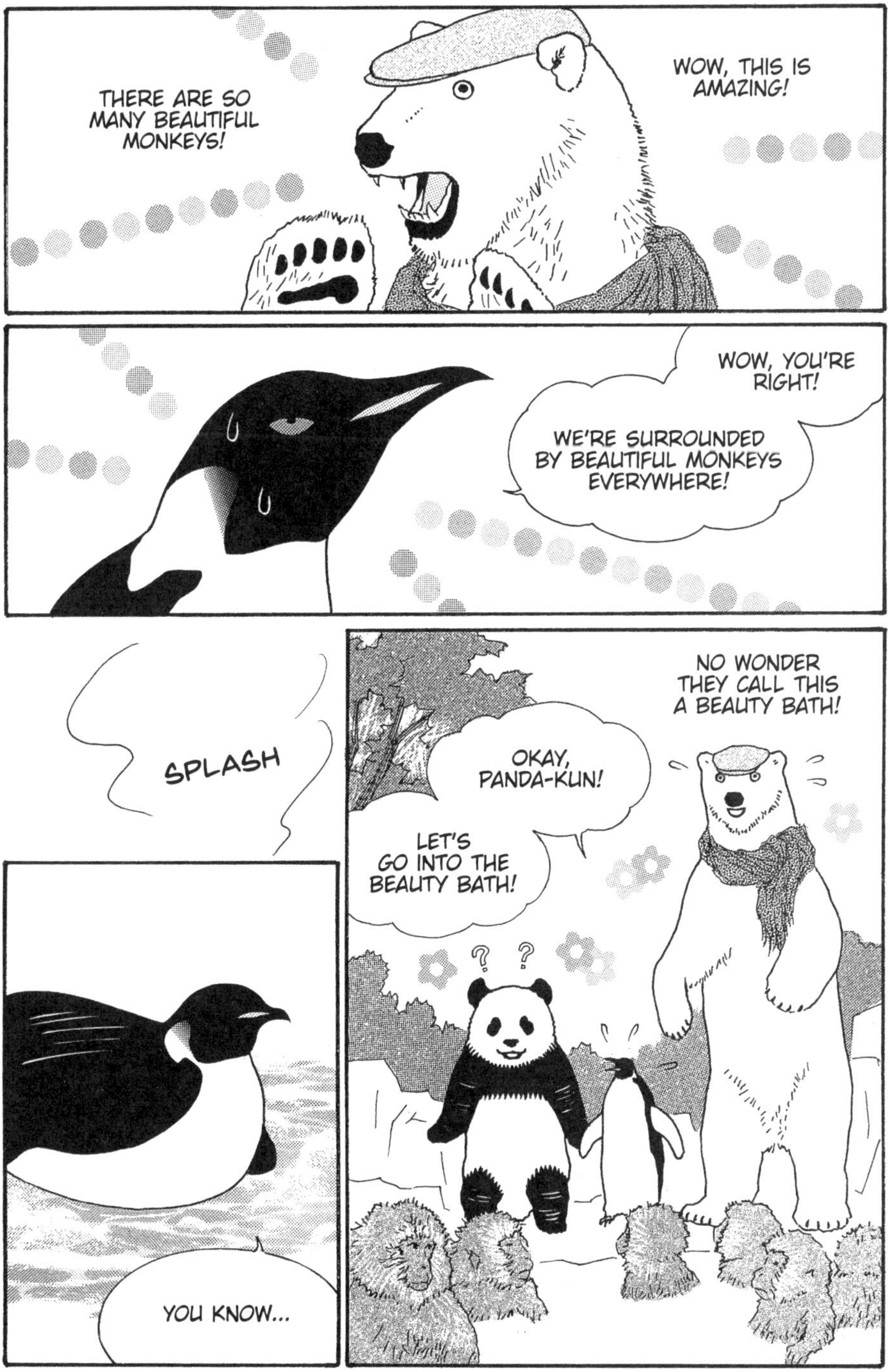
WOW, THIS IS AMAZING!
THERE ARE SO MANY BEAUTIFUL MONKEYS!
WOW, YOU'RE RIGHT!
WE'RE SURROUNDED BY BEAUTIFUL MONKEYS EVERYWHERE!
NO WONDER THEY CALL THIS A BEAUTY BATH!
OKAY, PANDA-KUN!
LET'S GO INTO THE BEAUTY BATH!
SPLASH
YOU KNOW...

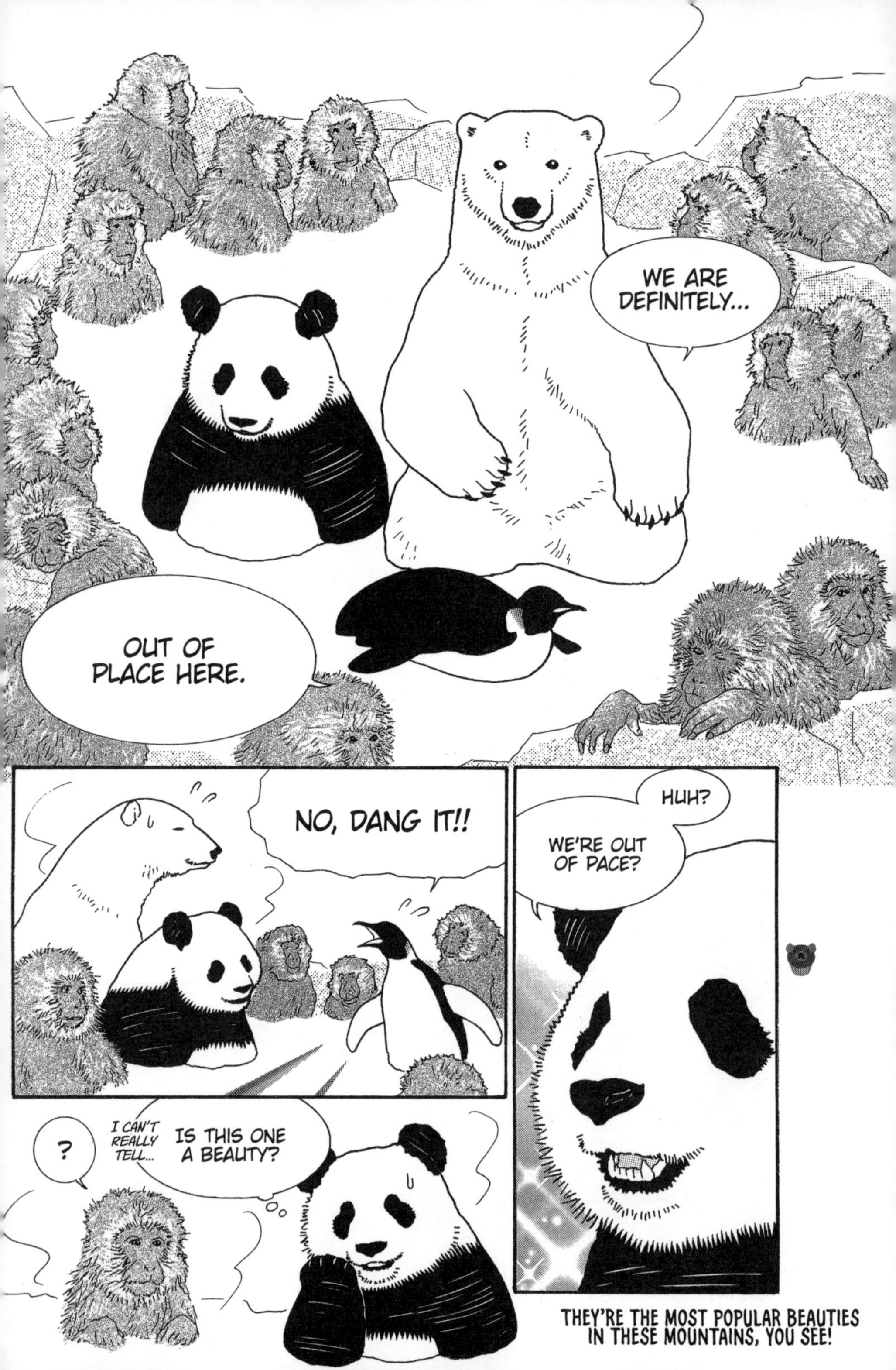
WE ARE DEFINITELY...
OUT OF PLACE HERE.
HUH?
WE'RE OUT OF PACE?
NO, DANG IT!!
IS THIS ONE A BEAUTY?
I CAN'T REALLY TELL...
?
THEY'RE THE MOST POPULAR BEAUTIES IN THESE MOUNTAINS, YOU SEE!

PING PONG!

Polar Bear Café

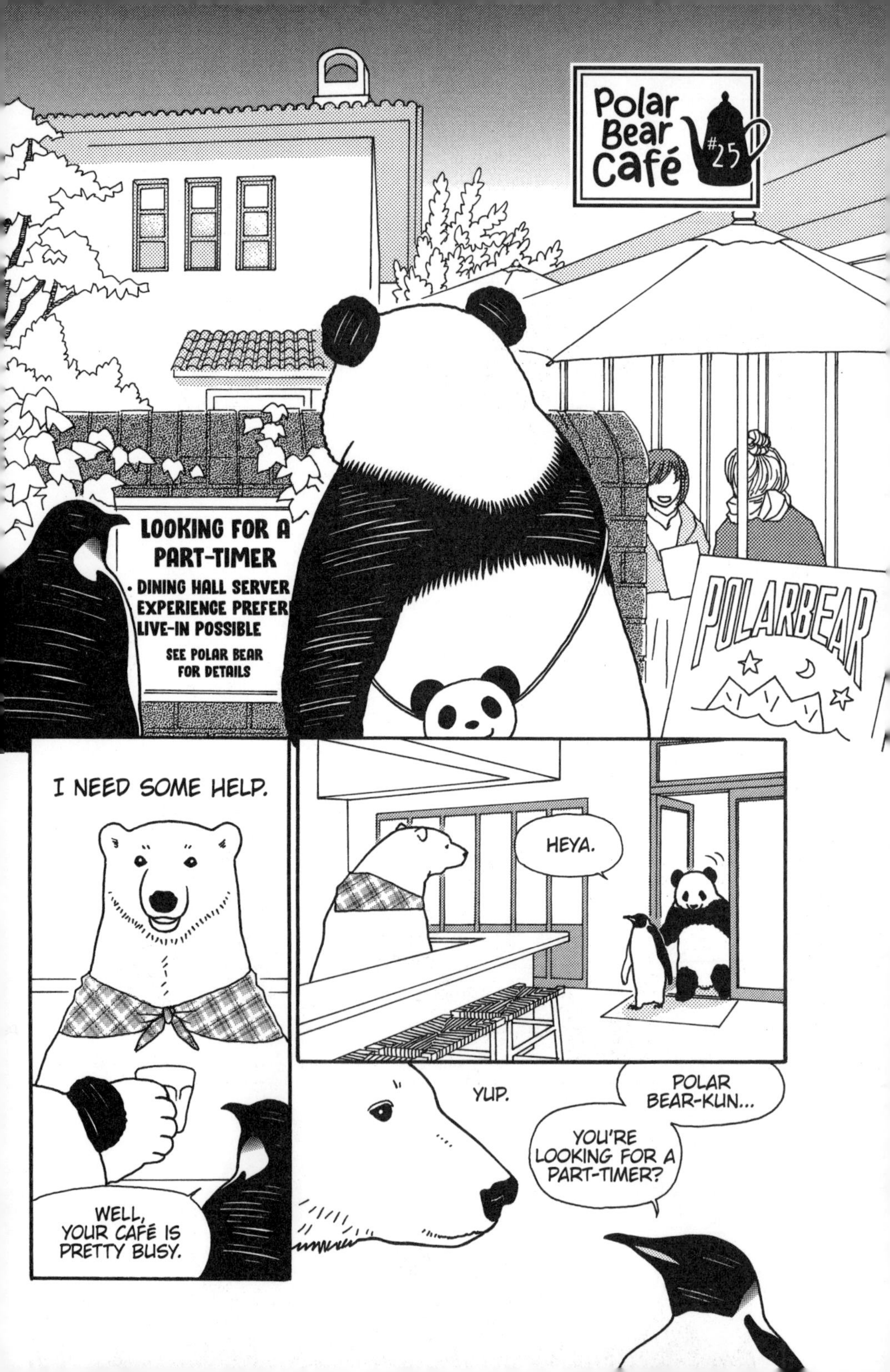

Polar Bear Café #25
LOOKING FOR A PART-TIMER
• DINING HALL SERVER
EXPERIENCE PREFER
LIVE-IN POSSIBLE
SEE POLAR BEAR FOR DETAILS
POLARBEAR
HEYA.
POLAR BEAR-KUN...
YOU'RE LOOKING FOR A PART-TIMER?
YUP.
I NEED SOME HELP.
WELL, YOUR CAFÉ IS PRETTY BUSY.

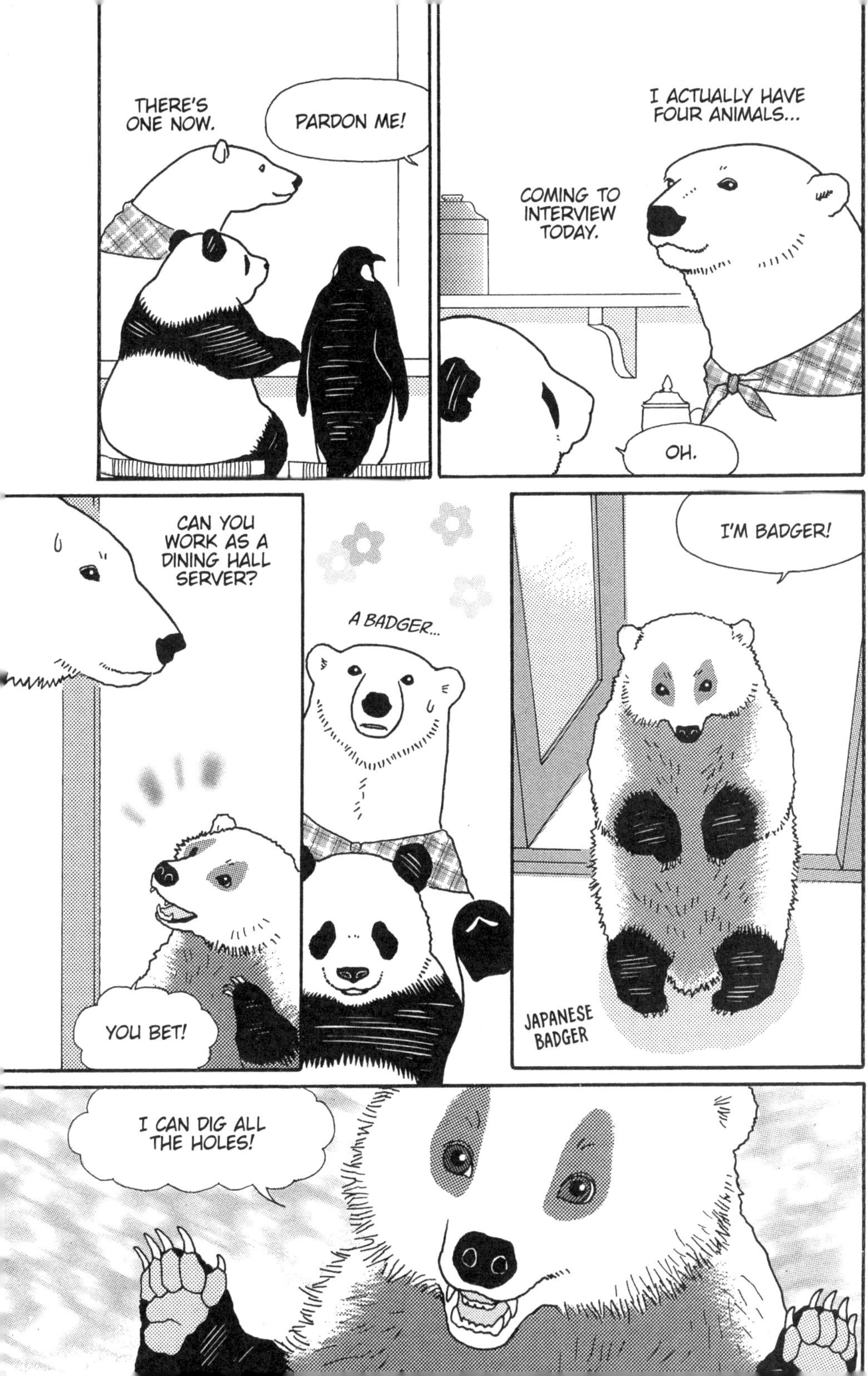
I ACTUALLY HAVE FOUR ANIMALS...
COMING TO INTERVIEW TODAY.
OH.
PARDON ME!
THERE'S ONE NOW.
I'M BADGER!
JAPANESE BADGER
A BADGER...
CAN YOU WORK AS A DINING HALL SERVER?
YOU BET!
I CAN DIG ALL THE HOLES!

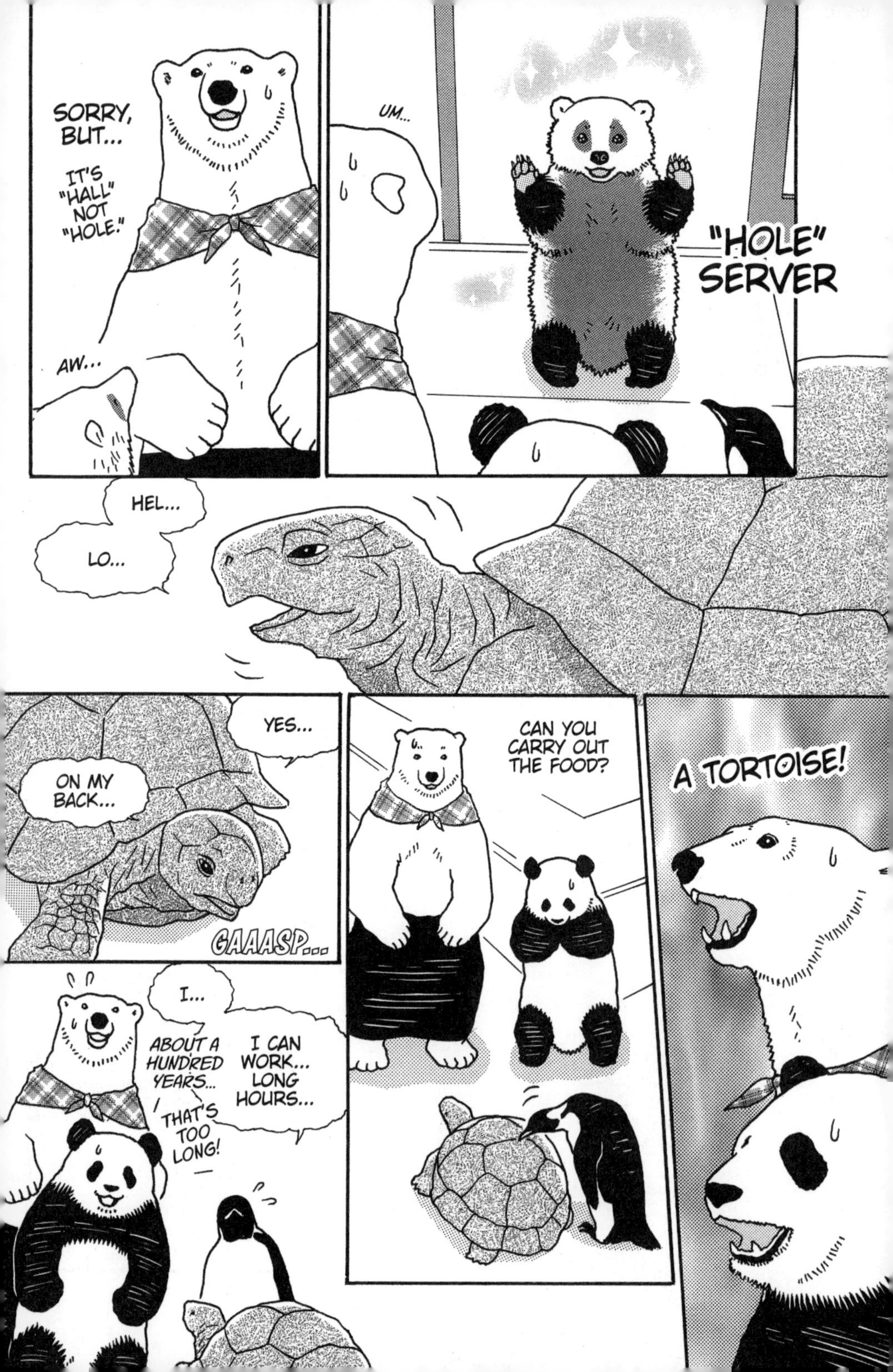
"HOLE" SERVER
UM...
SORRY, BUT...
IT'S "HALL" NOT "HOLE."
AW...
HEL...
LO...
A TORTOISE!
CAN YOU CARRY OUT THE FOOD?
YES...
ON MY BACK...
GAAAASP...
I...
I CAN WORK... LONG HOURS...
ABOUT A HUNDRED YEARS...
THAT'S TOO LONG!

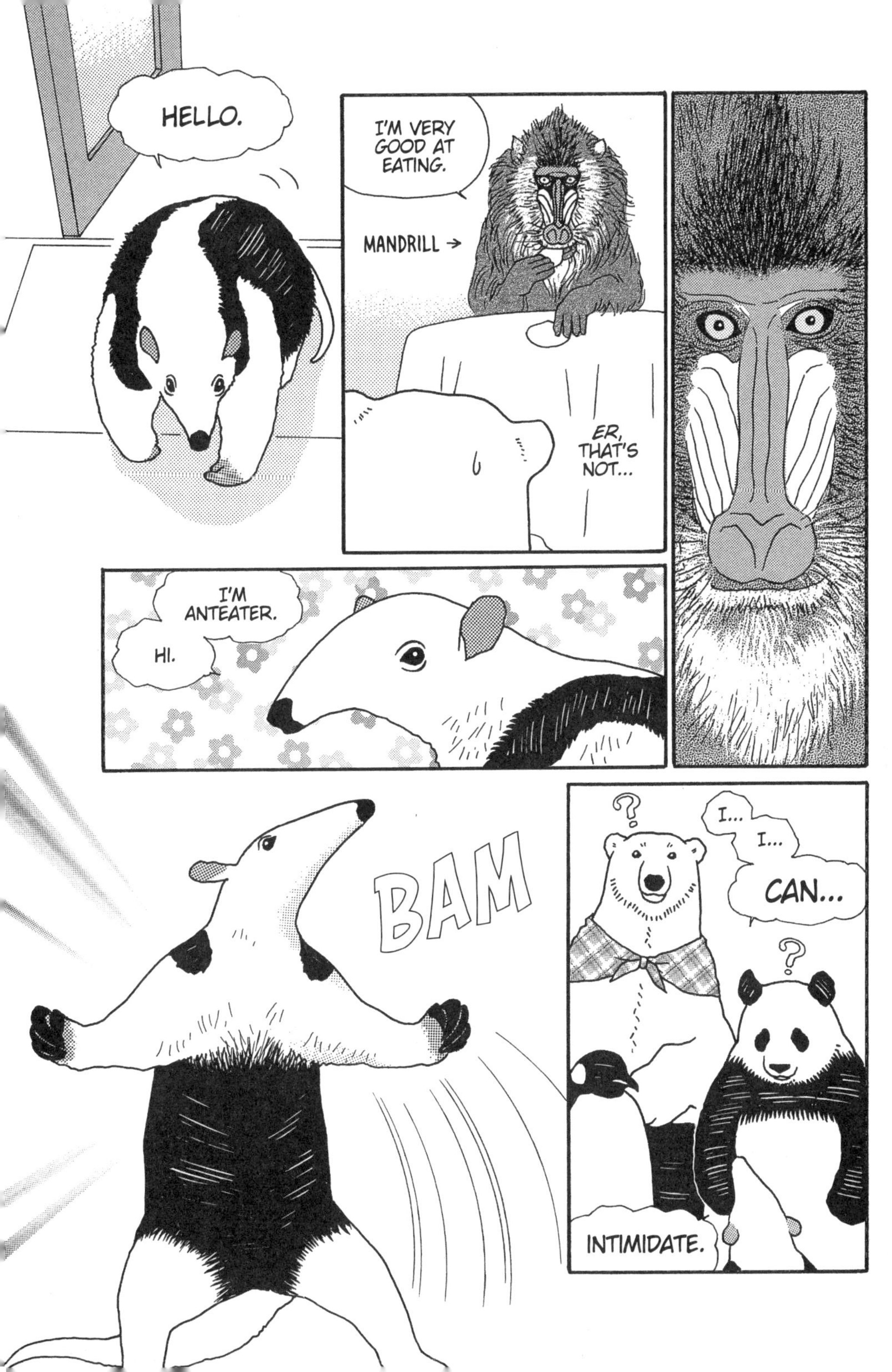

I'M VERY GOOD AT EATING.
MANDRILL →
ER, THAT'S NOT...
HELLO.
I'M ANTEATER.
HI.
I... I... CAN...
INTIMIDATE.
BAM

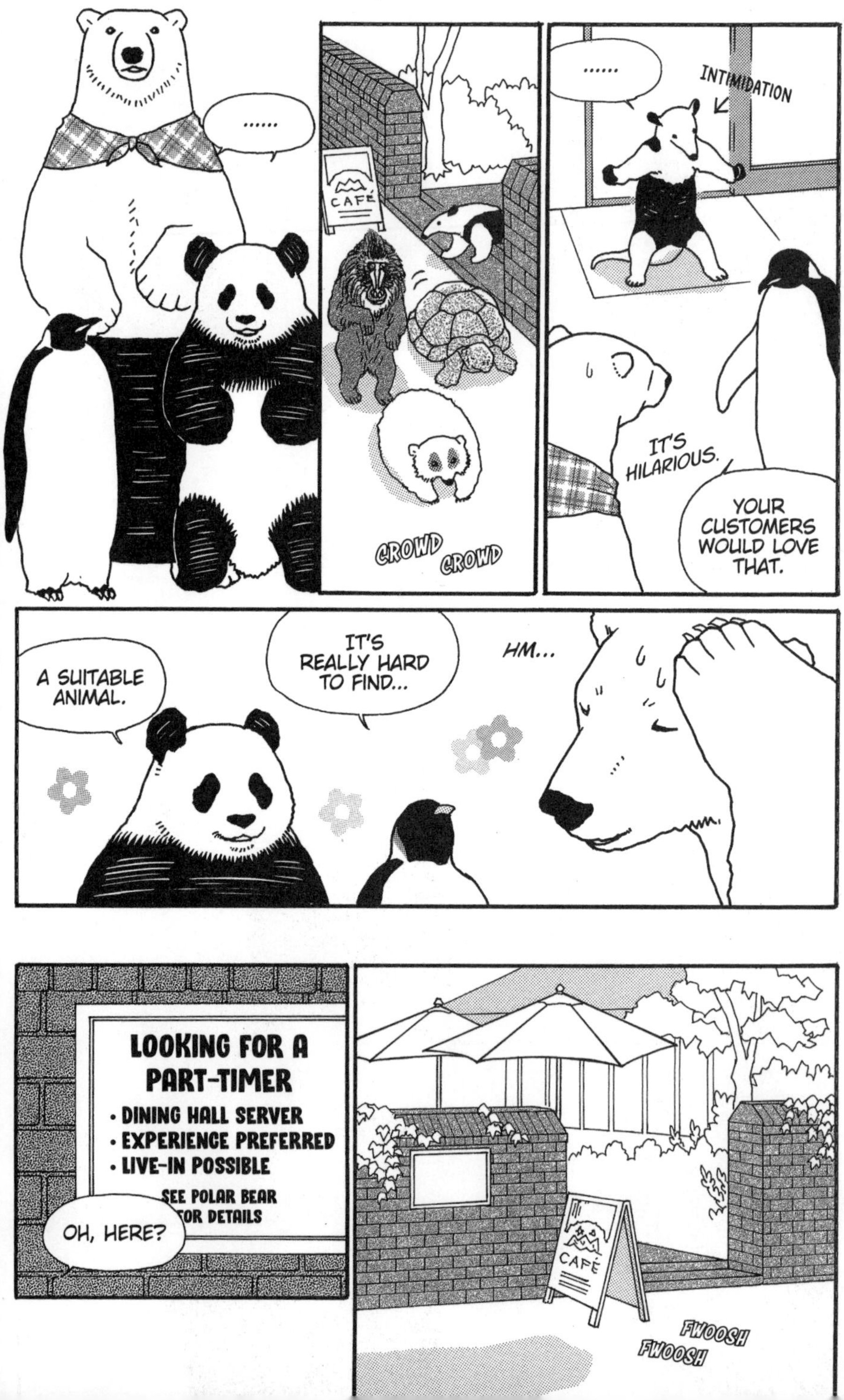
......
INTIMIDATION
IT'S HILARIOUS.
YOUR CUSTOMERS WOULD LOVE THAT.
CAFÉ
CROWD
CROWD
......
HM...
IT'S REALLY HARD TO FIND...
A SUITABLE ANIMAL.
CAFÉ
FWOOSH
FWOOSH
LOOKING FOR A PART-TIMER
• DINING HALL SERVER
• EXPERIENCE PREFERRED
• LIVE-IN POSSIBLE
SEE POLAR BEAR FOR DETAILS
OH, HERE?

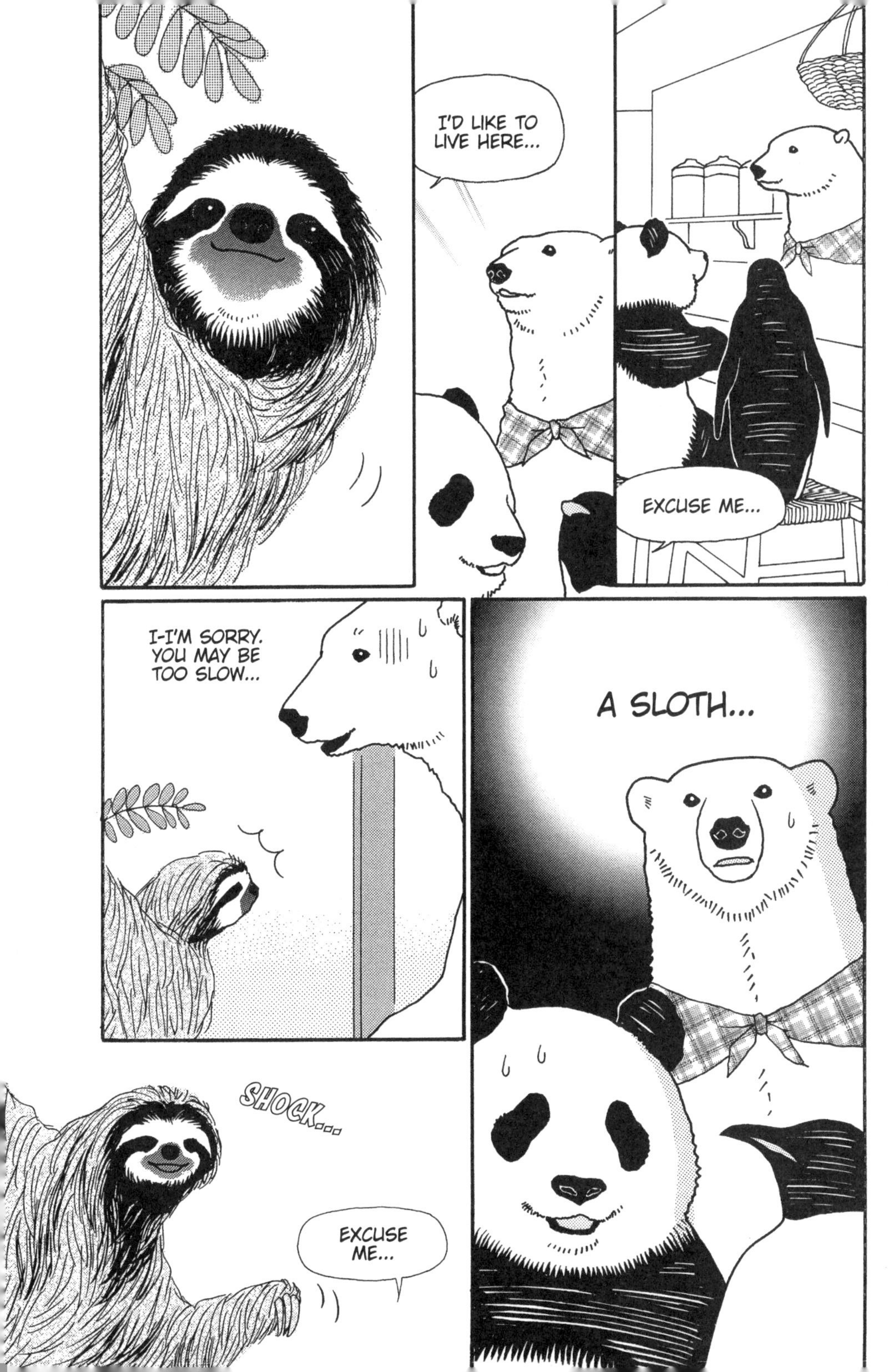
EXCUSE ME...
I'D LIKE TO LIVE HERE...
A SLOTH...
I-I'M SORRY. YOU MAY BE TOO SLOW...
SHOCK...
EXCUSE ME...

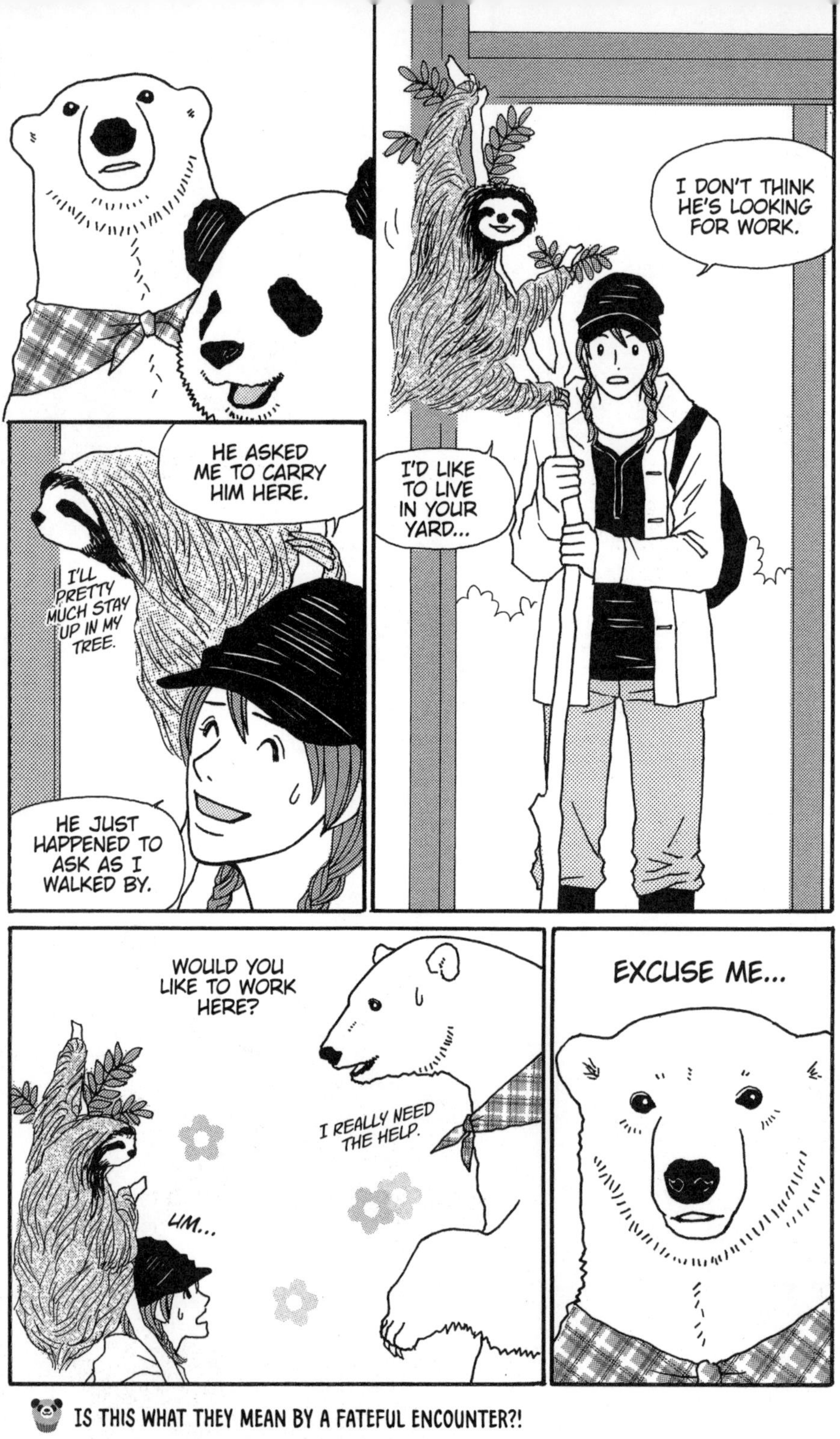
I DON'T THINK HE'S LOOKING FOR WORK.
I'D LIKE TO LIVE IN YOUR YARD...
HE ASKED ME TO CARRY HIM HERE.
I'LL PRETTY MUCH STAY UP IN MY TREE.
HE JUST HAPPENED TO ASK AS I WALKED BY.
EXCUSE ME...
WOULD YOU LIKE TO WORK HERE?
I REALLY NEED THE HELP.
UM...

IS THIS WHAT THEY MEAN BY A FATEFUL ENCOUNTER?!

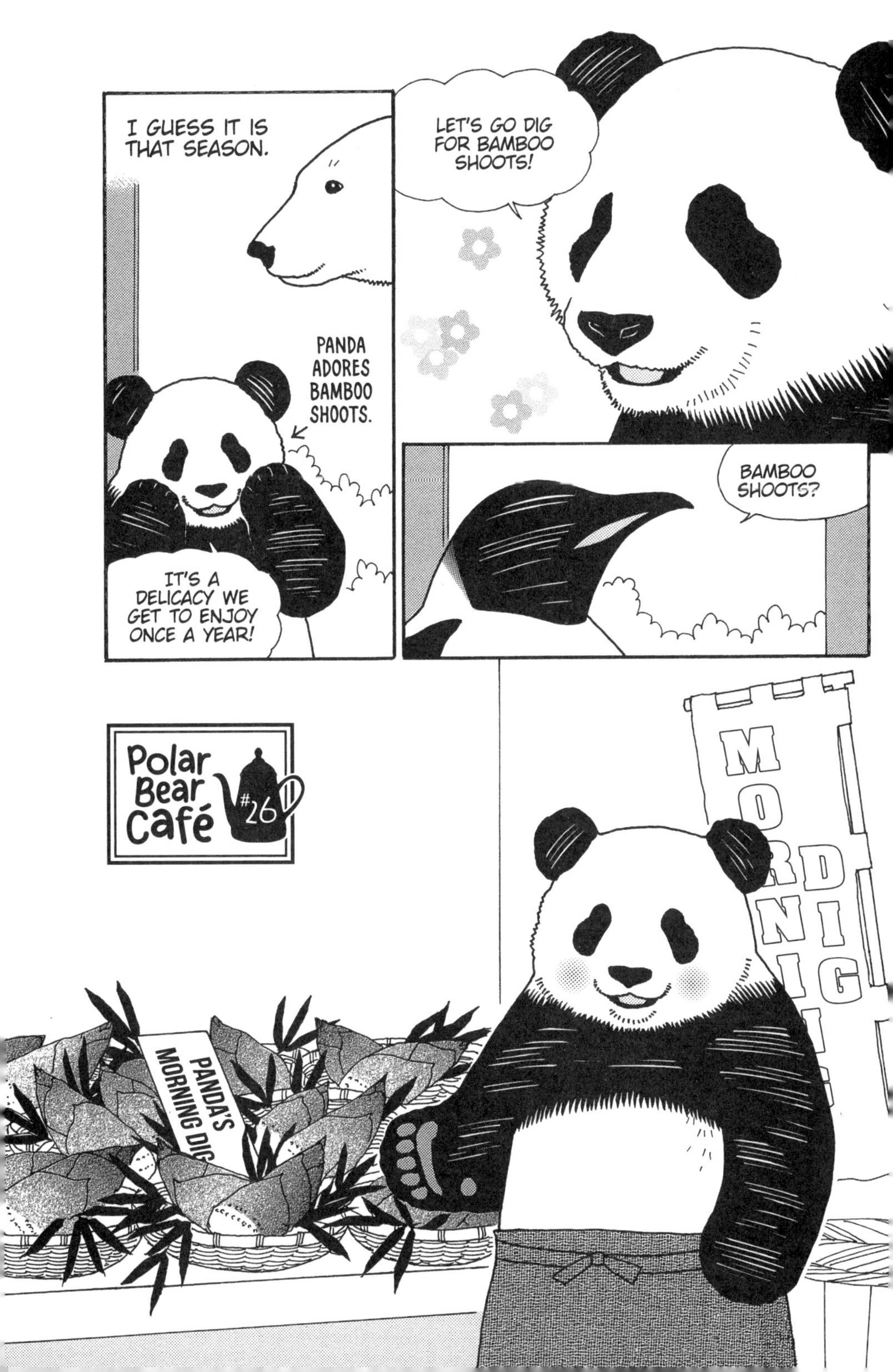
LET'S GO DIG FOR BAMBOO SHOOTS!
BAMBOO SHOOTS?
I GUESS IT IS THAT SEASON.
PANDA ADORES BAMBOO SHOOTS.
IT'S A DELICACY WE GET TO ENJOY ONCE A YEAR!
Polar Bear Café #26
PANDA'S MORNING DIG

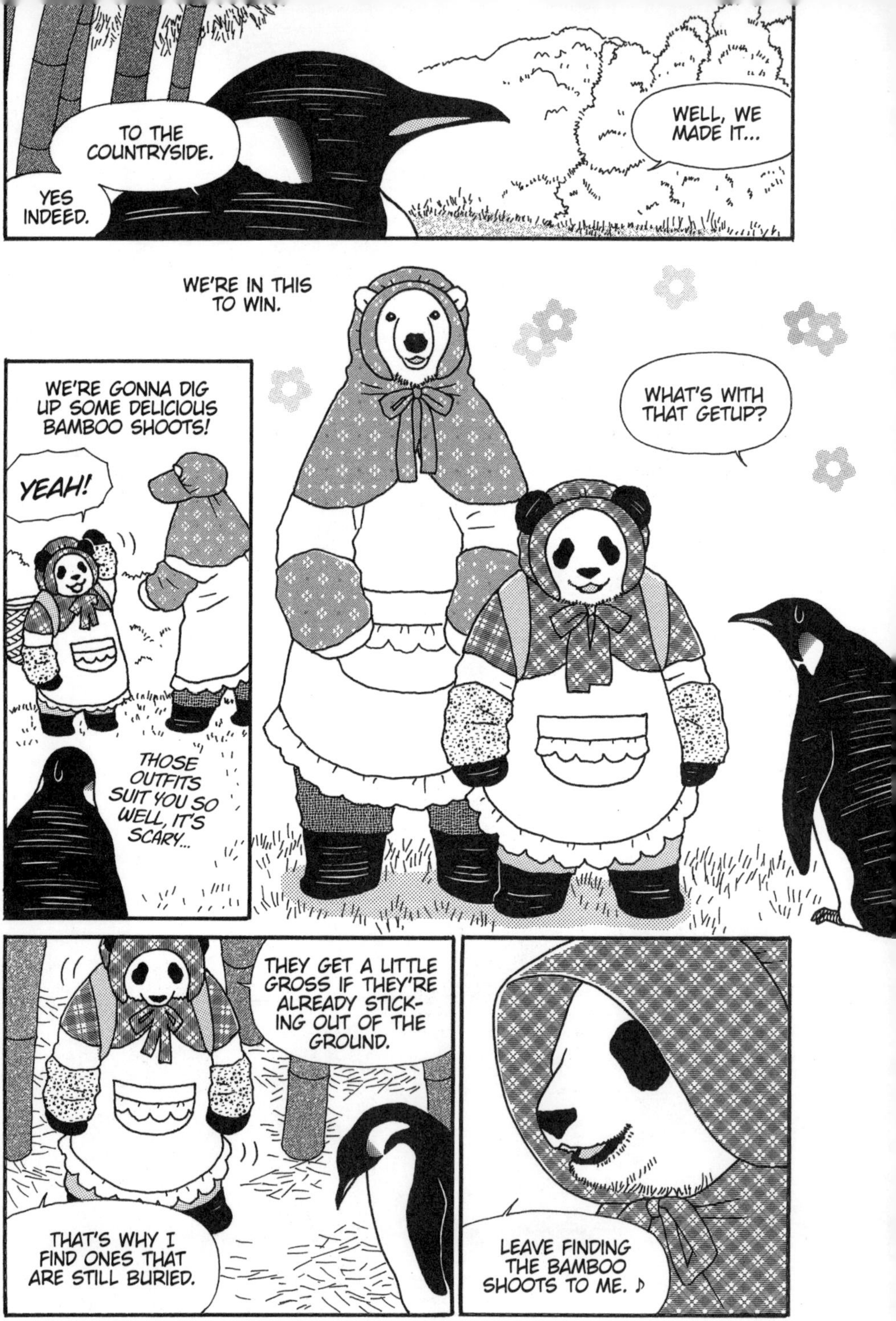
WELL, WE MADE IT...
TO THE COUNTRYSIDE.
YES INDEED.
WE'RE IN THIS TO WIN.
WHAT'S WITH THAT GETUP?
WE'RE GONNA DIG UP SOME DELICIOUS BAMBOO SHOOTS!
YEAH!
THOSE OUTFITS SUIT YOU SO WELL, IT'S SCARY...
LEAVE FINDING THE BAMBOO SHOOTS TO ME. ♪
THEY GET A LITTLE GROSS IF THEY'RE ALREADY STICK-ING OUT OF THE GROUND.
THAT'S WHY I FIND ONES THAT ARE STILL BURIED.

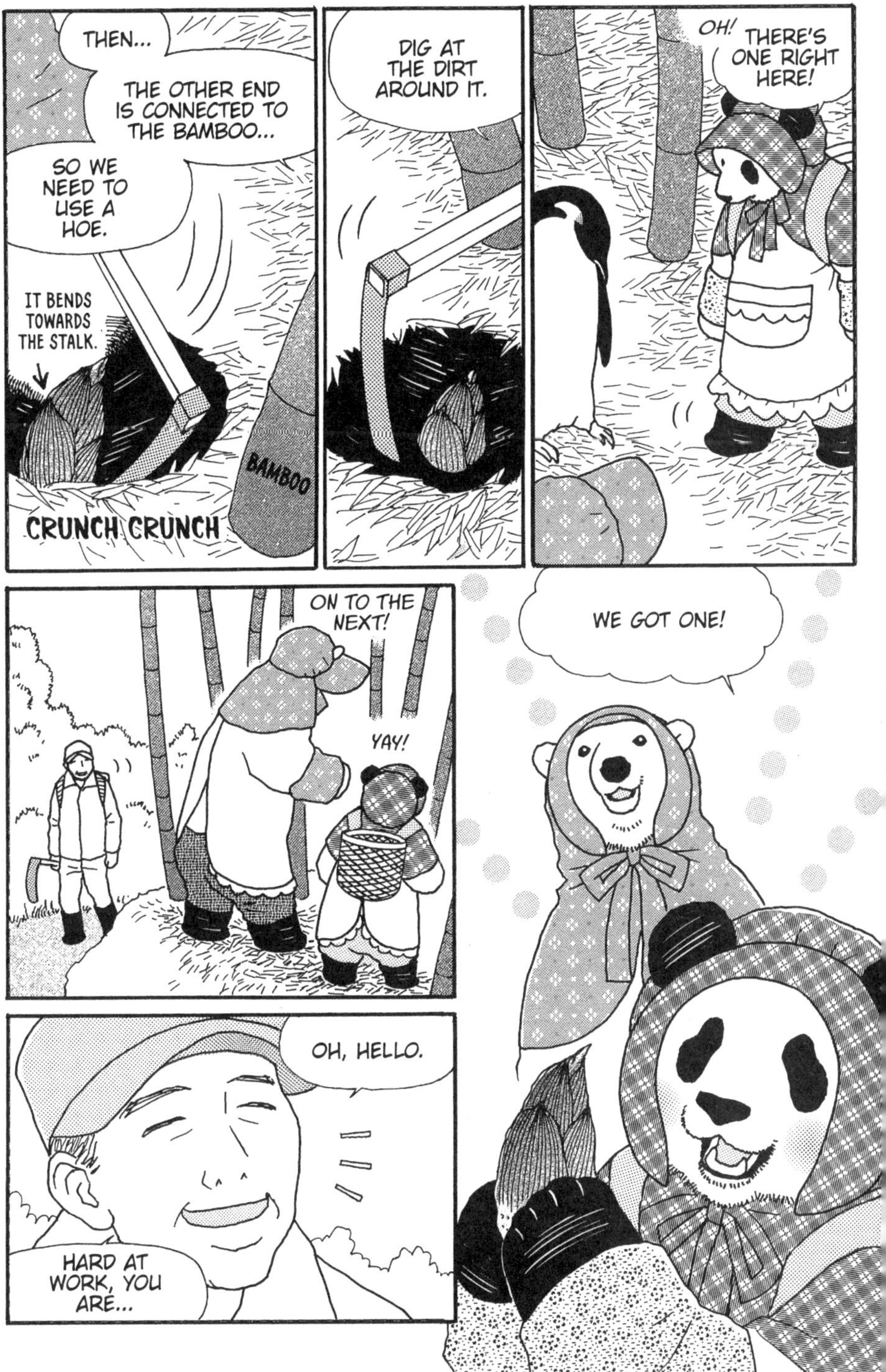
OH!
THERE'S ONE RIGHT HERE!
DIG AT THE DIRT AROUND IT.
THEN...
THE OTHER END IS CONNECTED TO THE BAMBOO...
SO WE NEED TO USE A HOE.
IT BENDS TOWARDS THE STALK.
BAMBOO
CRUNCH CRUNCH
WE GOT ONE!
ON TO THE NEXT!
YAY!
OH, HELLO.
HARD AT WORK, YOU ARE...

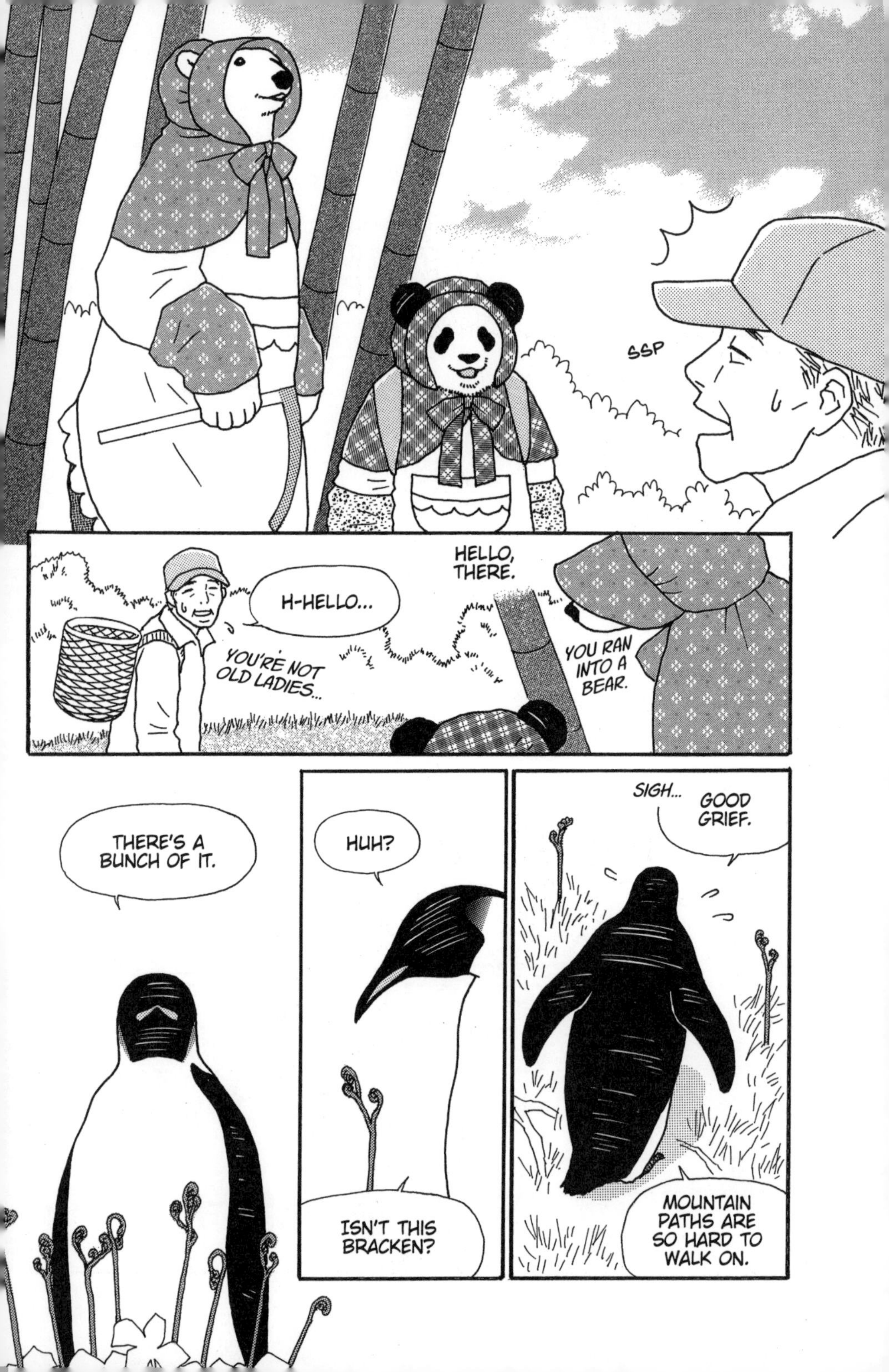
SSP
HELLO, THERE.
YOU RAN INTO A BEAR.
H-HELLO...
YOU'RE NOT OLD LADIES...
SIGH...
GOOD GRIEF.
MOUNTAIN PATHS ARE SO HARD TO WALK ON.
HUH?
ISN'T THIS BRACKEN?
THERE'S A BUNCH OF IT.

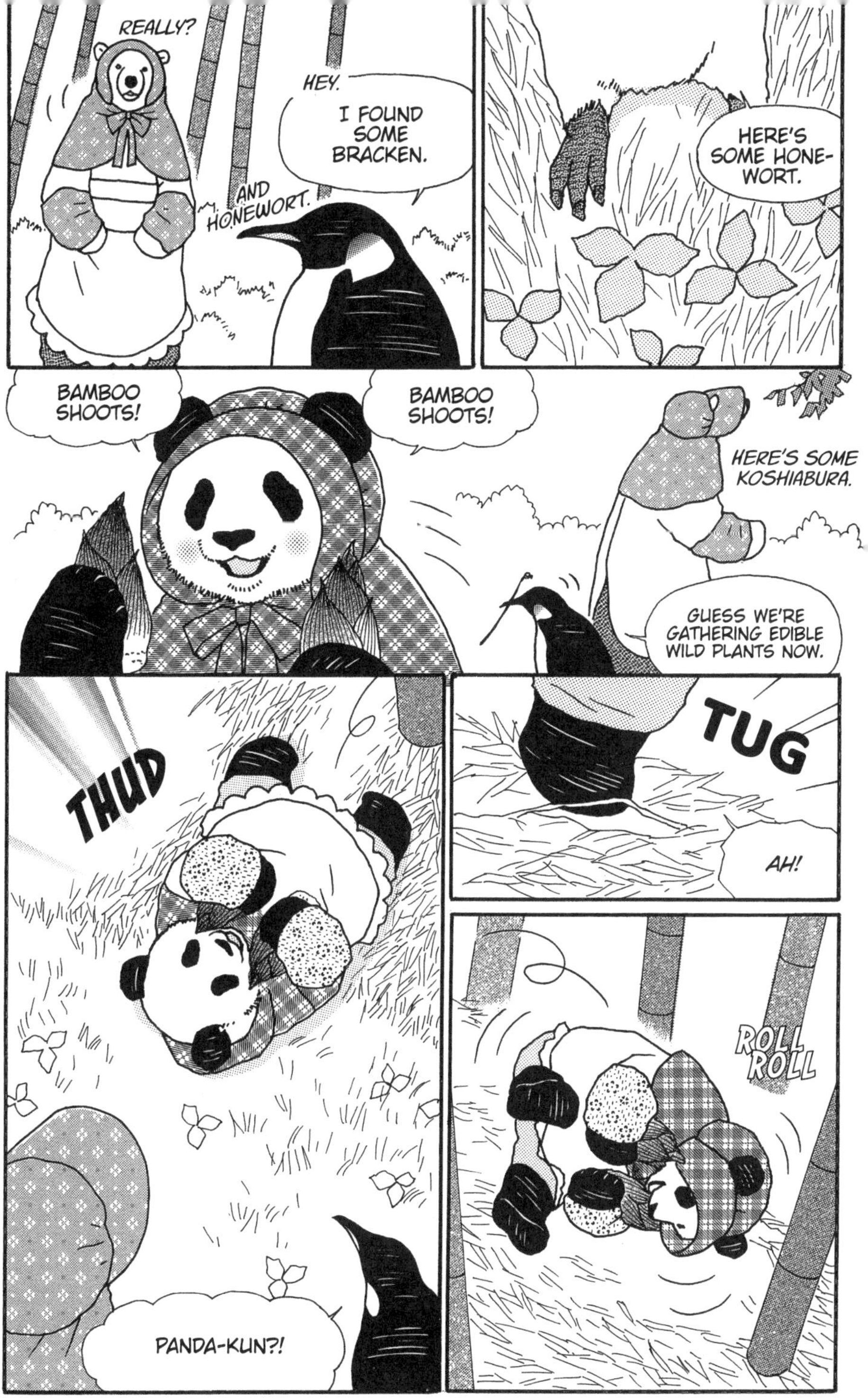
HERE'S SOME HONEWORT.
HEY.
I FOUND SOME BRACKEN.
AND HONEWORT.
REALLY?
HERE'S SOME KOSHIABURA.
GUESS WE'RE GATHERING EDIBLE WILD PLANTS NOW.
BAMBOO SHOOTS!
BAMBOO SHOOTS!
TUG
AH!
ROLL ROLL
THUD
PANDA-KUN?!

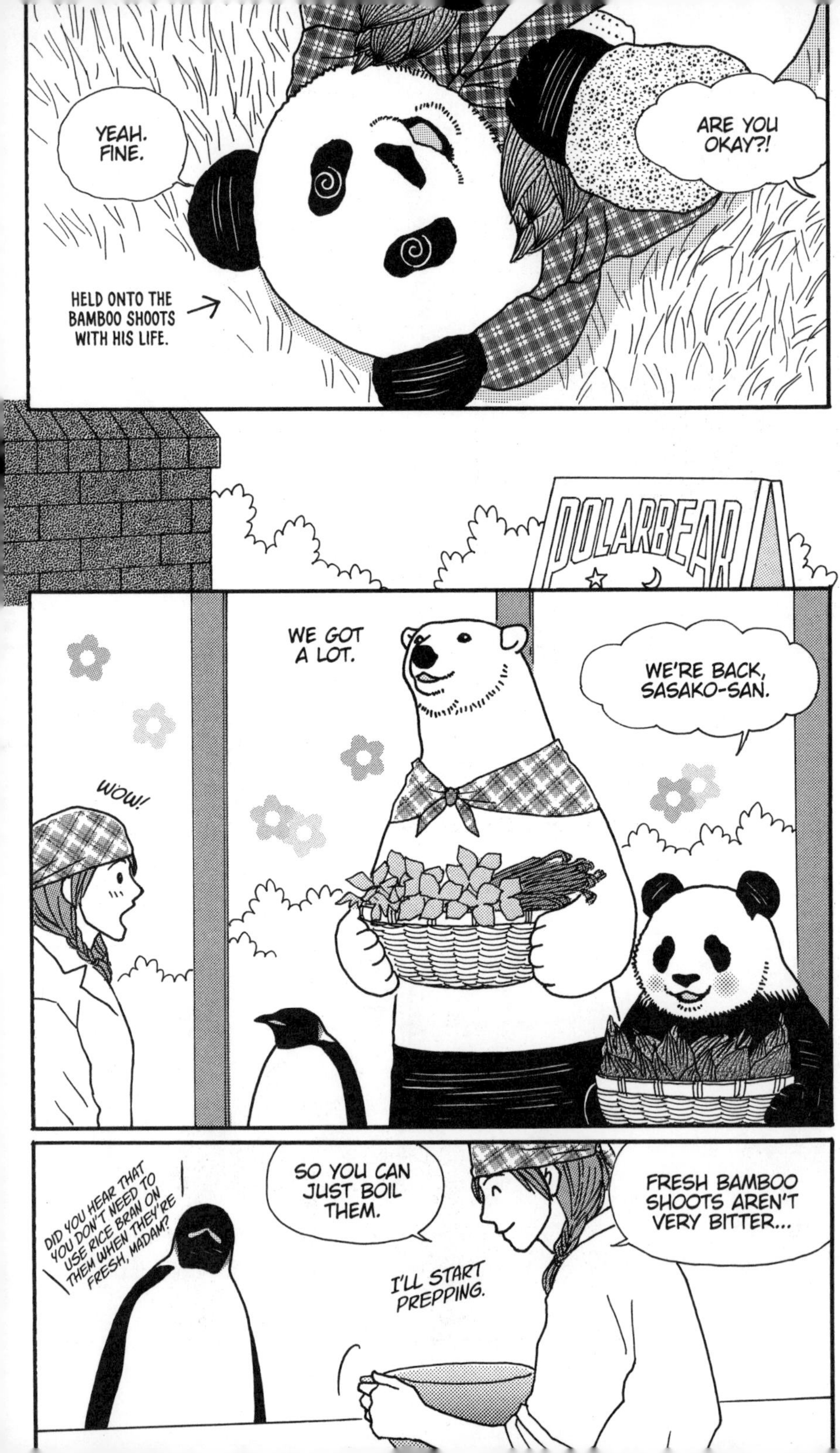
ARE YOU OKAY?!
YEAH. FINE.
HELD ONTO THE BAMBOO SHOOTS WITH HIS LIFE.
POLARBEAR
WE'RE BACK, SASAKO-SAN.
WE GOT A LOT.
WOW!
FRESH BAMBOO SHOOTS AREN'T VERY BITTER...
SO YOU CAN JUST BOIL THEM.
I'LL START PREPPING.
DID YOU HEAR THAT YOU DON'T NEED TO USE RICE BRAN ON THEM WHEN THEY'RE FRESH, MADAM?

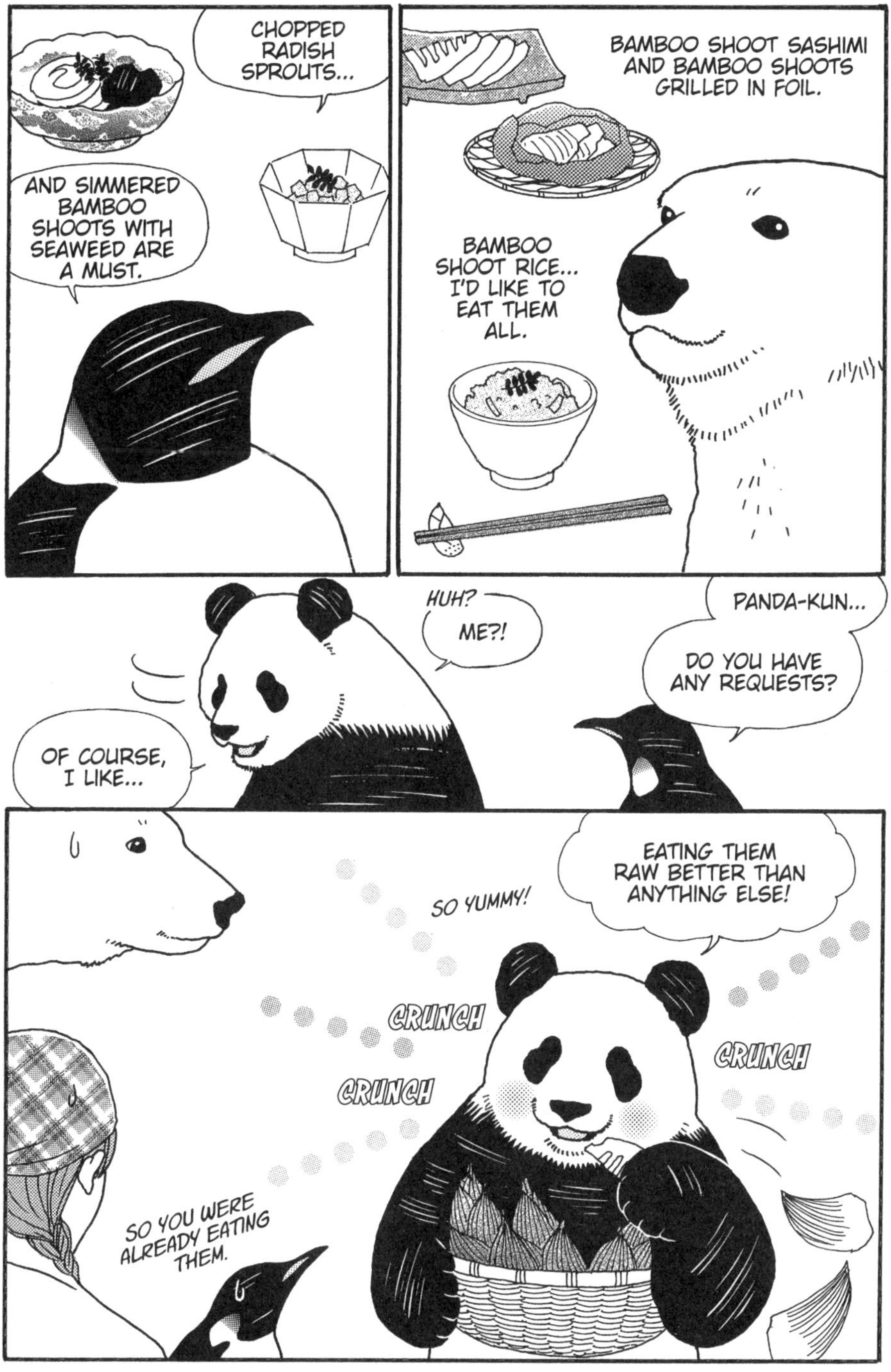
BAMBOO SHOOT SASHIMI AND BAMBOO SHOOTS GRILLED IN FOIL.
BAMBOO SHOOT RICE... I'D LIKE TO EAT THEM ALL.
CHOPPED RADISH SPROUTS...
AND SIMMERED BAMBOO SHOOTS WITH SEAWEED ARE A MUST.
PANDA-KUN...
DO YOU HAVE ANY REQUESTS?
HUH?
ME?!
OF COURSE, I LIKE...
EATING THEM RAW BETTER THAN ANYTHING ELSE!
SO YUMMY!
CRUNCH
CRUNCH
CRUNCH
SO YOU WERE ALREADY EATING THEM.

THAT'S NOT EXACTLY A RECIPE...

BFFS! ⟨BAMBOO FRIENDS FOREVER⟩

Polar Bear Café

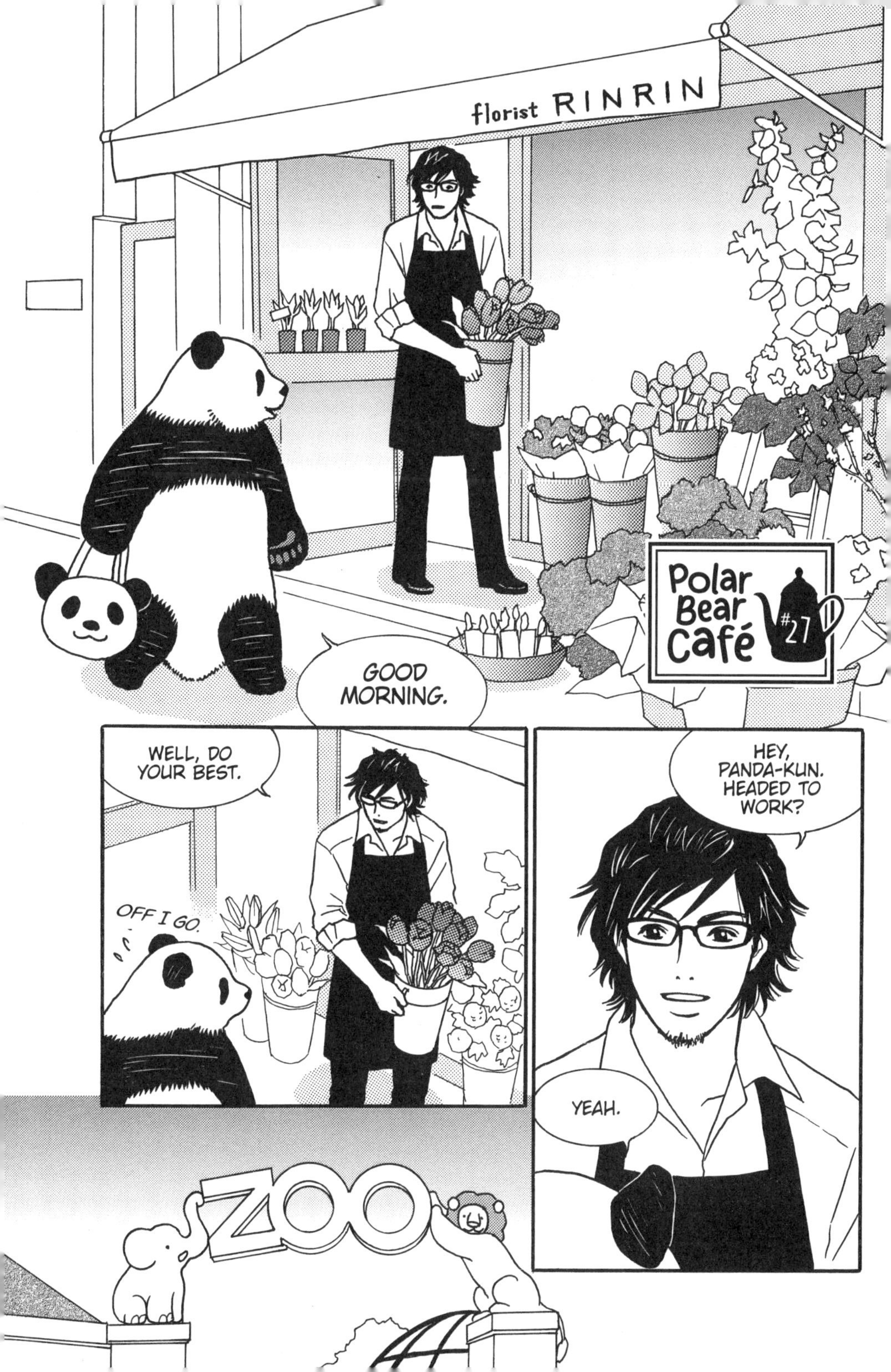
florist RINRIN
Polar Bear Café
#27
GOOD MORNING.
HEY, PANDA-KUN. HEADED TO WORK?
YEAH.
WELL, DO YOUR BEST.
OFF I GO.
ZOO

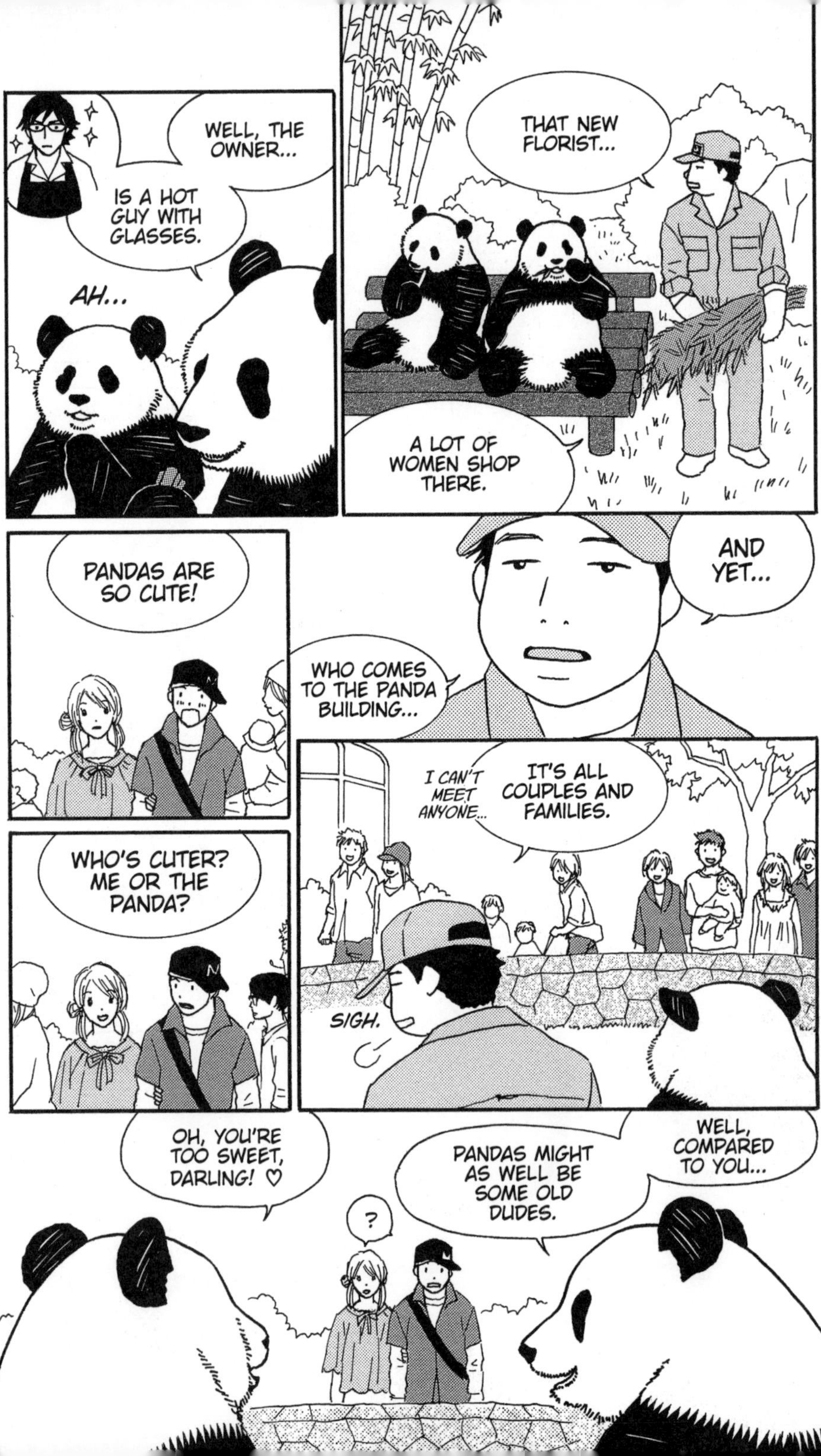
THAT NEW FLORIST...
A LOT OF WOMEN SHOP THERE.
WELL, THE OWNER...
IS A HOT GUY WITH GLASSES.
AH...
AND YET...
WHO COMES TO THE PANDA BUILDING...
IT'S ALL COUPLES AND FAMILIES.
I CAN'T MEET ANYONE...
SIGH.
PANDAS ARE SO CUTE!
WHO'S CUTER? ME OR THE PANDA?
WELL, COMPARED TO YOU...
PANDAS MIGHT AS WELL BE SOME OLD DUDES.
?
OH, YOU'RE TOO SWEET, DARLING! ♡

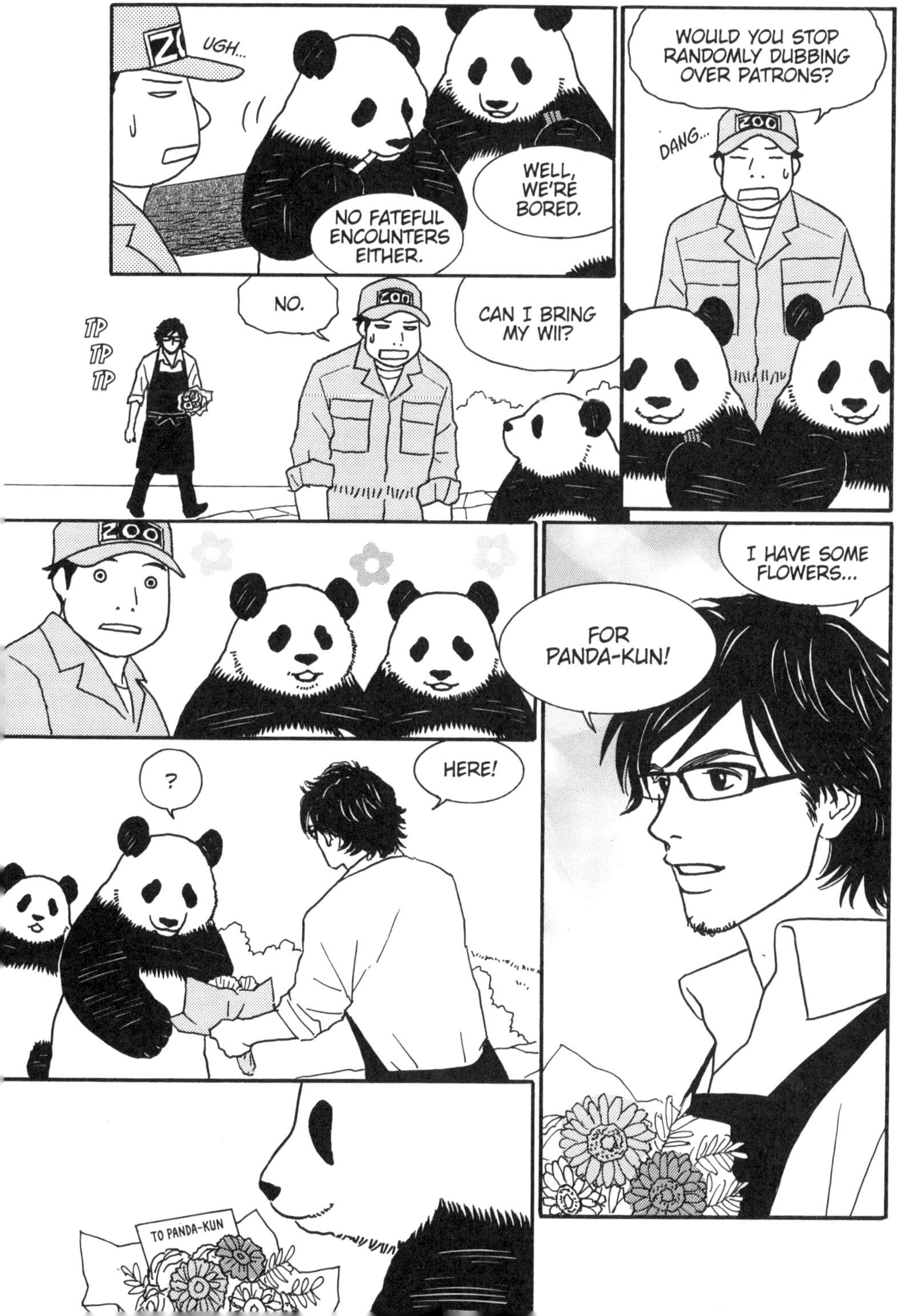
WOULD YOU STOP RANDOMLY DUBBING OVER PATRONS?
DANG...
WELL, WE'RE BORED.
NO FATEFUL ENCOUNTERS EITHER.
UGH...
CAN I BRING MY WII?
NO.
TP TP TP
I HAVE SOME FLOWERS...
FOR PANDA-KUN!
HERE!
?
TO PANDA-KUN

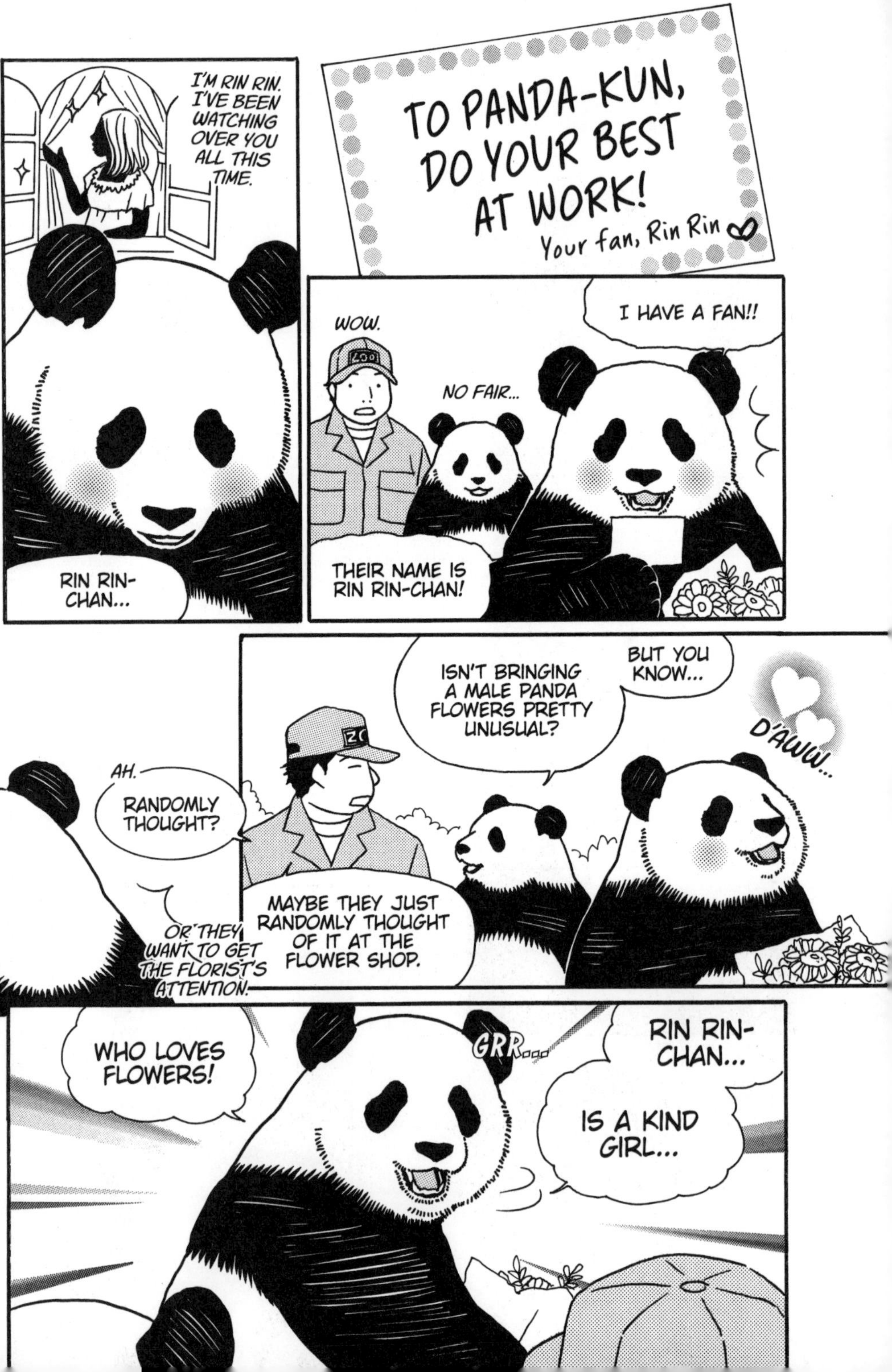
TO PANDA-KUN,
DO YOUR BEST
AT WORK!
Your fan, Rin Rin
I HAVE A FAN!!
WOW.
NO FAIR...
THEIR NAME IS RIN RIN-CHAN!
I'M RIN RIN. I'VE BEEN WATCHING OVER YOU ALL THIS TIME.
RIN RIN-CHAN...
D'AWW...
BUT YOU KNOW...
ISN'T BRINGING A MALE PANDA FLOWERS PRETTY UNUSUAL?
MAYBE THEY JUST RANDOMLY THOUGHT OF IT AT THE FLOWER SHOP.
AH.
RANDOMLY THOUGHT?
OR THEY WANT TO GET THE FLORIST'S ATTENTION.
RIN RIN-CHAN...
IS A KIND GIRL...
GRR...
WHO LOVES FLOWERS!

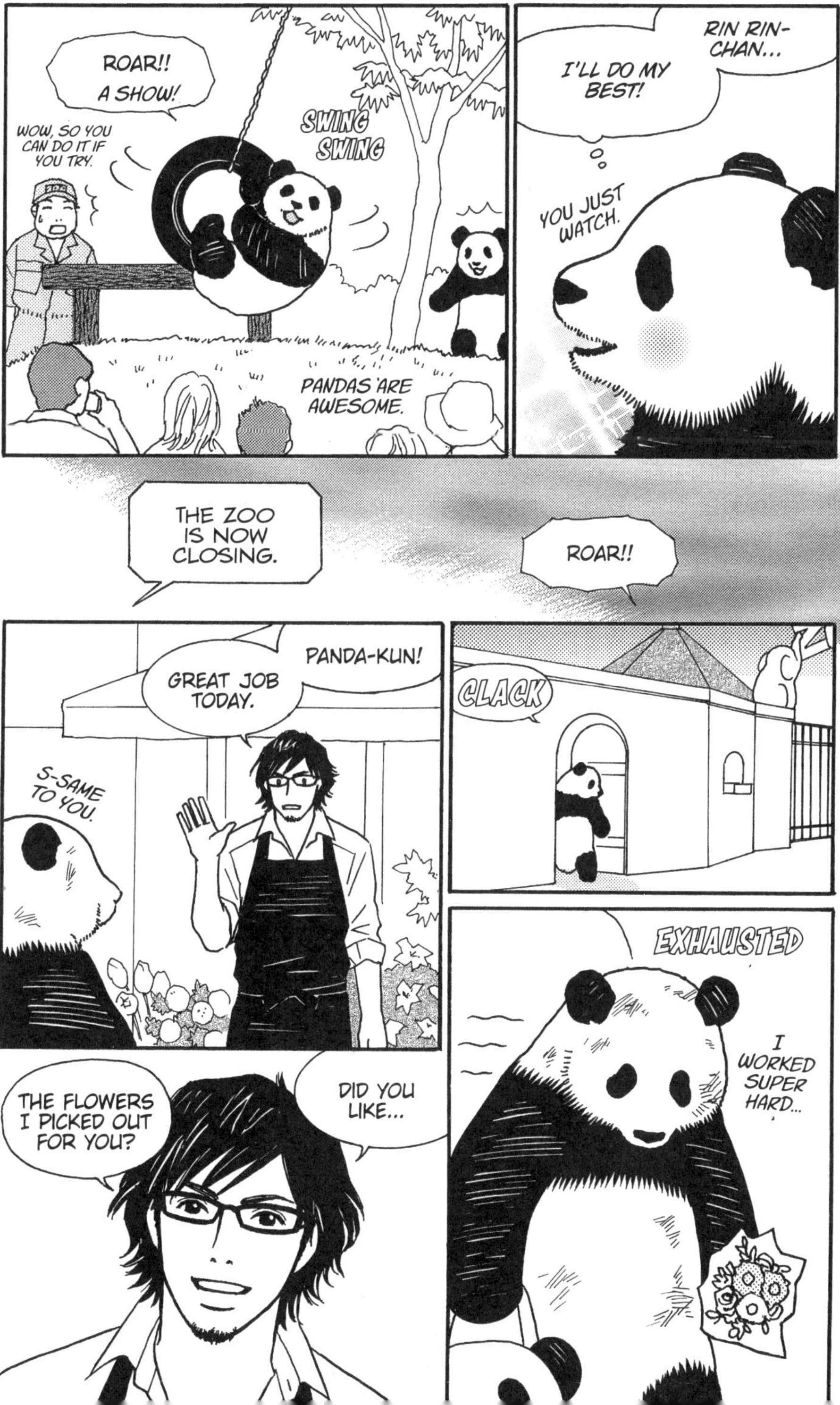

RIN RIN-CHAN...
I'LL DO MY BEST!
YOU JUST WATCH.
ROAR!! A SHOW!
WOW, SO YOU CAN DO IT IF YOU TRY.
SWING SWING
PANDAS ARE AWESOME.
ROAR!!
THE ZOO IS NOW CLOSING.
CLACK
PANDA-KUN!
GREAT JOB TODAY.
S-SAME TO YOU.
EXHAUSTED
I WORKED SUPER HARD...
DID YOU LIKE...
THE FLOWERS I PICKED OUT FOR YOU?

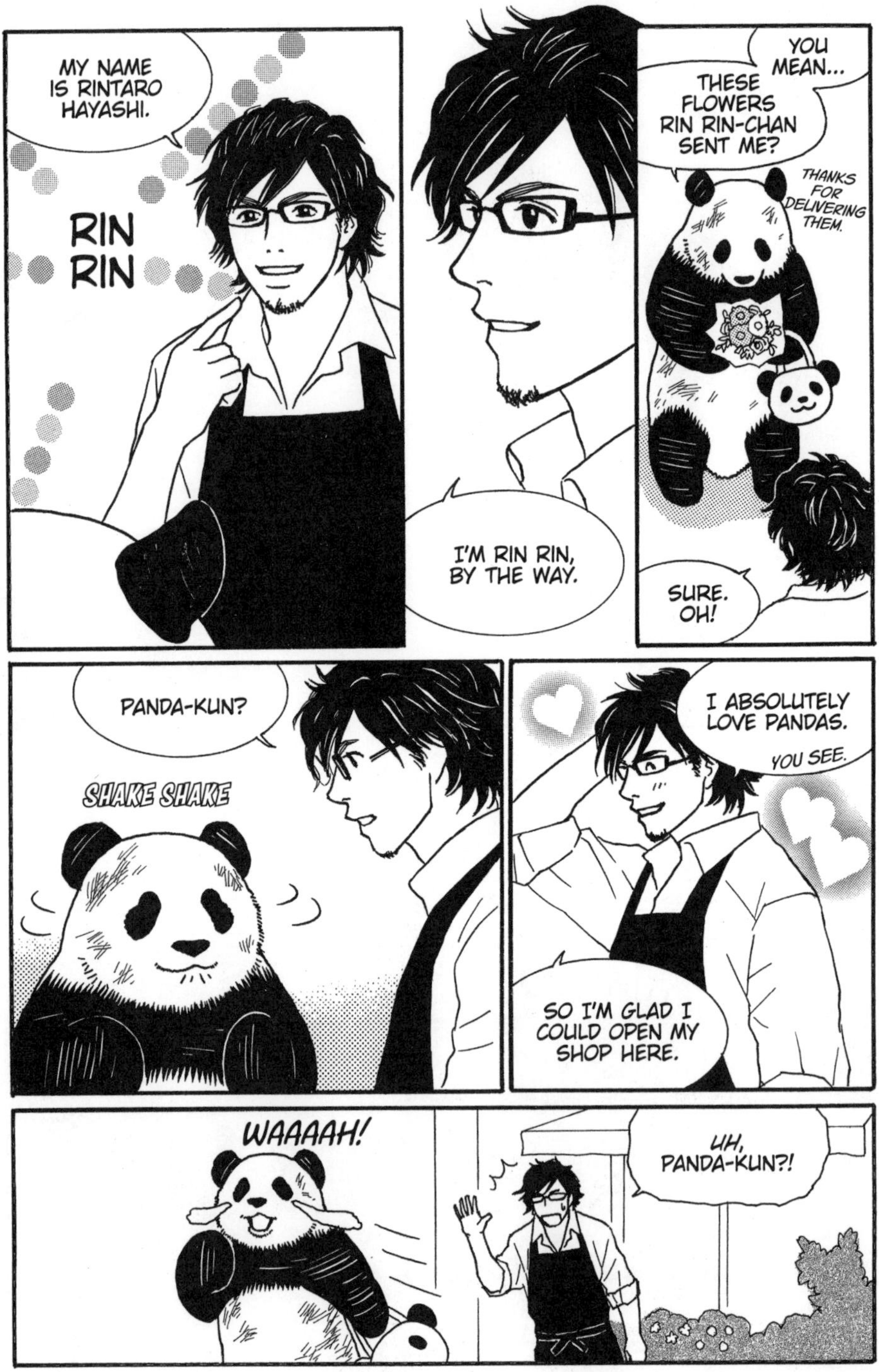
YOU MEAN... THESE FLOWERS RIN RIN-CHAN SENT ME?
THANKS FOR DELIVERING THEM.
SURE. OH!
I'M RIN RIN, BY THE WAY.
MY NAME IS RINTARO HAYASHI.
RIN RIN
I ABSOLUTELY LOVE PANDAS.
YOU SEE.
SO I'M GLAD I COULD OPEN MY SHOP HERE.
PANDA-KUN?
SHAKE SHAKE
UH, PANDA-KUN?!
WAAAAH!

WHAT A SHORT-LIVED DREAM...

Polar Bear Café #28

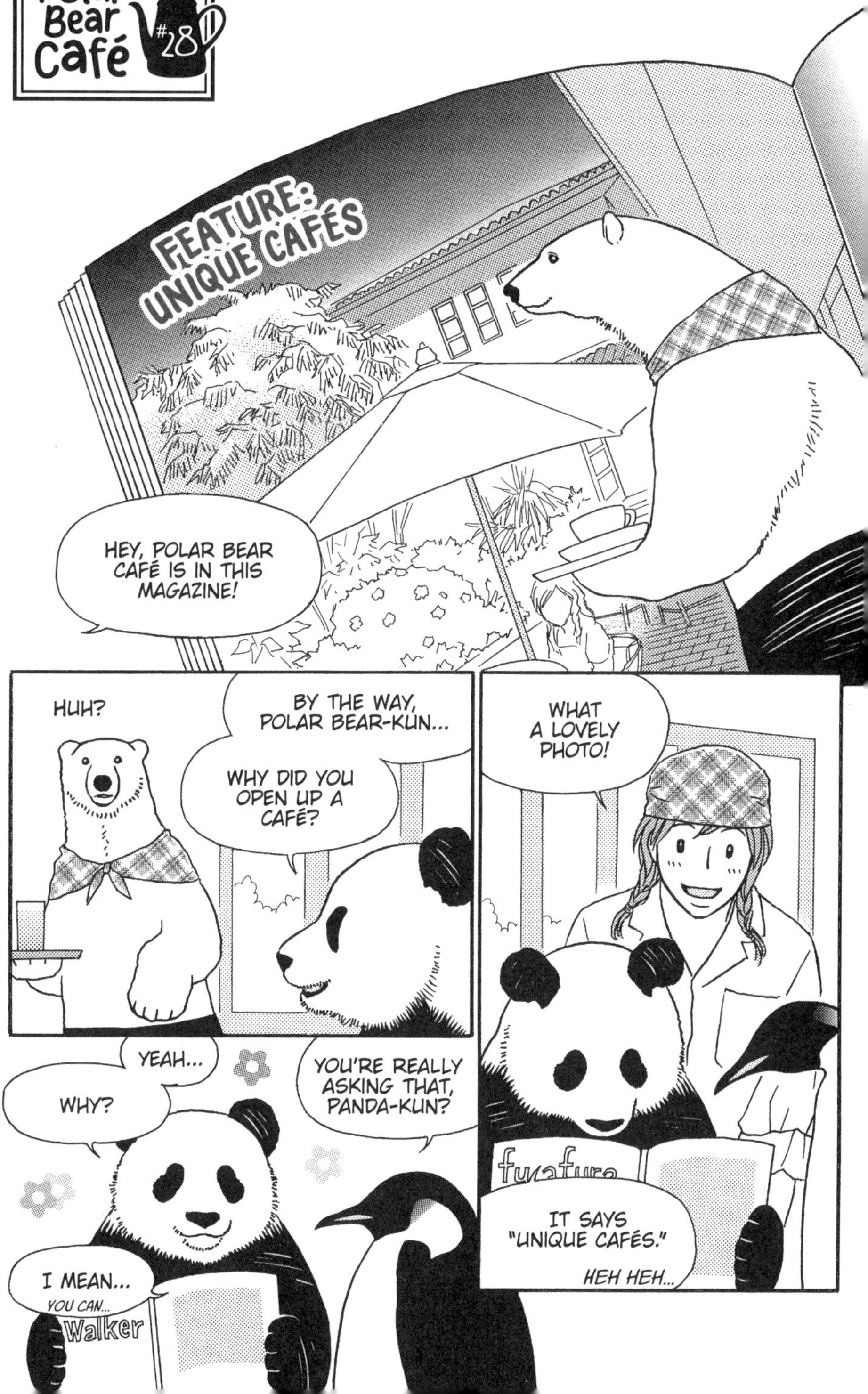
FEATURE: UNIQUE CAFÉS
HEY, POLAR BEAR CAFÉ IS IN THIS MAGAZINE!
WHAT A LOVELY PHOTO!
IT SAYS "UNIQUE CAFÉS."
HEH HEH...
BY THE WAY, POLAR BEAR-KUN...
WHY DID YOU OPEN UP A CAFÉ?
HUH?
YOU'RE REALLY ASKING THAT, PANDA-KUN?
YEAH...
WHY?
I MEAN...
YOU CAN...
Walker

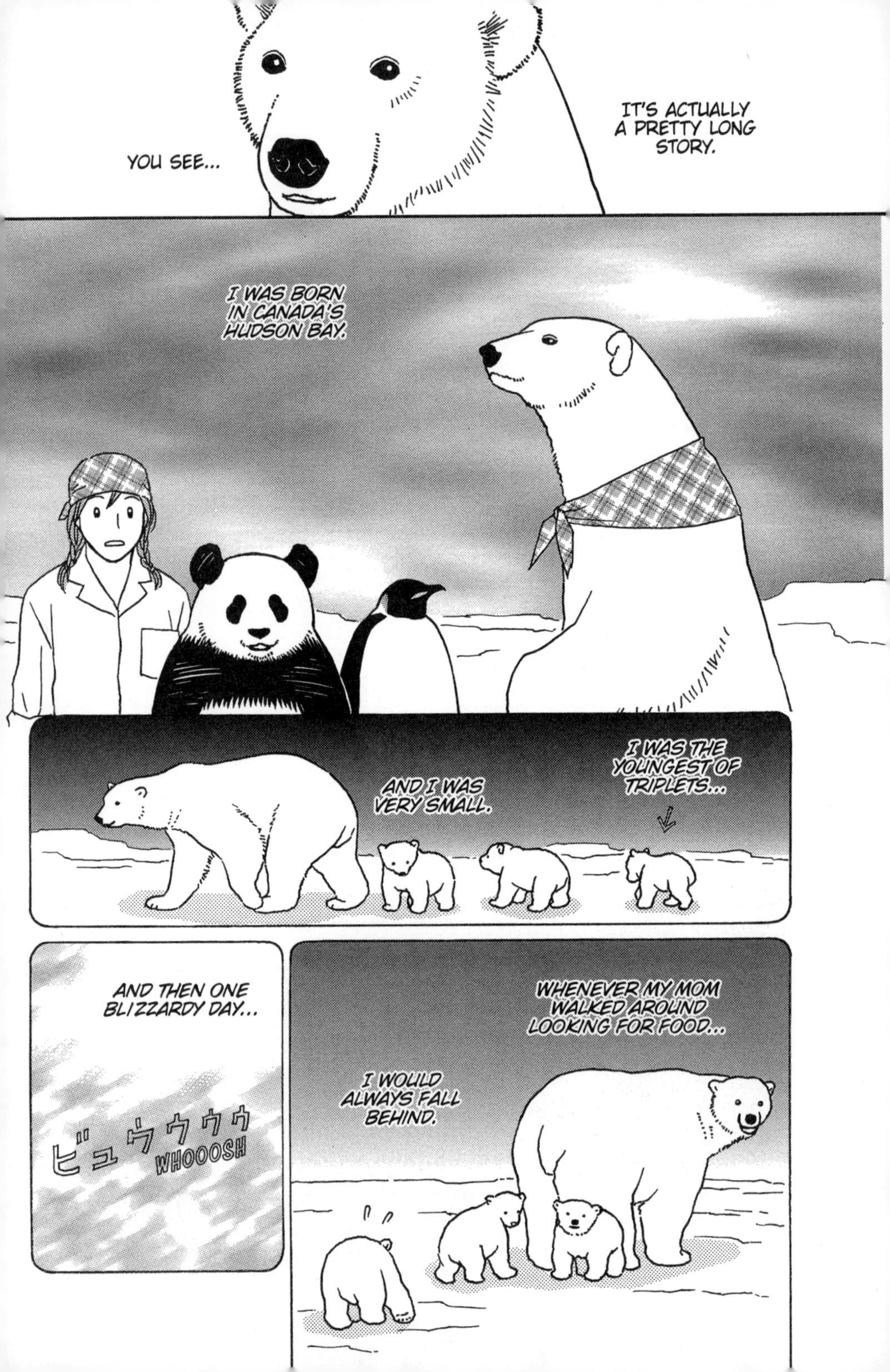
IT'S ACTUALLY A PRETTY LONG STORY.
YOU SEE...
I WAS BORN IN CANADA'S HUDSON BAY.
I WAS THE YOUNGEST OF TRIPLETS...
AND I WAS VERY SMALL.
WHENEVER MY MOM WALKED AROUND LOOKING FOR FOOD...
I WOULD ALWAYS FALL BEHIND.
AND THEN ONE BLIZZARDY DAY...
ビュウウウウ
WHOOOSH

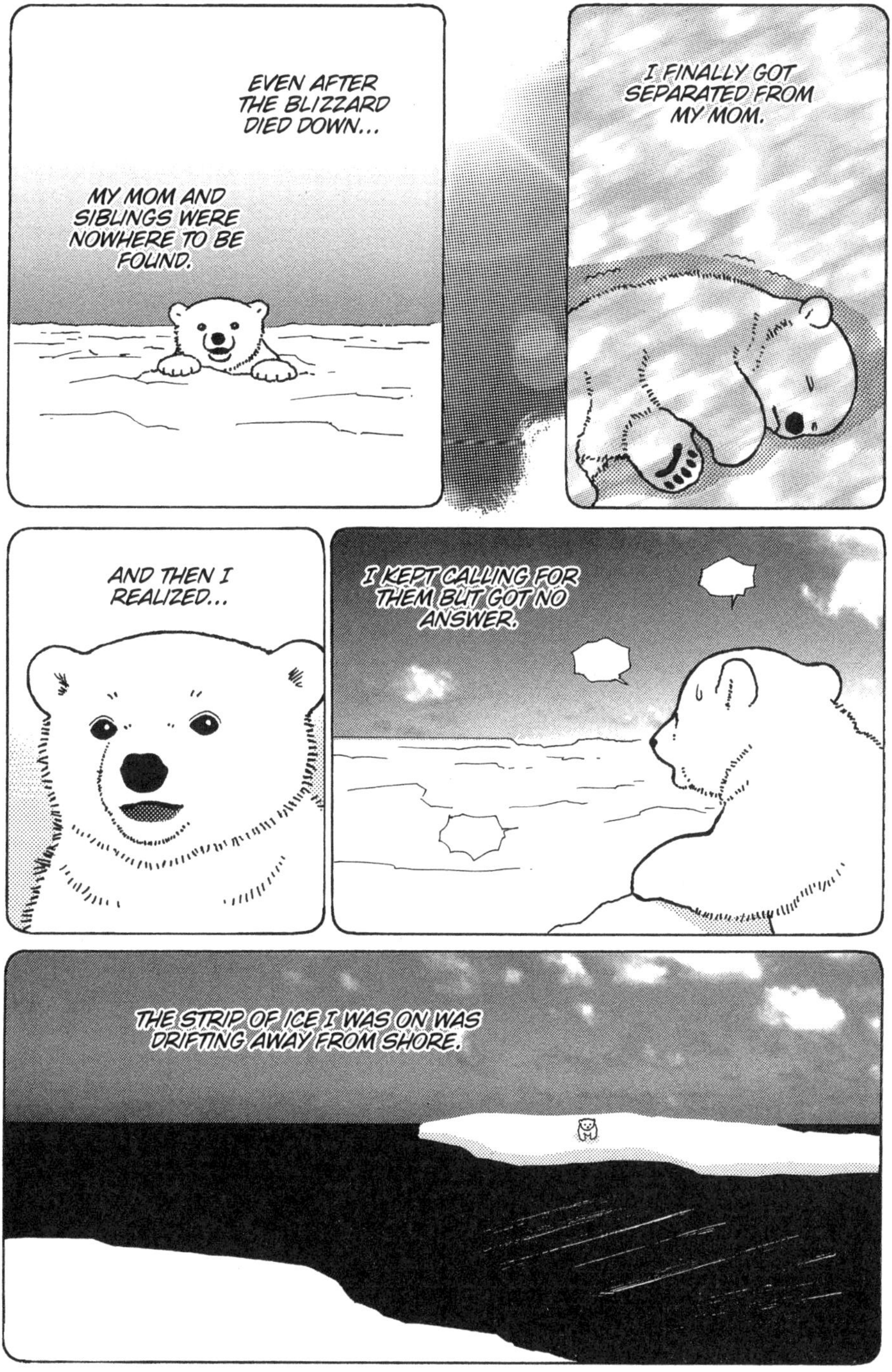
I FINALLY GOT SEPARATED FROM MY MOM.
EVEN AFTER THE BLIZZARD DIED DOWN...
MY MOM AND SIBLINGS WERE NOWHERE TO BE FOUND.
I KEPT CALLING FOR THEM BUT GOT NO ANSWER.
AND THEN I REALIZED...
THE STRIP OF ICE I WAS ON WAS DRIFTING AWAY FROM SHORE.

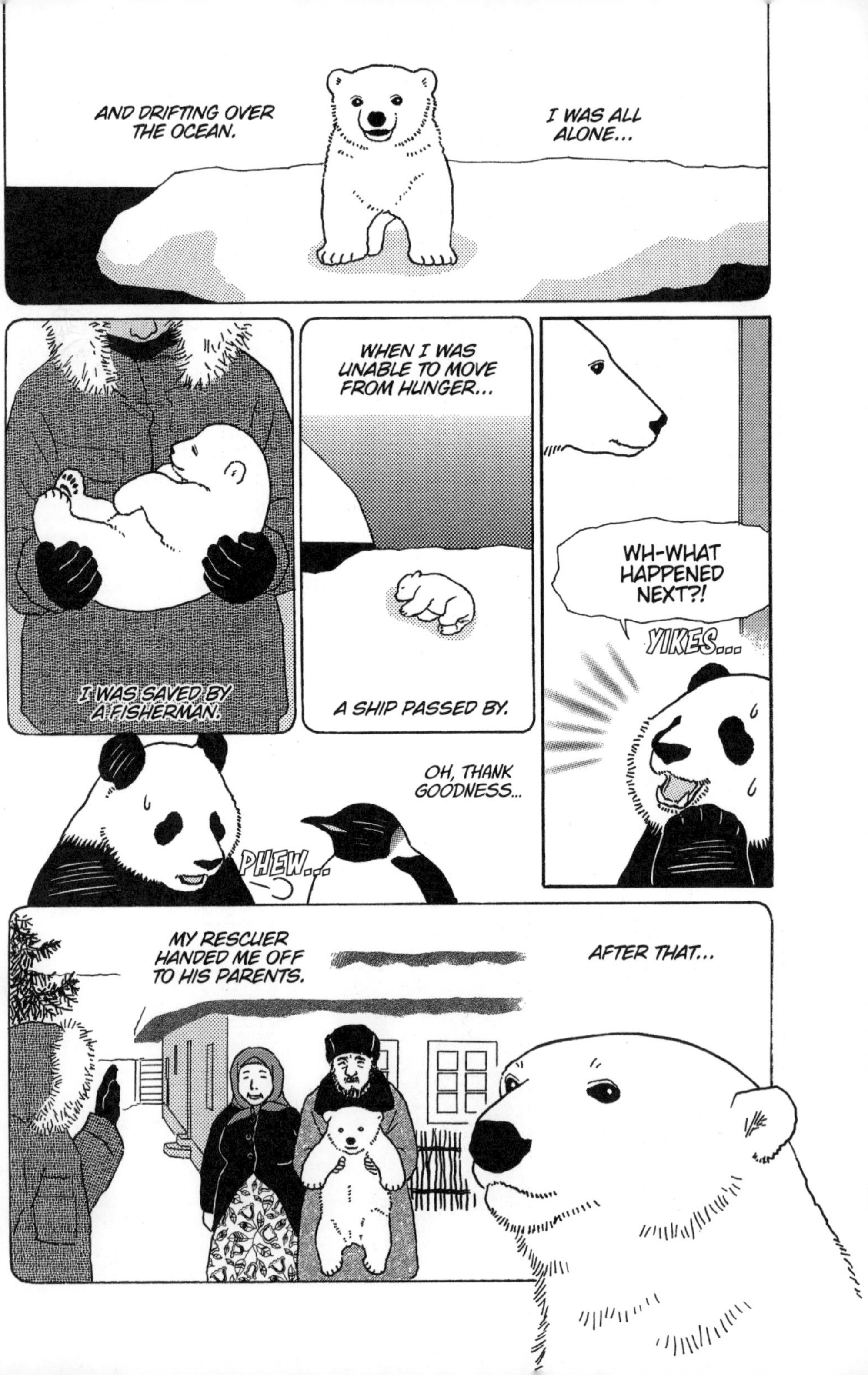

I WAS ALL ALONE...
AND DRIFTING OVER THE OCEAN.
WH-WHAT HAPPENED NEXT?!
YIKES...
WHEN I WAS UNABLE TO MOVE FROM HUNGER...
A SHIP PASSED BY.
I WAS SAVED BY A FISHERMAN.
OH, THANK GOODNESS...
PHEW...
AFTER THAT...
MY RESCUER HANDED ME OFF TO HIS PARENTS.

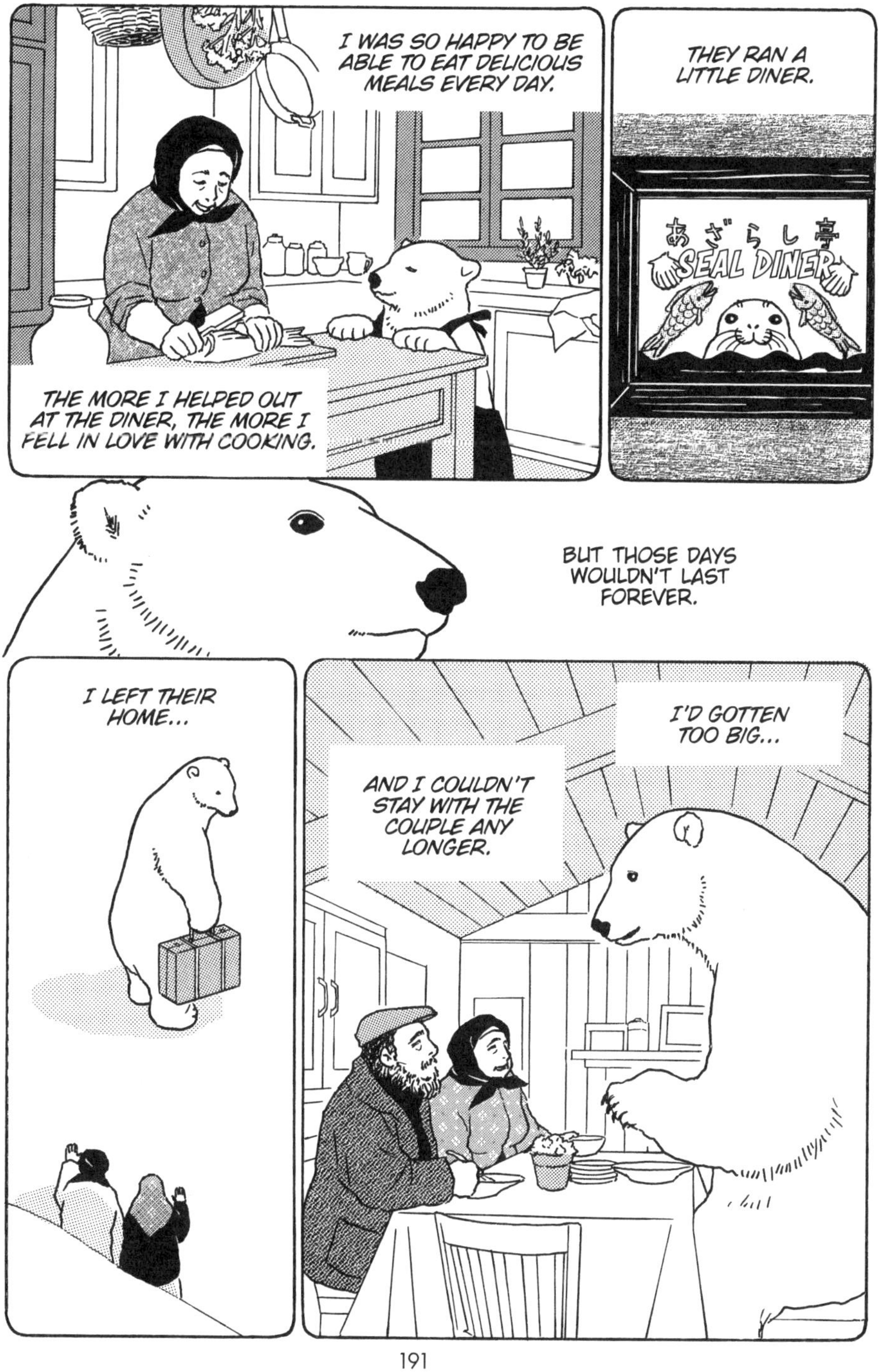
THEY RAN A LITTLE DINER.
あざらし亭
SEAL DINER
I WAS SO HAPPY TO BE ABLE TO EAT DELICIOUS MEALS EVERY DAY.
THE MORE I HELPED OUT AT THE DINER, THE MORE I FELL IN LOVE WITH COOKING.
BUT THOSE DAYS WOULDN'T LAST FOREVER.
I'D GOTTEN TOO BIG...
AND I COULDN'T STAY WITH THE COUPLE ANY LONGER.
I LEFT THEIR HOME...

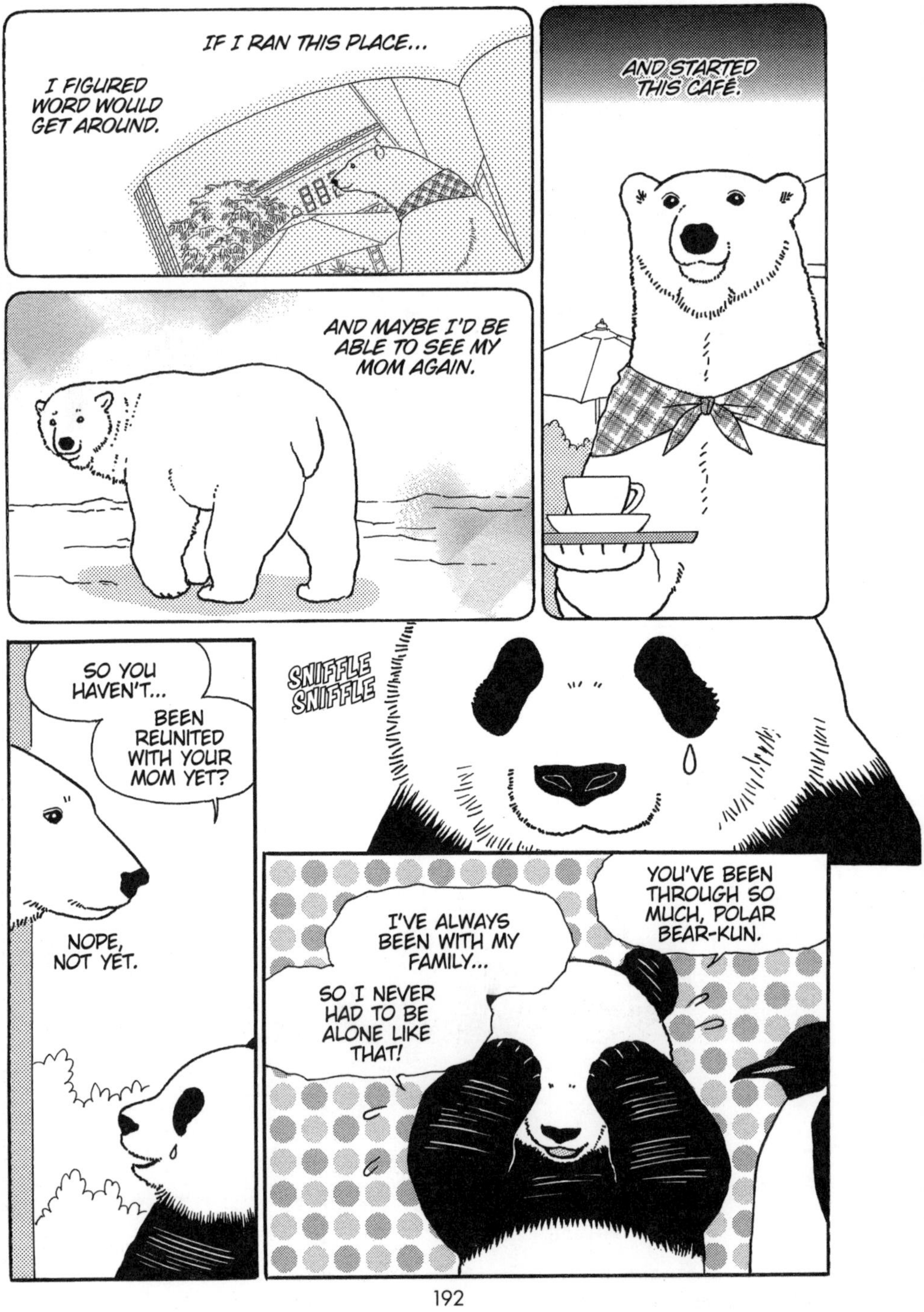

AND STARTED THIS CAFÉ.
IF I RAN THIS PLACE...
I FIGURED WORD WOULD GET AROUND.
AND MAYBE I'D BE ABLE TO SEE MY MOM AGAIN.
SNIFFLE SNIFFLE
YOU'VE BEEN THROUGH SO MUCH, POLAR BEAR-KUN.
I'VE ALWAYS BEEN WITH MY FAMILY...
SO I NEVER HAD TO BE ALONE LIKE THAT!
SO YOU HAVEN'T...
BEEN REUNITED WITH YOUR MOM YET?
NOPE, NOT YET.

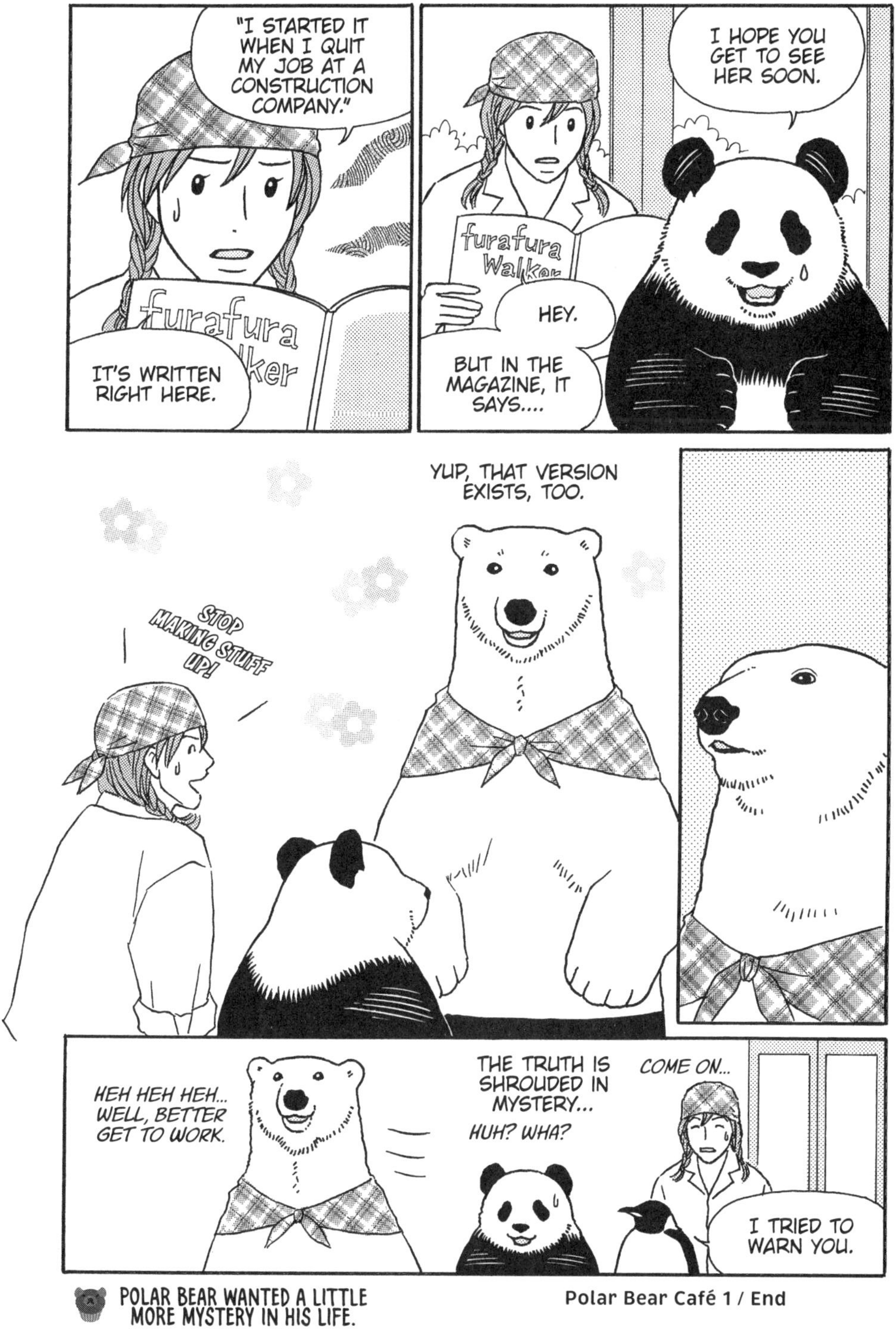
I HOPE YOU GET TO SEE HER SOON.
HEY.
BUT IN THE MAGAZINE, IT SAYS....
"I STARTED IT WHEN I QUIT MY JOB AT A CONSTRUCTION COMPANY."
IT'S WRITTEN RIGHT HERE.
furafura Walker
YUP, THAT VERSION EXISTS, TOO.
STOP MAKING STUFF UP!
COME ON...
THE TRUTH IS SHROUDED IN MYSTERY...
I TRIED TO WARN YOU.
HUH? WHA?
HEH HEH HEH... WELL, BETTER GET TO WORK.

POLAR BEAR WANTED A LITTLE MORE MYSTERY IN HIS LIFE.

Polar Bear Café 1 / End

THE CONSTRUCTION COMPANY VERSION

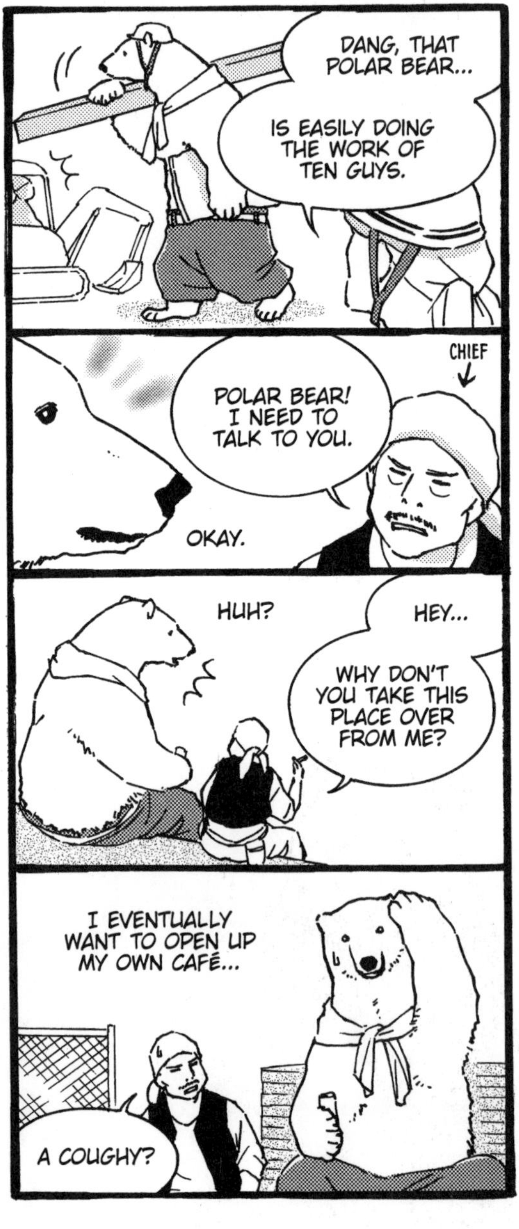
DANG, THAT POLAR BEAR...
IS EASILY DOING THE WORK OF TEN GUYS.
CHIEF
POLAR BEAR! I NEED TO TALK TO YOU.
OKAY.
HEY...
HUH?
WHY DON'T YOU TAKE THIS PLACE OVER FROM ME?
I EVENTUALLY WANT TO OPEN UP MY OWN CAFÉ...
A COUGHY?

Polar Bear Café

Polar Bear Café

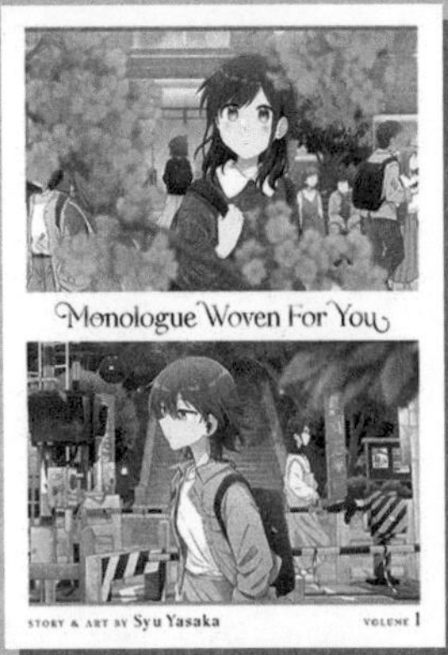
Monologue Woven For You
STORY & ART BY Syu Yasaka
VOLUME 1
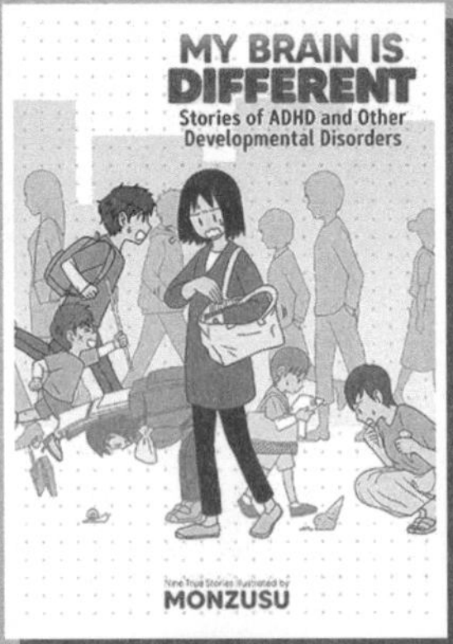
MY BRAIN IS DIFFERENT
Stories of ADHD and Other Developmental Disorders
MONZUSU
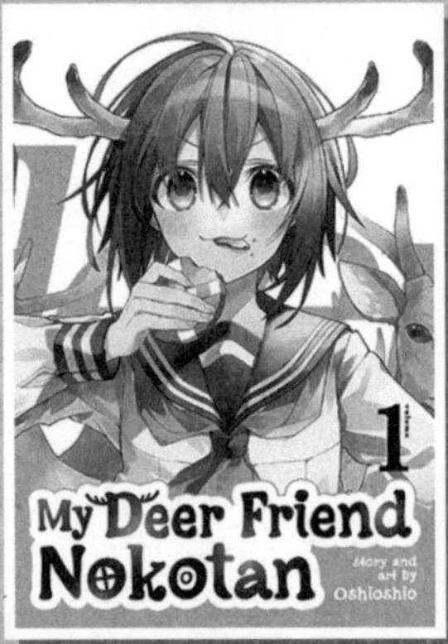
1
My Deer Friend Nokotan
Story and art by Oshioshio
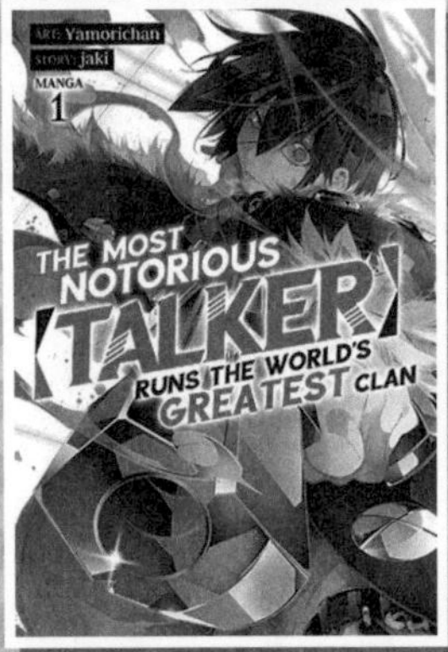
ART: Yamorichan
STORY: jaki
MANGA 1
THE MOST NOTORIOUS TALKER RUNS THE WORLD'S GREATEST CLAN
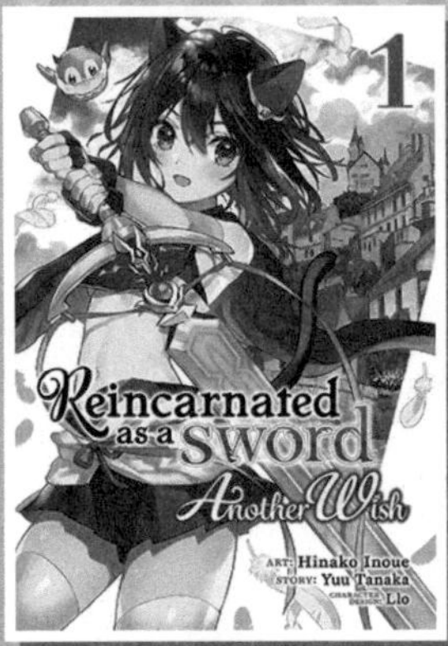
1
Reincarnated as a Sword
Another Wish
ART: Hinako Inoue
STORY: Yuu Tanaka
Llo
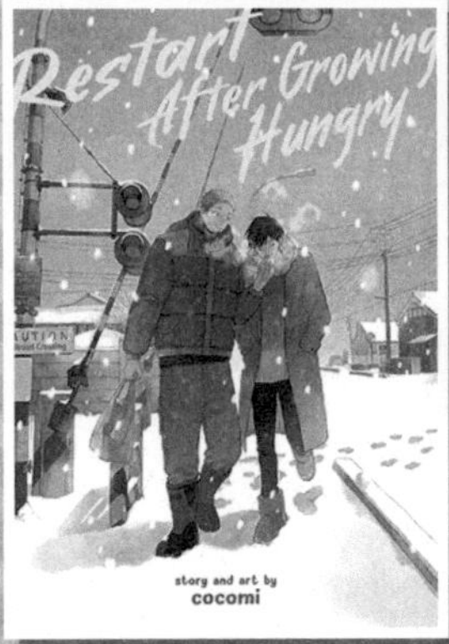
Restart After Growing Hungry
story and art by
cocomi
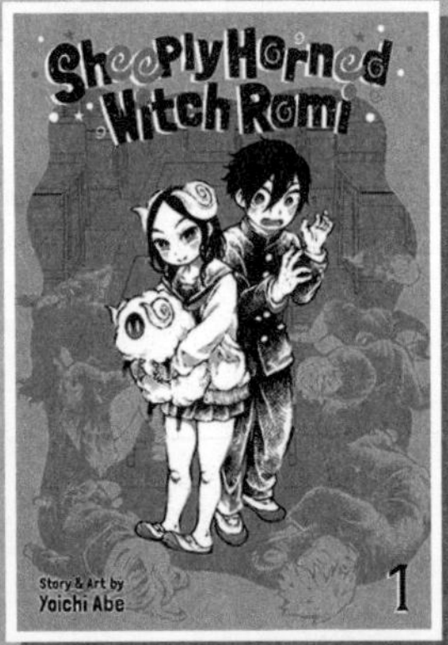
Sheeply Horned Witch Romi
Story & Art by
Yoichi Abe
1
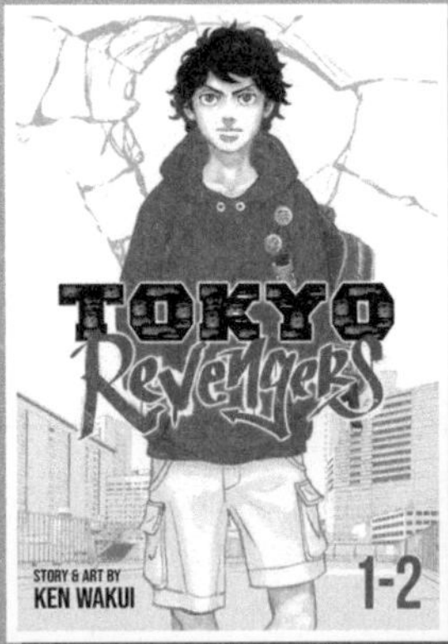
TOKYO Revengers
STORY & ART BY
KEN WAKUI
1-2
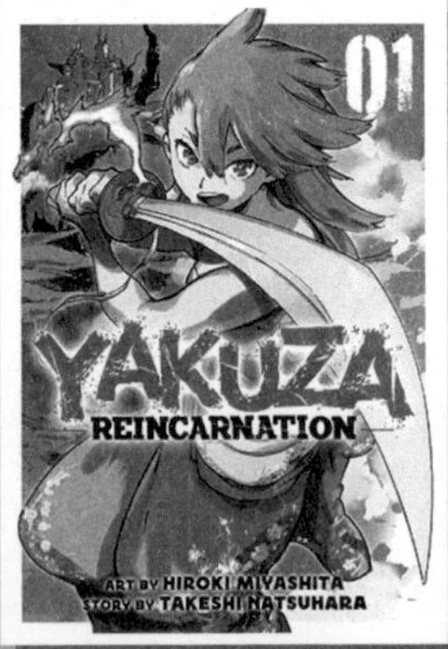
01
YAKUZA REINCARNATION
ART BY HIROKI MIYASHITA
STORY BY TAKESHI NATSUHARA

SEVEN SEAS ENTERTAINMENT PRESENTS

Polar Bear Café

story and art by **ALOHA HIGA** **COLLECTOR'S EDITION 1**

TRANSLATION
Michelle Tymon

LETTERING
Christa Miesner

COVER DESIGN
H. Qi

PROOFREADER
Danielle King

COPY EDITOR
Leighanna DeRouen

EDITOR
Linda Lombardi

PRODUCTION DESIGNER
Christina McKenzie

PRODUCTION MANAGER
Lissa Pattillo

PREPRESS TECHNICIAN
Melanie Ujimori
Jules Valera

EDITOR-IN-CHIEF
Julie Davis

ASSOCIATE PUBLISHER
Adam Arnold

PUBLISHER
Jason DeAngelis

ISBN: 978-1-68579-334-0
Printed in Canada
First Printing: January 2023
10 9 8 7 6 5 4 3 2 1

READING DIRECTIONS

This book reads from ***right to left***, Japanese style. If this is your first time reading manga, you start reading from the top right panel on each page and take it from there. If you get lost, just follow the numbered diagram here. It may seem backwards at first, but you'll get the hang of it! Have fun!!

1
2
3
4
5
6
7
8
9

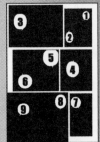

SPECIAL SHORT 1

PRINCE POLAR BEAR AND PANDERELLA

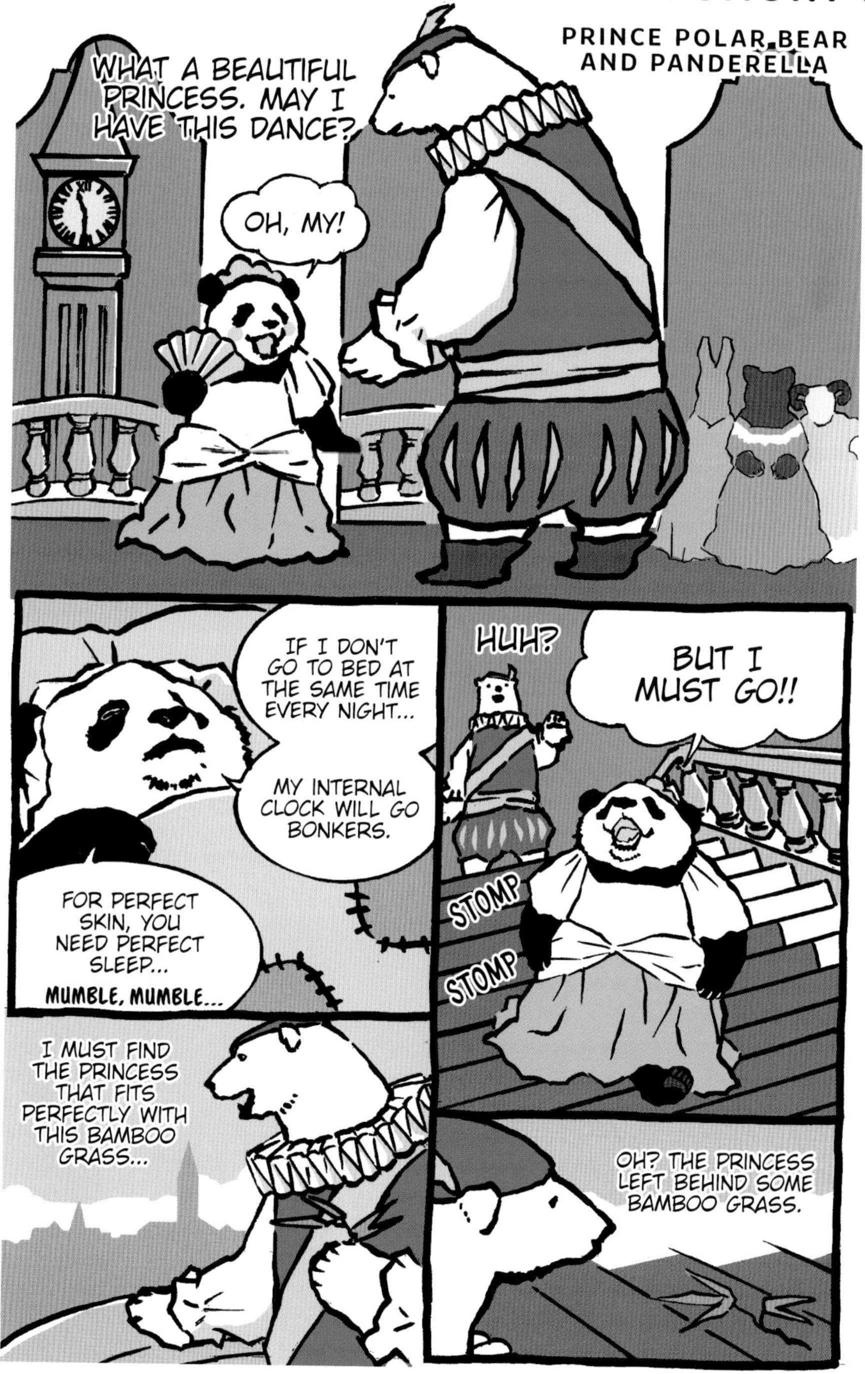

WHAT A BEAUTIFUL PRINCESS. MAY I HAVE THIS DANCE?
OH, MY!
BUT I MUST GO!!
HUH?
STOMP
STOMP
IF I DON'T GO TO BED AT THE SAME TIME EVERY NIGHT...
MY INTERNAL CLOCK WILL GO BONKERS.
FOR PERFECT SKIN, YOU NEED PERFECT SLEEP...
MUMBLE, MUMBLE...
OH? THE PRINCESS LEFT BEHIND SOME BAMBOO GRASS.
I MUST FIND THE PRINCESS THAT FITS PERFECTLY WITH THIS BAMBOO GRASS...

BETWEEN YOU AND ME, THE BAMBOO GRASS WAS JUST SOME LEFTOVERS.

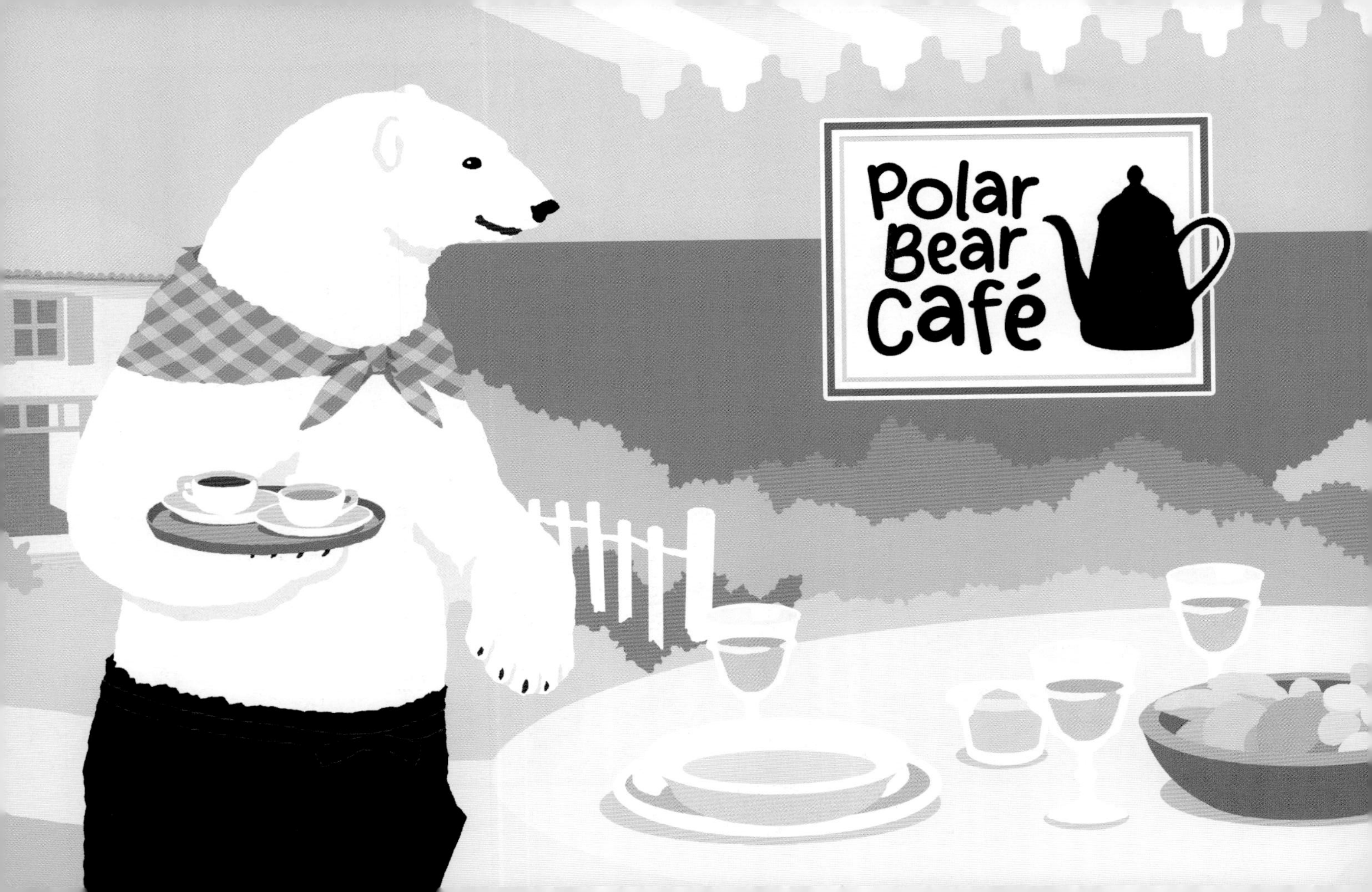
Polar Bear Café

LET'S MAKE AND PLAY WITH PAPER CRAFTS

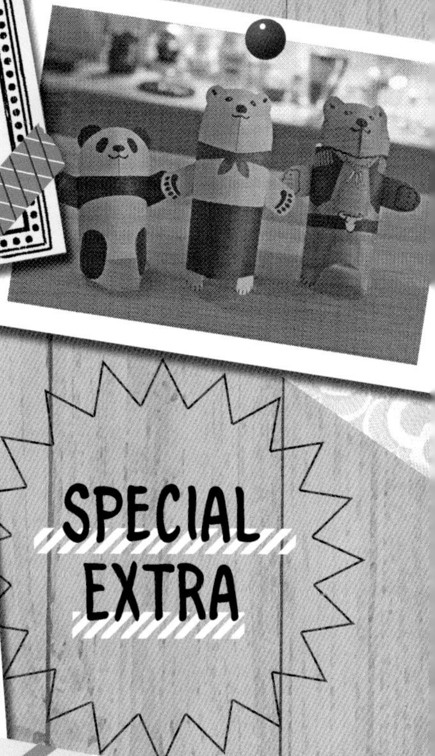

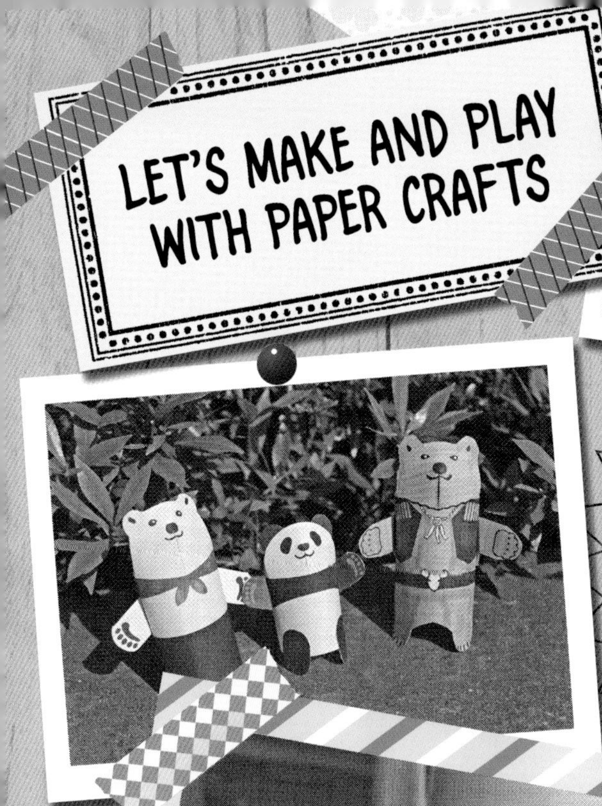

SPECIAL EXTRA

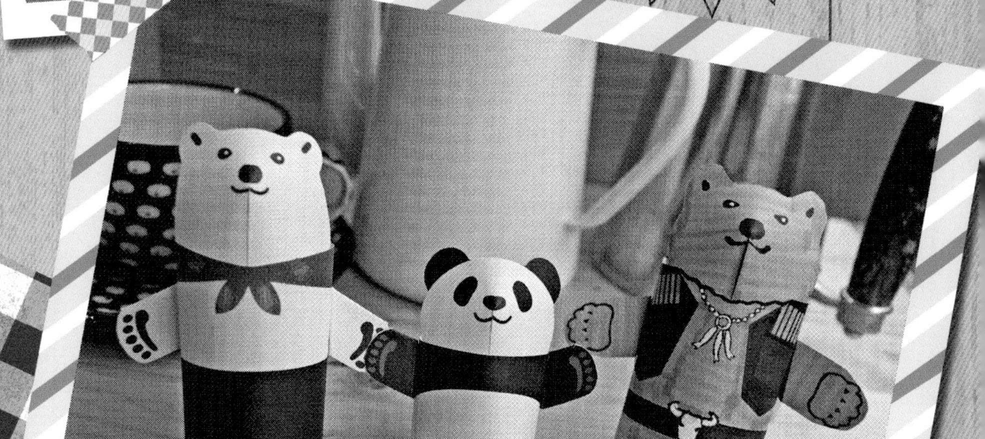

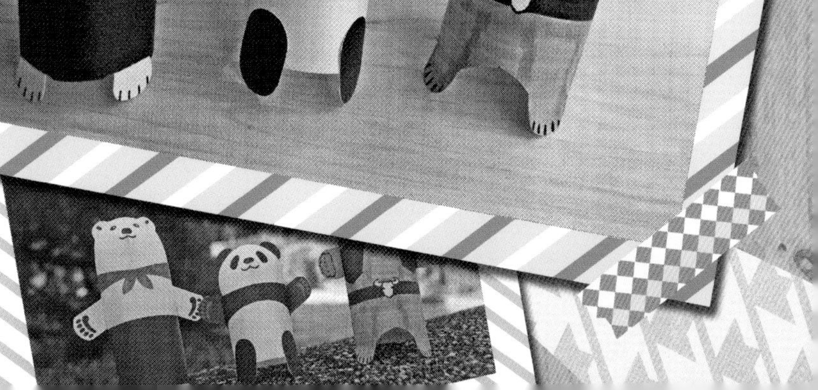

HOW TO MAKE

1. CUT OUT ALL THE PARTS ALONG THE LINES.
2. PUT GLUE ON THE PART UNDER THE NOSE AND CREATE A CONE SHAPE.
3. APPLY GLUE ONTO THE DESIGNATED PARTS OF THE BODY TO CREATE A CYLINDER SHAPE.

IT'S BEST TO MAKE AN ENLARGED COPY TO MAKE THIS.

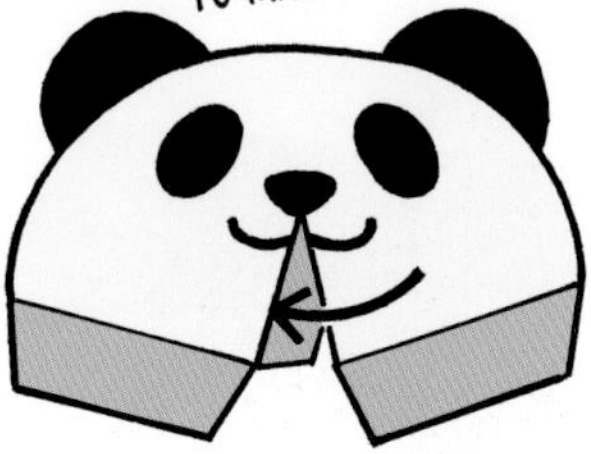

THE HEAD WILL BECOME 3D.

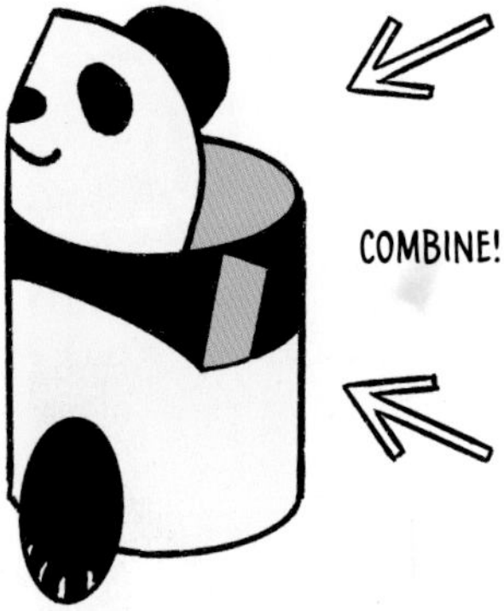

COMBINE!

FOLD BACK.

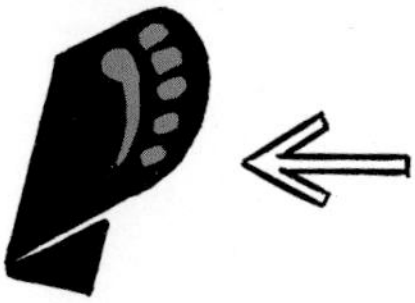

GLUE BOTH SIDES TOGETHER.

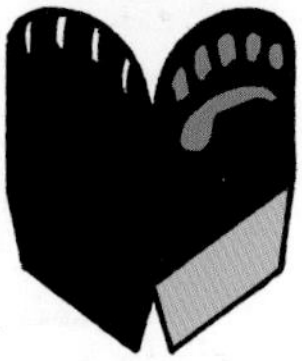

4. FOLD BACK THE HAND ON THE CENTER LINE AND MATCH UP THE BACK END TO THE BODY.
5. GLUE THE HANDS TO THE BODY.

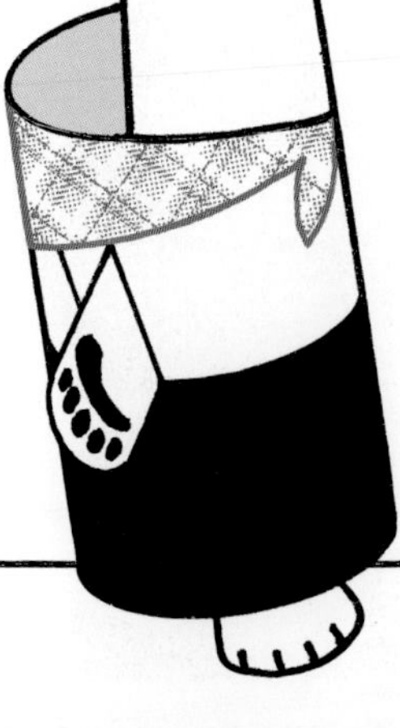

COMPLETE!

IT'S SUPER EASY!

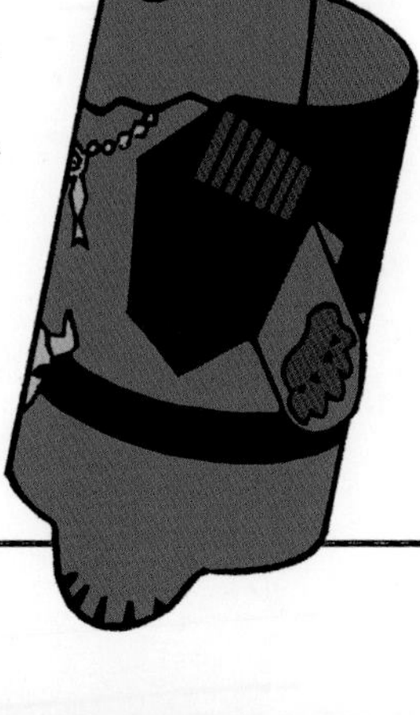

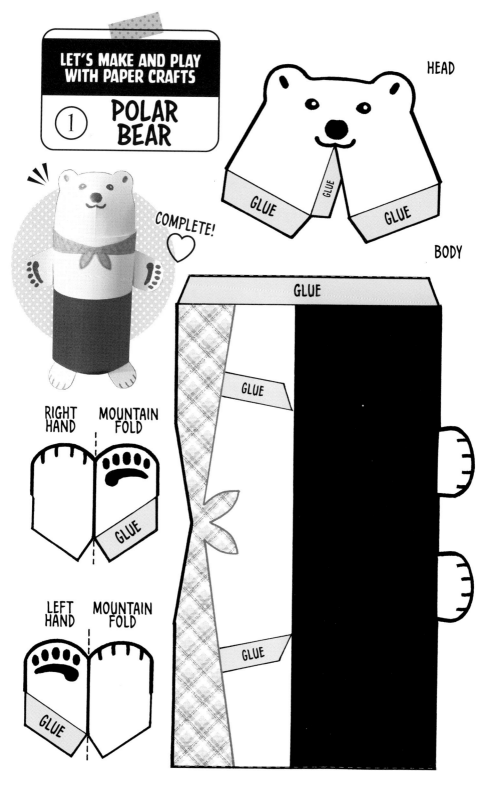

LET'S MAKE AND PLAY WITH PAPER CRAFTS

② PANDA

HEAD

GLUE
GLUE
GLUE

COMPLETE!

BODY

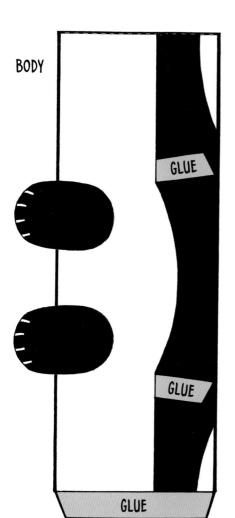

GLUE
GLUE
GLUE

RIGHT HAND

MOUNTAIN FOLD

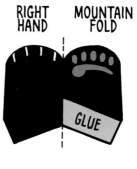

GLUE

LEFT HAND

MOUNTAIN FOLD

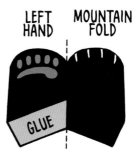

GLUE

LET'S MAKE AND PLAY WITH PAPER CRAFTS

③ GRIZZLY

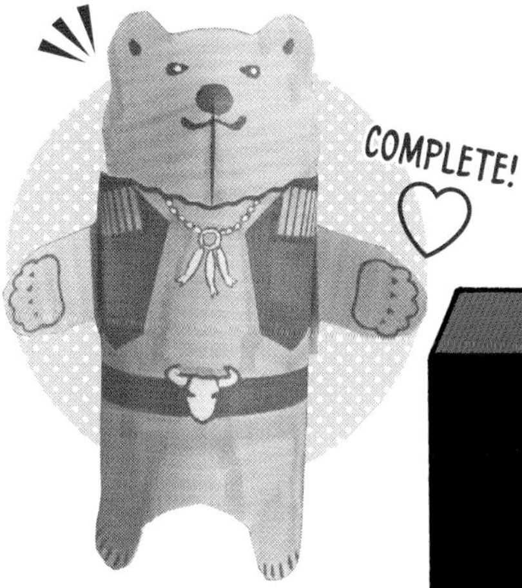
COMPLETE!

HEAD

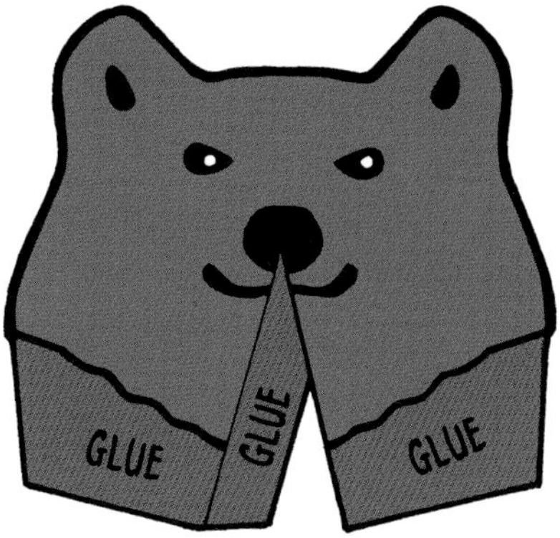
GLUE
GLUE
GLUE

BODY

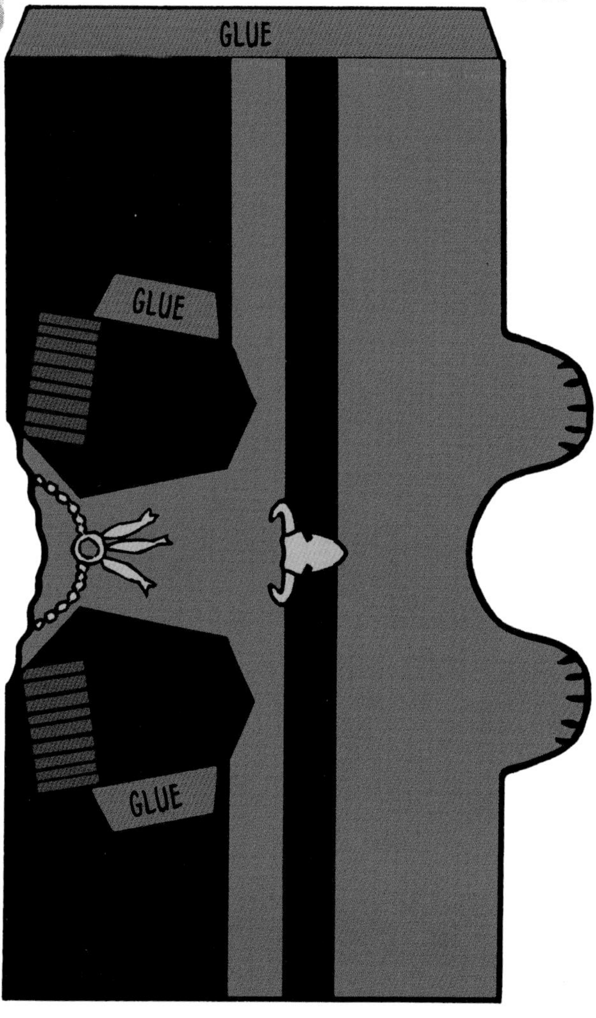
GLUE
GLUE
GLUE

RIGHT HAND

MOUNTAIN FOLD

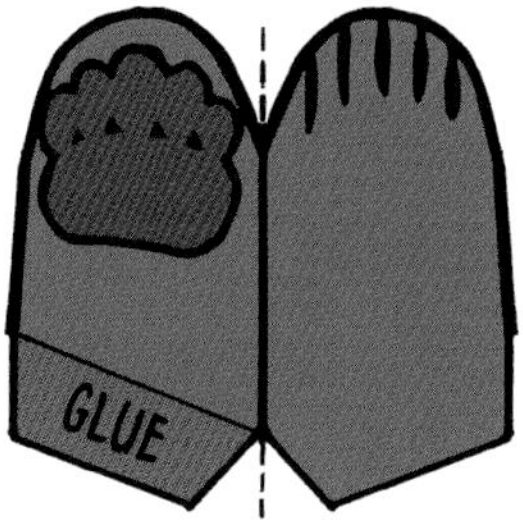
GLUE

LEFT HAND

MOUNTAIN FOLD

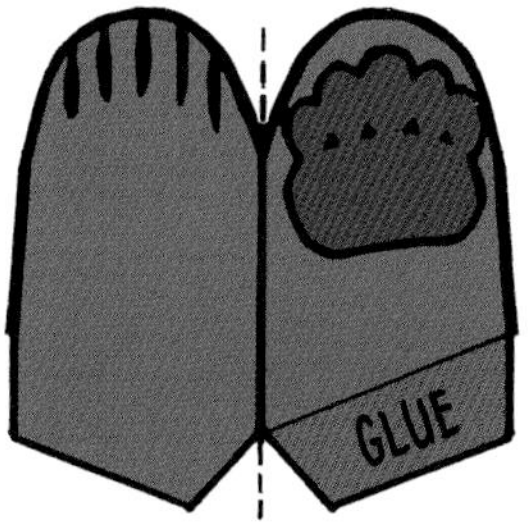
GLUE